LONDON BOROUGH OF ENFIELD
PUBLIC LIBRARIES

No. E 40877

This book must be RETURNED on or before the last date stamped below unless a renewal has been obtained by personal call, post or telephone, quoting the above number and the date due for return.

	-5. JAN. 1970	19. DEC. 1972		
13. JUL. 1968	14. FEB. 1970	8/73		
21. AUG. 1968				
20. SEP. 1968	-4. SEP. 1970			
31. OCT. 1968	-4. JAN. 1971			
-4. JAN. 1969				
	19. MAY 1971			
30. JAN. 1969				
	-9. OCT. 1971			
10. MAY 1969				
27. SEP. 1969	23. MAY 1972			
30. SEP. 1969	-3. JUL. 1972			

In the case of infectious illness, do not return books to the Library, but inform the Librarian.

THE FOUNDERS
OF PSYCHICAL RESEARCH

The Founders of Psychical Research

by
ALAN GAULD

Routledge & Kegan Paul
LONDON

*First published 1968
by Routledge & Kegan Paul Ltd.
Broadway House, 68–74 Carter Lane
London, E.C.4*

*Printed in Great Britain
by Butler & Tanner Ltd
Frome and London*

© *Alan Gauld 1968*

*No part of this book may be reproduced
in any form without permission from
the publisher, except for the quotation
of brief passages in criticism*

SBN 7100 6067 X

CONTENTS

PREFACE *page* vii
ACKNOWLEDGMENTS xi

PART ONE: THE ORIGINS AND FOUNDERS OF PSYCHICAL RESEARCH

I The Rise of Modern Spiritualism in America 1848–55   3
II The Genesis of Reluctant Doubt   32
III Spiritualism in England 1852–76   66
IV Early Investigations of the Sidgwick Group 1873–5   88
V Further Investigations of the Sidgwick Group 1876–80   115
VI The Foundation of the Society for Psychical Research 1882   137

PART TWO: THE WORK OF THE EARLY PSYCHICAL RESEARCHERS

VII Edmund Gurney and Phantasms of the Living   153
VIII Phantasms of the Dead   186
IX The Physical Phenomena   200
X Eusapia   221
XI The Mental Mediums   246
XII Myers' Theory of the Subliminal Self   275
XIII Myers' Cosmology and Theory of the Soul   300
XIV The Turn of the Century   313

CONTENTS

EPILOGUE 340
APPENDIX A: Early Experiments on Thought-transference Published by the S.P.R. 356
APPENDIX B: Critics of Mrs. Piper 361
APPENDIX C: Correspondence between Myers and Lord Acton on the Canons of Evidence to be Applied to Reports of 'Miraculous' Occurrences 364
INDEX 369

PREFACE

ALTHOUGH THIS STUDY centres upon the lives and work of three persons—Henry Sidgwick, Edmund Gurney and Frederic Myers—who were prominent in the Society for Psychical Research (the 'S.P.R.') during its early years, it is not a history of that Society. It passes over important aspects of the S.P.R.'s story and deals at some length with matters quite outside it.

I shall frequently have to give accounts of 'paranormal' phenomena; that is, of phenomena which, if indeed they occurred as narrated, would not be susceptible of explanation in terms of any generally recognised hypothesis. I am often in doubt myself as to their explanation; but if I were continually to emphasise this by inserting such words as 'alleged', 'ostensible', 'seeming', 'supposed' or 'putative' the effect would be ugly. I hope therefore that these qualifications will be taken for granted in all appropriate places. Only when I actually venture an opinion about the phenomena do I wish to commit myself, however tentatively.

REFERENCES

The following abbreviations are used throughout:

Capron   E. W. Capron, *Modern Spiritualism, its Facts and Fanaticisms, its Consistencies and Contradictions*. Boston, 1855.

Dial. Soc. Report   *Report on Spiritualism of the Committee of the London Dialectical Society*. London, 1871.

Fragments   F. W. H. Myers, *Fragments of Inner Life*. London, 1961. (First edition privately printed 1893.)

PREFACE

H.S.: A Memoir	A. S.[idgwick] and E. M. S.[idgwick], *Henry Sidgwick: A Memoir*. London, 1906.
Human Personality	F. W. H. Myers, *Human Personality and its Survival of Bodily Death*. 2 vols., London, 1903.
J.S.P.R.	*Journal of the Society for Psychical Research*. Vols. I– (*in progress*). London, 1884–.
Lewis	[E. E. Lewis], *A Report of the Mysterious Noises heard in the House of Mr. John D. Fox, in Hydesville, Arcadia, Wayne County*. Canandaigua, 1848.
Medium	*The Medium and Daybreak, A Weekly Journal devoted to the History, Phenomena, Philosophy and Teachings of Spiritualism*. London, 1876–82.
Phantasms	E. Gurney, F. W. H. Myers and F. Podmore, *Phantasms of the Living*. 2 vols., London, 1886.
Podmore	F. Podmore, *Modern Spiritualism, a History and a Criticism*. 2 vols., London, 1902.
Principles	W. James, *The Principles of Psychology*. 2 vols., New York, 1890.
P.S.P.R.	*Proceedings of the Society for Psychical Research*. Vols. I– (*in progress*), London, 1882–.
Spiritualist	*The Spiritualist, a Record of the Progress of the Science and Ethics of Spiritualism*, later *The Spiritualist Newspaper*. London, 1869–1880.
Spiritual Magazine	*The Spiritual Magazine*. Vols. 1–6, 1–9, London, 1860–74.
Tertium Quid	E. Gurney, *Tertium Quid: Chapters on Various Disputed Questions*. 2 vols., London, 1887.

MANUSCRIPT SOURCES

Of the MSS quoted:
1. The letters of F. W. H. Myers to Sir Oliver Lodge are in the archives of the S.P.R.

PREFACE

2. The letters from Henry Sidgwick to F. W. H. Myers, and Henry Sidgwick's MS Journal, are in the Library of Trinity College, Cambridge.

3. All other letters, papers, notebooks and diaries of, to or from F. W. H. Myers or his family are in the possession of his grandchildren unless otherwise indicated.

4. The letters from Edmund Gurney to William James are in the Houghton Library, Harvard University.

Other sources and references are given in footnotes.

ACKNOWLEDGMENTS

I SHOULD LIKE TO EXPRESS a particular indebtedness to Mrs. R. Goold-Adams, Mrs. E. Q. Nicholson and Mr. and Mrs. F. Brodie Lodge for making their family papers available to me, and for much kindness during my study of them; to Mr. W. H. Salter, who has been endlessly patient in answering, from his unique knowledge, my questions about the early history of the S.P.R.; to Professor C. D. Broad for allowing me to read an unpublished MS of his own, and for help in other ways; and to Dr. R. B. Joynson, whose comments on a draft of this work were particularly helpful.

For permission to quote from Prof. C. E. M. Hansel's *E.S.P.: A Scientific Evaluation* I have to thank Messrs MacGibbon and Kee. For access to and permission to quote from documents in their possession I must thank Miss Janine Dakyns; the Master and Fellows of Trinity College, Cambridge; Harvard College Library; the Council of the Society for Psychical Research; the Librarian of Bristol University Library; the Swedenborg Society; the Bodleian Library; and Yale University Library.

Among other persons and institutions to whom I am indebted are: the Librarian, University College, London; the Librarian, the London Library; New York Public Library; Mrs. Mark B. Packer; the Countess of Balfour; the Brotherton Library, University of Leeds; Mrs. F. Heywood; Lady Ruth Balfour; Miss Jemma Jebb; Admiral Hon. A. C. Strutt; the late Mr. E. O'Donnell; Mr. G. W. Lambert; Mr. A. H. Wesencraft; Mr. D. H. Newsome; Mr. Rollo Myers; Mr. Robert Stein; Dr. E. J. Dingwall; the late Edward Welbourne; Mrs. Laura Dale; Mr. T. H. Hall; Miss Vera Staff; Mr. George Brook; Mr. Fraser Nicol; Miss Ruby Yeatman; Mr. R. G. Medhurst; Mr. C. Sidgwick; Sir George Joy; Mr. D. S. Porter; Mrs. P. Osborn; and Rochester Public Library.

The Ghost in Man, the Ghost that once was Man,
But cannot wholly free itself from Man,
Are calling to each other thro' a dawn
Stranger than earth has ever seen; the veil
Is rending, and the Voices of the day
Are heard across the Voices of the dark.

TENNYSON

Part One

THE ORIGINS AND FOUNDERS OF PSYCHICAL RESEARCH

I The Rise of Modern Spiritualism in America 1848–55

IN THE SECOND QUARTER of the nineteenth century the more remote parts of New York State were curiously prolific of new religious movements. At least three of these movements—Mormonism, Adventism and Spiritualism—spread very widely and, in one form or another, they are known to most of us today. None of the three is more interesting than Spiritualism. The 'phenomena' characteristic of Spiritualism find many parallels in other religions and thus may have a bearing upon the psychology of religion in general; and certain of the episodes which have marked its history present puzzles of interest both to the philosopher and the amateur detective.

Not the least puzzling of these episodes is that with which modern Spiritualism began. On the 11th December 1847 a poor but respectable Methodist farmer, by name J. D. Fox, moved with his wife Margaret and his daughters Margaretta (aged fourteen) and Catherine (aged twelve) into a tiny wooden house in the village of Hydesville, New York State. In March 1848 the Foxes began to be disturbed at night by inexplicable rappings. The rappings came from the bedroom in which the whole family slept, but their immediate source could not be discovered. The noise 'was heard near the same place all the time. It was not very loud yet it produced a jar of the bedsteads and chairs, that could be felt by placing our hands on the chair, or while we were in bed.'[1] Matters came to a head on the evening of Friday, 31st March. The weather was cold, and there had been a light fall of snow. The Fox family had lost so much sleep during the previous fortnight that they

[1] *Lewis*, p. 5.

decided to go to bed early and take no notice of the rappings. Mrs. Fox's original statement, dated 11th April 1848, runs:

My husband had not gone to bed when we first heard the noise on this evening. I had just laid down. It commenced as usual. I knew it from all other noises I had ever heard in the house. The girls, who slept in the other bed in the room, heard the noise, and tried to make a similar noise by snapping their fingers. The youngest girl is about 12 years old; she is the one who made her hand go. As fast as she made the noise with her hands or fingers, the sound was followed up in the room. It did not sound any different at that time, only it made the same number of noises that the girl did. When she stopped, the sound itself stopped for a short time.

The other girl, who is in her 15th year, then spoke in sport and said, 'Now do this just as I do. Count 1, 2, 3, 4,' &, striking one hand in the other at the same time. The blows which she made were repeated as before. It appeared to answer her by repeating every blow that she made. She only did so once. She then began to be startled; and then I spoke and said to the noise, 'Count ten,' and it made ten strokes or noises. Then I asked the ages of my different children successively, and it gave a number of raps, corresponding to the ages of my children.

I then asked if it was a human being that was making the noise? and if it was, to manifest it by the same noise. There was no noise. I then asked if it was a spirit? and if it was, to manifest it by two sounds. I heard two sounds as soon as the words were spoken. I then asked if it was an injured spirit? to give me the sound, and I heard the rapping distinctly. I then asked if it was injured in this house? and it manifested it by the noise. If the person was living that injured it? and got the same answer. I then ascertained by the same method that its remains were buried under the dwelling, and how old it was. When I asked how old it was? it rapped 31 times: that it was a male; that it had left a family of five children; that it had two sons and three daughters, all living. I asked if it left a wife? and it rapped. If its wife was then living? no rapping; if she was dead? and the rapping was distinctly heard. [H]ow long had she been dead and it rapped twice.[1]

By now it was about half-past seven in the evening. The

[1] *Lewis*, pp. 6–7. A slightly different version of this testimony, dated 11th April 1848, is given by Leah Underhill (née Fox), *The Missing Link in Modern Spiritualism*, New York, 1885, pp. 5–10. I do not know its source. It is quoted in Conan Doyle's *History of Spiritualism*, London, 1926, Vol. I, pp. 61–5 as the original testimony.

Foxes called in various neighbours, who also heard the rappings. When William Duesler arrived about nine o'clock, he found, according to his statement, twelve or fourteen persons in the house. Some of them were too frightened to go into the haunted bedroom. Duesler questioned the supposed spirit still further by means of the primitive code which Mrs. Fox had established. The spirit alleged that his initials were 'C. B.', and that in life he had been a pedlar. He had been slain with a butcher's knife by a previous occupant of the cottage, a blacksmith named John C. Bell. Bell had taken $500 in cash which the pedlar had had about him, and also his trunk and pedlar's pack. The murder had been committed one Tuesday night about midnight, while the other inhabitants of the house, Mrs. Bell and a girl named Lucretia Pulver, were away.

The raps showed a rather curious familiarity with the concerns of the Foxes' neighbours, answering questions about them so readily that one witness, Chauncey P. Losey, remarked: 'I think that no human being could have answered all the questions that were answered by this rapping.'[1]

Mrs. Fox and the children spent the night with neighbours, Mr. Fox and a Mr. Redfield remaining behind. On the evening of the next day, Saturday, 1st April, large crowds gathered in and around the cottage. The rappings recommenced, and answered questions about the murder in much the same terms as before. Committees were chosen and placed in different parts of the house to guard against trickery. Various persons began to dig up the cellar, but after they had got down two or three feet water came in so fast that they had to desist. The noises began again on Sunday morning and continued throughout the day, ceasing in the evening. They were resumed on Monday night and occurred, perhaps spasmodically, for at least the next few weeks; without however conveying any fresh information of note about the deceased pedlar, except that his name was, supposedly, Charles B. Rosma.

In the middle of April a certain E. E. Lewis, a publisher of Canandaigua, collected statements from fourteen of the chief witnesses. He also obtained statements from five persons who had witnessed curious happenings in the house before the Foxes moved into it. One of these persons, Miss Lucretia Pulver,

[1] *Lewis*, pp. 21-2.

testified that she lived for a while with John C. Bell and his wife, and that one afternoon a pedlar, wearing a black frock coat and 'light coloured pants' and carrying a basket, had called at the house. 'Mrs. [Bell] was going to Lock Berlin to stay that night. I wanted to buy some things of the pedler [*sic*], but had no money with me, and he said he would call at our house the next morning and sell them to me. I never saw him after this. About three days after this, they sent for me to come back . . .'¹

Soon afterwards she began to hear knockings in the bedroom, and on one occasion she heard footsteps coming from the buttery. One evening Mrs. Bell sent her down to the cellar. She stumbled over a place where the cellar floor was uneven and loose. Mrs. Bell said that the unevenness was due to rats, and shortly afterwards 'Mr. [Bell] carried a lot of dirt into the cellar just at night, and was at work there some time.' Mrs. Bell said that he was filling up the rat holes.

Mrs. Anna Pulver testified that Mrs. Bell had told her of being disturbed one night by a sound like somebody walking about from one room to another. Mr. and Mrs. Weekman, who had lived in the house a year or so previously, stated that they had heard knockings and other strange noises there; and Mrs. Jane C. Lape, who had lived with the Weekmans, deposed:

> One day, about two o'clock P.M., while I was doing my work in the kitchen, I saw a man in the bed-room joining the kitchen. The bed-room door was open, and I saw the man distinctly . . . I had been in the kitchen some time at work, and knew that no one had gone into that room. The man stood facing me when I saw him. He did not speak, nor did I hear any noise at any time, like a person walking or moving about in the room. He had on grey pants, black frock coat and black cap. He was about middling size, I should think. I knew of no person in that vicinity who wore a similar dress. Mrs. Weekman was in another part of the house ... I was very much frightened and left the room, and when I returned with Mrs. W. there was no person there.²

Lewis published these statements towards the end of April 1848, in a pamphlet now of the utmost rarity.³ To this pamphlet he appended a certificate, signed by forty-four persons, testify-

¹ *Lewis*, p. 36. ² *Lewis*, p. 35. ³ See Preface, p. viii.

ing to the good character of John C. Bell, who had moved to the town of Lyons, Wayne county. Attempts to trace the pedlar or his family failed, and no formal charge was ever brought against Bell. Some later authorities state that David S. Fox (John D. Fox's son) and several other persons recommenced digging in the cellar of the Hydesville house in the summer of 1848; they unearthed some human teeth, some fragments of bone and some human hair. In November 1904 the disintegration of one of the cellar walls exposed to view 'human bones consisting of vertebrae, rib, arm and leg bones, a shoulder blade and collar bone'.[1]

So far as I am aware history tells no more of the intriguing story of the murdered pedlar; it has however a great deal to relate about the curious developments to which the 'Hydesville knockings' gave rise.

Most of the witnesses whose first-hand testimonies about the Hydesville knockings have come down to us believed that the Fox family could not have been responsible for them. Chauncey P. Losey said that the noise 'was unaccountable. It sounded as if it was in different places at different times.'[2] William D. Storer was even more definite:

> I cannot imagine any way by which this noise could be produced by any human agency. I have examined the premises very carefully, and can find nothing by which these sounds could be produced; no cord or wire, or anything of that kind by which anybody could produce these sounds by being at a distance.—There is no chance under the floor where anything could be secreted—no ceiling or anything of that kind.[3]

What appears particularly odd to anybody versed in the ways of modern psychical researchers is that no one seems to have suspected the Fox girls, Margaretta and Catherine. Indeed E. W. Capron asserts[4] that on one night at least the sounds continued

---
[1] See the account in the *Rochester Democrat and Chronicle* for 23 Nov. 1904, quoted by M. B. Pond, *The Unwilling Martyrs*, London, 1947, pp. 419–22. Doyle, *op. cit.* I, pp. 69–70, quotes a comparable account from the *Boston Journal* for 23rd Nov. 1904, and adds that a pedlar's tin box was also unearthed. House and box were eventually removed to the Spiritualist Camp at Lilydale, New York State.
[2] *Lewis*, p. 21.   [3] *Lewis*, pp. 25–6.   [4] *Capron*, p. 54.

whilst the girls were away from the house; though the original testimonies do not make it completely clear that this was so. After a few weeks however it became apparent that the phenomena now centred around the younger girl Kate. Sometime in the early summer of 1848 Kate was therefore packed off to stay with her widowed sister, Leah Fish, a music teacher at Rochester, New York State. Unfortunately the rappings then broke out in the presence of Margaretta, who was living with her brother David a few miles from Hydesville. Worse than this —as soon as Kate was established in Rochester they recommenced around her with greater strength than before. Mrs. Fish's house became the scene, so it is alleged, not merely of loud rappings, but of violent and totally inexplicable movements of objects. Rumours about these occurrences began to circulate, and Mrs. Fish's pupils to desert her. In despair she asked a Quaker named Isaac Post, who was an old friend of the family, to help her. Post sat with the family round a table and questioned the raps. Mrs. Fish mentioned to him that her brother David had obtained the name of the deceased pedlar by calling out the alphabet and noting which letters were responded to with raps. Post suggested that they should try this method again, and the raps spelled out 'We are all your deceased friends and relatives. Jacob Smith.' Jacob Smith was Mrs. Fish's grandfather.

When the Fox family heard of this startling development, which seems to have taken place in the autumn of 1848, they all proceeded to Rochester; and Rochester remained the principal abode of Mrs. Fox and her three daughters for most of the next two years. The Fox girls were soon besieged by, on the one hand, numerous spirits desirous of communicating with those still on earth and, on the other, uncomfortably large numbers of persons anxious to receive messages or to witness wonders. A visitor who was much impressed was E. W. Capron, of Auburn, who arrived in Rochester on 23rd November 1848. He made the following contemporary memorandum of one of his experiments:

> At another time, being present with Isaac Post, of Rochester, I tried the experiment of counting in the following manner. I took several shells from a card-basket on the table (small lake shells), closed my hand, and placed it entirely out of sight, and

requested as many raps as there were shells. It was done correctly. As I knew how many shells there were in my hand, I resolved to test it another way, to see if there was a possibility of my *mind* having any influence in the matter. I took a handful of shells, without knowing how many I took myself. Still the answers were correct. I then requested Mr. Post, who sat by the table, to put his hand in the basket, take out some shells without knowing the number, and pass them into my hand, which I immediately closed and placed in a position where none could see it. The number was told correctly as before.[1]

Capron became a frequent visitor to the Foxes; and, about late Summer 1849, Kate Fox went for a protracted stay at his home in Auburn, New York State. According to Capron's own journal, she produced at seances there a large number of remarkable phenomena, mostly however in the dark. These phenomena included object movements, the mysterious playing of a guitar, and touches from spirit hands. During one of these evenings, Capron says:

> ... a wish was expressed that we might see the hand that touched us. On looking towards the window (the moon shining through the curtain), we saw a hand waved to and fro before, and near the top of it. We could discern no other part of a form. This we have witnessed many times ourselves, and several have discovered distinctly the features of the persons whom they knew, and who had been dead for years.[2]

In November 1848 the spirits announced that, owing to the Fox family's continued resistance to their wishes and directions, they were about to depart. They did indeed depart for a short period, but they returned when Capron and a Quaker, George Willets, paid a visit. Capron and Willets were told: 'You all have a duty to perform. We want you to make this matter more public.' Following the directions of the spirits, Capron and Willets, eventually and with great reluctance, hired the Corinthian Hall, in Rochester, for the evening of Wednesday, 14th November 1849,[3] and advertised a public lecture

[1] *Capron*, p. 75. [2] *Capron*, pp. 105–6.
[3] *Capron*, p. 91, mistakenly gives the year as 1848; so does Underhill, *op. cit.*, p. 63. D. M. Dewey, *History of the Strange Sounds or Rappings heard in Rochester and Western New York*, Rochester, 1850, gives it as 1849 (p. 23); and so do E. W. Capron and H. D. Barron, *Explanation and History of the Mysterious Communion with Spirits*, Auburn, 1850, 1st Edn., p. 49. An account of the meeting can be found in the *Rochester Daily Democrat* for 16th Nov. 1849.

on the mysterious noises. The lecture, a simple history of the phenomena, was delivered by Capron, and afterwards the large audience was invited to elect a committee of five to test Margaretta and Leah Fish, the latter of whom had now seemingly developed mediumship herself. Kate was still at Auburn. On the following day the committee took the ladies, without prior warning, to the Hall of the Sons of Temperance, and subsequently to the home of a private citizen. The rappings were heard in both these places, not merely from the floor but upon walls and doors. At the next meeting the committee reported to the audience that they were quite unable to explain the phenomena. The audience then appointed a second committee, which consisted of some moderately eminent personages—Dr. H. H. Langworthy, Hon. Frederick Whittlesey, D. C. McCollum, William Fisher, all of Rochester, and Hon. A. P. Hascall (a former member of Congress) of Le Roy. 'At the next lecture this committee reported that they went into the investigation at the office of Chancellor Whittlesey, and they heard the sound on the floor, on the wall and door; that the ladies were placed in different positions, and, like the other committee, they were wholly unable to tell from what the sound proceeded or how it was made.'[1]

The audience at the second meeting appointed yet another committee. This committee in turn appointed a sub-committee of ladies which stripped and searched the sisters. The main committee then excluded all friends of the two sisters from the committee room, and stood Leah and Margaretta without shoes upon large feather pillows. Even under these conditions raps were heard both on the floor and on the wall. The committee reported these facts to a third, and packed, meeting, which thereupon broke up in rowdiness.

Newspaper reports of these meetings brought the Fox sisters far more than merely local fame, and the number of those coming to visit them increased still further. A vivid account of a visit to the sisters at this time was given by W. H. Macdonald in the *New York Excelsior*, a paper of which he was co-editor and co-proprietor, for 2nd February 1850:

The morning ... of the following day, we called upon them [Leah, Margaretta and Kate] again ... in a very light room,

[1] Quoted in Dewey, *op. cit.*, p. 25, from the *New York Weekly Tribune* of 8th Dec, 1849.

many questions were asked concerning ourself and were answered correctly, without a moment's hesitation. It is impossible that the correct answers to these questions could have been known to any person present, by ordinary methods of obtaining the information. Among these were the ages of ourself and wife, the number of our children living and dead, their ages, health, letters we expected, our success in business, etc.—all these queries related to the past, with one exception, and were solved with perfect correctness. A table standing in the room was moved without any visible agency (it will be recollected that it was in the day time, and the apartment was well-lighted), notwithstanding all our efforts to keep it stationary...

At interviews held with them on the two following days many questions were answered respecting many other gentlemen in our presence, and in all cases said to have been answered correctly. On one occasion the sounds proper to a carpenter's shop were heard apparently proceeding from the wall and table. Sawing, planing, pounding with a mallet, were imitated to the life.[1]

The Fox sisters had by this time added quite a wide variety of noises to their original repertoire. For some while past visitors had occasionally been startled by fearsome sounds re-enacting the pedlar's murder; sounds which were sometimes capped by a noise like the pouring of a quantity of clotted blood from a pail on to the floor. Judge Hascall of Le Roy and Mr. Summerfield, a lawyer of the same place, alleged that at a dark seance with the Foxes they had called for sounds to be made 'like a band of martial music'. The band was 'perfectly imitated' even to the beating of the bass drum and the roar of distant cannon.[2]

Not surprisingly, the sisters soon attracted the attention of P. T. Barnum, the showman. In the spring of 1850 they paid their first visit to New York,[3] staying at Barnum's Hotel, and giving exhibitions both there and at Barnum's Museum. Need-

[1] Quoted in Dewey, *op. cit.*, pp. 53–4; cf. a similar account by C. Hammond quoted in C. W. Elliott, *Mysteries; or Glimpses of the Supernatural*, New York, 1852, pp. 127–30.
[2] *Capron*, pp. 76–7.
[3] *Capron*, p. 172; Underhill, *op. cit.*, p. 128, says they arrived in New York City on 4th June, after excursions to Albany and Troy in April; but they are certainly attracting attention in New York City in April. See, e.g., the *New York Tribune* for 22nd April.

less to say the exhibitions were crowded. This association with Barnum certainly lends force to the views of those who regard the Fox sisters as out-and-out charlatans. However it must be added that during their stay in New York the sisters were several times invited to the homes of private, and indeed eminent, persons who were interested in the phenomena, and that these private demonstrations were even more remarkable than the public ones. Mr. Ripley, one of the editors of the *New York Tribune*, contributed to that paper a long account of a seance which the sisters held at the chambers of the Rev. Dr. Griswold, in Broadway. Among the guests of Dr. Griswold whose names Ripley felt he might without impropriety mention were J. Fenimore Cooper, George Bancroft, Rev. Dr. Hawks, Dr. J. W. Francis, Dr. Marcy, N. P. Willis, William Cullen Bryant, Mr. Bigelow of the *Evening Post*, Richard B. Kimball, H. T. Tuckerman and General Lyman. Several of those present, including Fenimore Cooper, received from the rappings correct information about the earthly lives of deceased persons upon whom they had fixed their minds. Ripley's account of the conclusion of the seance is as follows:

> The evening was now far advanced, and it was not thought desirable to continue the colloquies any further. At the suggestion of several gentlemen, the ladies removed from the sofa, where they had sat during the evening, and remained standing in another part of the room, producing a vibration on the pannels [*sic*] which was felt by every one who touched them. Different gentlemen stood on the outside and the inside of the door at the same time, when loud knockings were heard on the side opposite to that where they stood. The ladies were at such a distance from the door in both cases as to lend no countenance to the idea that the sounds were produced by any direct communication with them. They now went into a parlor, under the room in which the party was held, accompanied by several gentlemen, and the sounds were then produced with great distinctness, causing sensible vibrations in the sofa, and apparently coming from a thick hearth-rug, before the fireplace, as well as from other quarters of the rooms.[1]

---

[1] Quoted by Capron, pp. 174–5; also by Emma Hardinge [Hardinge-Britten], *Modern American Spiritualism*, New York, 1870, p. 65; cf. a somewhat different account quoted in A. Mahan, *Modern Mysteries Explained and Exposed*, Boston, 1855, pp. 114–16.

THE RISE OF MODERN SPIRITUALISM IN AMERICA

Horace Greeley, editor of the *Tribune*, and subsequently a candidate for the Presidency, had the Foxes to stay at his Turtle Bay home for several days. After their visit he declared in a letter to the *Tribune* that '... of those who have enjoyed proper opportunities for a full investigation, we believe that fully three-fourths are convinced, as we are, that these singular sounds and seeming manifestations are not produced by Mrs. Fox and her daughters, nor by any human being connected with them'.[1]

The exhibitions in New York were of course on a commercial basis. Capron states that for more than a year after the commencement of the rappings Mrs. Fish refused to take money from visitors; after that necessity forced her to accept 'voluntary contributions'. Since Capron was one of the visitors concerned, his word on this point must carry weight.[2] He asserts further that when the Fox sisters returned from New York to Rochester they fully intended to retire from public mediumship. But their house was so thronged with visitors that they found such a course impossible, and had no alternative but to 'make themselves servants of the public ... the same public who used their time, paying them for it, so that they might obtain the means of living'.[3] They became, in short, the first professional mediums; and they spent a good part of the next few years in touring the country and spreading the Word.

The rapidity with which Spiritualism spread across the United States in the eighteen-fifties is quite remarkable. It merits detailed investigation by a competent social historian. Doubtless the explanations offered by Podmore[4] are in fair measure correct. Podmore points out that during the decade prior to 1848 mesmerism, often joined with phrenology, had enjoyed a great popular vogue in the United States. The country contained numerous itinerant mesmeric lecturers and demonstrators, many of whom made a speciality of mesmeric cures of ailments; and these demonstrators had a large corps of trained subjects

[1] Hardinge, *op. cit.*, p. 72.
[2] Underhill, *op. cit.*, p. 103, says that they received their first money on 28th Nov. 1849.
[3] *Capron*, p. 182.
[4] *Podmore* I, pp. 202–20.

who would, when in trance, diagnose diseases, and otherwise exercise clairvoyant faculties. Mesmerism had a considerable press and a considerable public; and, when the potentialities of Spiritualism became clear, press and public, demonstrators and clairvoyants, readily attached themselves to it. Again, the citizens of the United States had a very long tradition of independent thought on religious matters. Many of them were literate enough to study and argue about religious pamphlets and propaganda; but few had had the opportunity of acquiring a higher education. Add to this a good deal of religious ferment, and a revival of sects—such as the Universalists and the Swedenborgians—whose adherents might be expected to sympathise with some aspects of Spiritualist doctrine, and the rapid spread of Spiritualism in the United States becomes quite comprehensible.

Whatever the explanation, there is no doubt of the fact. Spiritualism spread, if not like wildfire, at any rate fast enough to alarm the orthodox and move them to vigorous denunciations. It could hardly have progressed as it did if the Foxes had been its only messengers; but other mediums soon appeared on the scene. The rappings spread by a kind of contagion, those who came to witness the phenomena afterwards suffering comparable disturbances in their own homes. Indeed people who simply heard of the phenomena were liable to find themselves or their wives and daughters similarly visited. Thus before the end of 1848 rappings had broken out in several other Rochester families;[1] and Kate Fox's visit to Auburn in 1849 led to such percussions and repercussions that by the summer of 1850 the town contained, according to Capron's estimate, 50–100 mediums in various stages of development.[2] On 19th June 1852 *The Olive Branch*, a Methodist newspaper published in Boston, quoted a Catholic source as follows:

> Our readers . . . will hardly believe that this delusion has so spread over New England, and towns in other states of New England origin, that scarcely a village can be found which is not infected with it. In most small towns several families are possessed, the medium between the erratic ghosts and the crazy fools being, in some cases, a weak and half-witted woman, but

[1] *Capron*, pp. 66–7.   [2] *Capron*, p. 113.

in most instances, a little girl, whom her parents and friends have prostituted to this wicked trade.[1]

In 1853 Henry Spicer, an Englishman who was investigating the phenomena, stated that there were at that time 'not less than thirty thousand recognised media' in the United States.[2] His authority for this statement is not apparent; but he added that a friend has told him that there are no fewer than three hundred 'magnetic circles' in Philadelphia alone.

As the number of mediums increased, so the varieties of phenomena grew more numerous. Rappings remained the stock-in-trade, but table-tilting soon became very nearly as popular. Table-tilting was of course normally carried out with the hands of the sitters resting upon the table whilst it tapped out the messages; but there are in the literature numerous cases of the alleged independent movement, and even levitation, of tables and other objects. Podmore makes the following comment upon such cases:

> Very few critical accounts of the earlier seances have been preserved; but they are not needed. The accounts given by Spiritualists themselves, when they condescend upon detail, are sufficient to show that we need look for no other cause for the results described than trickery of the most trivial and vulgar kind—trickery for the most part too obvious to need a commentary.[3]

Podmore seems to me to exaggerate somewhat. It is true that the accounts which have come down to us from the eighteen-fifties frequently fail to give details which one would like to have on record; but unless we are to assume (and this is the direction in which Podmore's mind tends) that contagious imbecility and epidemic hallucinations were rampant in the United States of a century ago, it is in some cases not at all obvious what methods of trickery could have been employed. What for instance are we to make of an account, signed by four persons, of a sitting with the medium D. D. Home on 5th April 1852? The seance was held in a well-lighted room in a private

---

[1] A. Ballou, *An Exposition of Views respecting the Principal Facts, Causes and Peculiarities involved in Spirit Manifestations*, London, 1852, p. 145.
[2] H. Spicer, *Sights and Sounds: the Mystery of the Day*, London, 1853, p. 4.
[3] *Podmore* I, p. 228.

house; yet the table rocked violently, even when one of the company was seated upon it, and eventually it poised itself on two legs for some thirty seconds while nobody at all touched it.[1] And what of this, the most entertaining levitation story of the period that I have come upon:

> In the month of March, 1852, being at the home of Rev. J. J. Locke, in the town of Barre, Mass., one evening, as we were seated in a circle around a table,—I should say about a dozen persons being present, several of whom were strangers to us,—all were listening to some messages that were being spelled out by raps on the table (which stood independent from the touch of anyone), by the use of the alphabet. All was still and peaceful, the room well-lighted and no one expecting any thing unusual that I was aware of; when Mrs. Cheney's right hand began to rise very gradually and steadily, up, up,—higher and higher—till it seemed to raise her from the chair: still upward she was raised, until she swung in the open atmosphere between the floor and ceiling, and positively not coming in contact with any visible thing whatsoever.[2]

Much more obviously susceptible of an explanation in terms of crude and vulgar trickery were the phenomena afterwards called 'Materialisation' and 'Direct Voice'. These occurred almost exclusively in dark sittings. It was supposed that under certain conditions spirits might render themselves partially, or even wholly, visible and tangible (later on it became fashionable to suppose that they did so by clothing themselves in a sort of surrogate flesh, called 'ectoplasm', which they drew from the body of the medium). The hands and faces which appeared at Kate Fox's seances have already been mentioned. If spirits could materialise hands and faces, there seemed no reason why they should not also materialise lungs and vocal organs, and before long there were reports of spirits who actually spoke to sitters. The most celebrated early practitioners of these phenomena were the family of Jonathan Koons,[3] a farmer in the

[1] The testimony is quoted from the *Springfield Republican*, by Mahan, *op. cit.*, pp. 112–14.
[2] This is an extract from a letter from a Mr. S. F. Cheney to Rev. H. Snow, dated 26th April 1853. Mr. Snow quotes the extract in his *Spirit-Intercourse*, Boston, 1853, pp. 64–5, and vouches that Mr. Cheney is a 'worthy, Christian soul'.
[3] On the Koons family see *Podmore* I, pp. 246–9; Hardinge, *op. cit.*, pp. 307–33; and R. Hare, *Experimental Investigation of the Spirit Manifestations*, New York, 1855, pp. 295–307.

remote township of Dover, Ohio. In the darkness of Koons' seance room a band of spirits, with the family name of 'King',[1] sang, played musical instruments, rendered their hands visible by dipping them in phosphorus, and addressed the assembled company through a tin horn or trumpet, a device that in some form or another has remained almost mandatory for the Direct Voice ever since.

Even with phenomena of this class there are certain puzzles. The following account of a sitting with D. D. Home (in a private house) is given in a letter, dated 18th March 1853, to the *Hartford Times* of Connecticut:

> The gas light had been turned down, but sufficient light remained in the room to render ourselves, and most objects, quite visible, and the hands of the party, which rested on the table, could be distinctly seen. The spirits asked [by raps]:
> 'How many hands are there on the table?' There were six of us in the party, and the answer, after counting, was 'twelve'.
> *Reply*—'There are *thirteen*.'
> And there, sure enough, on that side of the table which was vacant, and opposite to the medium, appeared a *thirteenth* hand! It faded as we gazed, but presently up it came again—*a hand and an arm*, gleaming and apparently self-luminous; and it slowly moved... toward the centre of the table! To make sure that we were not deceived or laboring under a hallucination, we counted our own hands, which were all resting in sight upon the table. There it was, however, an arm and a hand, the arm extending back to the elbow, and there fading into imperceptibility. We all saw it, and all spoke of it, to assure each other of the reality of the thing. It emitted a faint but perceptible *light*. Presently it vanished, but we were soon permitted to see not only the same thing again, but the *process of its formation*. It began at the *elbow*, and formed rapidly and steadily, until the arm and hand again rested on the table before us. It was so plainly seen, that I readily observed it to be a *left* hand.[2]

The hand, by request, attempted to write. Then it picked up a bell from beneath the table, rang it some six feet away from

---

[1] During the rest of the century 'John King' appeared again and again through 'physical' mediums in England and America, and so did his daughter, 'Katie King', cf. below, pp. 81, 103n, 229. In life he was supposed to have been the buccaneer, Sir Henry Morgan.

[2] Hardinge, *op. cit.*, pp. 105–6.

the circle, and eventually brought it to the writer, who seized the hand instead.

It was a real hand—it had knuckles, fingers, and finger nails, and what was yet more curious . . ., it was soft and warm, feeling much like the hand of an infant, in every respect but that of size. But the most singular part of the strange occurrence is yet to be told—the hand melted in my grasp! Dissolved, dissipated, became annihilated, so far as the sense of feeling extended.

A natural outcome of the *rapprochement* between Spiritualism and mesmerism was the metamorphosis of the 'magnetic trance' into the 'mediumistic trance' in which the 'sensitive' or medium is especially open to spiritual influence. Once a medium was in trance, the spirits might, it was supposed, impress clairvoyant visions upon her[1] or, by 'controlling' her hand or vocal apparatus, induce her to deliver written or spoken teachings or messages. A great many spirit discourses and inspirational writings were produced in this way. Most of them are extremely tedious. The spoken discourses have the lilt and cadence and decorative phrasing of non-conformist pulpit oratory, without a touch of its fire. Even the most celebrated of the inspirational writings—Edmonds and Dexter's *Spiritualism* (1853), or Linton's *Healing of the Nations* (1858), are pedestrian at their very best. A great many such writings are epitomised in this sentence from a spirit sermon by Rev. H. Snow: 'We cannot dwell minutely upon the particulars which go to make up the sum total of the vastness of immensity.'[2] The spirits who supposedly inspired the discourses and writings all too often claimed famous names. Benjamin Franklin was ubiquitous, perhaps because his electrical skills made him seem a likely inventor of the 'Spiritual Telegraph'. Jefferson and Calhoun were frequent communicators, and so were Swedenborg, St. Paul and John the Baptist. Of their efforts one can only say that if the great minds of this world degenerate so much in the next the prospect for lesser fry is bleak indeed. The

---

[1] I say 'her' because female mediums seem for whatever reason to be commoner than male ones.
[2] *Op. cit.*, p. 116. It is only fair to point out that Mr. Snow later says that 'some parts of the spirit sermon were written not without violence to my critical taste' (p. 179).

Archangel Gabriel was often heard from, and in one circle at least the Saviour Himself communicated, casting his remarks in the form of such rhymed couplets as:

> Then in turn give me all your heart
> For Christ from goodness never will depart.[1]

However, it must be added that poems supposedly originating from famous deceased poets sometimes achieved an imitative accuracy which might still win them acceptance in a school magazine. A poem written by *soi-disant* Edgar Allen Poe begins:

> O, the dark, the awful chasm!
> O, the fearful Spirit spasm!
> Wrought by unresisted passion
> In my heart.
> Fancies joyous, but alluring,
> Love pure but unenduring,
> From time to time securing,
> Each a part.[2]

Of the numerous other modes of communication which one by one developed there is no space to write. The 'planchette' and the 'ouija' board are familiar to everyone, and with 'slate-writing' I will deal later (see pp. 201–7 below). Some idea of the variety of the 'phases of mediumship' can be obtained from this sentence describing the mediumistic activities of the Rev. C. Hammond, a former Universalist clergyman, author of several books of inspirational writings.[3] 'He . . . claims to be empowered or assisted by spirits to heal diseases, talk in unknown tongues, dance and perform various gymnastic exercises, such as shaking the arms and hands, perform Indian dances, whooping etc.'[4]

The teachings which the spirits imparted in these various ways consisted in large part of moral precepts and of exhortations to a nobler way of life; the sentiments expressed were in general thoroughly worthy, even though the style tended to

---
[1] *Capron*, p. 233.
[2] Spicer, *op. cit.*, p. 135. The Rev. T. Lake Harris' *Lyric of the Morning Land* (1855) and *Lyric of the Golden Age* (1856) are quite striking in places.
[3] C. Hammond, *Light from the Spirit World*, Rochester, 1852; *The Pilgrimage of Thomas Paine and others to the Seventh Circle*, New York, 1852.
[4] *Capron*, p. 100.

outfly the thought. More interesting were the teachings which concerned Man and the Universe. The cosmological pictures given by or through different mediums diverged from each other considerably on points of detail, but on the whole the generic similarities are more striking than the particular differences.

At death the spirit disengages itself from the body and floats for a while above it, still unconscious. What happens next is described by the spirit of Sweedenborg (*sic*) as follows:

> As it floats over the body . . . there come to it, drawn by their affections or by their duties, spirits possessing form and shape, beautiful beyond thought. They support this spirit-child until it recovers its consciousness . . . Then all the spirits whose lives are pure, whose mission being accomplished toward it, now take it by the hand, and bid it look around.[1]

As to the nature of the 'spirit' which quits its earthly tenement in this way there was at first some divergence of opinion. All communicators claimed to possess bodies which, to them, were every whit as substantial as the ones they formerly inhabited. Thus, on 13th August 1851, Swedenborg wrote through another medium, Isaac Post:

> At first I could scarcely realise that it was myself, I looked for my hands, and there they were, I looked for my feet, and they too were there; and so of every part of my body, nothing was lacking. I cast a view at my old frame, that had done me good service heretofore, it now seemed too worthless to be concerned about, I saw my friends with sadness in their countenances, moving gently about as though afraid of waking me. Could I have spoken, I would have said, Only put it where it will not annoy you.[2]

Some early writers seem actually to identify the spirit or soul with this quasi-physical body;[3] but within a few years a slightly more refined doctrine had become current. It distinguished between the 'spirit', or animating principle, and the 'soul', the subtle body which, in some sense, contains the spirit.[4] The soul

[1] G. T. Dexter and J. W. Edmonds, *Spiritualism*, New York, 1853, pp. 155-6.
[2] I. Post, *Voices from the Spirit World*, Boston, 1852, p. 41.
[3] Cf. Ballou, *op. cit.*, p. 16, and see *Podmore* I, pp. 391-2.
[4] See, e.g., Hare, *op. cit.*, pp. 390-2.

interpenetrates and vivifies the earthly body and thus forms a bridge between the spirit and the flesh. This simple scheme was often complicated by attempts to incorporate in it doctrines about the 'ether', a universal 'magnetic fluid' whose existence was widely held to have been proved by the experiments of mesmerists. The ether was a sort of half-way house between spirit and matter, and formed a medium through which they could reciprocally influence each other. Many writers held that the soul, or subtle body, must be composed of ether, but some placed a 'spiritual ether' between spirit and soul and a 'material ether' between soul and matter. Later on attempts were made to equate the ether with the 'luminiferous ether' of nineteenth-century physical science, and to suggest that whereas earthly matter and human bodies consist of ether vibrating at a low rate, spiritual matter and spiritual bodies are made of ether vibrating rapidly.[1]

The next world is, supposedly, divided into a number of 'spheres'—there are usually said to be six of them, making seven spheres in all if the earth is counted as the first. When a person dies, he is translated, or attracted, to that sphere where his moral affinities lie. There is no hell as such; but a person of debauched life will find himself automatically drawn to the second, or lowest sphere, where others of his kind dwell in degradation and squalor. More elevated spirits will gravitate to higher spheres. The scenery in these spheres resembles that of earth, but it is of surpassing beauty. The actual location of the spheres was a matter of some dispute. The spiritual spheres of Andrew Jackson Davis's *Principles of Nature* extend throughout, and indeed go to make up, the Universe as a whole. Spiritualists more commonly conceived the spheres simply as encircling the earth one above the other. Gridley says that the outermost boundary of the seventh sphere is about 30,000 miles above the earth's surface;[2] Hare's spirit friends gave the distance as 120 miles.[3]

Spirits of all but the lowest kind are generally pictured as

[1] A later work which had much influence was B. Stewart and P. C. Tait's *The Unseen Universe or Physical Speculations on a Future State*, London, 1875; it went through quite a few editions.
[2] J. A. Gridley, *Astounding Facts from the Spirit World*, Southampton, Mass., 1854, diagrams between pp. 96–7.
[3] Hare, *op. cit.*, p. 87.

engaged in occupations of an ennobling or unselfish sort; in 'guiding' those yet on earth, or those sunk in the degradation of the second sphere; in studying, in singing or in edifying discourse. The keynote is Progress. Every spirit, however base, can, and ultimately will, progress to the highest spheres. It is the duty of elevated spirits to assist the less advanced whenever they can.

Since spirits retain bodies like those they had on earth, distinctions of sex remain in the spheres; and a delicate question naturally arises as to the relation between the sexes in the next world. In the eighteen-fifties Spiritualists were not uncommonly accused of practising 'free love';[1] and without doubt some spirits gave curious accounts of their own activities in that direction:

> ... the male is generally and naturally positive to the female, so a spiritually enlightened wisdom often inclines them to assume the position of connubial commerce, not to produce a new existence, as on earth, but to supply the negative spirit with their own positive elements or, in other words, to multiply their own spiritual life in others ... .[2]

The spirits also commonly propounded moral and political ideas of a fairly advanced kind; and several communities outrightly socialistic derived inspiration from spirit teachings.

Of theology proper the communications contain, as Podmore remarks, very little; though persons of strong sectarian leanings occasionally received teachings mirroring their own views. God is frequently mentioned, and his beneficence is much dwelt upon, but He Himself is sometimes represented as dwelling so far beyond the lower spheres that no spirit capable of communicating with earth has ever seen Him. Elizabeth Twining, a Quaker, wrote through the hand of Isaac Post on 10th November 1851:

---

[1] Cf., e.g., *Podmore* I, pp. 292–3, and E. W. Fornell, *The Unhappy Medium: Spiritualism and the Life of Margaret Fox*, Austin, Texas, 1964, pp. 33–7. G. Lawton, *The Drama of Life after Death*, London, 1933, pp. 608–16, gives an account of a Spiritualist convention in 1858, at which several speakers favoured free love, and one young lady screamed out: 'Free love, free love, it is God's law, it is Heaven's command.'

[2] Gridley, *op. cit.*, p. 172. It is only fair to point out that in many ways Gridley's book is highly unorthodox.

I had somehow imbibed the idea that I should find my God whom I had endeavoured faithfully to serve, and from whom, I had all confidence that I had often received counsel, would be surrounded with glory unutterable . . . and from his exaltation I expected to receive the sentence of well done thou good and faithful servant, enter thou into the joy of thy Lord. Judge of my surprise on my arrival to my spirit home, I was welcomed with all the endearing affection that it is possible to conceive, I was surprised and delighted beyond my power to express, at my change; when I was fully assured that this was my continuing home, I enquired for the God who I had so faithfully served . . . my companions informed me they [k]new not any locality for him, they knew this, that they that do good, cultivate love and kindness, devote themselves to make others happy, are happy themselves while on earth, and must of necessity enter their renewed life in a condition to improve in all their ennobling virtues.[1]

A few Spiritualists adopted a positively anti-Christian tone; a good many however regarded Christ as human rather than divine, as an exemplar rather than a Redeemer. As to whether spirits below the seventh sphere may meet with Christ I have not been able to find any widespread consensus of opinion.

The principal teachings of early Spiritualism can all be found in the mesmeric literature of the decades prior to 1848; though they are, of course, much older than that. Jung-Stilling had postulated an ether which connects body and soul and links together the spiritual and material worlds; the famous Seeress of Prevorst, noted also for the curious physical phenomena said to occur in her presence, propounded some complex doctrines concerning the spiritual spheres; the somnambules studied by H. Werner were inspired to pronounce that the human constitution is threefold, consisting of a material body, a quasi-material soul and a spirit.[2] It is difficult to say whether in the New England of 1850 knowledge of these teachings was widespread enough to have influenced the development of Spiritualist doctrine. A work which was undoubtedly discussed so widely that almost any medium could have picked up its

---

[1] Post, *op. cit.*, pp. 106-7.
[2] J. H. Jung-Stilling, *Theory of Pneumatology*, tr. Samuel Jackson, London, 1834; J. Kerner, *The Seeress of Prevorst*, tr. C. Crowe, London, 1845; H. Werner, *Guardian Spirits, a Case of Vision into the Spiritual World*, tr. A. E. Ford, New York, 1847.

contents was Andrew Jackson Davis's *Principles of Nature* (1847). Davis, the 'Poughkeepsie Seer', a youth of small attainments, came in 1843 under the influence of a mesmerist, and began to fall into spontaneous trances during which the spirits of Galen and Swedenborg held discourse with him. The revelations with which they favoured him go to make up the book in question. It is beloved of Spiritualists because of the similarity of the views therein expressed to those which later became Spiritualist orthodoxy, and because it predicted that a new era of spiritual communion was about to burst on the world. Its two volumes of rhapsodical cosmology can be excelled in tediousness only by the same author's *The Great Harmonia* (5 vols., 1851). It might however be added that both are remarkable productions for a young man of little education.

Within a few years of the beginnings of modern Spiritualism, four different kinds of explanations of its characteristic phenomena had been propounded. They were in essence the explanations which in more developed forms are still put forward today. We may list them as follows:

1. The phenomena are explicable on quite ordinary principles; e.g. as the products of fraud or self-deception on the part of the medium, or of hallucination or illusion of sense or memory on the part of the witnesses.

2. The phenomena are not susceptible of any ordinary explanation, but are none the less not the work of spirits; an explanation of them is to be sought in terms of physiological or psychological laws as yet imperfectly understood.

3. The phenomena are to be taken at face value; they are the handiwork of spirits.

4. The phenomena are of diabolic origin.

The last of these hypotheses, though frequently heard in the early days of Spiritualism, is now so rarely put forward that I shall nowhere consider it. But some preliminary remarks about the others may be worth while at this stage.

It was of course widely suggested that the phenomena were fraudulent.[1] Suspicion did not fall upon the inspirational dis-

---
[1] See, e.g., Elliott, *op. cit.*; H. Mattison, *Spirit Rapping Unveiled!*, New York, 1855; C. G. Page, *Psychomancy*, New York, 1853.

courses and writings, for the activities of mesmerists had made the American public familiar with the idea that in certain aberrant mental states people might carry out actions for which they were not really responsible. But the rappings and other physical phenomena came under heavy fire. The Fox sisters, the 'great guns of rappism', were frequently accused of fraud, though so far as I am aware they were never actually detected in it. The most popular theory was that they somehow made the noises with their toes or their knees. In April 1851 a relative of the Foxes, Mrs. Norman Culver, stated in the *New York Herald* that when Margaretta was away she (Mrs. Culver) had offered to assist Catherine in the production of the phenomena.[1] Catherine had accepted the offer and had shown her how to make the knockings with her knees and toes. Raps could be made to 'sound distant on the wall' by making them louder, and looking earnestly at the spot where one wished them to be heard. Questions asked by sitters could usually be answered correctly if the enquirer himself called the alphabet; his 'countenance and motions' provided the clues. Unfortunately Mrs. Culver's statement attributes to Catherine a circumstantial but clearly erroneous account of how she and her sister bamboozled the Corinthian Hall committees by which, in fact, she was never investigated.[2] Spiritualists suggested that Mrs. Culver had a long-standing feud with the Foxes; and at any rate it is hardly possible to come to useful conclusions about the knockings on the basis of her allegations. Many years afterwards, in October 1888, Margaretta, with Kate's seeming concurrence, confessed at a public meeting in New York that the rappings had been fraudulent from beginning to end. Placing her stockinged foot upon a stool, she produced loud rappings which were accompanied, so a doctor on the platform avowed, by palpable movements of her muscles.[3] By this time however the sisters were confirmed alcoholics, were almost penniless and were bent upon ruining their sister Leah. Someone who knew (and disliked) Margaretta at this period said that 'for five dollars she would have denied her mother, and would have sworn to any

[1] *Capron*, pp. 421–3; Spicer, *op. cit.*, pp. 82–8.
[2] Joseph McCabe, *Spiritualism: a Popular History from 1847*, London, 1920, p. 43, says optimistically that Mrs. Culver 'made one or two slight but immaterial mistakes in detail'.
[3] See R. B. Davenport, *The Death-blow to Spiritualism*, New York, 1888, p. 177.

thing'.[1] Soon afterwards Kate denied that she subscribed to Margaretta's avowals, and Margaretta herself retracted them. The trouble with all toe, ankle and knee theories is the absolute failure of their proponents (including Margaretta Fox) to tell precisely how the joints or members could be manipulated so as to reproduce the famous rappings in a convincing way. Quite a few people who could crack their toes or their knees came forward to give public demonstration of their powers;[2] but no toe-cracker of whom I have heard could tap out a rhythm in the least comparable to that which any one of the Fox sisters could produce on a good day. The sisters could obtain not just regular rappings, but arpeggios and cadenzas of raps at a rate not unlike that of a musician playing a fast passage. It is difficult indeed to believe that the human being has ever existed who could work his toes to this tune.[3]

Yet even if we discard these notions, and instead suppose that the Fox sisters concealed rapping machinery under their dresses, difficulties remain. How *did* they manage to convince so many persons that the rappings came from walls or doors which were well away from them, but which they could none the less hardly have 'prepared' in advance? Some rooms and some pieces of furniture exhibit odd acoustic effects; but so far as I can discover there is no *general* acoustic principle by which raps made in one place can be made to sound as though they came from another. Did the sisters accomplish the trick by 'directing their gaze earnestly' to the desired spot? Such methods have certainly been known to work with excited and uncritical believers; but the Fox sisters baffled even alert and intelligent persons who were doing their best to catch them out. And there is yet another difficulty. The Fox Sisters were very far indeed

[1] Fornell, *op. cit.*, p. 181.
[2] Cf. the interesting account of his own abilities in this direction by M. Petrovo-Solovovo, *J.S.P.R.* VI (1893), pp. 120–2.
[3] Cromwell Varley (a noted electrical engineer and a Fellow of the Royal Society) said that Kate Fox produced for him 'a chorus of raps such as fifty hammers, all striking rapidly, could hardly produce' (*Dial. Soc. Report*, p. 165). Sir William Crookes said that he had heard 'a cascade of sharp sounds as from an induction coil in full work' (*Researches in the Phenomena of Spiritualism*, London, 1874, p. 86). The violence of the blows was also sometimes such as to rule out toe- or knee-cracking. Crookes (*op. cit.*, p. 87) said that the raps which Kate produced were 'sometimes loud enough to be heard several rooms off'. Cf. R. D. Owen, *The Debateable Land*, 2nd edn., London, 1874, pp. 274–7.

from being the only persons in whose presence the rappings took place; even a quick glance at, say, Emma Hardinge's *Modern American Spiritualism* (1870) will convince the least credulous on this point. Indeed so numerous were rapping mediums in the early days of Spiritualism that if we are to suppose them all fraudulent we have almost to begin thinking in terms of some new kind of hysterical ailment.

Those who held that the phenomena of Spiritualism could be dealt with in terms of physiological or psychological laws as yet imperfectly understood usually nailed their colours to the mast of the Odic or Odylic Force supposedly revealed by the mesmeric researches of von Reichenbach.[1] Odic Force was a descendant of the universal magnetic fluid by reference to whose motions Mesmer and his disciples had explained the effects of animal magnetism; it was supposed to resemble electricity and magnetism closely in some respects, e.g. in possessing polarity and the power of attracting or repelling other bodies. Individuals of certain physical temperaments might under certain circumstances have their nerve centres charged with this force; if the lower centres became charged the force might discharge itself in the form of unintelligent rappings and movements of objects; if higher centres became charged the phenomena would manifest a corresponding intelligence. If the force flowed from one person's nervous system to another's, the thoughts and wishes of the first person could cause the second to execute corresponding actions or to produce corresponding rappings. Thus a medium amidst a circle of sitters might automatically express their thoughts and wishes as rapped or written messages from deceased friends and relations. This scheme of things may seem ludicrous today; but some of its expounders were far from being cranks.

Spiritualists generally accepted some part of the odylic theory, though often with considerable variations of terminology. It could readily be squared with their own doctrines about an odylo-magnetic ether, and it provided moreover a convenient backdoor through which nonsensical or erroneous

[1] See, e.g., Mahan, *op. cit.*; E. C. Rogers, *Philosophy of Mysterious Agents*, Boston, 1853; and Richmond's part of S. B. Brittan and B. W. Richmond, *A Discussion of the Facts and Philosophy of Ancient and Modern Spiritualism*, New York, 1853. For Baron K. von Reichenbach's theories, see his *Physico-Physiological Researches*, London, 1850; and *Podmore* I, pp. 117–19.

'communications', which were presumably the result of contamination from the sitters, could be expelled from the Mansion of Truth. Spiritualists simply tacked on to the theory the notion that spirits too could manipulate the odylic forces of the medium's nervous system so as to produce writing, speaking, raps, etc.[1] The spirits themselves frequently confirmed this general view.

Unfortunately, by admitting that sitters could influence communications, Spiritualists made it extremely difficult for any communicator known to a sitter to establish his independent existence. The only kind of communication which would seem to rule out the possibility that the medium might be obtaining all her information from the mental activity of those around her would be one in which a spirit gave about himself correct information of which no one present was aware. Such cases are infrequent in the early literature. An example is a communicator who appeared in 1853 at a circle in the township of Waterford, New York State, the medium being Mr. John Prosser of that town. The communicator claimed to be the spirit of an old Revolutionary soldier, and to have been over a hundred years old when he died. His remarks were recorded by a member of the circle, Elisha Waters:

> Now, this is every word true I'm telling ye. I'll tell ye, so that if you've a mind to take a little pains, you can find out that this is *jest* exactly as I tell it ye. I lived at Point Pleasant, New Jersey, and if you want to know, you *jest* ask if old Uncle John Chamberlain didn't speak the truth . . .
>
> My friends, I did not expect to speak with you again, but I want to give you this as a test. I died on Friday, the 15th day of January, 1847, and I was the father of eleven children. Now, if you've a mind to take a little pains, you will find this is all jest as I tell it ye. I don't talk as you do, but if you like to hear an old man, I will come again.[2]

A letter addressed to the postmaster of Point Pleasant, New Jersey, produced the following reply:

> With pleasure I will give thee a correct account, for I have known him well for fifty years, and lived a neighbour to him. He deceased January 15th 1847, aged one hundred and four

---

[1] See, e.g., Hare, *op. cit.*, pp. 94–5. [2] *Capron*, pp. 284–5.

years. He had seven children that lived to be married; three of them have deceased and left children. He has four daughters living at this time; three of them are neighbours to me; the oldest daughter is a widow, seventy-eight years old; three have husbands; one of them lives twenty miles from me. As they have very little learning, they request thee to correspond with me . . .

THOMAS COOK

However, cases of this kind present difficulties of interpretation, which will be touched on later.[1]

The possibility that the veridical information which communicators sometimes gave about themselves might in fact have come from the minds of the sitters did not seem to worry the many thousands of willing believers; neither did the suggestive observation, sometimes made, that meaningful messages would dwindle into nonsense when the hands and face of the relevant sitter were concealed from the medium. The number of Spiritualists grew and grew. By 1853 ten Spiritualist periodicals were established in the United States. In 1855 an enthusiast claimed that there were 2,500,000 Spiritualists in the country;[2] in 1859 a Catholic Convention put the number at 11,000,000.[3] These figures must be greatly exaggerated;[4] but even so there can be no doubt about the astonishing success of early Spiritualism. Its success however seems to have been mainly among the relatively unlettered. Of eminent persons who were converted to Spiritualism there were only a few: Judge J. W. Edmonds, a Judge of the Supreme Court of New York; N. Talmadge, formerly Governor of Wisconsin; Robert Hare, professor emeritus of chemistry at the university of Pennsylvania; Professor J. J. Mapes, an agricultural chemist; and Harriet Beecher Stowe, the authoress of *Uncle Tom's*

[1] Cf. pp. 250–1 below.
[2] Rev. W. R. Hayden, quoted in W. Howitt, *The History of the Supernatural*, London, 1863, Vol. II, p. 177.
[3] Hardinge, *op. cit.*, p. 273. Cf. *Podmore* I, p. 303.
[4] The earliest reliable figures are those of the Census Report of 1890, which puts the number of persons affiliated to Spiritualist Churches at 45,030. See Lawton, *op. cit.*, p. 146. But it must be remembered (*a*) that the number of Spiritualists had probably declined a good deal during the previous thirty years, and (*b*) that, as Lawton points out (*op. cit.*, p. 156), there may well be ten to fifteen non-enrolled Spiritualists for every enrolled one.

Cabin. But a number showed a more or less serious interest. One such was Abraham Lincoln;[1] and another was Wild Bill Hickok, Marshal of Abilene and celebrated gunfighter.[2] The spirits who warned Wild Bill of impending danger and guided the aim of his double-action .44s can hardly have come from the same sphere as the reformed generals who lectured the Quaker, Isaac Post, on pacifism and the wickedness of war.

Of attempts to study the phenomena scientifically, to prove them *in extenso* in an orderly and impartial way, there were at this period practically none. Almost the only investigations which could properly be called experimental were, as Podmore remarks, some of those conducted by Robert Hare.[3] Hare's work, unsatisfactory though it was, remained on its own for many years. In March 1869 William James, then a senior of the Harvard medical school, wrote as follows in a review of Epes Sargent's *Planchette: the Despair of Science* (a distinctly uncritical survey of Spiritualism and its phenomena):

> The present attitude of society on the whole question is as extraordinary and anomalous as it is discreditable to the pretensions of an age which prides itself on enlightenment and the diffusion of knowledge. We see tens of thousands of respectable people on the one hand admitting as facts of everyday certainty what tens of thousands of others equally respectable claim to be an abject and contemptible delusion; while other tens of thousands are content to stand passively in the dark between these two hosts and in doubt, the matter meanwhile being—rightfully considered—one of really transcendent interest.[4]

---

[1] On Abraham Lincoln and Spiritualism, see Fornell, *op. cit.*, pp. 118-23, and Nettie Colburn Maynard: *Was Abraham Lincoln a Spiritualist?*, London, 1917. Among the Lodge papers in the S.P.R. archives is a letter from a Dr. Ridgley Martin, of North Baltimore, Ohio, to W. R. Bradbrook, of Ipswich. It is dated 9th Dec. 1926. Dr. Martin describes how he attended a seance with Lincoln at Springfield, Illinois. Lincoln's mother and his sweetheart communicated, and at the end of the seance he remarked 'all religionists are more or less spiritualists'. On the suggestion by Conan Doyle (*op. cit.*, I, p. 146) that Lincoln's famous proclamation was influenced by the spirits, see W. F. Prince's 'The Aetiology of a Psychical Legend', *J.S.P.R.* XXVI (1930), pp. 148-57.

[2] R. O'Connor, *Wild Bill Hickok*, London, 1962, p. 233.

[3] Some of Hare's experiments resembled the later ones by Crookes described below (pp. 86-7). See Hare, *op. cit.*, pp. 40-55, and *Podmore* I, pp. 233-6.

[4] Quoted from *The Boston Daily Advertiser* of 10th March 1869 in G. Murphy and R. O. Ballou, *William James on Psychical Research*, London, 1960, p. 21.

James thought that what was needed was proper experimentation. But it was not until the eighteen-eighties that a systematic and extended enquiry was set afoot. Even then the participants were few in number. They were however men of remarkable ability and of undoubted dedication; and they were impelled by the belief that behind these doubtful phenomena there might obscurely lie truths not just of philosophical interest, but of immediate relevance to the welfare of suffering humanity.

II The Genesis of Reluctant Doubt

ON SUNDAY, 30th March 1851, was held Britain's first and only religious census. The worshippers at Divine Service in churches and chapels throughout England and Wales were counted by whoever was in charge; and from the figures thus obtained it was estimated that 7,261,032 persons had attended at least one service on that day. The population of England and Wales in 1851 was 17,927,609; and after deductions had been made for those whose duties, place of residence or physical condition precluded attendance the number of persons who could have gone to church but did not was put at 5,288,294.[1] The totals cannot be regarded as anything other than rough approximations, but they do suggest quite strongly that well over half the people who were in a position to attend Divine Service on that Sunday did so. What most impressed contemporaries however was not the number of worshippers, but the number of absentees; and it is possible that had the census been conducted a few years earlier or a few years later the percentage of reported attendance might have been higher. Today the figures prompt quite different reflections. No doubt quite a few of those who attended church did so simply from expediency; but even so there can hardly be the smallest doubt that sincere religious belief was far more widely disseminated in 1851 than it is at the present time.

It also seems likely that in 1851 religious belief, or at any rate strong religious belief, was distinctly more widespread than it had been fifty years before. To say that there had been a 'religious revival' would be over-simplification; there had been

[1] I have taken these figures from G. Kitson Clark's *The Making of Victorian England*, London, 1962, p. 149.

THE GENESIS OF RELUCTANT DOUBT

a number of interlinked revivals forming as it were the wavetops of an inflowing tide. But the facts are pretty clear. It is not possible to quote figures for church attendance—the religious census of 1851 was unique—but some statistics concerning the erection of new places of worship are very suggestive. Since the beginning of the century the Anglicans had built 2,698 new places of worship, the Congregationalists 2,330, the Baptists 2,137, and the old Methodists 10,182. These new places of worship had provided between them 5,041,440 new sittings.[1]

Various explanations of the growth in religious belief and observance during the first half of the nineteenth century have been put forward. Some have regarded it as an effect of the Romantic Revival; but a theory which can link Hannah More with Madame de Staël is surely capable of explaining anything.[2] Others have seen it as a continuation and amplification of the earlier Methodist revival in a country shaken by the excesses to which unbelief had led on the Continent. There can at least be no doubt that, despite internal schisms, the Methodist movement continued to make rapid progress, and that the Evangelical party which attained such influence in the Church of England between 1800 and 1830 resembled the Methodists in many ways. Both Evangelicals and Methodists would probably have subscribed to some such creed as this: Man is by inheritance radically sinful[3] and deserves no mercy from his Maker. But for the intercession of the Saviour he would be irretrievably lost. In consequence of that intercession, salvation can by God's grace be attained. It can be attained through faith in the living Christ, and only through faith in the living Christ. Participation in the sacraments, however frequent, does not confer Grace; nor can a lifetime of good works procure salvation. Good works without faith are like decorations on a tomb: they catch the eye but do not profit the man within.[4]

[1] Kitson Clark, *op. cit.*, p. 171.
[2] Though one must admit the similarity of *The Shepherd of Salisbury Plain* to certain of the *Lyrical Ballads*.
[3] Augustus Toplady, a noted early Evangelical, is said to have calculated that a man who lives out his allotted span will commit eighty thousand million sins in the course of his life. Presumably it paid to die young.
[4] In the light of the doctrine of 'justification by faith' one can understand the morbid preoccupation with death-bed and condemned-cell scenes characteristic of so much Methodist and Evangelical literature. If one did not sustain one's faith

The faith which saves and justifies is a direct and personal transaction between a man and his Saviour. No one need, or can, mediate between them. The Bible is God's Very Word, and a proper study of it is the surest road to deliverance. The Bible speaks of One who will judge the quick and the dead; it speaks of a Saviour and of salvation, but it speaks also of consignment to the Abyss. Its words are not intended as allegories. Christ is as real a figure as the Archbishop of Canterbury, and a far more frequent visitor to all parts of his Province. Heaven and Hell are actual localities. The Day of Judgment will take place as surely as the next Assizes and will be followed by even speedier executions.

It would however be misleading to present the similarities between Evangelicalism and Methodism as primarily similarities of belief. The most important similarity lay not in a set of beliefs but in a way of believing. The true Christian, so Evangelicals and Methodists both felt, should not merely be regular in his observances, should not merely set aside certain times for the exercise of his religion; he should *live* Christianity. He should be marked at all times by his earnest yet happy demeanour; by the holy zeal with which he performs even the humblest offices of life; by his continuing attempts to draw others to the paths of righteousness; by his abiding sense that every moment of time not spent in God's service must at the last be accounted for.

The similarities of tone between the Methodists and the Evangelical wing of the Church of England were so great that contemporaries frequently failed to distinguish between them; and it is hardly possible to regard the latter as other than in some sense a child of the former. No doubt Methodism likewise inspired or at least influenced the revivals in the various nonconformist sects, though why the ground should have been so particularly fertile at that time is another and a larger question. The Methodist and the Evangelical movements differed however in at least one noteworthy respect. The Methodists had been forced to work outside the established Church, and they found only a few friends amongst the wealthy or educated; the Evangelicals made a determined and almost political attempt

---

until the very hour of dissolution, one's soul might be forfeit. No quantity of good works could outweigh ultimate backsliding.

to take over the established Church, and they won support from many influential persons. By 1812 an Evangelical was Prime Minister, and the Church Missionary Society, a leading Evangelical organisation, numbered among its vice-presidents five peers, nine M.P.s and Sir Thomas Baring, the wealthy merchant banker.[1] By the eighteen-twenties the influence of Evangelicalism was being strongly, though perhaps indirectly, felt in University Senior Common Rooms. Among Oxford Fellows of the eighteen-twenties and eighteen-thirties who had come from Evangelical homes were Manning, Macaulay, J. H. Newman, Francis Newman, Jowitt, Mark Pattison, Robert Isaac Wilberforce, Hurrell Froude, Edward Pusey and John Keble. First at Oxford, then at Cambridge, the younger dons and the would-be dons found it increasingly natural not just to take religion seriously, but to make it the very pivot of their lives. Dons of an older and more wordly generation listened uneasily while their juniors discussed Baptismal regeneration, ecclesiology or visits to the Holy Land.[2] By the eighteen-thirties Evangelicalism had begun to affect the whole life of the nation[3] in ways too pervasive to be disentangled here. Many writers have suggested that it was from the zeal and influence of the Evangelicals, and even from the legislation which they brought about, that some of the factors most characteristic of the Victorian middle-class way of life derived. Halévy says that Evangelical religion was 'the moral cement of English society', and G. M. Young asserts:

> Evangelicalism had imposed on Society, even on classes which were indifferent to its religious basis and unaffected by its economic appeal, its code of Sabbath observance, responsibility and philanthropy; of discipline in the home, regularity in affairs; it had created a most effective technique of agitation, of private persuasion and social persecution.[4]

Once the Evangelical movement had lost its first crusading ardour, there was little about it to retain the allegiance of a

[1] Ford K. Brown, *Fathers of the Victorians*, Cambridge, 1962, p. 270.
[2] D. H. Newsome, *Godliness and Good Learning*, London, 1961, p. 17, quotes from V. H. H. Green a story that when the future Dean Stanley was describing a visit to the Holy Land to some clerics of his College, an elderly Fellow was heard to remark 'Jerusalem be damned. Give us wine, women and horses.'
[3] E. Halévy, *A History of the English People 1830–41*, London, 1927, p. 165, says that the summit of Evangelical influence was attained in the year 1833.
[4] G. M. Young, *Victorian England: Portrait of an Age*, 2nd edn., Oxford, 1953, p. 5.

sensitive or intelligent man. The children and grandchildren of its early leaders tended to desert it. Many of them were drawn away by the Oxford Movement of the eighteen-thirties and eighteen-forties, an attempt by refined and scholarly people, partly reacting against Evangelicalism, to make the doctrines and sacraments of Christianity seem once again mysterious, to exhibit the Church as a developing institution whose present could be illuminated by its past, and whose future might still have revelations to unfold. But few of those who had been brought up in the ways of Evangelicalism ever lost its stamp completely. The *earnestness* which had once been so especially characteristic of Evangelicals and Methodists could by 1840 or so be found amongst families which had altogether shed their Evangelicalism; moreover it had spread by force of example or through moral pressure to families with no Evangelical connections at all.

It is indeed the pattern of family life which Evangelicalism disseminated so widely[1] that seems in retrospect its most important legacy. Central to that pattern of life was a way of bringing up children about which much has been written. Religion was made not just part of what a child had to be taught, but that around which, at greater or lesser distance, every kind of lesson revolved. Some have represented the regime as one of misery and oppression which frowned upon the slightest enjoyment and brutally punished the most trivial breaches of discipline.

> Before Ernest could well crawl he was taught to kneel; before he could well speak he was taught the Lord's prayer, and the general confession. How was it possible that these things could be taught too early? If his attention flagged or his memory failed him, here was an ill weed which would grow apace, unless it were plucked out immediately, and the only way to pluck it out was to whip him, or shut him up in a cupboard, or dock him of some of the small pleasures of childhood.

Samuel Butler was not the only eminent Victorian whose childhood was made wretched by over-zealous parents; Augustus Hare, Mark Pattison and John Ruskin are other obvious examples. Even that celebrated chapter of Mrs.

---

[1] But which no doubt originated amongst Methodists. See Paul E. Sangster's *Pity My Simplicity*, London, 1963.

Sherwood's *The Fairchild Family* in which Mr. Fairchild punishes his children for quarrelling with each other by whipping them (while he recites rhythmic moral verses), lecturing them about Cain and Abel, and taking them to a gibbet where the corpse of a fratricide hangs in chains, may not have been entirely fictional. An elderly gentleman of my acquaintance can recollect hearing around the year 1890 the childhood reminiscences of a very old lady of Evangelical descent who told him that on hanging mornings at Newgate prison[1] she and her brothers and sisters had always been birched after breakfast to remind them of the certain doom which awaited the ungodly.

Not all religious parents however were such brutes as Theobald Pontifex and Mr. Fairchild. There were homes, and Evangelical homes, of a gentler and more cultivated kind, in which faith had to be professed freely or not at all, and example was held a better teacher than violence. Many parents felt it a duty to be, not heavy-handed and forbidding, but always, and whatever the circumstances, cheerful and kindly, believing that the Christian should at all times be recognised by the inward joy and the outward charity which faith brings in its train. Their households could be very happy places to grow up in. Discipline, though firm, was loving. Children were watched constantly, were encouraged and exhorted; but they were never neglected or cruelly punished. Above all they could take pleasure in the simpler sorts of religious observance. Bible-reading and family prayers, hymn-singing and scripture lessons, might seem to a half-comprehending child almost like grown-up rituals or games whose performance brought especial pleasure to that Friend and Protector who, though out of sight, was always close, and particularly close on Sundays.

Such households were far commoner than hostile accounts of Evangelicalism and the Victorian nursery might lead one to suppose.[2] Those whose childhoods were happiest found least cause to write about them; and studies based on contemporary fiction or propaganda are bound to reflect the views of

[1] The Middlesex gibbet was removed from Tyburn to Newgate in 1783. It remained outside Newgate prison until 1856.
[2] O. Chadwick, *The Victorian Church*, London, 1966, says (p. 446): 'We find many examples of pious evangelical children of pious evangelical homes, a father–son relationship of perfect naturalness and friendship, in families like Bickersteth, Moule, Villiers, Sumner, Ryle, Wilson.'

extremists.[1] The children of (say) James Stephen, Charles Russell or Archibald Campbell Tait were shown the greatest kindness and solicitude.[2] So were those of the Rev. Frederic Myers (1811–51), perpetual curate of St. John's, Keswick, a clergyman who in the eighteen-forties held, though he did not noise abroad, views that even in the freer atmosphere of the eighteen-sixties would have placed him among the 'Broad' churchmen.

Myers owed the living of St. John's to John Marshall, a local landowner whose immense fortune came from his Leeds flax-mills. In 1842 Myers married John Marshall's youngest daughter, Susan Harriet (b. 1811), a girl of piety and good sense. There must have been a considerable disparity in their fortunes, but the Marshalls do not seem to have opposed the match. Myers was a man of some intellectual and literary gifts,[3] earnest in his ministration, and zealous in the improvement of his parish. He was especially concerned to educate his parishioners; and he was no less concerned over the education of his own three children, Frederic William Henry (b. 1843), Ernest James (b. 1844) and Arthur Thomas (b. 1851). In later years Frederic attributed his life-long love of classical literature in part to the excellence of his father's early teaching.

The religious education of these children however seems to have been largely their mother's responsibility. She recorded her endeavours in this and other directions in a Journal, still surviving, which runs from 12th February 1844, when her eldest son was a year and six days old, to 18th September 1851, by which time her husband had been dead for two months. The eldest child, Freddy, who is of course the Journal's most prominent figure, was a precocious youngster and absorbed what his mother told him with absolute conviction and a burning interest.

On 26th November 1845 Susan Myers noted that she was thinking of giving young Freddy his first religious instruction—he was then two years and nine months old.

[1] Cf. M. Maison, *Search your Soul, Eustace*, London, 1961.
[2] See N. L. Annan, *Leslie Stephen: His Thought and Character in Relation to his Time*, London, 1951; G. W. E. Russell, *The Household of Faith*, London, 1902; W. Benham, ed., *Catharine and Craufurd Tait*, London, 1879. Catharine Tait's memoir (in Benham, *op. cit.*) of her five little daughters, all of whom died of scarlet fever in 1856, is profoundly moving. Some extracts are quoted by Newsome, *op. cit.*, pp. 76–8.
[3] See the article on him, in the *Dictionary of National Biography*.

I began, I think, speaking of heaven as a happy place to which he might some day go if he was a good boy. 'Is it very far away, Mamma—heaven? Bee wd. rather stay here.' 'But every body in heaven is quite good & quite happy Freddy'—'Bee not quite good—Bee stay here Mamma'—I told him that indeed he was not quite good but that there was someone whom he must ask to make him good—some one that his Papa & I went to church (if it was Sunday) to prey to & ask Him to make us good & that this was God. He looked very attentive and then said— 'Is he a man, God?' No I said he was far better and kinder than any man cd be. 'Bee didn't see him go to church Mamma—did you see him, did Papa?' No I said no one cd. see God but He saw us & wd. hear us when we prayed—that he gave us all we had—bright sun, beautiful flowers etc—and was very kind to us— that I had a great deal more to tell him sometime about God and about a very good book He had given us called the Bible.

A few months later she made him repeat a short prayer, 'but though he was quiet and attentive and not irreverent I don't think he entered into the feelings of really addressing God'.

When he was just over four years old he began reading the Bible; his mother described his reactions in a passage which some might think curiously prognostic of her son's future character and interests:

> He is sadly shocked and grieved when good men do anything wrong and seems hardly able to understand how it should be so. And of the bad people he always hopes 'they were very sorry and grew good at last'—All his thoughts have a *hopeful* tendency, and he loves the *bright* side of everything. In speaking of sorrow for the death of any good person, he asks—'But would not God make him an angel in heaven?' 'Yes, I hope so'—'Oh then Mamma, *that* is very *happy*!' Indeed he seems to have a sort of realizing vision of angels which makes them quite familiar to him. 'I had such a *beautiful* dream Mamma—I saw such a bright angel standing near me.'

At about this time there occurred an incident which left a lasting impression on little Freddy:

> One day he came to me after his walk scarcely able to refrain from tears, telling me he had seen 'such a sad thing! a little mole that a cart had gone over & killed.' Then his face cleared up & he said very earnestly 'But Mamma I *do* think that little mole's soul is gone to heaven—don't you?' 'No my child—that

mole had not a soul at all you know—' and 'Oh Mamma'—
& then he could not refrain from a burst of tears, when his
comfort was taken from him.

Freddy remembered this occurrence forty-five years later
when he came to write his autobiography:

> To this day I remember my rush of tears at the thought of that
> furry innocent creature, crushed by a danger which I fancied
> it too blind to see, and losing all joy for ever by that unmerited
> stroke. The pity of it! the pity of it! and the first horror of a
> death without resurrection rose in my bursting heart.[1]

He was clearly a child of unusual sensitiveness in a number of
different ways. In his autobiography he recalled the influence
which his surroundings had upon him in childhood:

> It was in the garden of that fair Parsonage that my conscious life
> began. *Ver illud erat.* The memories of those years swim and
> sparkle in a haze of light and dew. The thought of Paradise is
> interwoven for me with that garden's glory;—with the fresh
> brightness of a great clump and tangle of blush-roses, which
> hung above my head like a fairy forest, and made magical with
> their fragrance the sunny inlets of the lawn. And even with
> that earliest gaze is mingled the memory of that vast background
> of lake and mountain; where Skiddaw—οὑμὸς κιθαιρών—hid
> his shoulders among the clouds, while through them his head
> towered to heaven; and Causey Pike and Catbells, with the vale
> of Newlands between them, guarded that winding avenue into
> things unknown,—as it were the limitary parapet and enchan-
> ted portal of the world. Close to Parsonage is Castelet, a little
> hill from which Derwentwater is seen outspread, with Borrow-
> dale in the distance. I can recall the days when that prospect
> was still one of mysterious glory; when gleaming lake and
> wooded islands showed a broad radiance bossed with gloom, and
> purple Borrowdale wore a visionary majesty on which I dared
> scarcely look too long.[2]

That these recollections were not coloured by an adult
passion for Wordsworth is shown by Susan Myers' Journal entry
for 12th October 1847:

> He is not grateful or humble as I sh. like to see him. I am afraid
> he has too much *prosperity*—for it is difficult to refrain from

---

[1] *Fragments*, p. 8.   [2] *Fragments*, p. 7.

giving pleasure to a being so joyous & so easily delighted as he is. Very simple things are matters of almost [ec]stasy to him— a new flower, a new walk, a bright moon unexpectedly caught sight of—his lessons if skilfully managed—a new book always— a bit of poetry which takes his fancy when he comes to it—these he likes 'so *very very* much—I cannot tell how much Mamma'— And along with this delight is a proportionate pain when he is disappointed in anything he has set his heart upon—or when his will is crossed, or his fancy, in anything.

Such excessive sensitivity was not, Susan Myers thought, matched by any intellectual eminence:

> I do not see anything remarkable in his intellect so far—good sense and a *very* good memory seem to be his gifts. But we might be thankful for even much less than he has if we may but be permitted to see his moral nature developing as we could wish— and the early influence of the grace of God upon his heart.

But Freddy's moral nature did not altogether develop as his mother wished. Despite listening to her teachings and reading a chapter of the Bible every day, he remained careless of parental instructions, and was arrogant and overbearing with other children. On the other hand his memory was indeed remarkable; in November 1848 he learned one of Macaulay's *Lays* (560 lines) by heart to please his uncle Whewell.[1] And his mother seems to have underestimated his intellect. At the age of five he composed upon the text 'Not slothful in business fervent in spirit serving the Lord, Rejoicing in hope patient in tribulation continuing instant in prayer, Distributing to the necessities of saints given to hospitality'[2] a little sermon whose platitudinousness and sonority ring so true that they might well inspire grave doubts as to the quality of his father's preaching. And the questions which he asked in this dialogue are remarkably subtle for a five-year old:

> Freddy delights much in dwelling on the idea of Heaven— 'all people good, none naughty—& as happy as if it were always Christmas Day—But they're *quite* different, the happiness that is on *earth* and that in heaven—are they not?'—'Not

---

[1] William Whewell (1794–1866), author of *History of the Inductive Sciences* (1837) and *Philosophy of the Inductive Sciences* (1840), master of Trinity College, Cambridge, 1841–66, married Susan Marshall's sister Cordelia.
[2] Romans xii. 11–13. Freddy's punctuation.

quite of a different kind' I said—'for what will make us most happy in heaven'—'Oh to love God & Jesus Christ—and that we may do here—but then we shall so *very very* much more then. And shall we love *every*body, people that we never saw or heard of before?'—'Yes—every one in Heaven'—'Then'—with a little doubtfulness—'will the black people have their black skins when they come to heaven?'—I said 'yes—probably—but every one will look beautiful there, because they will look so good'—'Yes & so *bright* too—I wonder whether any angels move about in those bright clouds and make them so shiny.'

'But can you tell Mamma, why God made only *2* places—one so very good as heaven, & the other so very bad as hell—& why not another, not *quite* so bad, for those who are a *little* good?' I said 'God gives us all our choice here on earth whether we will choose good or evil & tells us this is one only time.' 'Then Mamma where do you think that little baby of Aunt C.'s who died before it had any name will go?—won't it go to heaven, for you know it had no time to choose?'

On his sixth birthday, 6th February 1849, Freddy was induced to set down a series of resolutions, some of which would have satisfied the most fervent Evangelical:

1. To strive more to please God and to be his true servant.
2. To follow Christ and follow dear Papa as he followed Christ.
3. To have more of that love which St. Paul describes I Cor. XIII.
5. To remember always that GOD sees me and that I shall have to render an account of all my works to HIM.
12. To remember that NOW is the appointed time and that it may be too late to repent even today.

The preoccupation with death and the afterworld which Freddy had, as a result of his mother's teachings, by then acquired would now strike the most religious people as altogether morbid, and at times it undoubtedly caused him great unhappiness.

One day at Torquay [in the spring of 1850] I was talking to them [Freddy and Ernest] about their cousin Harry and his illness & death—& how the doctor desired him to be kept so quiet, & not to know how ill he was—'Oh what a pity' Freddy said—'there would be no *last words* then—none like Bp. Shirley's repeating that beautiful hymn the last day' ('I praised the earth etc' [)] 'Then' I said 'if you were very ill wd. you like me to tell you?'—'Oh Mamma—I shd. not like it—I think *you* wd. be so very unhappy if I died'—and this thought quite upset him & he burst into tears. 'But' I said—'I shd. be comforted if I thought you loved Jesus Christ—and were with him in heaven—' 'Yes but I cd. not come back to tell you I was happy—Oh I wish we could all die at once & go to heaven together '& he was still weeping.

Susan Myers was not good at temporising to assuage Freddy's worries, and her attempts in this direction were sometimes unfortunate, as he recalled many years later:

> I had a second shock of pain at seven or eight years old. My mother, who shrank from dwelling on the hideous doctrine of hell, suggested to me that perhaps men who led bad lives on earth were annihilated at death. The idea that such a fate should be possible for any man seemed to me appalling. I remember where I stood at the moment, and how my brain reeled under the shock.[1]

Curiously enough the death of his father in July 1851 gave him no such anguish as this merely speculative suggestion. His firm and completely literal belief that his father was now with Jesus and the angels blunted the edge of his sorrow and enabled him to be a very real source of comfort to his mother. On 18th September 1851 she noted in her Journal:

> I cd. not have believed that a child of 8 yrs. old could have given such sympathy & such comfort in deep sorrow as I have had from Freddy . . . when we first entered this sad house & I was overpowered with grief he began with a full heart & trembling voice to repeat to me 'Blessed [are the] dead [that] die in the Lord'—'The Ld. gave & the Ld. hath taken away' 'He maketh sore & bindeth up. He woundeth and His hands make whole.' Once when I said 'there can never be joy again'—or something like it—he said 'You know God *can* do everything— & He might give us, just once, such a vision of Him as shd. make us happy all our lives after.'

'But,' she added, with remarkable clear-sightedness, 'I see great danger in trusting to mere excitement of feeling in him.'

Probably few children were as sensitive or as precocious as Freddy. But there is no doubt that many of those born into

---

[1] *Fragments*, p. 8.

educated homes between, say, 1825 and 1850 were brought up rather as he was. Religion and religious observances were made the central point not just of lessons but of life. A child might come to believe that should he die, his parents' most loved and trusted friend, the Lord Jesus, would personally conduct him to a place of everlasting bliss; and might wonder, as Freddy Myers did, why Heaven was not visible when the clouds rolled back. The emotional security in which such an upbringing, if not too harsh, could enfold a child is nowadays, and to an adult, almost unimaginable. Loss of faith entailed not just a poignant realisation that all one's hopes and all one's memories must one day pass into the shadows; it cut one instantly adrift from a loved and sheltering world in which one's place and obligations admitted of no doubt, and one's path ahead, however arduous, was clear.

The faith of children who were born into such households during the second quarter of the nineteenth century was to be severely tested. These children grew to maturity in a period when, for the first time in almost two hundred years, the discoveries and speculations of scientists and scholars were coming into marked and public conflict with the teachings of Christianity. It was, tragically enough, the most sensitive and the most intelligent Christians who were most liable to succumb. Many of them ranked their loss of faith as the most dreadful catastrophe that had ever befallen them. J. A. Symonds' complaint is mild:

> The sensation of God disappeared from me without the need of God being destroyed. But this is not merely a personal history, it is the history of the age in which we live, of the age of disintegration of old beliefs.[1]

Some, like Otho Laurence in Mallock's *New Republic* (1877), would have echoed Clough's *Easter Day*:

> Ah Well-a-day, for we are souls bereaved!
> Of all the creatures under heaven's wide cope
> We are most hopeless who had once most hope,
> And most beliefless who had once believed.

* * *

[1] Quoted by L. E. Elliott-Binns, *Religion in the Victorian Era*, London, 1936, p. 283.

THE GENESIS OF RELUCTANT DOUBT

Until the year 1859 it had been quite easy for religious people to think that science was on their side. Many of the leading scientists of the early and middle nineteenth century were profoundly religious; and parents could readily believe that studying elementary science would not merely keep their children out of mischief, but instil into them a proper appreciation of the craftsmanship which the Author of the Universe had put into his handiwork. It is true that some sensitive persons felt uneasy at the direction which certain sciences—particularly, of course, geology—were taking; in 1851 Ruskin wrote to a friend:

> If only the geologists would let me alone, I could do very well, but those dreadful hammers! I hear the clink of them at the end of every cadence of the Bible verses.[1]

Tennyson, too, expressed similar anxieties in well-known stanzas of *In Memoriam* (1850). Yet he was able, whether logically or not, to dissolve those anxieties in the course of the poem; and his optimism was shared by many thinking people of the time.

If science at all weakened religion in the eighteen-forties and eighteen-fifties, it was not so much through direct clashes (though there were clashes)[2] as indirectly, by the creation of an atmosphere in which honest doubt was almost bound to spring up. In the eighteenth and early nineteenth centuries the members of scientific societies had, to the general way of thinking, very often been figures of fun, scarcely distinguishable from astrologers and alchemists. But in the second quarter of the nineteenth century various scientific and technical achievements gained wide publicity and fired people's imaginations with the power and the possibilities of science. Obvious examples are: the development of the electric telegraph; the first measurement of the distance of a fixed star; the discovery of the planet Neptune by a combination of theoretical and observational techniques; and Owen's reconstruction of the *moa* from

[1] Quoted by L. E. Elliott-Binns, *English Thought 1860–1900: The Theological Aspect*, London, 1956, p. 175 n.
[2] Robert Chambers' *Vestiges of Creation* (1844) created of course a sensation and an outcry; but those who exclaimed would, as A. D. White has justly remarked (*A History of the Warfare of Science with Theology in Christendom*, New York, 1930, Vol. I, p. 66), have been better engaged in putting up thanksgivings for Chambers' account of evolution, and prayers that it might prove true.

a small piece of bone. The process reached a kind of peak in the Great Exhibition of 1851, which brought recent advances in technology to the notice of even quite humble and uneducated persons.

These developments could not fail to arouse, at least in younger people, very considerable optimism as to what scientists might in the future achieve through their methods of empirical investigation. A faith in empirical methods leads naturally to an empiricist philosophy. And so when John Stuart Mill produced in his *Logic* (1843) the most closely reasoned empiricist treatise to appear for over a hundred years, the younger intellectuals were very ready to listen to him. He was read and discussed first of all at Oxford, which the Dissolution of the Oxford Movement had left in a state of flux. He took longer to penetrate Cambridge, but by the late eighteen-fifties he had attained there, and more generally throughout the country, an influence greater perhaps than any other philosopher has ever enjoyed, and certainly greater than he was himself ever to enjoy again.

The dominant themes of Mill's *Logic* are two: Firstly that we have no legitimate source of information about the world except our own senses and inferences based ultimately upon them—'intuition' and 'faith' are not valid grounds for belief. Secondly that it ought to be possible through a study of the nature of valid inference to construct (was was hitherto lacking) a proper methodology for the social sciences, the sciences which above all others should be capable of alleviating the lot of mankind (a function which Mill and his followers thought that religion had conspicuously failed to perform). Something of the tenor of Mill's influence upon the younger men at Cambridge in the early eighteen-sixties may be gathered from this account of it by Henry Sidgwick, one of the ablest of them:

> ... I will begin by sketching briefly the ideal which, under the influence primarily of J. S. Mill, but partly of Comte seen through Mill's spectacles, gradually became dominant in my mind in the early sixties:—I say 'in my mind', but you will understand that it was largely derived from intercourse with others of my generation, and that at the time it seemed to me the only possible ideal for all adequately enlightened minds. It had two aspects, one social and the other philosophical or

THE GENESIS OF RELUCTANT DOUBT

theological. What we aimed at from a social point of view was a complete revision of human relations, political, moral, and economic, in the light of science directed by comprehensive and impartial sympathy; and an unsparing reform of whatever, in the judgment of science, was pronounced to be not conducive to the general happiness . . .

As regards theology . . . What was fixed and unalterable and accepted by us all was the necessity and duty of examining the evidence for historical Christianity with strict scientific impartiality; placing ourselves as far as possible outside traditional sentiments and opinions, and endeavouring to weigh the *pros* and *cons* on all theological questions as a duly instructed rational being from another planet—or let us say from China— would naturally weigh them.[1]

These young men would not necessarily have rejected traditional religious beliefs; but their rejection of the traditional way of believing was a step towards so doing.

Sidgwick's own career illustrates the religious doubts and difficulties which troubled many of his contemporaries and successors. He was born in 1838 and went to school at Rugby. His small size and slim build kept him from achieving any athletic distinctions, but his other gifts soon became apparent. His cousin and future brother-in-law, E. W. Benson, later Archbishop of Canterbury, was a master at the school and for some years exercised a profound influence upon him. When Sidgwick went up to Trinity College, Cambridge, in 1855, he ardently desired to follow Benson into the Church, and his University career was of a kind which might have given him a brilliant start. He won several of the more important university prizes, and in 1859 was Senior Classic, First Chancellor's Medallist and 33rd Wrangler.[2] Later in the same year he was elected to a College Fellowship. It is true that at this period of his life he was (except with his family and close friends) painfully reserved and shy; but before very long, and largely as a result of severe self-discipline, he overcame this handicap, and there can be little doubt that had he pursued an ecclesiastical

---

[1] *H.S.: A Memoir*, pp. 39–40.
[2] According to Leslie Stephen, *Sketches from Cambridge by a Don*, London, 1865, p. 38, a high place in either of the two Triposes could in effect obtain at least £5,000 for the man concerned, 'besides an amount of glory of which it is difficult to make an exact valuation'.

career the highest offices in the land would have been open to him. Yet by February 1860 he was writing to a friend 'My own great difficulty at present is whether I can put such fetters on the free expression of my religious belief as seems to be expected of a clergyman.'

An important cause of the waning of Sidgwick's clerical ambitions seems to have been his election in 1857 to membership of the 'Apostles', a small but extremely select discussion society founded in the early part of the century. The spirit of the society gradually came to absorb and dominate Sidgwick completely and to influence the whole direction of his life:

> I can only describe it as the spirit of the pursuit of truth with absolute devotion and unreserve by a group of intimate friends, who were perfectly frank with each other, and indulged in any amount of humorous sarcasm and playful banter, and yet each respects the other, and when he discourses tries to learn from him and see what he sees. Absolute candour was the only duty that the tradition of the society enforced. . . .
>
> . . . after I had gradually apprehended the spirit as I have described it, it came to seem to me that no part of my life at Cambridge was so real to me as the Saturday evenings on which the apostolic debates were held; and the tie of attachment to the society is much the strongest corporate bond which I have known in life. I think, then, that my admission into this society and the enthusiastic way in which I came to idealise it really determined or revealed that the deepest bent of my nature was towards the life of thought—thought exercised on the central problems of human life.[1]

It would not have been possible for someone so much affected by the spirit of the Apostles, and so much influenced by Mill, to ignore the results, gradually filtering through from Germany, of the new 'higher' criticism of the Bible. German scholars had for some time past been applying to the Bible methods of historical and textual criticism originally developed in the elucidation of classical texts. Their enquiries had cast considerable doubts on such fundamental matters as the Mosaic authorship of the Pentateuch, the trustworthiness of parts of the New Testament narratives, and the genuineness of various Pauline epistles. It took a considerable time for the results of

[1] *H.S.: A Memoir*, pp. 34–5.

German criticism to reach the educated English public. The first clear hints of approaching trouble came perhaps from various articles by leading freethinkers and learned Unitarians published in the *Westminster Review* in and after 1852,[1] when George Eliot and John Chapman[2] assumed charge of it. An increasing restlessness began to develop among the more liberal-minded and intelligent clergy. They could hardly help accepting many of the conclusions of the higher criticism, but they did not think these conclusions fatal to true religion. They were naturally alarmed lest the majority of Churchmen, by holding fast to narrow, fundamental beliefs, should estrange themselves more and more from contemporary thought. Benjamin Jowett expressed his fears upon this point in a volume called *Essays and Reviews* which he and six other liberal Churchmen published in 1859 as a kind of 'Broad Church' manifesto:

> It is a mischief that critical observations which any intelligent man can make for himself, should be ascribed to atheism or unbelief. It would be a strange and almost incredible thing that the Gospel, which at first made war only on the vices of mankind, should now be opposed to one of the highest and rarest of human virtues—the love of truth. And that in the present day the great object of Christianity should be, not to change the lives of men, but to prevent them from changing their opinions; that would be a singular inversion of the purposes for which

---

[1] Especially influential was an article by James Martineau (April 1853) on *Creed and Heresies of Early Christianity*, which expounded the view of Baur of Tübingen, a neo-Hegelian, that the New Testament contains unmistakable evidence of a division in the early Church between a Judaising school, headed by St. Peter, and a Universalist school, headed by St. Paul. The Catholic Church represents an Hegelian synthesis of the two antithetical viewpoints; it is Pauline in its Universalism, but Petrine in clinging to an authoritative set of laws and customs. The Fourth Gospel, far from being an eyewitness account of the Ministry of Christ, is a second-century reinterpretation of his career and teachings in the light of the aforesaid synthesis. *The Acts of the Apostles* is likewise a second-century work, mostly fictional, and written to conceal the schism. Some account of Baur's views was also given in two fairly 'popular' works, R. W. Mackay's *Progress of the Intellect* (1850), and his *Rise and Progress of Christianity* (1854).

[2] Chapman (1821–94) published George Eliot's translation of Strauss's *Life of Jesus* (1846) and the two books by R. W. Mackay referred to in the previous footnote, so he was quite influential in disseminating knowledge of German Biblical criticism. He also published, curiously enough, the English edition of Andrew Jackson Davis's *Principles of Nature*, a work whose hostility to the Church made it, the Swedenborgian J. J. G. Wilkinson wrote to Henry James Sr. on 23rd Jan. 1848, 'a kind of new Koran to one section of the Unitarians' (letter in the Archives of the Swedenborg Society).

Christ came into the world. The Christian religion is in a false position when all the tendencies of knowledge are opposed to it. Such a position cannot be long maintained, or can only end in the withdrawal of the educated classes from the influences of religion.[1]

Jowett's remedy for these dangers is that Scripture must be interpreted like any other book; and some of the other essayists were even more radical in their tone. *Essays and Reviews* was for a time overshadowed by Darwin's *Origin of Species*, which had appeared shortly before it. However, in October 1860 Frederic Harrison, a young positivist, reviewed it in the *Westminster*, under the heading of 'Neo-Christianity'. He hailed the book with delight as evidence that Christianity was about to die of self-inflicted wounds. That a book written by Christians, and mostly by clergymen, should rouse a freethinker to enthusiasm scandalised the orthodox beyond measure and, though the authors at once became famous, or at least notorious, they were subjected not merely to abuse but to active persecution. It seemed to conservative Christians quite appalling that at a time when the impregnable rock of Holy Scripture was being undermined by Darwin and his allies, a group of those whose sacred duty should have been to shore it up again had conspired to hammer their wedges not under it but into it.

The reactions of the orthodox disgusted Sidgwick and those of his friends who, like him, thought honesty the highest of intellectual virtues. He addressed a letter to *The Times* on the subject, and was rather surprised that on 20th February 1861 it was published:

> What we all want is, briefly, not a condemnation but a refutation. The age when ecclesiastical censures were sufficient in such cases has passed away. A large portion of the laity now, though unqualified for abstruse theological investigations, are yet competent to hear and decide on theological arguments. These men will not be satisfied by an *ex cathedra* shelving of the question, nor terrified by a deduction of awful consequences from the new speculations. For philosophy and history alike have taught them to seek not what is 'safe', but what is true. What has hitherto appeared ... [is] calculated only to alienate the men I speak of. And yet these men cling with all their

---

[1] *Essays and Reviews*, 7th edn., London, 1861, p. 374.

THE GENESIS OF RELUCTANT DOUBT

hearts to Church of England Christianity! As a learned divine (Mr. Westcott) expresses it, they love their early faith, but they love truth more.

We want, then, a reply which will take each essay separately, discuss it fully and fairly, entering into the writer's point of view. ... All the friends of the essayists know that the only ground upon which they have met is a belief in the advantage of perfectly open discussion and perfectly impartial investigation. If they can be met and refuted on their own ground, the publication of the book will have been a blessing to the Church; for we cannot ignore the fact that the thoughts they have expressed have long been floating vaguely through the minds of many. The way in which they have hitherto been handled will increase their influence, I think, upon the mass of English laity; it will increase their influence, I am sure, upon the youth of England.[1]

The refutation for which Sidgwick asked was not forthcoming, and he began with great perseverance and earnestness to seek his own answers to the problems which had been raised. He pursued a serious course of philosophical reading, and went in some detail into such historical questions as he hoped would give him 'important aid in answering the great questions raised by the orthodox Christianity from which my view of the Universe had been derived'. These questions appear to have been mostly ones concerned with the credibility or otherwise of the supernatural elements in the Gospel stories, it being still widely held at that time that Christ's miracles were his 'credentials':

Was Jesus incarnate God, miraculously brought into the world as a man? Were his utterances of divine authority? Did he actually rise from the grave with a human body glorified, and therewith ascend into heaven? Or if the answers to these questions could not strictly be affirmative in the ordinary sense of the term, what element of truth, vital for mankind, could be disengaged from the husk of legend, or symbolised by the legend, supposing the truth itself capable of being established by human reasoning?[2]

In 1862 Sidgwick read Renan's *Études d'Histoire Religieuse* and derived from it '... the conviction that it was impossible really

---

[1] H.S.: A Memoir, pp. 64–5. [2] H.S.: A Memoir, pp. 37–8.

to understand at first hand Christianity as an historical religion without penetrating more deeply the mind of the Hebrews and of the Semitic stock from which they sprang'.[1] This conviction led him to spend a good part of his spare time during the next three years in studying Arabic and Hebrew. He visited Germany, then the centre of such researches, and for a while even had thoughts of putting in for one of Cambridge's two Chairs in Arabic. That his historical and textual studies were not superficial may be seen from his review of Seeley's *Ecce Homo* in the *Westminster* for July 1866. But by the end of 1864 he had ceased to believe that such endeavours would help him to answer the problems which haunted him. Why he reached this conclusion is not specifically stated in his biography or his published writings, but what hints there are[2] suggest that particularly bothersome to him was a dilemma over the evidence for the miraculous events connected with the ministry of Christ and the foundation of Christianity. This dilemma may perhaps be stated as follows:

Either the occurrence of 'miracles' is (in the light perhaps of modern scientific knowledge) absolutely incredible. In that case we must reject as untrustworthy all portions of the Bible which narrate miraculous events. But if we do this not merely will we deprive Christianity of those parts of its 'evidences' which have in past times most struck plain men; we will be in danger of casting doubt on the accuracy of almost every other passage in the Bible, including the vital chapters of the New Testament. For there is generally speaking no reason for dismissing the 'miraculous' parts of the Bible except that they narrate miracles; their textual qualifications are no different from those of other parts. If one portion of text with those qualifications has to be dismissed, other portions of text with similar qualifications (i.e. much of the rest of the Bible) cannot readily be accepted.

Or miraculous events are not to be rejected as inherently incredible, but are to be allowed to take the place which they have always held among the supports of Christianity. In this

---

[1] *H.S.: A Memoir*, p. 36.
[2] See esp. his *Miscellaneous Essays and Addresses*, London, 1904, pp. 2–10; and *H.S.: A Memoir*, pp. 345–8. Cf. pp. 153–61 of C. D. Broad's 'Henry Sidgwick and Psychical Research', *P.S.P.R.* XLV (1938), pp. 131–61.

case a further set of difficulties arises. Recent historical and textual criticism has shown beyond doubt that most of the evidence for the New Testament miracles (not to mention the Old Testament ones) can not unfairly be described as remote and hearsay. The evidence for these miracles is, considered just as *evidence*, not obviously stronger than the evidence for other, non-Christian, miracles; indeed it is quite certainly far weaker than the evidence for, let us say, the miraculous events associated with modern Spiritualism. If we *are* prepared to admit the occurrence of miracles, we have no reason to continue to regard Christianity as a religion whose supernatural credentials are in any way unique.

Abandoning all hope that historical enquiry would remove his religious difficulties, Sidgwick plunged back into philosophy and theology; and in 1867 he was appointed College lecturer in Moral Science. He had indeed never abandoned philosophical and theological studies even during the period of his historical and linguistic endeavours; and the continual swinging of his opinions from left to right of centre and back again would be almost comical could one not infer the intensity of effort and the expenditure of feeling which lay behind it.[1]

January 1862 had found him re-reading Comte. 'I have rather less sympathy with his views than before,' he wrote to E. M. Young, 'but his life is a fine evidence of the power of enthusiasm even in the nineteenth century. I tried to fancy being a Positivist and adoring Gutenberg, the inventor of printing, but I found the conception impossible.'[2] By May of the same year he was writing to J. J. Cowell:

> I have given up a good deal of my materialism and scepticism, and come round to Maurice and Broad Church again; not that I expect exactly to stay there, but I feel that I must learn all that they have got to teach me before I go any further. I have been deeply impressed by the impotence of modern unbelief in explaining the phenomena which Christians point to as evidence of the Holy Spirit's influence. 'The wind bloweth where it listeth, etc.,' is as true now as it ever was. I used to think that one explained the difference between the religious and irre-

---

[1] A résumé of his reading and the changes in his opinions will be found on pp. xv–xxi of the 6th (1901) edition of his *Methods of Ethics*.
[2] *H.S.: A Memoir*, p. 74.

ligious man by using words like 'enthusiasm'; but science can no more bridge over this difference than she can the difference between a man and a brute.¹

But within a month he was complaining to another friend, Graham Dakyns, that Mansel, a leading Broad Churchman, talked of revelation 'as if the Bible had dropped from the skies ready translated into English; he ignores all historical criticism utterly'. 'At present', he concluded, 'I am only a Theist; but I have vowed that it should not be for want of profound and devoted study, if I do not become a Christian.'² At the end of 1862 he broke from Mill and utilitarianism and moved towards the position which he later consolidated in *The Methods of Ethics* (1874). To Dakyns he wrote in December 1862:

> You know I want intuitions for Morality; at least one (of Love) is required to supplement the utilitarian morality, and I do not see why, if we are to have one, we may not have others. I have worked away vigorously at the selfish morality, but I cannot persuade myself, except by trusting intuition, that Christian self-sacrifice is really a happier life than classical insouciance.³

Philosophy however, like history, failed to lead him back to Christianity. His hopes of returning were, curiously enough, boosted by the publication in 1866 of Seeley's *Ecce Homo*. Sidgwick's review of this work for the *Westminster* was highly critical; none the less, as he wrote to Graham Dakyns in April or May 1866:

> I have had the work of Christ put before me by a powerful hand, and been made to recognise its extraordinary excellence as I have never before done; and though I do not for a moment relinquish my right to judge it by the ideal, and estimate its defects, partialities, etc., yet I do feel the great need that mankind have of a pattern, and I have none that I could propose to substitute. Hence I feel that I should call myself a Christian if I were in a country where . . . [at this point the letter is torn].⁴

But this partial *rapprochement* with Christianity did not last and, in June 1869, Sidgwick felt impelled to take a step which he had long contemplated. He resigned his Fellowship and assistant tutorship at Trinity, on the grounds that he could not continue

---
¹ *H.S.: A Memoir*, p. 79.
² *H.S.: A Memoir*, pp. 81, 82.
³ *H.S.: A Memoir*, p. 90.
⁴ *H.S.: A Memoir*, pp. 145–6.

in that assent to the doctrines of the Church of England which had been a condition of his appointment. However, his standing with the College was such that he was immediately appointed to a lectureship in Moral Sciences (at £200 a year), so that his action did not, as it might have done, end his Cambridge career, but only involved him in a substantial loss of income.

He did not at that time definitely secede from the Church of England; indeed I do not know whether he ever took such a step. He continued for the rest of his life to lean somewhat hesitantly towards Theism. Only in terms of the existence of a supreme and supremely moral Being, guiding all things to good ends, could he conceive why his knowledge of Duty should be to him as insistent as his knowledge of the physical world. To an enquirer he wrote in 1880:

> I cannot resign myself to disbelief in duty; in fact, if I did, I should feel that the last barrier between me and complete philosophical scepticism, or disbelief in truth altogether, was broken down. Therefore I sometimes say to myself 'I believe in God'; while sometimes again I can say no more than 'I hope this belief is true, and I must and will act as if it was.'[1]

Both Sidgwick and his friends saw the epitome of his life-long search for Truth in a stanza from one of his favourite poems, Tennyson's *The Voyage:*

> For one fair Vision ever fled
> Down the waste waters day and night,
> And still we follow'd where she led,
> In hope to gain upon her flight.
> Her face was evermore unseen,
> And fixt upon the far sea-line;
> But each man murmur'd, 'O my Queen,
> I follow till I make thee mine.'

By the time when he resigned his Fellowship, Sidgwick had become a leading figure in Cambridge, though he had not yet attained the national and international reputation which publication of *The Methods of Ethics* brought him. Not that he had a large following among the undergraduates; moral sciences students were not numerous, and his lectures were too careful and too well-thought-out to be easy listening. His influence was,

[1] *H.S.: A Memoir*, p. 348.

at least in the late sixties and early seventies, strongest in a small but important circle constituted by the younger and more liberal-minded Fellows, particularly of his own College, Trinity, together with some of the brighter undergraduates. The sources of his influence were various. The religious doubts which had begun to worry him in the early eighteen-sixties were worrying many others by the end of the decade. His own perplexities were common knowledge, and his honesty and sincerity were beyond doubt. Young men who knew Sidgwick, and who were troubled as he had been, turned to him as a matter of course for sympathy and advice. Such sympathy and advice he gave freely; and in a more general way his personality and conversation, and his powers in debate, made him a natural leader of advanced thinking in the University.[1] It was in argument and discussion with his friends that Sidgwick was at his best.[2] He never made the smallest attempt to dominate a discussion, or to set himself up as a Panjandrum, and he would listen with attention and even humility to any viewpoint, however gauche or stumbling, which was honestly propounded.[3] But having listened to it, he would himself assemble and refurbish the most telling arguments upon both sides, add new arguments of his own, for and against, parade them all for a more rigorous inspection, and one by one dismiss them from his service. For such work his mind was perhaps the subtlest instrument of its day and age. It could discriminate and divide, check and find flaws, where cruder engines could hardly even begin to operate. To an onlooker this process might be fascinating. To Sidgwick himself it was less than satisfactory. He may have enjoyed arguing, but he was not one of those philosophers who argue simply for sport. The questions about which he disputed were often the questions to which, more than anything else in life, he desired answers. And answers were not forthcoming. Few arguments could stand his scrutiny, and

[1] On Sidgwick's influence, see W. Heitland's article on 'Cambridge in the Seventies' in H. Granville-Barker (ed.), *The Eighteen-seventies*, Cambridge, 1929, pp. 254–78.

[2] On Sidgwick, as a teacher and conversationalist, see the opinions quoted in *H.S.: A Memoir*, pp. 303–19. There are many references to him in books of reminiscences.

[3] His nephew by marriage, Admiral the Hon. A. C. Strutt, has described to me the patience with which Sidgwick listened to and commented upon the views on the nature of conscience which he put forward at the age of fifteen.

those that did had an unfortunate knack of counterbalancing each other. Sidgwick's friends thought that his detachment and his absolute candour were those of a saint, and after his death they did not hesitate to say so; but it is not through detachment that saints win their way to inward peace, nor is candour perhaps generally conducive to happiness.

Sidgwick's appearance and manner increased the effect of his conversation. His person was small and finely wrought, but a magnificent beard, which grew white with the passage of time, added a touch of the patriarch to his looks. His voice however was very gentle, and a nervous stammer which had afflicted him since childhood was heightened in moments of excitement and, by delaying some of his most pungent remarks, gave them an added force when they finally burst forth. During an argument he would be alive with interest and humour and would illustrate his points with quick gestures of his beautiful hands; but in moments of repose, or when he was tired or absorbed in thought, his face would lapse into an expression of almost childlike wistfulness.

Although Sidgwick's disposition was profoundly religious and his mind singularly acute, and although his personality gave him in his immediate circle something of the status of a religious teacher, his influence on the friends who so much admired him was none the less generally in the direction of unbelief. He would dearly have liked to offer them fare more satisfying than a mere judicial evaluation of opposing views; but he could not. In August 1873 he told one of them that he feared that 'during the years in which we have exchanged thoughts I have unwillingly done you more harm than good by the cold corrosive scepticism which somehow, in my own mind, is powerless to affect my "idealism", but which I see in more than one case acting otherwise upon others'.[1] Whilst Sidgwick may well have helped his friends to become wiser, or even better, men, I greatly doubt if he helped them to be happier.

Sidgwick's religious doubts had begun to take shape in the late eighteen-fifties and early eighteen-sixties; scientific advances

[1] *H.S.: A Memoir*, p. 283.

and empiricist philosophy did not directly inspire them, but rather constituted a background out of which they arose. However, the group of young men whom he so much influenced were mostly a little younger than he, and the rapid growth in the eighteen-sixties and seventies not perhaps so much of scientific discovery as of popular science, or rather of science for the educated layman, played a more direct part in the fermentation of their doubts.

Especially important were certain discoveries in the field of physiology. During the middle years of the nineteenth century a good deal of evidence had accumulated to suggest that mental activity of any kind is always accompanied by changes in the brain. This did not of course prove that brain-states are the causes of mind-states. The mind-state might equally well be the cause of the brain-states; and it is particularly hard to suppose that the *Intellect* and the *Will*, whose workings seem so spontaneous, are the outcome simply of antecedent and purely mechanical brain activities.

There began however to come to light phenomena which suggested that a prior mental act may not be necessary even for actions which seem without doubt to be intelligent; the obvious inference being, of course, that if such mental acts are unnecessary, if the brain can work very well without them, when they do occur they are mere by-products of the cerebral machinery. The phenomena in question were first partially uncovered in the eighteen-thirties and eighteen-forties by Marshall Hall of Nottingham. Hall found that the decerebrate animals could execute reflex movements of a biologically adaptive kind so long as their spinal cords remained intact. Since a brain and hence, presumably, consciousness, seemed unnecessary for such movements, the view that they can occur only as a result of 'Acts of Will' was considerably shaken. W. B. Carpenter, author of the leading physiological text-book of the day, *Principles of Human Physiology* (1842, 4th edn. 1852),[1] and of the leading text-book on the physiology of the nervous system, *The Principles of Mental Physiology* (1874), was prepared to go even further. Carpenter held that 'a careful analysis of the sources

---

[1] Carpenter's *Animal Physiology* (2nd edn. 1847), a fairly popular work, gives a concise account of Marshall Hall's experiments (pp. 354–62). Hall's findings, however, were received by most of his contemporaries with hostility and distaste.

from which many of even our ordinary actions proceed, will show that the Will has no direct participation in producing them; and that they are, psychologically speaking, the direct manifestations of Ideational states excited to a certain measure of intensity or, in physiological language, *reflex actions of the Cerebrum*'. He supports this thesis with accounts of cases of table-tilting, planchette-writing, pendulum-swinging and so forth, in which intelligent messages are spelled out without the operator having the least conscious awareness that he is himself responsible for them. Carpenter also has some entertaining stories of people carrying out complex actions quite unconsciously; the most notable is perhaps that of a Parliamentary reporter who continued to note down a speech correctly after he had fallen asleep. In an appendix to his *Mental Physiology* Carpenter described the recent experiments of David (later Sir David) Ferrier on the electrical stimulation of the bared cerebral cortices of various anaesthetised animals. Ferrier found that localised stimulation of the cortex could produce quite complex patterns of movements, including even patterns commonly associated with emotional states, and Carpenter thought that such facts confirmed his views about the possibilities of automatic action mediated by the cerebrum.

Carpenter himself, curiously enough, was a religious man and upheld the freedom of the will; however the facts which he cited had obvious appeal to those who favoured a mechanistic view of man. In a celebrated article 'On the Hypothesis that Animals are Automata, and its History', published in the *Fortnightly Review* in 1874, T. H. Huxley, after mentioning some of the highly adaptive reflex behaviour which a decerebrate frog is capable of executing (e.g. the removal of a drop of oil from its body by whichever one of its feet is not held down), describes the case of a human patient reduced by damage to the parietal lobe of the brain to a state of seeming automatism. Despite his affliction, this patient could dress, undress, smoke, sing and execute other actions for which conscious volition is usually deemed necessary. Huxley concludes that consciousness, whether of brute or of man, is a by-product of the working of the brain. We need not suppose it capable of modifying that working. Well might those of a religious turn of mind find Huxley's arguments disturbing. If mental phenomena are inexorably dependent upon prior events in the brain, what room is left for that subtle entity, the soul, which is some day to shed its worn-out garment, the body, as a quickening seed sheds the husk which once sheltered it?

The most famous of all occasions of dispute between religion and science was, of course, Darwin's theory of evolution (1858). The horror which Darwin's theory inspired among his contemporaries was due only in part to its conflicting with the Biblical account of Creation, and hence casting doubt in the direct inspiration of Holy Writ in general. If the worst came to the worst, the practice of giving allegorical interpretations to parts of the Scriptures had an ancient and respectable history. The horror was due rather to two other factors. Firstly, Darwinism seemed to imply that there had been no Fall and, if there had been no Fall, what was the point of an atonement? Secondly, Darwinism undercut the traditional arguments from Design upon which so many Victorians had based the faith in a benevolent, and indeed progressive, Deity. For instance Paley had suggested, in a well-known passage, that the intricate mechanism of the eye could only have been contrived by a sort of Cosmic optician; Darwinians could reply that these mechanisms might have evolved from less intricate ones by processes of natural selection favouring those mutants best adapted to their environments.

Darwin himself did not at first make any attempt to apply his theory of evolution to man. Others however had no such hesitations; and it was not long before a further disturbing possibility became evident, to wit, that the theory might be applied even to those social and moral[1] aspects of human nature which theologians had thought their especial preserves. 'Evolutionary Ethics' came of course to be associated most particularly with the name of Herbert Spencer. But Darwin's *Descent of Man* (1871) was probably more influential than anything Spencer ever wrote. In the *Descent of Man* Darwin argued that any species of animal which had, by the ordinary processes of evolution, acquired well-marked social instincts (such instincts might be thought to have survival value for many

---

[1] And political. Walter Bagehot's *Physics and Politics* (1869), an ingenious account of the evolution of different forms of political organisation, attracted a good deal of notice. It was first published in the *Fortnightly Review*.

THE GENESIS OF RELUCTANT DOUBT

kinds of creatures) 'would inevitably acquire a moral sense or conscience as soon as its intellectual powers had become as well, or nearly as well, developed, as in man'. Owing to his condition of mind man

> ... cannot avoid looking both backwards and forwards, and comparing past impressions. Hence after some temporary desire or passion has mastered his social instincts, he reflects and compares the now weakened impression of such past impulses with the ever-present social instincts; and he then feels that sense of dissatisfaction which all unsatisfied instincts leave behind them; he therefore resolves to act differently for the future,—and this is conscience. Any instinct, permanently stronger or more enduring that another, gives rise to a feeling which we express by saying that it ought to be obeyed. A pointer dog, if able to reflect on his past conduct, would say to himself, I ought (as indeed we say of him) to have pointed at that hare and not have yielded to the passing temptation of hunting it.[1]

A species whose social instincts were markedly different from those of man might develop notions of right and wrong very different from our own:

> If, for instance, to take an extreme case, men were reared under precisely the same conditions as hive bees, there can hardly be a doubt that our unmarried females would, like the worker-bees, think it a sacred duty to kill their brothers, and mothers would strive to kill their fertile daughters, and no one would think of interfering.[2]

The corrosive effect which the vindication of such views might have upon certain religious beliefs is obvious. If Darwin is right, man's moral sense, far from being the unique gift from God which Butler and other theologians had thought it, is no more divine than any other human faculty; and its deliverances are not eternal and unchanging but, in the setting of the Universe at large, merely local and transitory. Miss F. P. Cobbe voiced the feelings of many when, reviewing the *Descent of Man* in the *Theological Review* for April 1871, she exclaimed 'These doctrines appear to me simply the most dangerous which have ever been set forth since the days of Mandeville ...

[1] Charles Darwin, *The Descent of Man*, 2nd edn., London, 1874, pp. 610-11.
[2] *Ibid.*, p. 99.

theories whose validity must prove the *in*validity of all the sanctions which morality has hitherto received from powers beyond those of the penal laws.'

Thinkers of an outlook different from Miss Cobbe's, however, could draw from Darwin's work not the conclusion that civilised morality was in danger of collapse, but the view that since morality depends ultimately upon social and not upon religious instincts, morality needs no buttressing by religion. Those rationalists and freethinkers who continued to cherish Mill's hope that a developed science of sociology might carry mankind with giant strides towards the millennium found in the extension of Darwinism to society new possibilities for at last achieving a scientific moral code. In the society of their dreams presumably moral doubts would be resolved by the pronouncements of grave scientists rather than by the thin bleatings of the still, small voice of God.

A. W. Benn suggests[1] that the climax of English rationalism was reached in the year 1877. By 1880 or so the new Oxford idealist philosophy was becoming better known, and many people felt that T. H. Green and F. H. Bradley were trimming the talons of the brash empiricists who had so wounded religious susceptibilities during previous decades. It is of course probable that the number of professed unbelievers continued to increase for the rest of the century, but there is little doubt that rationalism, *earnest* doubt, attained its period of greatest intellectual ascendancy in the mid-eighteen-seventies. Some of the notable books which provided it with ammunition have already been mentioned. Perhaps one should add to the list various archaeological and anthropological works, of which Tylor's *Primitive Culture* (1871) is perhaps the best known. Tylor attempted to provide, in his theory of animism, a naturalistic explanation of the origin of religious belief. Not too different in spirit were Robertson Smith's influential articles on Biblical subjects for the Ninth Edition of the *Encyclopaedia Britannica*. Robertson Smith accepted the 'advanced' conclusions of scholars like Ewald, Kuenen and Wellhausen concerning such points as the origins of the Pentateuch and Psalms and the dating and origins of the Gospels. Winwood Reade drew together both these tendencies

[1] A. W. Benn, *The History of English Rationalism in the Nineteenth Century*, New York, 1962, Vol. II, p. 387.

in his well-known *Martyrdom of Man* (1872), a pocket history of the human race which combines a quasi-scientific explanation, resembling Tylor's, of the origins of religious belief, with a singularly unflattering account of Judaism and Christianity.

An agency which brought the views of scientific rationalists to the notice of many at this period was the *Fortnightly Review*, which was founded by G. H. Lewes in 1866 and came under the management of John Morley in 1867. In 1866 it printed Alexander Bain's 'The Intellect viewed Physiologically' and Tylor's first exposition of his theory of animism. In 1867 it began to serialise Bagehot's articles on 'Physics and Politics'. In 1869 it published H. C. Bastian's 'The Physiology of Thinking' and T. H. Huxley's 'The Physical Basis of Life'. In 1872 came Galton's 'Statistical Enquiry into the Efficacy of Prayer'. Galton examined the longevity of persons whose health is widely prayed for—and found it no greater than that of the common run of people. He remarked that missionary ships, though the objects of many prayers, do not receive especially favourable rates from insurance companies, even from Quaker ones. 1874 saw Huxley's 'Animal Automatism', and the famous paper on 'Body and Mind', in which W. K. Clifford asserted:

> But the fact that mind and brain are associated in a definite way, and in that particular way that I have mentioned, affords a very strong presumption that we have here something which can be *explained*; that it is possible to find a reason for this exact correspondence. If such a reason can be found the case is entirely altered . . . we should have the highest assurance that Science can give, a practical certainty on which we are bound to act, that there is no mind without a brain.

In 1876 came G. H. Lewes' two articles on 'Spiritualism and Materialism', and Leslie Stephen's 'Agnostic's Apology', an impassioned attack upon the ethical standards of Christianity. In 1877 appeared Tyndall's 'Science and Man' and Stephen's 'The Scepticism of Believers'.

These articles, all of which reflected or expounded in one way or another the agnostic tendencies of recent science, were read and discussed by intelligent people throughout the country, and their effect was considerable. 'It is said that in tropical forests one can almost hear the vegetation growing,' wrote W. H. Mallock in 1877. 'One may almost say that with us one can hear faith decaying.'[1] This is no doubt too strong a way of putting it; none the less faith was undoubtedly decaying quite widely among a large number of the more able younger men, and not least amongst the Trinity set of whom Sidgwick was the centre. Sidgwick himself was too clear-headed a thinker to fall under the spell of the various muddled systems of 'Evolutionary Ethics',[2] and though he must of course have felt the difficulties which now faced the view that a mind might survive in a disembodied state, I doubt if he would have been much impressed by swashbuckling pedantry like Clifford's. But the dissemination of scientific knowledge had a marked influence upon some of his contemporaries and juniors. Scepticism based on science flowed into and reinforced the older stream of doubt stemming from historical and ethical considerations. Their joint effect may be traced in the fact that whilst the outstanding Cambridge men of the eighteen-forties—B. F. Westcott, C. B. Scott, J. Llewellyn Davies, J. E. B. Mayer, Lord Alwyne Compton, E. H. Bickersteth, C. F. Mackenzie, Charles Evans, J. B. Lightfoot, E. W. Benson and F. J. A. Hort[3]—all took Orders (three of them becoming great clerical headmasters and six bishops), the outstanding Cambridge intellectuals of the eighteen-seventies—the Trinity group centring on Henry Sidgwick and Henry Jackson, and including Frederic Myers, G. W. and A. J. Balfour, Walter Leaf, Edmund Gurney, Arthur Verrall, F. W. Maitland, Henry Butcher and George Prothero—tended towards agnosticism or hesitant Deism.[4] Most of these doubters came from homes that were religious but not oppressively so—Sidgwick, Myers, Gurney, Butcher and Prothero were the sons of clergymen, Leaf and the Balfours had Evangelical backgrounds—and several were greatly distressed by the doubts which assailed them. It must indeed have been no trivial affliction to find that the faith which had from childhood guided one's actions and sheltered one from the cold fear of death was in danger of crumbling utterly away. W. H. Mallock was

---

[1] W. H. Mallock, 'Faith and Verification', *The Nineteenth Century* IV (1878), p. 673.

[2] See his article 'The Theory of Evolution in its Application to Practice' *Mind* I (1876), pp. 52–67; and cf. his cool review of Miss Cobbe's *Darwinism in Morals and Other Essays, Academy* III (1872), pp. 230–1.

[3] Fenton John Anthony Hort—what a first line for a limerick!

[4] I have taken the names from Newsome, *op. cit.*, pp. 27, 229.

perhaps dramatising only a little in the article quoted above when he went on:

> Now what I say is, that this loss of faith, complete as it may be, is a thing bitterly regretted by many, who are most ready to own to it. They may often sneer at faith, and say it will never come back to them; and this bitterness against it may often seem a sign of their being glad to get rid of it. But it is as the bitterness of a woman against her lover, which has not been the cause of her deserting him, but which has been occasioned by his deserting her. To men in a condition like this, a strange blankness has come over human life. They may hear others vociferating that it is solemn; they feel quietly that it is only sad. It is not serious, it is only not amusing. This state of mind and its prevalence is very apt to be overlooked, because it is not a state of mind that, in common intercourse, readily finds utterance ... there are many about us, though they never confess their pain, and perhaps themselves hardly like to dwell on it, whose hearts are aching for the God that they no longer can believe in.[1]

Few of these reluctant doubters were content to rest in unbelief. Many of them sought, and not a few obtained, answers to their doubts; some of course through philosophical speculations, but others through empirical enquiries of a novel and quite extraordinary kind. Whether or not the answers or partial answers which these empirical enquiries gave were adequate can perhaps never be fully decided, at least in this world; but the story of the enquiries makes up one of the most curious chapters in the history of human endeavour.

[1] Mallock, *loc. cit.*, p. 674.

III Spiritualism in England 1852–76

UNTIL THE EARLY EIGHTEEN-SEVENTIES English Spiritualism was a rather pale reflection of its American counterpart, and there is no point in recounting its history in detail. Its path was to some extent prepared by the growing curiosity about mesmerism and its phenomena which marked the eighteen-forties. The leading mesmeric periodical, the *Zoist* (1843–56), a journal with some scientific status, published quite a few accounts of supposed cases of mesmeric clairvoyance. In a little book called *Somnolism and Psycheism* (1849) Dr. J. Haddock published accounts of the next world which his mesmeric subject, Emma, a girl totally unable to read or write, had dictated in a state of 'exstasis'. Emma's revelations bore a marked resemblance to those of Swedenborg and of Andrew Jackson Davis. So too did the revelations which Alphonse Cahagnet heard from his mesmeric subjects and set down in his *Arcanes de la Vie Future Dévoilés* (1847–8; English translation *The Celestial Telegraph*, 1850). W. Gregory, author of *Letters on Animal Magnetism* (1851), a most influential work, speaks highly of both Haddock and Cahagnet; though he thinks that Andrew Jackson Davis obtained the leading ideas of his *Principles of Nature* through thought-transference from those around him.

Along with the interest in mesmerism went an interest in the ghost stories which German occultists had regarded as tying in with the phenomena of mesmerism. Mrs. Crowe's *Night-Side of Nature* (1848), which included many of the more interesting German cases, had a considerable sale. In 1851 was founded at

Cambridge a Society to conduct 'a serious and earnest enquiry into the nature of the phenomena vagurely called supernatural', and a number of distinguished persons became members.[1]

When Mrs. W. Hayden, an American professional medium, visited England in October 1852, she found quite a few educated people anxious to witness the mysterious spirit rappings which occurred in her presence. Mrs. Hayden charged a guinea a sitting, and her performances were for the monied few; but in the early part of 1853 a craze for table-tilting spread across the country, and table-tilting was a pastime which anyone could afford.[2] The craze originated on the Continent, where it had been inspired by the strange happenings in America, and it captured England to such an extent that invitations were issued for 'tea and table-tipping'. On 19th May 1853 J. J. G. Wilkinson, a noted Swedenborgian, wrote to Henry James (Senior):

> Nothing is talked of here but table mowings [sic] and spirit rappings. There is, so far as I know, no class of persons of importance who are not yet penetrated with this odd-looking movement. The only people who are actually *contra* are the stony materialists & the gassy philosophers: both of them hate this noise which the approaching spiritual world makes with its big toes. The pious Atheists too want Mrs. Hayden and her coadjutor to be put in prison: she is, they say, blasphemous; and degrades the mighty dead by summoning them to her table: as if the meanest degradation were not infinitely superior to the annihilation to which Man has been consigned by Philosophers and Atheists.[3]

Wilkinson was right in remarking that there was 'no class of persons of importance' which had not yet been penetrated by the movement. On one occasion Queen Victoria and Prince Albert tried their hands, and soon made the table spin.[4]

Rappings and table-tiltings received a good deal of notice in the press, most of it unfavourable; for instance G. H. Lewes gave an account in the *Leader* of a sitting with Mrs. Hayden at which, by hesitating at appropriate letters as he passed his hand over the alphabet, he induced the raps to spell out

---

[1] W. H. Salter, *The S.P.R.: an Outline of its History*, London, 1948, pp. 5-6.
[2] On Mrs. Hayden and the table-tilting craze, see *Podmore* II, pp. 3-21.
[3] Archives of the Swedenborg Society.
[4] E. Longford, *Victoria R.I.*, London, 1964, p. 339.

detailed communications from a fictitious 'Nelly Sorel', and finally to assert that Mrs. Hayden was an imposter. Several Evangelical clergymen[1] published pamphlets attributing the phenomena to diabolic agency. The Rev. E. Gillson, of Bath, held by means of his table converse with a lost soul, who expected in the course of ten years to be bound with Satan and all his crew and cast into the abyss. The following excerpt from Mr. Gillson's narrative was very popular with contemporary reviewers:

> I then asked, 'Where are Satan's headquarters? Are they in England?' There was a slight movement.
> 'Are they in France?' A violent movement.
> 'Are they in Spain?' Similar agitation.
> 'Are they at Rome?' The table seemed literally frantic.

There were however a few men of scientific attainments who were prepared to look into these curious phenomena. In *The Times* of 30th June 1853, and the *Athenaeum* for 2nd July, Faraday described some ingenious experiments which he had carried out to show that table-tilting is due to unconscious muscular action by the sitters, and not to outpourings of odylic force[2] or to the strong shoulders of spirits underneath the table. Faraday placed a movable top upon an ordinary table and was able to demonstrate that this movable top, on which the hands of the sitters were laid, always began to move *before* the table tilted.[3] Augustus de Morgan, the mathematician, and Robert Chambers, the author of *Vestiges of Creation*, were both impressed by Mrs. Hayden's performance, but neither was prepared to declare himself in favour of a Spiritualistic explanation. Indeed the only distinguished English convert to Spiritualism at this time was Robert Owen, the veteran social reformer, who received from the spirits much valuable information concerning social justice in this world and the next.[4]

---

[1] N. S. Godfrey, *Table-moving Tested and Proved to be the Result of Satanic Agency*, London, 1853; Do., *Table-turning, The Devil's Modern Masterpiece*, London, 1853; E. Gillson, *Table-talking: Disclosures of Satanic Wonders*, Bath, 1853.

[2] See above, p. 27.

[3] The odic theory had been popular with pamphleteers. See, e.g., W. R. Birt, *Table-moving Popularly Explained*, London, 1853; [F. Roubaud], *Practical Instructions in Table-moving*, London, 1853; Anon., *Table Moving by Animal Magnetism Demonstrated*, London [1853].

[4] See Podmore, *Robert Owen*, London, 1923, pp. 600-12, and *Podmore* II, pp. 18-19.

After Faraday's exposé interest in Spiritualism declined; but it revived briefly in the summer of 1855 when D. D. Home, most famous of all mediums, came to England from America.[1] Home, who was then aged twenty-two, stayed for some months in the home of Mr. Thomas Rymer, an Ealing solicitor, and gave there a large number of sittings to friends of his host and to distinguished callers. He never charged for his services, and his sitters were quite frequently privileged to witness the most astounding events, often in good light—levitation of tables and other objects, playing of musical instruments by unseen hands, the actual materialisation of spirit hands, and so forth. Home also possessed considerable talents as a straightforward clairvoyant medium. Towards the end of 1855 he left the country, and Spiritualism was thereafter pretty much obscured from the public eye. Two Spiritualist periodicals enjoyed a brief existence —the *Yorkshire Spiritual Telegraph*, organ of a small Spiritualist community at Keighley, Yorkshire, ran from April 1855 to 1857, and then, under the name of the *British Spiritual Telegraph*, until 1859; the *Spiritual Herald* ran from February to July 1856. Both had to rely heavily upon news from America; the editor of the *Herald* wrote sadly in his last issue:

> The periodical has failed for want of English manifestations, or for want of English courage. We should have preferred filling our pages with our own national facts, but we could not procure them.

It was not, however, that there were no 'national facts'; there were such facts, but knowledge of them was confined to a few people most of whom at first avoided publicity. These people had usually been impressed by Mrs. Hayden or by Home, or even simply by the table-tipping epidemic, and had continued to experiment on their own. Some of them un-

[1] On Home, see *inter alia*, J. Burton, *Hey-day of a Wizard*, London, 1948; D. D. Home, *Incidents in My Life*, London, 1863; Do., *Incidents in My Life*, Second Series, London, 1872; Do., *Lights and Shadows of Spiritualism*, London, 1877; Mme D. D. Home, *D. D. Home, His Life and Mission*, London, 1888; Do., *The Gift of D. D. Home*, London, 1890; Viscount Adare, *Experiences in Spiritualism*, privately printed, 1870; reprinted as *P.S.P.R.* XXXV (1926), pp. 26–285; P. P. Alexander, *Spiritualism: A Narrative with a Discussion*, Edinburgh, 1871; E. J. Dingwall, *Some Human Oddities*, London, 1947, pp. 187–93 (for bibliographical information); Podmore, *passim*, but esp. II, pp. 223–43; and references given below (pp. 71n, 210–216). H. Wyndham's *Mr. Sludge the Medium*, London, 1937, is not reliable.

doubtedly believed that they had obtained results—for example, raps and other physical phenomena, automatic writing and speaking, and clairvoyant visions of spirits. The most important of the enquirers were probably those mentioned in Mrs. Howitt Watts' *Pioneers of the Spiritual Reformation*[1]—Mr. and Mrs. Alaric Watts, Mr. and Mrs. William Howitt, J. J. G. Wilkinson, Robert Chambers, Mr. and Mrs. Newton Crosland, Professor and Mrs. Augustus de Morgan, Professor and Mrs. Nenner, the Rev. James Smith, Dr. Doherty, Dr. Ashburner, Benjamin Coleman and W. M. Wilkinson. They were by no means all negligible or obviously ridiculous persons, and one—de Morgan—was a man of transcendent ability. Howitt, a Quaker, was already noted as a prolific writer on literary and historical subjects; he was converted to belief in the phenomena by a seance held at the de Morgans'. Various forms of mediumship developed in his own family, and he became the most energetic of Spiritualism's early advocates in this country.

The late eighteen-fifties was indeed almost the only period in which English Spiritualism was able to develop in relative independence of its American counterpart. The admixture of symbolical Christianity with Swedenborgianism presented in (say) Mrs. Newton Crosland's *Light in the Valley* (1857), a work based largely on her own visions and automatic writings, W. M. Wilkinson's *Spirit Drawings* (1858), and Mrs. de Morgan's *From Matter to Spirit* (published in 1863, but dealing with phenomena from the eighteen-fifties), are fairly far removed from the more down-to-earth main stream of American and later English Spiritualism.

After 1859 Spiritualism in Britain began to spread more rapidly. Its phenomena and doctrines reverted to American models, and it would be tedious to describe them in detail. It may however be of some interest to ask through what channels and what agencies Spiritualism was disseminated, and why it caught on, as, in a modest way, it undoubtedly did.

One of the most important factors behind the revival of Spiritualism in England was the return in 1859 of the celebrated medium D. D. Home. Home was a constant globe-

---

[1] London, 1883, p. 246.

trotter, but during the eighteen-sixties he resided in England for extended periods, and he circulated very widely in some sections of high society. He was, as Miss Jean Burton has aptly put it,[1] the perfect house guest. He was slim and spiritual-looking, his conversation was refined, his manners were pleasing. He had, it was true, a touch of vanity and affectation; but then his talents, and not just his mediumistic talents, were considerable. He was a gifted musician, and his readings and recitations, both public and private, brought him not unmerited applause. It is scarcely surprising that hostesses loved him. He was not strictly speaking a professional medium; he never charged for his sittings, whatever gains he made from them being indirect and in the way of hospitality and gifts. Nor does there seem to be any reliable first-hand account of his being detected in fraud.[2]

Home was well known not merely in Society, but to the Press; wherever he went he was news, and the phenomena which occurred in his presence were widely reported. Particularly influential was an article entitled 'Stranger than Fiction' which Robert Bell, a noted dramatist and journalist, published in the *Cornhill Magazine* for 1860. Amongst other wonders, Bell described how in a darkened room he had seen the outline of Home's prone body against the window curtains as the medium floated from one side of the window to the other.

No doubt it was because of Home's successes that various other American mediums, of assorted talents and specialities, visited England during the eighteen-sixties; and no doubt the activities of these visitors helped the further spread of Spiritualistic beliefs and practices. It was however a long time before native professional mediums appeared on the scene in any number. Mrs. Mary Marshall, of London, who began to practise in 1858, was almost on her own for about a decade (though she was sometimes assisted by her niece or her son).

---

[1] *Op. cit.*, p. 51.
[2] On this question see Count Perovsky-Petrovo-Solovovo's 'Some Thoughts on D. D. Home', *P.S.P.R.* XXXIX (1930), pp. 247–62, and the comments by Hereward Carrington, *J.S.P.R.* XXVI (1930), pp. 109–11. On the erroneous story that Robert Browning detected Home in fraud see Betty Miller's very interesting article 'The seance at Ealing' in the *Cornhill Magazine* for Autumn 1957. She shows that the tale grew in the telling quite as far beyond recognition as any story of a marvel might have done.

She produced physical phenomena of a calibre very modest by American standards, and for more 'advanced' phenomena required darkness, or near-darkness; none the less several persons who subsequently became prominent Spiritualists owed their initiation to her.[1] A later influence was Kate Fox, who came to England in 1871 and was feted by Spiritualists. Many accounts of her phenomena found their way into print.[2] Like Home, Kate moved among genteel people, and in December 1872 she married Mr. H. D. Jencken, an English barrister interested in Spiritualism. At the wedding breakfast the loaded table is said to have reared up on two legs, whilst raps spelled out 'Jencken is his own master no longer'.[3]

The number of persons who actually witnessed Home's or Mrs. Marshall's phenomena must however have been relatively small, and even the circle of those who knew one or more of the witnesses can hardly have been very large. It was from books, and even more from the Press, that many obtained their first knowledge of Spiritualism. Of course the Press was for the most part far from friendly to Spiritualism, and so considerable importance attached to the foundation in January 1860 of the *Spiritual Magazine*, a fairly reputable Spiritualist monthly. Its

---

[1] The following is an amusing incident in connection with Mrs. Marshall's mediumship. Mr. Benjamin Coleman, a noted Spiritualist, was staying with a Mr. Willmore and, at the latter's request, asked Mrs. Marshall and her daughter round to the house. Coleman was out at the time of the visit. When he came back, late at night:

Willmore, in great excitement came to me, and begged that I would come down stairs immediately for he did not know what to do; he said, his wife, his daughter, and Miss Lee were all in hysterics. I followed him at once, and upon entering the room, a small three-legged table met me at the door, *no one touching it*, and made me a graceful bow as if to say, 'How do you do?' One of the females was on the sofa screaming; and the others in different parts of the room throwing themselves about in a state of great distress. I went up to the other end of the room to Miss Lee, the table following me and standing by my side whilst I endeavoured to calm her. I had nearly succeeded in doing so, when the table made a jump at her and threw her again into violent hysterics; her screams were responded to by the other females. Matters looked so serious that I felt it necessary to take a decided part with the table, and seizing it with both hands, I lifted it into the centre of the room, and said, 'Now spirits, you have done quite enough, I command you to leave this place in God's name.' They appeared to obey my injunction . . . (*Dial. Soc. Report*, pp. 141–2).

[2] For Lord Rayleigh's experiences see his Presidential Address to the S.P.R., *P.S.P.R.* XXX (1919), pp. 275–90.

[3] *Spiritualist*, 1st Jan. 1873.

editors were T. Shorter and W. M. Wilkinson, but its tone was set by William Howitt, the chief contributor, a man of wide, if not entirely accurate, learning. Howitt looked upon Spiritualism as a supplement to Christianity, and his articles were often of an historical and even quite scholarly kind. The *Spiritual Magazine* ran for fifteen years and was able to attract sympathisers who would have been repelled by most of the American periodicals. In November 1869 appeared *The Spiritualist*, later called *The Spiritualist Newspaper*, which interested itself particularly in scientific investigations of the phenomena. Its editor, W. H. Harrison, was not without scientific gifts, and it achieved a fair standard of reporting and lay-out. It became linked with the British National Association of Spiritualists, a society founded in 1874 by some of the more educated Spiritualists for the undogmatic and non-sectarian study of Spiritualism.

But though the *Spiritual Magazine* or some other periodical might arouse or sustain an interest in Spiritualism, mere descriptions of the phenomena could not be so effective in convincing the unconvinced as personal experience. A good deal of the spread of Spiritualism seems to have been through a kind of 'infection'. Someone would sit with an established medium, say Home or Mrs. Marshall, or with some private 'home circle', and would be 'affected'—that is, pass into a trance—or be told that he possessed mediumistic gifts. Or perhaps he would receive messages striking enough to arouse his curiosity in good earnest. At all events, he would be sufficiently impressed to start his own 'home circle'. Some member of the circle would then develop mediumship, and the circle would itself become a centre from which the 'infection' could be transmitted. Various private mediums[1] obtained almost as much celebrity, if not as Home, at any rate as Mrs. Marshall—for instance Mrs. Everitt of Pentonville, said to be the first medium in England to develop (in 1867) the 'direct voice' Mrs. Guppy, the protégée of Alfred Russel Wallace (himself a convert of Mrs. Marshall's); and Edward Childs, who had originally developed at Mrs. Everitt's circle.

It was at this period still the physical phenomena—especially raps and table-movements conveying 'evidential' messages—

[1] Cf. *Podmore* II, pp. 63–77.

by which conversions and the arousal of interest were chiefly effected.[1] There were however many other kinds of phenomena going on in private circles; for instance trance writing and speaking, clairvoyant visions of spirits, and so on. These phenomena obtained much less publicity than the physical effects, perhaps because people no longer felt quite confident that if a medium exhibited in trance powers of thought and expression beyond her normal range the explanation must be sought in some intelligence external to her own. Different kinds of manifestation would sometimes accompany each other, raps punctuating automatic writing, or clairvoyants 'seeing' the spirits who made the raps. It is now of course quite impossible to sort out the respective parts played in these goings-on by hallucination, suggestion and the possibly paranormal, though psychologically the question is of great interest.

The agencies which spread Spiritualism amongst the relatively well-to-do during the eighteen-sixties and early eighteen-seventies are thus fairly clear. Why such people should have been receptive at this time is a much more difficult question. No doubt many of them had, if not a proper appreciation of the issues raised by Darwinism and by rationalist criticism of the Bible, at any rate a general feeling that the faith of their fathers could do with buttressing and revivification. Nor I think would they have lacked a certain vague optimism, characteristic of their class and their time, as to the Creator's beneficent intentions for the Progress of Mankind; an optimism so much in harmony with Spiritualistic teachings that it would have formed a natural soil for them.

Spiritualism however spread far outside the somewhat limited circle of those who might come across Home, or the Howitts, or the de Morgans, or even Mrs. Everitt or Mrs. Guppy, or who could afford a visit to the Marshalls or a subscription to the *Spiritual Magazine*. The typical venue of a Spiritualist meeting was not a genteel parlour, but a Mechanics' Institute or a Temperance Hall. By the mid-eighteen-sixties Spiritualism was gaining a considerable foothold amongst artisans and the more educated working men, and these pretty soon came to constitute the bulk of its supporters. Part of its spread amongst

[1] On this point cf. the accounts in *An Exposition of Spiritualism*, London, 1862, and in *Dial. Soc. Report* (1871).

working people was perhaps along the enormous grapevine constituted by the country's millions of domestic servants—there are quite a few cases on record of home circles centring round a maid. A further important influence was that of 'inspirational' lecturers and speakers, who came at first chiefly from the United States. Amongst them were Emma Hardinge (later Hardinge-Britten), who returned to England from the United States in 1865 and toured the country many times, attracting large audiences; and Mrs. Cora L. V. Tappan (formerly Cora Hatch), who visited England in 1873. Native exponents of the same arts began to appear, many of them non-professional and many, according to Mrs. Hardinge-Britten:

> ... miners, pit men, weavers and factory hands, who, notwithstanding the unceasing toils of the week, cheerfully devote themselves to the duties of the Spiritual Rostrum on the Sunday; and though they are simply 'children of the people', and wholly untrained to such work, their rude natural eloquence, heightened by the afflatus of the spirit intelligences that speak through their lips, produces a much deeper influence upon audiences of their own class, than the metaphysical arguments of more polished speakers could do.[1]

One of the earliest and most celebrated of the native practitioners was J. J. Morse, once a pot-boy in a public-house, who had certainly 'developed' by 1870. Sometimes these speakers would discover their gifts through attending a trance address by some established speaker, and being affected themselves; for instance W. J. Colville began his career through hearing one of Mrs. Tappan's orations. The discourses which the spirits delivered through the best of such speakers not infrequently contained some underlying thread of rational argument; but all too often the thread was broken or hopelessly buried by the flood of sonorous sentences.

Whereas among the middle classes Spiritualism was commonly looked upon as a supplement to Christianity, working-class Spiritualism tended to set itself up as an alternative to Christianity. It was, too, sometimes linked with radicalism and even socialism—the spirits commonly expressed very advanced views upon social questions.

[1] E. Hardinge-Britten, *Nineteenth Century Miracles*, New York, 1884, p. 165.

The working-class wing of the Spiritualist movement found an able lecturer and propagandist in James Burns. Burns was active in the 'Association of Progressive Spiritualists of Great Britain', which was founded in 1865; and in April 1867 he started a monthly magazine, *Human Nature*, to be its organ. The subtitle of this magazine, as Podmore observes, sufficiently indicates its scope and character: 'A monthly Journal of Zoistic Science and Intelligence, embodying Physiology, Phrenology, Psychology, Spiritualism, Philosophy, the Laws of Health and Sociology.' Burns and his associates were very active in propagandising, and in setting up Spiritualist Sunday Schools (known as 'Spiritual Lyceums'), and in 1868 the Hon. Secretary of the A.P.S.G.B. was able to report that he had 'received upwards of 1,900 letters from persons in all classes of society, and had distributed a considerable amount of Spiritualist literature'.[1] Burns shortly instituted a weekly paper, the *Medium and Daybreak*, which came to enjoy the largest circulation of any Spiritualist periodical.

It is not at all difficult to understand why Spiritualism gained ground among the relatively poor. The endeavours of several generations of 'missionaries to England' had made them increasingly aware of religion and religious issues, and had at the same time helped to spread literacy amongst them more widely than ever before. If a man was literate enough to read his Bible with the right degree of uncritical fervour, he was literate enough to read Spiritualist or, for that matter, secularist, literature with a similar uncriticalness. Spiritualism was comforting, cosy, humane. Compared at any rate with the fiercer Christian sects it had a great deal to offer plain men: oratory quite as colourful as any the nonconformists could provide, but without the disquieting undertones; word not of a Day of Judgment, but of reunion with those we love; talk not of man's sinfulness, but of the eternity of moral progress which awaits him; above all miracles not distant and dubious, but worked here and now by ordinary people.

What needs an explanation is not why Spiritualism spread, but why it did not spread farther and faster, and why it spread most particularly in certain regions and among certain rather limited sections of the community. That it spread more slowly

[1] *Spiritual Magazine* 1868, pp. 426-7.

in Britain than in America may perhaps be set down to the greater strength of orthodoxy in Britain, and to the widespread hostility of the British Press. To explain why it was markedly regional in its successes, winning ground especially in the Yorkshire and Lancashire industrial towns, and also in Northumberland, Durham, Nottingham, Derby and Glasgow, and why it drew its converts mostly from nonconformity and the sects, and particularly from the Methodists,[1] would require detailed investigations of the social conditions and the religious histories of the individual regions concerned.

Thus from the early eighteen-sixties to at any rate the mid-eighteen-seventies (when there were some rather devastating exposures of prominent mediums) Spiritualism in England made continued progress amongst persons of many ranks of life. How many convinced Spiritualists the country contained is difficult to say; but the existence of four fairly successful periodicals suggests that the number of active Spiritualists must have been well into five figures. The numbers of those influenced by Spiritualism, or at least interested in it, may have been perhaps ten times greater. Spiritualist meetings could certainly attract large crowds, even though we may need to make allowances of exaggeration by enthusiastic reporters. To give a few examples: in 1867 the audience at a Glasgow meeting numbered 300 or 400;[2] in August 1871 2,000 people attended a demonstration near Bradford;[3] in 1873 J. J. Morse drew an audience of 800 at the Trades' Hall, Glasgow;[4] in 1874 over 1,200 attended a meeting at Darlington.[5] And such figures perhaps do not reveal the full extent of the interest in a religion whose essential practices could be carried out round a dining-room table.

So far I have said very little about the Spiritualistic 'manifestations' in Britain. These manifestations were in general so

---

[1] I base these statements simply on the provincial notes in the leading Spiritualist periodicals of the time. On the regional distribution of Spiritualism cf. Hardinge-Britten, *op. cit.*, pp. 222–5. Mrs. Hardinge-Britten, a celebrated touring speaker, would have been in a good position to know.
[2] *Spiritual Magazine* 1867, p. 497.
[3] *Medium*, 16th Aug. 1871.
[4] *Spiritual Magazine* 1873, p. 474.
[5] *Medium*, 31st July 1874.

similar to the American ones that there is not much point in describing them; but shortly after the year 1870 came two developments which require notice.

The first of these was the appearance on the scene of the Rev. William Stainton Moses (1839–92). Moses, an Oxford graduate, had been ordained in 1863, and had for some years lived the ordinary life of a country curate. In 1870 he became interested in Spiritualism through reading Robert Dale Owen's *Debateable Land*. Shortly afterwards he moved to London and became a master at University College School. In 1872 he joined his close friends, Dr. and Mrs. Stanhope Speer, in forming a 'home circle'. They shortly obtained remarkable physical phenomena (which are dealt with later on) and, next year, Moses began to produce automatic writings, whose serialisation in *The Spiritualist* (from 15th October 1873) under the pseudonym of 'M. A. Oxon.' attracted a good deal of attention. A large part of these writings (the originals of which are still preserved) were of didactic character and supposedly came from a group of spirits of the eminent dead; so eminent, in fact, that Moses withheld their real names lest their teachings be received with incredulity. They communicated under the sobriquets of Imperator, Rector, Doctor, Prudens,[1] and so forth, and their teachings, later reprinted under the titles *Spirit Teachings*, and *More Spirit Teachings*, differ from others of the same kind chiefly in their unrhetorical style. They present a cosmology altogether in the main Spiritualist tradition, together with ethical and theological teachings of a liberal but unexciting kind. It needed not, as Podmore remarked, that a spirit should descend from the seventh sphere to preach views which could be heard from any Unitarian pulpit.

The relative literary merit of *Spirit Teachings* has made it the Bible of British Spiritualism, or at least its leading piece of patristic literature. However, Moses' automatic writings are important to us for somewhat different reasons. In amongst them are various cases of 'evidential' communications—communications, that is, containing correct information about deceased persons which, on the face of it, could not have been

---

[1] 'Imperator' was the prophet Malachi; 'Rector', St. Hippolytus; 'Prudens', Plotinus; 'Doctor', Athenodorus. Cf. A. W. Trethewy, *The 'Controls' of Stainton Moses*, London, n.d.

known to the medium; such information was sometimes also communicated by raps or table-tilts. Moses published a number of these cases in *The Spiritualist*, and subsequently in a small book called *Spirit Identity* (1878). A well-known example is the case of Abraham Florentine. On 1st and 2nd September 1874 a certain Abraham Florentine communicated by table-tilts. He said that he had fought in the American war of 1812, and that he had died on 5th August 1874, aged 83 years, 1 month and 17 days. Enquiries made in the United States confirmed his assertions, though he had understated his age by ten days. 'Evidential' cases of this quality were then rare, and Moses' standing and high character made them impressive, even to persons who might otherwise have been sceptical. Moses was a serious, solid-looking man of middle height, and those who knew him and had listened to his earnest conversation found it extremely difficult to imagine him in the role of liar or of practical joker. On 9th May 1874 he talked with, and showed his notebooks to, two enquirers of high academic standing, Edmund Gurney and F. W. H. Myers; both of them felt that if Spiritualistic phenomena could be attested by a person of such pre-eminent respectability and such monumental seriousness of mind, there must indeed be something in them worthy of investigation.

Unfortunately in many of Moses' 'evidential' cases one cannot rule out the possibility that he somewhere read or heard the relevant information, did not consciously note it, or else speedily forgot about it but subsequently reproduced it when in a state of dissociation. It has been discovered,[1] for instance, that the ten-day error in Abraham Florentine's statement of his age at death is matched by a similar error in obituary notices of him in American papers. There would just have been time for these newspapers to have reached England before the sitting at which Florentine first appeared; though there is of course no evidence that Moses actually read them.

The second development which requires notice is even more startling. 'Materialised' spirit hands—visible and tangible—and also materialised arms and faces (not to mention materialised mouths and vocal organs), had occasionally been reported even in the very early days of Spiritualism. It was commonly

[1] By Dr. E. J. Dingwall. See *J.S.P.R.* XX (1921), pp. 148-52.

supposed that the spirits were able to manifest themselves in this way by drawing 'power', or some spiritual substance, from the body of the medium. 'Full-form materialisations' however were hardly ever noted in the early days of Spiritualism; Home indeed claimed to have produced them in the mid-fifties, but the phantom figures observed in his presence may well in many cases have been hallucinatory. A considerable sensation was therefore created in Spiritualist circles by reports that in 1861 Kate Fox had at dark sittings repeatedly conjured up the materialised form of the deceased wife of Charles Livermore, a wealthy New York[1] banker. The materialisation had been unhesitatingly recognised by Mr. Livermore, and was solid to the touch. Nothing even remotely like these manifestations was heard of in England until the early eighteen-seventies; but in and after the year 1872 a gradual approach to them began. First in the field was that enterprising amateur, Mrs. Samuel Guppy.[2] Mrs. Guppy introduced the prototype of what came to be known as the 'Punch and Judy' cabinet. The basic idea was that the medium should be placed on her own inside a completely light-tight compartment. In such a confined and darkened space sufficient 'power' might (it was supposed) be built up for the construction of a materialised figure able to stand scrutiny in the light (light was supposed to hinder the accumulation of 'power'). A suitable cabinet might be made out of wood and resemble a sentry box; or it might be made out of curtains hung on a frame or arranged so as to seclude some part of the room. At first the spirits were only able to stand enough light to show their faces at an aperture (hence the name 'Punch and Judy' cabinet); but gradually they (or the mediums) grew sufficiently solid (or sufficiently bold) to emerge completely from the cabinet. In the more striking cases the medium might be tied down inside the cabinet, the knots sealed, etc.; and the ties would be found intact at the end of the sitting. Investigators however were rarely permitted to look inside the cabinet and examine the medium whilst the materialisation was also in view. The first and most famous case in

[1] See R. D. Owen, *op. cit.*, pp. 385–401; and, on the development of 'materialisation' phenomena in America, E. Sargent, *The Proof Palpable of Immortality*, 2nd edn., Boston, 1876. A related development was that of 'spirit photography'.

[2] See *Podmore* II, p. 96; and W. H. Harrison in *The Spiritualist* for 15th March 1872.

which this is said to have taken place occurred on 29th March 1874, when William Crookes (later Sir William), the noted chemist, was allowed to inspect by the light of a phosphorus lamp both the entranced form of a young medium, Miss Florence Cook of Hackney, and that of her materialised (and completely solid) spirit guide, 'Katie King'.[1] But this seance (unlike others of Crookes' sittings with Miss Cook, at which however medium and materialisation were not with certainty perceived together) took place not at Crookes' home, but at that of the medium; and Crookes' own account of the circumstances and of the precautions taken is so sketchy that one can hardly form any proper opinion as to what was going on.[2]

By this time the number of professional mediums practising in England had markedly increased; a fact shown up strikingly in the advertisement pages of Spiritualist periodicals.[3] Among the professional mediums of the eighteen-seventies who produced materialisations were F. Herne, C. Williams, Mr. and Mrs. Nelson Holmes (visitors from America), A. Rita, Bastian, Taylor, the Misses Wood and Fairlamb, 'Dr.' F. Monck and W. Eglinton.[4] These mediums often sat in pairs, sometimes by threes. A non-professional, Miss Mary Showers, daughter of a general in the Indian army, also obtained considerable publicity.[5] Nearly all the persons named were at one time or another accused of fraud, some (including Miss Showers) in the most incriminating circumstances; though the various exposures did not by any means always convince the faithful.

[1] Crookes, *op. cit.*, pp. 106-7.

[2] Mr. Trevor Hall has argued that Crookes was using his 'experiments' with Florence Cook as a cover for an affair with her. See his *The Spiritualists*, London, 1962. However, the evidence on which he bases his assertions is severely criticised by R. G. Medhurst and K. M. Goldney in their paper 'William Crookes and the Physical Phenomena of Mediumship', *P.S.P.R.* LIV (1964), pp. 25-157, and elsewhere. Dr. E. J. Dingwall's *The Critics' Dilemma*, Crowhurst, Sussex, 1966, supports Mr. Hall. I do not propose to enter into the controversy, since I am only concerned here with Crookes' reports as part of the contemporary scene.

[3] A French lady who advertised in the *Medium and Daybreak* during 1875 said that she was 'a SOMNAMBULIST by birth, and very lucid' and that she could be 'CONSULTED for all diseases, Researches, etc.'

[4] See *Podmore* II, pp. 95-115; and cf. the very informative series of sixteen articles on 'Stainton Moses and Contemporary Physical Mediums' by R. G. Medhurst, *Light* LXXXIII (1963) to LXXXVI (1966).

[5] On Miss Showers, see Dingwall, *op. cit.*, pp. 54-69 (an account utilising the researches of Mr. M. Gilbert).

The summit of possible achievement, so far as materialisations are concerned, would of course be that a complete materialisation should come into being in good light and with the medium in full view, and that it should disappear or disintegrate under the same conditions. This astonishing effect—the most bizarre ever reported—was actually obtained during the eighteen-seventies on a number of occasions by at least two mediums: 'Dr.' F. Monck (formerly a Baptist preacher), and W. Eglinton.[1] The phenomena were much the same in both cases. Here is an account by Mr. William Oxley of a startling seance with Monck:

> A fair light from a gas-lamp enabled us distinctly to see all objects in the room... Dr. Monck, still in trance and controlled by Samuel, drew aside the curtains and showed himself and the form of Lillie standing in mid air fully four feet away from himself; he then closed the curtains, and, reopening them to their extremities, nothing but himself was visible. He next stood close to the table, the curtains still being opened, and from his right side there issued a thin white vapour, which gradually assumed a form, at first as of gossamer outline like a garment or robe, which became more dense or opaque; then appeared the head with a crown adorned by a luminous lily; and finally the full materialised form of Lillie, who spoke to us; she was about three feet high, with her feet resting on the table, and while thus standing Dr. Monck, or rather Samuel through him, handled the drapery, showing us that it was real and material. This was repeated three times, the materialised form

---

[1] On Eglinton see below, pp. 201–7. On Monck, in addition to the numerous references in Spiritualist periodicals of the eighteen-seventies, see W. P. Adshead, *Dr. Monck in Derbyshire*, London, 1877, and T. Colley, *Later Phases of Materialisation*, London, 1877 (both reprints of articles); G. Sexton, 'Personal Experiences of Dr. Monck's Mediumship', *Spiritual Magazine*, 1874, pp. 97–105; 'Dr. Monck's Mediumship', *Light*, 1906, pp. 331–41; R. G. Medhurst, 'Stainton Moses and Contemporary Physical Mediums: II Francis Ward Monck', *Light*, 1965, pp. 145, 146–50. In 1876 Monck, who was staying in a private house for the purpose of giving sittings, was discovered to have materials for faking phenomena in his baggage, and in 1877 was sent to prison for three months. In 1907 Monck was the occasion of an action brought by J. N. Maskelyne, the conjuror, against the Rev. T. Colley, who had been a close friend and supporter of Monck. Colley had offered £1,000 to anyone who could repeat Monck's performances. Maskelyne claimed the money. Colley said that Maskelyne had not duplicated the phenomena. The court upheld Colley, largely because of the testimony of A. R. Wallace. Colley, incidentally, asserted that the paraphernalia found in Monck's baggage were *his*, and were used for giving demonstrations of methods of fraud.

gradually dissolving each time before our eyes. The fourth time, when the form was fully completed, Lillie floated up two feet above the curtain, which was partially drawn, and while Dr. Monck was clapping his hands and looking up and speaking to her, Lillie moved her lips and bowed to us several times, she then descended and stood in mid air about a foot away from the medium, and dissolved away while we were all gazing at the wondrous scene.[1]

Quite a number of other people—seemingly sane, and including no less a person than Alfred Russel Wallace—testified that they had witnessed this effect with Monck or Eglinton. Some of their accounts are even more remarkable than the one just quoted.

By the mid-eighteen-seventies the main issues had become pretty clear-cut. Either one had to accept the occurrence of astonishing and incredible physical phenomena, of a kind which had hitherto escaped detection; or one had to admit that the senses or the memories of seemingly sane people could deceive them in preposterous and unprecedented ways. Either one had to admit that Stainton Moses and others could be influenced by the surviving spirits of deceased persons, or at least that they possessed telepathic or clairvoyant powers of a sort quite unknown to science; or else one had to suppose them capable, in a state of dissociation, of reproducing passages from newspapers or works of reference of which they had not the least conscious recollection. Whatever view one took, the fact remained that phenomena had come to light which merited further investigation. It was therefore unfortunate that almost to a man the orthodox scientists of the day turned their backs on the matter. T. H. Huxley's reply to a request from the London Dialectical Society that he should join a committee to investigate Spiritualistic phenomena has become famous:

> ... supposing the phenomena to be genuine—they do not interest me. If anybody would endow me with the faculty of listening to the chatter of old women and curates in the nearest cathedral town, I should decline the privilege, having better things to do.

---

[1] *Spiritualist*, 12th May 1876.

And if the folk in the spiritual world do not talk more wisely and sensibly than their friends report them to do, I put them in the same category.

The only good that I can see in a demonstration of the truth of 'Spiritualism' is to furnish an additional argument against suicide. Better live a crossing-sweeper than die and be made to talk twaddle by a 'medium' hired at a guinea a seance.[1]

Even the two distinguished scientists who became Spiritualists—Alfred Russel Wallace and Cromwell Varley—carried out little in the way of systematic investigation. There was some justification for the complaint voiced in a *Times* leader of 26th December 1872:

> That in a generation which boasts itself to be one of exact science and plain matter-of-fact a belief should have been so long-lived, and should have grown even to such proportions that Mr. William Howitt, one of its chief fanatics, can number its adherents at 'twenty millions', and that it should have attained to such an age and vitality without its falsity having been demonstrated to the satisfaction of all but the very ignorant is strange indeed. It is evident either that the subject is surrounded by unusual difficulties or that in this matter our scientific men have signally failed to do their duty by the public, which looks to them for its facts. We believe the latter to be the case.

There had as a matter of fact by 1872 been just two serious attempts at methodical and scientific investigation of the phenomena; though neither of them had been anything like satisfactory. The first was an investigation of Spiritualism by a committee of the London Dialectical Society, a society whose purpose was that of 'affording a hearing to subjects which are ostracised elsewhere', especially ones of a 'metaphysical, religious, social or political character'.[2] The committee, set up in 1869, had over thirty members, mostly professional men, but including also Alfred Russel Wallace. It heard evidence and received communications (not of the extra-mundane variety) from most of the leading English Spiritualists, and also from

---

[1] *Dial. Soc. Report*, pp. 229–30.
[2] Salter, *op. cit.*, p. 9. For some sidelights on the Dialectical Society, see Bertrand and Patricia Russell (eds.), *The Amberley Papers*, London, 1937, Vol. II, pp. 115–18, 167–73.

several mediums, including D. D. Home. Its *Report*, published in 1871, is a valuable source-book for the student of the contemporary Spiritualist scene. The committee also divided itself up into six sub-committees for the purpose of practical investigation; though in the upshot only sub-committees One and Two had anything of interest to relate.

Sub-committee No. 1 held forty meetings at the private residences of its members. It employed no professional mediums, the 'mediums' being members of the committee itself; and it obtained in light inexplicable movements of heavy dining-room tables and other objects, and intelligent raps upon tables or the floor. One of its more startling experiments, that of 28th December 1870, is described in the contemporary minutes as follows:

> All chairs were then turned with their backs to the table, and nine inches away from it; and all present *knelt* on the chairs, with their wrists resting on the backs, and their hands a few inches above the table.
>
> Under these conditions, the table (the heavy dining-room table...) moved four times, each time from four to six inches, and the second time nearly twelve inches.
>
> Then all hands were placed on the backs of the chairs, and nearly a foot from the table, when four movements occurred, one slow and continuous, for nearly a minute.
>
> Then all present placed their hands behind their backs, kneeling erect on their chairs, which were removed a foot clear away from the table; the gas also was turned up higher, so as to give abundance of light, and under these test conditions, distinct movements occurred to the extent of several inches each time, and visible to every one present.[1]

Sub-committee No. 2 had rather similar experiences. Both sub-committees averred that at the start of the investigation the majority of their members had been sceptical. But it must be added that sub-committee No. 2 had only four members, whilst the most active members of sub-committee No. 1 seem to have been those already disposed to believe; and that the standard of reporting of both sub-committees leaves a great deal to be desired.[2] The publication (1871) of the majority

[1] *Dial. Soc. Report*, pp. 390–1.
[2] *Podmore* II, p. 150, points out some small discrepancies between the seance account quoted above and the description of the same seance in the report of the

report which, though moderate in tone, was favourable to the phenomena, caused something of a stir; indeed it caused indignation—not least, apparently, among the other members of the Dialectical Society.

A stir was also created in the same year (1871) when William Crookes published, in the *Quarterly Journal of Science* (of which he was himself editor), an account of some experiments which, in company with various friends and assistants, he had conducted with D. D. Home and a non-professional medium, Mrs. Clayer,[1] always, he says, by 'ample light'.

The most interesting kinds of experiment were these:

1. D. D. Home, held hand and foot and closely watched, would stand beside a horizontal mahogany board, without touching it. One end of the board was pivoted; the other was suspended from a spring balance. The board, still untouched by any visible agency, would be depressed a number of times; its movements being automatically recorded on a moving smoked-glass plate by means of a needle attached to the pointer of the balance.

2. A piece of parchment was stretched lightly across a circular hoop of wood. By means of a lever movements of the parchment were registered on a moving smoked-glass plate. (*a*) Mrs. Clayer's hands would be placed and held on the board on which the apparatus stood; but without touching the actual apparatus. Rapid percussive sounds would be heard coming from the parchment, and corresponding movements would be marked on the smoked-glass plate. (*b*) D. D. Home's hand was held by Crookes some 10 inches above the parchment, his other hand being held by a friend of Crookes'. The parchment drum was pressed slowly up and down, there being this time no percussive sounds.

---

sub-committee and concludes that they invalidate the whole character of the investigation. Podmore also says (p. 151) that only in the minority report of the Chairman, Dr. James Edmunds, was there any trace of critical handling of the materials. However, there is something very curious in Edmunds' attitude to the whole business. Subsequent correspondence in *The Spiritualist* (e.g. 15th Oct. 1871) revealed that the medium through whom some of the most startling effects (including the ones quoted above) were obtained was Dr. Edmunds' wife, and that the sittings had been held in his own home in his absence!

[1] N. Fodor, *Encyclopaedia of Psychic Science*, London [1933], p. 2, gives this as her name, or perhaps pseudonym. Crookes does not name her.

As a result of these experiments Crookes was violently attacked by some of his scientific colleagues, especially by W. B. Carpenter, who even hinted, in the *Quarterly Review* for October 1871, that the Fellows of the Royal Society had had much hesitation in electing Crookes to their number. Crookes replied vigorously, and in the *Quarterly Journal of Science* for January 1874 gave some account of other phenomena which he had witnessed with D. D. Home and with Kate Fox-Jencken. These included raps, object movements, levitation of furniture and of human beings, and the appearances of lights, hands and faces. Crookes' descriptions of these happenings are singularly abbreviated and wanting in detail—one suspects that he felt his own word as to their genuineness was guarantee enough—though many years later he published his detailed notes of some of them (see below, pp. 213–15). However, the country had heard a lot about Spiritualism since 1871, and Crookes' further report caused serious comment even in quite academic circles, especially when it was republished, together with his other papers on the subject, as *Researches in the Phenomena of Spiritualism* (1874).

Several of those who were prominent in subsequent investigations of such matters owed either the first arousal or a decisive re-arousal of their interest in them to Crookes' experiments. They included Lord Rayleigh; William, afterwards Sir William, Barrett, Professor of Physics at the Royal College of Science, Dublin; Arthur Balfour, one of Henry Sidgwick's ablest pupils; and Sidgwick himself.

IV Early Investigations of the Sidgwick Group 1873-5

SIDGWICK'S INTEREST in the phenomena of Spiritualism was not a new one. In his undergraduate days he had joined the old University Ghost Club and had collected various stories for it. The growth of Spiritualism in the early eighteen-sixties excited his curiosity, and in July 1863 he and a college friend, J. J. Cowell, had some inconclusive sittings with a professional medium. Cowell became much interested in Spiritualism and discovered that he himself possessed the gift of automatic writing. He invited Sidgwick to his home to study the phenomena. They failed to find anything in the statements written down which might not have been due to 'unconscious cerebration' on Cowell's part, but the writings were punctuated by some curious and intelligent raps, which, Sidgwick told Graham Dakyns in a letter of April 1864, 'were perceived by the sensoria of myself and Cowell, sitting at a small table, certainly not in consequence of any physical force exercised by us on the table'.[1]

No doubt Sidgwick's interest in Spiritualism at this time was related to his general concern with the evidence for miracles. He continued his investigations at intervals during the next few years with results, so far as I can discover, similarly inconclusive. When Crookes' experiments were first published, Sidgwick was preparing his *Methods of Ethics*; he was worried by the fact that an individual's duty and his happiness seem inevitably to diverge and doubted whether a reasoned moral code could be established on the basis of merely mundane sanctions. Under these circumstances his ethical studies were bound to lead him to further reflections upon the problem of an after-

[1] H.S. A Memoir, p. 106.

life. His concern with ethical matters had always taken a practical turn, and it was perhaps inevitable that he should be stirred into further empirical investigations by Crookes' startling and seemingly authoritative claims. But I very much doubt whether Sidgwick's investigations would have been so extensive or so prolonged as they in fact were had it not been for the influence upon him of a person whose temperament was far more eager than his own, namely Frederic Myers.

Myers' mother had settled in Cheltenham after her husband's death and had sent her sons as day-boys to Cheltenham College. Frederic's teachers seem to have felt that his classical scholarship was not always so exact as it might have been,[1] but they were impressed by his fluency in composition. When he was only fourteen he sent in three entries for the College's English verse prize (the subject was 'Belisarius'), and his poems were placed first, second and fourth.[2] For a lad of that age they display an extraordinary feeling for words:

> As some faint meteor in the pale-starred even
> Gleams from the heavens on a joyless tract,—
> A tract of wide waste lands, and solitary,
> Save beasts that howl beneath a cloud-wrapt night,
> And reddens for a moment, and is gone;
> And the wind moans, and the far bittern booms,
> And the reeds shiver, and the marsh-fed willows
> Sway their lank arms awhile, and all is still:
> So gleamed a smile across his haggard face,
> A smile that only lit his desolation.

In 1859 he entered a poem in a national competition inaugurated to mark the centenary of Robert Burns' birth; his entry was placed second, and a writer in the *Manchester Guardian* said that it was as fine as anything which Chatterton had written at a similar age.[3]

When Myers went up to Trinity in October 1860 as a minor scholar his reputation had preceded him; and in the following year the success of his University Prize Poem, *The Prince of Wales at the Tomb of Washington*, made him locally famous.[4]

[1] Myers' school reports are still in existence.
[2] Two of them are reprinted in his *Collected Poems*, London, 1921, pp. 49–68.
[3] *Collected Poems*, p. 69.
[4] Its slightly fulsome tones were parodied by W. J. Lawrance in *The Undergraduate at the Tomb of the Trinity Cook*, Cambridge [1863].

Those who knew him at this time might well have prophesied that he would become one of the most notable poets of his age. He did not quite live up to this early promise, and eventually he almost abandoned poetry; none the less his character and career have to be understood in the light of the side of his nature from which the poetry sprang. He was endowed in the highest degree with that capacity for *delight* which, in the wake of the Romantic Revival, seemed to many the most essential mark of a poet.[1] To Myers a scene or a painting or a line of verse might bring an enjoyment so intense that it verged on pain; a poignant sense that what now confronted him fell hopelessly short of an Ideal Beauty of which it was but the shadow and the promise. So powerfully could he be gripped by an emotion that the ecstasy or the despair of a moment might almost seem to transcend itself and to partake of something universal and timeless.

To Myers' undergraduate contemporaries he appeared an eccentric and a *poseur*. His extreme sensibility led him to express his feelings in an unrestrained way and to dramatise scenes and incidents which others were likely to find merely trivial or silly.[2] It led also to an arrogance and a vanity which made him widely unpopular, for his emotions had to him at times a momentous, a cosmic import, and he could hardly help regarding himself as singled out by Fate, for some high destiny. His pride was augmented by his early successes; and he was perhaps not unaware of possessing personal advantages—a tallish (though somewhat plump) figure, a handsome face and silky beard, a delicately flexible voice—denied to many others. Few liked him, and some detested him. His closest friend during his early years at Cambridge was Arthur Sidgwick, a clever young classic in the year above him. Their relationship was of an emotional and aesthetic kind, and its intenseness may well have caused unfavourable comment, so adding to Myers' unpopularity.[3]

---

[1] His own essay on Shelley, *Collected Poems*, pp. 22-33, may convey something of what I mean.

[2] There are some curious examples of this tendency in *Fragments*.

[3] Phyllis Grosskurth, *John Addington Symonds*, London, 1964, quotes (pp. 114-15) a letter from J. A. Symonds to H. G. Dakyns (the original of which I have seen) which says that Myers and Arthur Sidgwick were 'assailed by the same disease' (i.e. homosexuality) as Symonds. I have noticed one or two points in Myers'

Myers possessed not merely keen sensibilities but a fine intellect. He turned himself, by diligent study, into an outstanding classical scholar, and the range of his other interests was very wide. He did exceptionally well in his various examinations, and he won a series of important university prizes. A good part of his subsequent history centres around the conflicts between these two parts of his being, the emotional and the intellectual. The emotional and poetic side of him felt that everyday events and scenes are somehow reflections of a deeper order of things from which they take their meaning and by which they are in some obscure way harmonised and guided to good ends. His intellectual side often found the greatest difficulty in accepting this scheme. Much of his life was passed in search for some rational justification of the beliefs to which his inmost nature prompted him. Without such justification he could never wholeheartedly accept the beliefs; yet without the beliefs his world seemed empty of joy and his life bereft of all significance.

During Myers' later schooldays, and his first three years at Cambridge, these divergent tendencies were to a large extent reconciled in an enthusiasm for classical literature and the Greek way of life. Philological and textual studies satisfied his intellect and revealed to him writings which seemed but intensifications of his own being; whilst in the religious views of Plato and Virgil he found much to accord with his own predispositions. Even at school he had read and memorised classical literature with an avidity which can have had few parallels among lads of his age:

> That early burst of admiration for Virgil of which I have already spoken was followed by a growing passion for one after another of the Greek and Latin poets. From ten to sixteen I lived much in the inward reciting of Homer, Aeschylus, Lucretius, Horace, and Ovid. The reading of Plato's Gorgias at fourteen was a great event; but the study of the Phaedo at sixteen effected upon me a kind of conversion. At that time, too, I

---

letters which are consistent with, though they do not exactly support, the notion that Myers went through such a phase; and cf. the second passage from *Fragments*, p. 10, quoted below. But he had certainly developed normal tendencies within a few years. I think that homosexuality was not rare amongst young university classicists in those restricted days.

returned to my worship of Virgil, whom Homer had for some years thrust into the background. I gradually wrote out Bucolics, Georgics, Aeneid from memory; and felt, as I have felt ever since, that of all minds known to me it is Virgil's of which I am the most intimate and adoring disciple . . . The discovery at seventeen, in an old school-book, of the poems of Sappho, whom till then I had known only by name, brought an access of intoxicating joy. Later on, the solitary decipherment of Pindar made another epoch of the same kind.[1]

None the less he came in later years to feel that this course of life had not been entirely suitable for him. Even as a child he had been, as his mother noted, self-willed and unusually emotional, and the early death of his father removed a source of discipline whose loss was not counterbalanced by exposure to the severities of boarding-school life. The fervid Hellenism of his university days did not supply the needed corrective. The classics, he was to write thirty years afterwards

> drew from me and fostered evil as well as good; they might aid imaginative impulse and detachment from sordid interests, but they had no check for lust or pride.[2]

In the natural course of events an undergraduate of Myers' undeniable prominence would have been invited to join the Apostles; but though Arthur Sidgwick, who was a member, used to press his claims, the other Apostles could never stomach him, and he was not elected. The Apostles might have cut Myers back to size; but as it was he consorted mainly with the rowing set (he was an enthusiastic but not remarkable oarsman) before whom he could play the oracle unchallenged.

He was perhaps somewhat chastened in 1863 by an unfortunate *contretemps* in which he was landed by his own egotism. In the previous year he had won the University's Camden medal for Latin verse. Whilst composing his entry for the next competition he came across a volume of past Oxford prize poems, and he began to cull from it such lines as he thought worthy of preservation and force them in to his own poem. In so doing he was following what he conceived was Virgil's practice, and he made no secret of his activities to his friends, to whom he would remark in Virgil's words 'Aurum colligo e stercore

---

[1] *Fragments*, p. 10.   [2] *Fragments*, p. 10.

Ennii' (I am collecting gold from Ennius' dungheap). Custom, of course, sanctioned and even applauded the working of tags from other writers into one's own verses; but in appropriating a large number of complete lines (enough to make up about a quarter of his poem) he was clearly transgressing the accepted rules of the game. Although before the competition he had handed a copy of his entry with the borrowed lines marked to a graduate of Trinity, he very foolishly did not acknowledge them in the copy which he formally submitted. His poem was awarded the prize; but another competitor, getting wind of the insertions, tracked them down and complained to the Vice-Chancellor, at the same time withdrawing his own entry. There was a considerable rumpus, which ended in Myers resigning the prize. His appropriation of other people's lines was represented by his numerous enemies as a piece of straightforward cheating. This was not the view taken by the authorities but the imputation stuck, and the episode was still held against him in Cambridge circles even forty years later.[1]

Myers' Hellenic enthusiasms seem to have reached and passed their height during the summer of 1864. In February 1864 he was placed second in the first class of the Classical Tripos and, after graduating, he set out to travel in Greece and Asia Minor —no easy venture at that time. The actual sight of the Aegean lands in a curious way dissolved the passionate dreams of their departed loveliness which he had for so long cherished. Of Sicyon, where once Praxilla sang, there remained but a few, lonely ruins; not even the faintest murmuring of Sappho's voice was borne by the sea-breezes along the shores of Lesbos.

> I climbed to the summit of Syra,—
> More like a man
> Flying from something that he feared, than one
> Who sought the thing he loved.

For gazing thence on Delos and on the Cyclades, and on those straits and channels of purple sea, I felt that nowise could I come closer still; never more intimately than thus could embrace that vanished beauty. Alas for an ideal which roots itself in the past! That longing cannot be allayed; it feels 'the insatiability which attends all unnatural passions as their inevitable punishment'. For it is an unnatural passion; the

[1] On this episode, see G. C. Coulton, *Fourscore Years*, Cambridge, 1943, pp. 106-8.

world rolls onward, not backward, and men must set their hearts on what lies before.[1]

When he returned to England in June 1864 Myers swung away from Hellenism. In October he was second in the first class of the Moral Sciences Tripos, being placed so high largely for his political economy. He then sought to obtain an extra year in which to take the Natural Sciences Tripos. He would no doubt have obtained another first class;[2] but the requisite dispensation was not granted him. He may have had thoughts of a medical career[3]—his brother Arthur took up medicine a few years later, after gaining a first in classics—and he certainly attended classes in chemistry, pathology and botany, so laying the foundations of that general knowledge of science which later so impressed his friends. However, this project too was abandoned, and in 1865 he accepted a Fellowship and College Lectureship in classics at Trinity.

As the spring tide of Myers' Hellenism ebbed away it left him with no great moving force to uphold and guide his life. He had never actually cast off Christianity, and he had of late years begun to show serious interest in it; but the *Phaedo* rather than the New Testament had been his sacred text, and now that his Greek ideal had faded he was left for the first and only time in numb indifference to both past and future. During a tour of Canada and the United States in the summer of 1865 he swam late one night across Niagara below the falls:

> As I stood on a rock, choosing my place to plunge into the boiling whiteness, I asked myself with urgency, 'What if I die?' For once the answer was blank of emotion. I have often looked back on this apathy in the brief interspace of religions as my only subjective key to the indifference which I observe in so many of mankind . . . I emerged on the American side, and looked back on the tossing gulf. May death, I dimly thought, be such a transit, terrifying but easy, and leading to nothing new? *Coelum non animum mutant* may be true of that change as well.[4]

---

[1] *Fragments*, p. 11.
[2] Even this feat would not have remained a record for long. In 1867–8 H. M. Gwatkin (1844–1916), later Dixie professor of ecclesiastical history, obtained four first classes—in classics, mathematics, moral sciences and theology.
[3] He certainly toyed with the idea in 1871.
[4] *Fragments*, p. 12.

To a man of Myers' eager temperament sustained indifference was not possible; his pent-up enthusiasm was sooner or later sure to find some line of discharge. And it so happened that a ready line of discharge was at that point presented to him by the crusading Christianity of Mrs. Josephine Butler,[1] the still young and beautiful wife of George Butler, Vice-Principal of Cheltenham College, and later Principal of Liverpool College. Mrs. Butler later, of course, became famous for her work among prostitutes and her campaign against the Contagious Diseases Acts. At this time however she was chiefly engaged in what might be described as the spiritual seduction of promising young men. Her religion was emotional rather than dogmatic, and her methods of conversion were simple. Having aroused her quarry by her exciting concern for his welfare, she would flatter him with an earnest account of her own inner trials and victories—an account delivered perhaps at twilight whilst she lay with her slim form stretched out upon a sofa—and at last capture him by a well-staged *dénouement*. She might, for instance, call him into her room to find her kneeling in pale beauty before her mirror, devoutly praying for his salvation.[2] Only men with the coolest heads could resist such an appeal; and Myers was not one of them. During the next few years he met or visited Mrs. Butler repeatedly, and his way of life changed so much that his friends hardly knew him. One of them, Richard Jebb, noted in his Journal for 26th February 1866: 'Myers devotes himself to self-discipline. He never goes anywhere. He gets up at 6.30 and goes to bed at 10.00. His days are spent in reading *Ecce Homo* and in thinking.'[3] In September of that year Myers underwent not, I think, so much a conversion—he was already the keenest of converts—as a moment of illumination, a sensible inflowing of Divine Grace. For some while thereafter his life was one sustained rapture, a rapture which he was only too eager to share with others. 'If you think of me,' he wrote to Arthur Sidgwick on 5th October 1866,

> think of me as of . . . one who after night and sloughs of the valley is lifted into a nobler aether and lucent morning on the

---

[1] A recent biography of Mrs. Butler is E. Moberly Bell, *Josephine Butler*, London, 1962.

[2] Cf. Symonds' experiences, Grosskurth, *op. cit.*, pp. 83–4.

[3] Caroline Jebb, *Life and Letters of Sir Richard Claverhouse Jebb*, Cambridge, 1907, p. 81.

hills,—who sees before him a prospect dimmed indeed here and there with mists of degradation; flecked by storms of passionate remorse, but free, and infinite, and unspeakable, and lit by an unimagined sun—

I could not have conceived the existence of such happiness as I have experienced this summer; I hardly venture to look forward to the future, dazed with excess of light.

Myers seems to have maintained and, *mirabile dictu,* even increased this fervour during the following year. In a letter of 14th July 1867 he told Arthur Sidgwick 'the belief in her which I had when at Rugby was an infidel apathy as compared with the passionate intensity of my belief in her now. I cannot prove the difference: no words that I could use were too strong even before: but the dictionary ends sooner than the soul.' Myers' worship of Christ was not perhaps quite distinct in his own heart from a worship of Mrs. Butler; and his enthusiasm for her brought some sharp comments from his friends.

The most extended records of this phase of Myers' beliefs are two long and intensely personal religious poems, *St. Paul* (1867) and *St. John the Baptist* (1868). *St. Paul,* the better of the two, enjoyed a great success in its day, though it is now perhaps best remembered through Stephen's wicked parody in *Lapsus Calami.* Its hectic movement and intricate rhythms, a little reminiscent perhaps of Meredith's *Love in the Valley,*[1] can still carry the reader along for at least a few pages. Henry Sidgwick, who was keenly interested in poetry, described it to James Bryce in a letter of 28th December 1867 as 'very fine poetical rhetoric—consummate except for excess of artifice, and *occasional* lapses into bad taste'; and this seems to me a very fair judgement.

Sidgwick and Myers had by then been acquainted for several years; in fact Sidgwick had coached Myers in classics during the latter's first year at Cambridge. Sidgwick was at that time intensely shy—the social gifts which he later displayed were the result of painful self-discipline—and he was not popular with the undergraduates. In an unpublished *Account of my Friendship with Henry Sidgwick*[2] Myers noted:

[1] Meredith reviewed *St. Paul* in the *Fortnightly* for 1868. See *Fortnightly Review* III, pp. 115–17. Henry Sidgwick reviewed it in the *Spectator* for 4th Jan. 1868. For a hostile analysis of *St. Paul* see the letter of P. Gosse quoted on pp. 14–15 of E. Charteris's *Life and Letters of Sir Edmund Gosse,* London, 1931.

[2] Written 18th Oct. 1873, possibly for Annie Marshall, wife of his cousin, Walter Marshall.

He was of course an admirable scholar, but he taught with great coldness & was generally accused of unwillingness to take trouble with his pupils, & selfish indifference to their success. He was rarely seen by undergraduates, except in Chapel, where his distant and frigid air, and his habit of 'eating his beard',—shovelling it by handfuls into his mouth, while he gazed coldly thro' halfshut eyes at the Freshmen opposite him,—used to inspire the said Freshmen with a feeling of uneasy dislike rising in the most sensitive among them to actual hatred. 'That old goat was there eating his beard again,—I should like to punch his head', may be taken as a typical Freshman remark on the subject.

In company Myers used to defend Sidgwick for Arthur Sidgwick's sake, but he shared in the general dislike of him, feeling him aloof and anaemic; and when, in February 1861, at their last coaching, Sidgwick said: 'I hope I shall not lose sight of you,' Myers received the remark with some disdain, feeling that he might as easily lose sight of the rising sun.[1] Although they met occasionally in the next six years, it is not until 1868 that references to Sidgwick in Myers' diary suggest a growing acquaintanceship.

Even then their relations were for some while a little uneasy. Myers made occasional attempts to lure Sidgwick into Mrs. Butler's fold; though it is hard to imagine anyone less likely than Sidgwick to be captured by that perfervid prophetess. Myers' arguments can perhaps be guessed from the following letter, written to Arthur Sidgwick a few years previously in an attempt as much, perhaps, to dispel his own doubts as to dispel his friend's:

> I am well aware that in such controversy as we had at Rugby I when defending Christianity was uniformly defeated, and I have no expectation even if I knew all about the arguments on both sides, instead of being as ignorant as I am, that I should find much good result from that sort of reasoning, but I cannot resist writing to say that the moral evidence in favour of Christianity becomes, immediately the will is thoroughly

---

[1] But Sidgwick was still interested in Myers. In a letter to Graham Dakyns written about May 1861, he said: 'I send by the book post a volume of poetry. I want you to read the poem on the death of Socrates, by Myers (when *15* at Cheltenham)—and, if you will, to show it to Tennyson and ask his opinion. I would not do this if I did not think it *very extraordinary*.'

subjected, quite overwhelmingly strong. I, even I, wretched and half-hearted beginner as I am can almost say already that I know the thing is true. How do I know? How do I know that Virgil is a great poet? I cannot prove it to Jackson & yet how absolutely I *see* his deficiency. How do you know that Bach was a great musician? You cannot prove it to me and yet how clearly you feel that it is I who have a sense wanting, not you who have subjective fancies on the subject. I tell you that whatever else I know or do not know [erasure] I know to what extent I can resist them of my own strength of will under every variety of circumstances. The whole mental process is one in which as you well know I have cause to take a desperate interest. And I am beginning to know in an equally unmistakeable manner what it is to have a strength not my own infused into me, as I believe, by the Holy Spirit of God.

You cannot say that your critical analysis *disproves* Christianity. It merely fails to prove it on external grounds. The gospel of John, for instance, Rénan supposes genuine tho' untrustworthy, Strauss (if I mistake not) a 2nd century compilation. You cannot say that criticism is conclusive against the gospel of John, as it is against the letters of Phalaris. If the grand initial difficulty of believing that God became man was got over I believe the difficulties of detail would be far from invincible. And that grand initial difficulty is to certain persons, to certain states of mind, the greatest argument in favour of the religion. Who is right? Consider that if the thing is true for one person, it is true for another, if it is true for Mrs. Butler it is true for you.

No threats need be held out as to the consequence of disregarding it if true. The more thoroughly you feel that love is everything that matters the more would it agonize you with shame if once you thought that you had possibly been rejecting such love as the gospels tell of.

Nothing on earth would rejoice me so much as your conversion. Great heavens what a prospect! Leagued on Earth with all those whose love is best worth having in a bond closer than any freemasonry, enrolled among the countless 'species of one genus

        All with foreheads bearing LOVER
        written above the earnest eyes of them.'

and after death—! and all this as I believe to be had merely for the asking, surely this is God.[1]

---

[1] This letter is dated 5th May 1865; it suggests that Myers' interest in Chris-

The growth of Myers' doubts was slow and agonising. In his autobiography he passes quickly over his loss of faith, as though even the memory was still painful to him:

> There is no need to retrace the steps of gradual disillusion. This came to me, as to many others, from increased knowledge of history and of science, from a wider outlook on the world. Sad it was, and slow; a recognition of insufficiency of evidence, fraught with growing pain. Insensibly the celestial vision faded, and left me to
>
> > pale despair and cold tranquillity
> > Nature's vast frame, the web of human things,
> > Birth and the grave, that are not as they were.[1]

When, in February 1869, an attack of pneumonia put his life in danger, Myers realised that he was no longer a Christian; and for the next few years he vacillated between complete agnosticism and a troubled half-belief. His doubts caused him great distress. He needed a religious belief more intensely perhaps than most men can readily understand. Hitherto his life had held significance for him because he had conceived it as enacted, so to speak, against the backcloth of eternity; now he began to see himself as a puppet whose gyrations had only the appearance of meaning, and who would before long be put away for ever. The thought of personal extinction was dreadful to him, and he could not understand how anyone could feel otherwise.[2] It was not merely that the prospect of annihilation seemed to rob his life of all its point and purpose; he loved life, he loved experience for its own sake so keenly that he found the idea of its coming to an end unbearable. And without the restraints imposed by religious belief his love of experience was prone to degenerate into a mere sensuality by which, whatever reason might say, he afterwards felt himself degraded.

Myers' unhappiness was at its worst in 1869 and 1870.[3]

---

tianity had been at any rate brewing for a good while before the crisis of Sept. 1866. It is quoted in a slightly bowdlerised form in Myers' *Fragments of Poetry and Prose*, London, 1904, pp. 25–7.

[1] *Fragments*, p. 13.

[2] Gwen Raverat describes (*Period Piece*, London, 1952, p. 189) how Myers once touched her Uncle Frank [Darwin] and said: 'Frank, let me *feel* you: a man who really does not WANT immortality.'

[3] The feelings of this period are expressed in two of his better poems, the sonnets *Would God it were Evening* and *Would God it were Morning*.

During those years he turned increasingly to Sidgwick as to a guide who, though unable to find shelter, was at least undismayed by the cruel winds of doubt.

The friendship which sprang up between these two might seem at first sight a most unlikely one. Sidgwick was ascetic and cool-headed, a political and academic liberal and a practical reformer. Myers, by contrast, was not merely a man pulled this way and that by turbulent emotions and irrepressible sensuality; he was at this period of his life a snob, a name-dropper, an archtory.[1] Sidgwick once remarked to him: 'My difficulty about you is that feeling that you deviate from the Type in a direction opposite to mine.'[2] Yet there were many things to draw them together. On a workaday level was the fact that both were much occupied with educational questions. Sidgwick was active in the movement for Women's Education, and later on was concerned in many other educational matters. In 1869 Myers resigned his lectureship at Trinity to work on behalf of the movement for the higher education of women, and in 1872 he became a school inspector (he was appointed to the Cambridge district in 1875, and retained the post until shortly before his death).[3] On a deeper level they had many further points of contact. Sidgwick of course had no 'message' for his disciples; he could not offer them a panacea for philosophical bewilderment, or a quick formula for solving moral problems. 'Feeling that the deepest truth I have to tell is by no means "good tidings",' he later noted in his journal, 'I naturally shrink from exercising on others the personal influence which would make men [resemble] me, as much as men more optimistic and prophetic naturally aim at exercising such influence. Hence as a teacher I naturally desire to limit my teaching to those whose bent or deliberate choice it is to search after ultimate truth; if such come to me, I try to tell them all I know.'[4] It was only to those very few persons—and Myers was one of them—who preferred Truth, however grim, to illusion, however soothing, that Sidgwick could give of his inner self; and it was only

[1] See the extraordinary letter in which in 1868 he advocated capital punishment for habitual criminals—Una Taylor, *Guests and Memories*, Oxford, 1934, pp. 258-60.
[2] *H.S.: A Memoir*, p. 273.
[3] In the summer of 1885 he applied, or at least thought of applying, for the Chair of English Language and Literature at Oxford.
[4] *H.S.: A Memoir*, pp. 395-6.

through such persons that he could hope to spread and to perpetuate his own intellectual and moral ideals. To the perplexities of an honest doubter he would listen with ready understanding and deep sympathy; in most cases he had himself once entertained the same thoughts and himself once felt the same distress. On 11th March 1871 Myers wrote to him:

> My confidence not only in *your* criticism of Clough &c. but in the general possibilities of discovering a man's mind from his writings is greatly increased by the astounding precision with which you insert your pen's point between the convolutions of my cerebral hemispheres. Give you a few more historical facts, & there wd. be nothing secret in me wh. should not be revealed . . . Anyhow I am greatly obliged to you, & it is most satisfying & delightful to feel that there is anyone in the world who takes the trouble to understand one.

Myers' appreciation of Sidgwick's trouble and understanding was boundless, and was expressed with all the gratitude and admiration of which his ardent nature was capable. When Myers became engaged to be married Sidgwick wrote to his bride-to-be:

> For many years Frederic Myers has been as dear to me as the dearest of brothers—there is no one so qualified to enrich and make brighter and nobler the lives of those he loves . . . One might guess from his poetry the ardour and depth and fulness of his feeling, and his sensitiveness to all things fair and great and high; but the unwavering loyalty and tender observant sympathy that I have had from him in a friendship that has been without the smallest cloud from the first beginning— that can only be shown in life and not in verse.

It was, by a strange paradox, above all else Myers' desire to believe which made him cleave so hard to Sidgwick, that perennial doubter. His excursion into Mrs. Butler's heady realm had ended disastrously, and he could not endure even the thought of again suffering so sharp a disappointment. Yet he was only too keenly aware that the inner needs which had lured him into building on sand might do so again. There was, he felt, no one better qualified than Sidgwick to rescue him from the pitfalls of wishful thinking, and no one with whom, if all else failed, he would more readily face the waking nightmare of total unbelief.

It was not just upon dogmatic or theological issues that Myers sought Sidgwick's help. To a man so torn between the carnal and the eternal problems of everyday conduct were peculiarly urgent. In his autobiography he said:

> The effect of agnosticism upon me was wholly evil. During this phase only can I remember anything of deadness and bitterness;— of scorn of human life, of anger at destiny, of cynical preference of the pleasures of the passing hour.[1]

He rather enjoyed (I suspect) alarming Sidgwick with the details of these passing hours. On 1st May 1872 Sidgwick wrote plaintively to him:

> ... it would delight me much to know that you were prosperously betrothed; not from the vulgar desire to reach the end of Vol. III ... but in order that Cupid may
>
> 'Get his sop and hold his noise'
>
> and leave room for other enthusiasms and impulses of self-development.

Never was such a point more tactfully put. Sidgwick's own way of life was strict, but his views upon other people's lapses, though stern,[2] rarely led him to sever a friendship, and he sought to sway Myers by suggesting that his conduct was unbecoming or even dangerous, rather than by preaching at him. He brought him into the society of George Eliot and the *earnest* agnostics; and whether or not one admires earnestness, there is no doubt that Myers needed its restraining influence. Myers once said that there was no moral height to which he might not, in certain circumstances, have risen, and no depth to which he might not conceivably have sunk. I believe that this was very nearly true; and that it was in fair measure due to Sidgwick's example and influence that Myers did not sink.

What Myers most urgently needed however was not just moral and philosophical guidance, but a purpose or occupation to help him overcome the feeling that life is in the last

---

[1] *Fragments*, p. 36.

[2] See the story, Grosskurth, *op. cit.*, p. 128, of Sidgwick locking the manuscripts of Symonds' pederastic poems in a box and ceremonially throwing the key into the Avon. Judging by the specimens in Symonds' MS. autobiography (in the London Library) the bottom of a river (though not perhaps the Avon) would on purely literary grounds have been a suitable place for the poems themselves.

resort altogether barren and pointless. His ardent temperament and dramatising tendencies would hardly have been satisfied by anything less than devotion to some Great Cause; and best of all to a Cause which seemed to offer him at least the hope of recovering the beliefs which he had lost. Exactly when he first discussed Spiritualism with Sidgwick is uncertain,[1] but the occasion left an indelible impression upon him.

> In a star-light walk which I shall not forget . . . I asked him, almost with trembling, whether he thought that when Tradition, Intuition, Metaphysic, had failed to solve the riddle of the Universe, there was still a chance that from any actual observable phenomena,—ghosts, spirits, whatsoever there might be,—some valid knowledge might be drawn as to a World Unseen. Already, it seemed, he had thought that this was possible; steadily, though in no sanguine fashion, he indicated some last grounds of hope; and from that night onwards I resolved to pursue this quest, if it might be, at his side.[2]

Myers seems to have carried out his own first experiments in these directions during 1872 and 1873, I think in private circles with his friends; and in the autumn of 1873 he came across his 'first personal experience of forces unknown to science'.[3] In October 1873 he suggested a joint investigation to Sidgwick, who replied (with Crookes' papers fresh in his mind):

> . . . As for spirit-rapping I am in exactly the same mind towards it as towards Religion. I believe there is something in it: don't know what: have tried hard to discover and find that I always paralyze the phenomena; my taste is strongly affected by the obvious humbug mixed with it which, at the same time, my

---

[1] In his obituary of Sidgwick, *P.S.P.R.* XV (1901), pp. 452–62, Myers says (p. 454) that it was on 3rd Dec. 1869; but in *Fragments* (p. 14) he gives the date as 13th Nov. 1871. The latter is probably correct, since his diary entry for that day reads 'H.S. on ghosts'. 'On ghosts?' is pencilled after 'H.S.' in the diary entry for 3rd Dec. 1869.
[2] Myers, *loc. cit.*, p. 454.
[3] His diary entry for 20th Nov. 1873 reads 'John King shakes hands', and this may have been the occasion referred to. If so the medium was perhaps C. Williams. See Mrs. Myers' story in *Light* LIV (1934), p. 332. She says that her husband told her of a seance with Williams at which a big, hairy hand came down from the ceiling. Myers seized it in both of his; it diminished in size until it resembled a baby's hand, and finally melted away in his grasp. Cf. *J.S.P.R.* XXXI (1939), p. 79.

reason does not over-estimate. John King is an old friend, but as he always came into the dark and talked at random, our friendship refrigerated. Still I shall be glad to accompany you on any favourable opportunity . . .[1]

They had a number of sittings in the early part of 1874, mostly in private circles composed of their own friends, though occasionally with paid mediums. On 9th May 1874 there occurred an event which decisively influenced the whole course of Myers' life. Accompanied by his friend Edmund Gurney, another of the younger Trinity Fellows, he went to the home of his aunt, Lady Mount-Temple, to meet Stainton Moses. Moses, a man of university education, gave them a first-hand account of the strange phenomena of which he was the focus; and they could not but feel impressed by his 'manifest sanity and probity'. 'He spoke frankly and fully; he showed his note-books; he referred us to his friends; he inspired a belief which was at once sufficient, and which is still sufficient, to prompt to action.'[2] On his return Myers persuaded Sidgwick to join him in organising a 'sort of informal association' for the investigation of the phenomena; into this association were sooner or later drawn Edmund Gurney, Walter Leaf and Lord Rayleigh (all Fellows of Trinity); Arthur Balfour and his sisters Eleanor and Evelyn (Lady Rayleigh); the John Hollonds;[3] and various others. Up till this time Sidgwick's investigations of Spiritualism and related phenomena had been fitful, waxing and waning as his opinions vacillated; but for much of the rest of his life he was to be constantly prodded into action by the eager and relentless Myers.

The first mediums with whom Sidgwick and his group of friends seem to have had sittings were two professionals, C. Williams, who specialised in strong physical phenomena and materialised 'John King' and other spirits, and a dainty and charming visitor from America, Annie Eva Fay.[4] Mrs. Fay made at first a con-

[1] *H.S.: A Memoir*, pp. 284–5.
[2] *Human Personality* II, pp. 223–4.
[3] John Hollond, a contemporary of Myers' at Trinity, was M.P. for Brighton 1880–5.
[4] On the career of Mrs. Fay, see E. J. Dingwall, *The Critics' Dilemma*, pp. 40–5. She had a clever vaudeville mind-reading act, as well as the physical effects here

siderable impression on Myers and Sidgwick. She came to Britain early in 1874 and gave exhibitions on the stage, in her own apartments and in the houses of those who cared to employ her. Most of her seances were of the following kind. In the first half she would sit on a stool or chair with her neck secured to a staple in a post or wall behind her, and her hands tied to a similar staple lower down. Objects, including musical instruments, would be placed on her lap or near at hand; the lights would be lowered, and a curtain pulled in front of her. The objects would be thrown around and the musical instruments played. The second part of her performance would be a fairly orthodox dark sitting; the sitters would be grouped in a circle round her, and she would clap her hands or surrender them to neighbours to show that she was not engaged in trickery. Meanwhile her spirit guides, John D. Hull and William Howes, would tweak sitters' beards and clothes and noses, play upon the musical instruments, displace objects and chat to the company in the direct voice.[1]

There does not seem to be the slightest reason for regarding Mrs. Fay's performances as anything other than conjuring.[2] Such a conclusion was at least strongly suggested by the sittings which various of Sidgwick's friends had with her in the autumn of 1874, seemingly at Balfour's town house 4 Carlton Gardens. Instead of tying both of Mrs. Fay's hands to one staple with a single cord or strip of linen (this had been the usual procedure at her seances), the sitters tied each of her hands to a separate staple. Phenomena ceased.[3]

It is not clear whether Myers and Sidgwick participated in these sittings. Myers' diaries show that he had sittings with Mrs. Fay in June, November and December 1874, and seemingly also in January 1875. He was sometimes accompanied by Sidgwick or by Crookes and at least once by Edmund Gurney. By the end of November 1874, and despite the results at

---

described, and she seems to have adjusted her claims as to the part which the spirits played in the manifestations to the audience before whom she was performing.

[1] See, e.g., J. N. Maskelyne, *Modern Spiritualism*, London [1876], pp. 120–3.

[2] On Mrs. Fay's methods see J. W. Truesdell, *The Bottom Facts concerning the Science of Spiritualism*, London, 1884, pp. 240–75.

[3] See p. 48 of Mrs. Sidgwick's 'Results of a Personal Investigation into the Physical Phenomena of Spiritualism', *P.S.P.R.* IV (1886), pp. 45–79.

Carlton Gardens, he was writing about 'Eva' in quite extravagant terms: 'The moral evidences of her candour', he wrote to Sidgwick on 26th November 1874, 'constantly increase. Each accession of intimacy with her leads me to an increased respect for her uprightness, courage and kindness.'

Myers and Sidgwick did their best to persuade Lord Rayleigh, already a famous physicist, to undertake a sustained investigation of Mrs. Fay. Mrs. Fay said (quite possibly correctly) that Sidgwick was too fidgety to make a good sitter, and perhaps because of this he retired from the enquiry. Myers replied to him (3rd December 1874) in phraseology harking back to his Butler days:

> But pledge not yourself *never* to witness her revelations, for I hope that that sweet and noble one may be permitted to remain yet some 30 or 40 years in the form, & may under God's providence be a leading agent in bringing Life and Immortality to light.

However, these elevated hopes were soon dashed. Rayleigh, though not impressed by what he had seen of Mrs. Fay at Carlton Gardens, was sufficiently struck by Myers', and also Crookes', accounts of her, to invite her as a paid guest to his country house, Terling Place, Essex, in January 1875. What exactly happened is not clear, but from a letter of Rayleigh's to Myers dated 15th January 1875 it seems likely that for some rather obscure reason Mrs. Fay withdrew from the agreement at the last moment. She was not, so far as I know, again investigated seriously by any member of the Sidgwick group, which had by this time developed other interests.[1]

Even Myers seems shortly to have lost his faith in her, and his reaction was so violent that he struck through her name where it appeared in his diary. What disillusioned him so much I have not discovered. In a letter to Sir Oliver Lodge, dated 15th March 1892, he describes Mrs Fay as 'an undoubted cheat',

---

[1] But Crookes, who had shown signs of wanting to monopolise investigations of Mrs. Fay for himself, continued to investigate her. On his famous 'electrical test' with her see Medhurst and Goldney, *loc. cit.*, pp. 94–105, and C. Brookes-Smith, *J.S.P.R.* XLIII (1965), pp. 26–31; and C. J. Stephenson, *P.S.P.R.* LIV (1966), pp. 407–11.

During the next quarter of a century the Sidgwick group investigated many physical mediums; and the same pattern of events was repeated a number of times. Myers would become enthusiastic about such-and-such a medium; the Sidgwicks would acquiesce far enough to support or participate in an investigation; and everyone would in the end be more or less disappointed. It would be tedious indeed to run through the details of all the investigations, even if full records remained. Myers sat, often several times, with practically every famous medium, public or private, of that time; and the Sidgwicks sat with many of them. I shall single out for special treatment the various series of experiments, stretching over several years, which the group conducted with certain Newcastle mediums; these mediums were in any case probably the most interesting with whom they had sittings at this time.

In the early eighteen-seventies Newcastle possessed a rising Spiritualist Association. Its leaders were Mr. Mould, a corn merchant, Mr. Armstrong, a florist and seedsman, and T. P. Barkas, a dentist and author of *Outlines of Ten Years Investigations into Modern Spiritualism* (1862). This society engaged as its official mediums two local girls (who had 'developed' in private circles): Miss C. E. Wood and Miss Annie Fairlamb; in 1874 they are said to have been aged nineteen and eighteen respectively.[1] These young ladies frequently sat as a pair, and they soon began to produce materialisations—first hands and faces peeping through the curtains of a cabinet, and before long full forms stepping out of it. Accounts of their performances attracted notice in the Spiritualist press. The principal materialisations were their own spirit guides; who were, as was commonly the case, either children or very childish. They included a little coloured girl called 'Pocky' or 'Pocha' (short for 'Pocahontas'), 'Georgie', 'Willy', 'Maggie', 'Cissie' and 'Benny'.

Early next year another group of Newcastle mediums began to receive publicity.[2] This was the Petty family, of whom the chief operators were Mrs. Petty and her sons Willie and Joseph,

---

[1] See *Spiritualist*, 27th March 1874. There are a good many references to the Newcastle Society and mediums in the Spiritualist press for this and the following year.
[2] *Spiritualist*, 19th Feb. 1875. Letter from J. Hare.

then aged seventeen and fourteen respectively. In addition to 'light physicals'—object movements, playing of musical instruments, raps, etc.—the Pettys began to work up materialisation phenomena. The chief spirits who manifested through them were 'Emma', a child, Mrs. Petty's control, and 'Chico', a negro, Willie's guide.

Whether the Sidgwick group got to hear of the Newcastle mediums from Spiritualist friends, or simply read about them in the Spiritualist press, I do not know. But by the end of November 1874 Sidgwick and Myers were making plans to visit them. An introduction was effected through Hensleigh Wedgwood[1] who knew Barkas and, suitable terms having been arranged, Sidgwick, Gurney, Myers and Leaf visited Newcastle in various combinations and permutations during January, February and March 1875. They had sittings with the two girls, Miss Wood and Miss Fairlamb, and with the Petty family. The sittings with the girls were the more interesting, and I shall concentrate on them; but the general pattern of all the sittings was much the same. They seem to have been held in Barkas' house, he being regarded as honest. The mediums retired into a cabinet made of curtains on a wooden frame, where they sat on a dais or lay on mattresses. Then threads were tied round their necks and wrists, the knots being sealed, and the other ends of the threads were affixed to the wall or the floor, and likewise sealed. The sitters—who usually, if not always, included members of the Newcastle Society—sat outside the cabinet, the room being dimly illuminated. The company would then sing hymns, generally of a dismal sort, often for hours; Sidgwick and his friends remembered the tedium of it for the rest of their lives. (On one occasion Sidgwick tried to relieve the monotony of the hymns by reciting poetry instead; the spirits found Swinburne an acceptable substitute for Moody and Sankey.)[2] Eventually one or more figures, clad in white and gauzy drapery, would emerge, move around in the gloom for a while, and return to the cabinet. After a further pause, and perhaps more hymns, the company would enter the cabinet and

---

[1] Hensleigh Wedgwood (1803–91), a cousin of Darwin's, was noted as a philologist. He was converted to Spiritualism about 1873 and was a founder-member of the S.P.R.

[2] Cf. Charlotte Leaf, *Walter Leaf 1852–1927*, London, 1932, pp. 94–5.

find the knots and seals still unbroken. Here is an account of what was probably a typical sitting:

> Just returned from seance of 8 PM Feb 17, at Dr. Barkas' Dentistry. Present: Myers, Gurney, Mr. Mould & 4 other members of the Newcastle Association.
>
> Mediums: {Miss Fairlamb
>   „ Wood
>
> Mediums tied as follows {silk round neck: knot sealed: other end of piece nailed into wooden partition: seal made over nail and silk. Silk round wrist very tight: knot sealed: other end of piece nailed to partition or floor: seal made over nail and silk.
>
> They lie down in cabinet: Low Light.
> 'Pocky' after many promises to appear comes faintly from door of cabinet not wholly disengaging herself from it. Her form is indistinct. She moves her arms much as on Monday. [i.e. to and fro beneath her veil.] She stands nearly disengaged from cabinet and blows kisses which are distinctly heard. She retires into the cabinet and speaks through the medium, saying she will appear more strongly soon.
> After a long pause she comes out again: embraces Mould repeatedly: then kisses Gurney two or three times: pauses to materialise her lips: at last succeeds; so that whereas her first kisses to G. were given through drapery, her last kiss is with uncovered lips. She lets me feel her hand and places her hand on the back of mine. She tears down some baize from the partition. She stands at the corner of the cabinet conversing by raps on the cabinet. I ask if she is making these raps with her hand? No. With any part of the body? No. By some force? No. Is another spirit doing it? Yes. It was 'Benny'. Then at our request all the spirits present (as subsequently explained by Pocky) began to rap: viz. Benny, Geordie and Cissy. We heard three distinct simultaneous rappings or systems of raps, 2 within the cabinet, one outside, near or (as stated by Pocky) upon the door into the passage— these raps become loud and wandering. They cease. Mould had remarked that when Pocky leant over him to kiss Gurney he felt no body; nothing but drapery. Asked whether her trunk is materialised she replies that it is not—only head hands and some kind of legs—not regular feet.
> She retires to a point near the cabinet but quite outside it, so

that wall of room is plainly visible between her and cabinet. She then dematerialises herself—sinking away into a slight white mark on the ground in about half a minute. This mark soon disappears.

When the mediums have recovered we enter and examine seals and knots. We do this carefully. All is unbroken, though the nails had been driven so thoroughly through the substance of the silk that a slight push severed the silk from nails and seals.

(F. W. H. Myers
Edmund Gurney)[1]

The investigators found these results encouraging, Myers at first being particularly excited; and they contracted with Miss Wood and Miss Fairlamb for further sittings to be held in London. The mediums arrived early in April 1875 and stayed nearly three weeks, lodging in Alexandra Square. After six or eight sittings, much of the pattern described above, and probably held in Myers' lodgings in Bolton Row, Mayfair, the locale was moved to Arthur Balfour's house, 4 Carlton Gardens, where his sister Eleanor (who was his housekeeper) seems to have had a leading hand in the arrangements. Since it did not seem impossible that during long hours in the cabinet someone might be able to duplicate the seals on the knots, the mediums were now secured by means of long leather straps fastened round their waists and ankles with combination padlocks, and attached at the other end, likewise by combination locks to marble pillars (the 'cabinet' was a small room opening out of a drawing-room where the observers sat; it contained an ornate mantelpiece). This new method of fastening, for whatever reason, obviously required some getting used to, and phenomena at the first three sittings were sparse and not reassuring. The most exciting sitting was the third, that of Saturday, 17th April. At the end of the sitting Miss Wood was left talking wildly, apparently under the impression that she had shot someone and was in gaol. She had eventually to be escorted to her lodgings at 6.15 a.m., quiet, but still suffering from the same delusion. Whether the performance could have been put on was not clear.

---

[1] This document, obviously a copy, is in the Library of Trinity College, Cambridge. It is illustrated by a plan showing that the 'cabinet' had been set up in a corner of the room, with the sitters in a line facing it.

The fourth and last seance[1] seems to have been held on the evening of Sunday, 18th. Miss Fairlamb was on her own, no doubt because of Miss Wood's recent late night. On this occasion an 'undoubtedly material human figure came to the doorway [of the cabinet], stood there with its right foot on the chair and allowed two members of the circle to come close to it and touch it'. Unfortunately it was discovered that the belt round Miss Fairlamb's waist had not been fastened sufficiently tightly to exclude the possibility that she might have got free.

At the end of May 1875 the Petty family arrived in Cambridge for three weeks of sittings. These sittings attracted a good deal of interest—'Lots of applications for admission,' Sidgwick wrote to Myers on 25th May, 'indeed I believe people are beginning to think it is a part of the Cambridge Festivities, and want to know who gives tickets'—but they also attracted a good deal of comment, most of it unfavourable Something of the nature of the comment, and also of the sittings, may be gathered from a letter which Mrs. Richard Jebb wrote to her sister in June 1875.

> Term is over now and we have settled down into quietness with a little variety furnished by a set of spiritual séances, the most arrant nonsense and imposture in my mind but it amuses those great geniuses who think they can see some distances into a mill stone. Henry Sidgwick and Fred Myers . . . are the head of the investigation as they call it, but they both seem as easy to delude and as anxious to believe as any infant.
> This is no affair of table turning and question answering. The medium, in this case a boy of sixteen, whose father and mother sit in the circle, is tied with tapes and laid on a mattress in a cabinet with a curtain tied over the opening instead of a door. He is supposed to be tied so that he cannot come out of the closet, and while he is entranced the spirit makes itself evident by a faint tall light. I have only given them my company twice, finding sitting in a dark room for two hours rather dull, since I had no faith to bear me up.[2]

---

[1] Mrs. Sidgwick, *loc. cit.*, p. 50, states that there were only four sittings. Myers' diary entry for 19th April, however, reads 'Cissy grows out of Miss F.', which suggests that he had an extra sitting with Miss Fairlamb.
[2] Mary Reed Bobbitt, *With Dearest Love to All: the Life and Letters of Lady Jebb*, London, 1960, pp. 110–11.

However, Sidgwick took a rather different view of the sittings than that imputed to him by Mrs. Jebb. 'When your letter came', he wrote to Graham Dakyns on 27th June, 'I was just going in for three weeks of experiments—all of which failed, or nearly so: the "phenomena" would not come under the conditions we wished to impose.'[1]

Miss Wood and Miss Fairlamb came to London again on 5th July 1875. Sittings were again held at Carlton Gardens. This time yet another method of control was adopted. The medium, not tied in any way, lay on a hammock inside the cabinet. The hammock was suspended by a rope which ran over a pulley on the ceiling and down to a spring balance so placed that one of the observers could keep a constant eye on it. The person watching the balance could at any time lower the hammock; this of course being to prevent the medium from keeping a constant pull on the hammock by fastening it to the floor. Very little happened until the twelfth and last sitting, on Saturday, 24th July, when Miss Fairlamb was in the hammock and Sidgwick watching the balance.

> After some time Miss Wood went into the cabinet for a few moments 'to give power,' as it was said, and took in a light chair with her. Of course the cabinet was, to the best of our belief, destitute of furniture, or of any objects which could be placed in the hammock, and so far as we knew the mediums were never alone there before the séance began. After Miss Wood had joined the circle again, the weight went down to about 60 lb.—a very little over. Then a form came out and kissed me through the white veil in which it was wrapped. Miss Wood was still in her seat, and this kiss could not have been given by Miss Fairlamb without leaving the hammock, and at the moment it was given Mr. Sidgwick lowered the hammock a few inches without producing any change in the weight indicated. So far things looked promising, for a certain fall of weight was not to be taken in itself as a presumption against the genuineness of the phenomena, since it is thought by some Spiritualists that the medium may lose weight during a materialisation. Afterwards Miss Wood was called up to the form, which looked small and did not move very easily—it might have been a woman on her knees—and led it to various members of the circle. Two other

[1] *H.S.: A Memoir*, p. 298.

forms afterwards came out in succession; the weight remaining approximately constant. When the last had retired, the disentrancement began, Miss Wood going again into the cabinet to help it.[1]

Miss Balfour thereupon asked Miss Fairlamb to submit to a search, but she declined absolutely, which of course rendered the whole test useless. As Sidgwick said to Myers (who was not present at the later sittings) in a letter on 25th July:

> Now Miss Wood had been called in to the cabinet before ghost came out; and had been allowed to take in a chair with her: therefore she might have brought in weight. Thus test became inconclusive without searching: but when searching was refused it became—what? I should add that we all thought the movements of the small figures just like those of a girl on her knees.
>
> This is where we are. I need not say that I am *unconvinced* of the girls' fraud: but I expect the Hollands [sic] are convinced and the Misses Balfour regard the probability as painfully heavy. A. J. B. was not there . . .

On 31st July Sidgwick went up to Newcastle to explain their views to Blake and Armstrong. However, the Newcastle Spiritualists apparently suggested reasons (not difficult to guess) why Miss Fairlamb might justifiably have been unwilling to be searched; and in consequence some further sittings were undertaken at Cambridge in late August and early September 1875. These sittings however were for the most part inconclusive, and some suspicious features were noted—for instance it was found that a form which emerged from the cabinet did so only as far as the limits imposed by the fastenings would permit.

By this time Myers seems to have been the only one of the group who had any residual faith in the two mediums. In October 1875 he visited Newcastle yet again, accompanied by the John Hollonds and Alexander Aksakov, a Russian who was intensely interested in psychical phenomena. Their first seance—for which Miss Wood was the medium—was held on Thursday, 14th October, in a hall used by the local Spiritualists, and in the presence of some twenty-five of them. Myers' account to Sidgwick was enthusiastic:

[1] Mrs. Sidgwick, *loc. cit.*, pp. 51–2.

We have just had a séance at the Hall.
BENNY BROUGHT MISS WOOD OUT. BOTH WALKED AND TALKED.

Miss W. with Pocky's voice, Benny in a low whisper. I touched both;—both were solid. *If* the Newcastle folk are trustworthy the thing is done. There is a new cabinet at the hall into which a confederate might conceivably be introduced from a closet—but if so it is with the knowledge of Armstrong etc. The 27 people who formed the circle were dimly visible all the time —not all of them visible to me, but Blake and Armstrong vouched for those whom I could not see.

The rest of the sittings were almost all total failures; none the less this one experience of Myers' seemed to justify further investigations. These however were delayed for a number of reasons until the end of the following year.

V Further Investigations of the Sidgwick Group 1876–80

IN DECEMBER 1875 Sidgwick announced his engagement to Arthur Balfour's sister, Eleanor, who had taken part in some of the investigations just described. They had been drawn together not merely through their researches into Spiritualism, but by a common interest in the furtherance of higher education for women. Nora Balfour was then aged thirty, small and delicately made, a listener rather than a conversationalist. 'I feel sure that you will come to love her,' Sidgwick wrote to his mother, 'she is very quiet and undemonstrative; but so sweet and simple and calm and helpful.' Some of these qualities, together with an unostentatious but overwhelming sense of duty to her fellows, had no doubt been fostered in her by her mother, Lady Blanche Cecil, an earnest and unrelenting Evangelical, for whom charity (but a real charity) began away from home. Lady Blanche, however, also fostered intellectual qualities. She did not hold narrow or sectarian views about her children's education, but encouraged them to read widely on all sorts of subjects. Two of them, Arthur and Gerald, became notable philosophers, and the premature death of a third, Francis, deprived the country of perhaps its most promising biologist. Despite her reserved exterior, Nora's abilities were quite as distinguished as those of her brothers. She had a particular bent for the mathematical sciences, which enabled her to give valuable assistance to her brother-in-law, Lord Rayleigh, with whom she wrote some joint papers. Later on, when she was Principal of Newnham College, the same talents proved of great assistance in more mundane business.[1]

[1] See Ethel M. Sidgwick, *Mrs. Henry Sidgwick, A Memoir*, London, 1938. For

Henry Sidgwick and Nora Balfour were married in April 1876. This of course made Sidgwick brother-in-law to a future Prime Minister; and through his sister's marriage to E. W. Benson he was already brother-in-law to a future Archbishop of Canterbury. To say that the Sidgwicks had friends in high places would be an enormous understatement. They were also, I should guess, among the most intellectual couples of the century; as intellectual as, say, the Leweses or the Grotes. It is however hard to think of anyone less like Mrs. Grote, that 'grenadier in skirts', than Mrs. Sidgwick. There was probably not a single occasion in the whole of Mrs. Sidgwick's adult life on which she talked assertively or acted flamboyantly. 'She is not exactly perfect,' Sidgwick wrote to his mother around the time of his marriage, 'any more than other people, but it *is* true that whatever defects she has are purely negative: all that is positive in her is quite quite good. I cannot even imagine her doing anything wrong.'

Myers too had had occasional thoughts of marriage, especially during the climax or climaxes of his agnosticism; and on at least one occasion he had proposed and been refused. Of late years, however, he had abandoned the idea; and his reasons for so doing will need examination, since they influenced the whole subsequent course of his life.

Myers' mother (it will be remembered) was a member of the immensely wealthy Marshall family.[1] The Marshalls had spent some part of their fortune in buying estates for themselves in the Lake District; and it was there that Susan Marshall had met the Rev. Frederic Myers. Susan Marshall was the daughter of the John Marshall (1765–1845) who had built up the family fortune, and she was the aunt of the John Marshall (1830–81) who in the eighteen-seventies was the titular head of the family. One of this John Marshall's brothers, named Walter James Marshall (b. 1837), had married in 1866 Annie Eliza, the twenty-one year old daughter of a Yorkshire clergyman and landowner, the Rev. J. R. Hill. The marriage produced five children; but it did not turn out happily. Both

---

further information about the Balfour family see Kenneth Young's *Arthur James Balfour*, London, 1963.

[1] On the Marshalls see W. G. Rimmer, *Marshalls of Leeds: Flax-Spinners 1788–1886*, Cambridge, 1960.

Walter and Annie were troubled with ill-health, and Walter became liable to alternating moods of almost pathological depression and excitement which were a source of constant anxiety to his wife. Walter's brother John seems to have been incapable of conducting his own affairs, and both of Annie's sisters died insane. If ever the stars ordained disaster for a marriage, it was for theirs. In the hope of improving matters, Walter and Annie passed a good deal of their time in various health resorts, English and continental. In the early months of 1871 they were at Vevey, in the Canton of Vaud. Myers, who had been in Italy, stayed with them for a few days in late February. He had of course known Walter, who was his first cousin, since they were children, and Annie at least since the time of her marriage. But it was only now that she seriously attracted his attention. Annie used to confide in Myers' mother, an extremely practical lady, and during walks beside the Lake of Geneva she told Myers himself something of her troubles. He was greatly struck by the courage and the absence of bitterness with which she faced a future that seemed to hold no hope of any break in the clouds. Some years later he visited Vevey again and remembered their talks:

> For here she stood, and here she spoke, and there
> Raised her soft look thro' the evening's crimsoned air;
> And all she looked was lovely; all she said
> Simple, and sweet, and full of tears unshed;
> And my soul sprang to meet her, and I knew
> Dimly the hope we twain were called unto.[1]

It was over a year before he saw her again, but after that their relationship developed rapidly. In January 1873 he stayed with Walter and Annie at Scarborough, and rode and walked with them by the sea; at the end of March she came to stay with his mother at Cheltenham, and there were more walks and talks. Myers was increasingly impressed by the steadfastness and the sweetness of disposition which she showed under the most trying circumstances; his admiration for her turned to affection and, in the summer of 1873—at Hallsteads, the beautiful Ullswater home of his uncle, Arthur Marshall—to love. Annie had little enough to comfort her, and Myers'

[1] *Fragments*, p. 24.

unfailing kindness was one of the few bright spots in an otherwise bleak existence. She returned his love; but it was love of a rather different kind, perhaps, to anything he had known before. This stanza from a poem which he wrote in 1873 seems to describe a particular incident:

> I had guessed not, did I not know, that the spirit of man was so strong
> To prefer irredeemable woe to the slightest shadow of wrong;
> I had guessed not, had I not known, that twain in their last emprize,
> Full-souled, and awake, and alone, with the whole world's love in their eyes,
> With no faith in God to appal them, no fear of man in their breast,
> With nothing but Honour to call them, could yet find Honour the best,—
> Could stay the stream of the river and turn the tides of the sea,
> Give back that gift to the giver, thine heart to the bosom of thee.[1]

It is hard to get any very clear picture of Annie. The references to her in family letters are mostly brief; and in Myers' autobiography, where she is called 'Phyllis', she is lost to sight behind the ripe clusters of superlatives—'that fountain of vivifying joy' is a sample expression. She must have been good-looking—the 'sea-like sapphire of her eyes' was to haunt Myers' memory. She was certainly a sensitive and highly cultivated person, whose natural gaiety and kindliness was not quite overshadowed by her misfortunes. In addition to her domestic troubles, she had financial worries occasioned by continual visits to health resorts, and she suffered too from religious doubts closely akin to Myers'.

Myers' infatuation with Annie began at a time when his experiments in Spiritualism were first suggesting to him that he might at last have discovered in the imprisoning wall of agnosticism a panel which would give way before his frenzied beating. She was to him already, as it were, a small hint of the divine in an otherwise godless Universe; and soon his love for her became inextricably blended with his newly found religious hopes. She became at once a symbol and a manifestation of a

[1] *Fragments*, p. 19.

hidden world of timeless realities, a world once apprehended by Plato, and now obscurely revealed by the strange phenomena of Spiritualism.

> ... so soon as I began to have hope of a future life I began to conceive earth's culminant passion *sub specie aeternitatis*. I felt that if anything still recognisable in me had preceded earth-life, it was this one profound affinity; if anything was destined to survive, it must be into the maintenance of this one affinity that my central effort must be thrown. I was like a half-drunken man suddenly sobered by the announcement that he has come into a fortune. The first impulse was the mere resolve that nothing here on earth should prejudice that chance of happiness to be. Ogier and the Queen of France, in William Morris' poem, foreseeing possibilities too great to risk, looked each on the other
>
>> But for one moment; for too wise were they
>> To cast the coming years of joy away.
>
> Still more for me was there a sense that this was but the first moment of an endless passion; a sense of desperate reality, of age-long issues;—nay, as of the very crisis and visible morn of Fate. From that hour the moral victory was won;—achieved with steadfastness, though not yet with more than steadfastness; with no inward felicity in such obedience to the highest law ...
>
> Among the pure ideas which men in some dim fashion discern on earth, 'Wisdom,' says Plato, 'we cannot see, or terrible had been the love she had inspired.' To me it seemed as though I then saw Virtue clear. An effect was wrought upon me which neither Mrs. Butler's heroic Christianity nor Henry Sidgwick's rightness and reasonableness had ever produced. And although in my own heart I still felt the recurrent conflict between the savage and the sage,—between the half-human instinct and the deliberate choice of upright man;—yet in this one matter the impulse which prompted me to virtue became like the impulse of self-preservation itself. I knew in the deep of the heart that Virtue alone was safe, and only Virtue lasting, and only Virtue blest; and Phyllis became to me as the very promise and earnest of triumphant Virtue.[1]

It is clear *what* effect Annie had upon Myers; but *why* she had this effect is far from clear. Part of the answer may be that she herself showed 'mediumistic' tendencies or, as Myers might

[1] *Fragments*, pp. 38-9.

have put it, was especially responsive to spiritual influences. In his diary Myers notes that at several seances which they attended together she was 'affected'; and in August and September 1874 both participated with others of their family in a series of sittings at Hallsteads at which raps and table levitations were obtained without the assistance of any paid medium.[1]

Walter's and Annie's private troubles continued with fluctuations and occasional improvements throughout most of 1873, 1874 and 1875. In August 1873 Myers accompanied Walter on a cruise to the Canary Islands, and Walter's health improved for a while. The improvement did not last. On 26th May 1874 Myers wrote to Sidgwick that 'Walter was better, but far from well'; but shortly afterwards, on 13th June 1874, he reported 'W. is worse again & many troubles of various kinds hang over that unhappy household.' The following summer Walter and Annie spent a good deal of time at Old Church, a house in the grounds of Hallsteads, and Walter improved again; but in February 1876 he and Annie were at Torquay (Myers also went down there) hoping that things would better themselves.

Myers did whatever he could to help Annie. He saw her quite frequently in London (she and Walter had a house at 23 Thurloe Square) or in the Lake District; occasionally he took Walter off her hands for a day; and he wrote to her regularly. Only a few fragments of his letters now remain; they are not at all in his usual epistolary style, and were undoubtedly written with the object of distracting her from her cares. Here is part of one which he sent her in October 1873:

> Then I went back to town & thence to Wykehurst with Gurney, & found Herbert Spencer there, & the Huths very nice. Gurney is at present arguing with Mrs. Huth about Thackeray, who is one of the articles of Mrs. Huth's creed. Herbert Spencer has been exhausted by an argument with me as to whether School Inspectors were necessarily, & by the very fact of their existence, not only useless but noxious. This he proved with much satisfaction to all present, but soon became dizzy with excitement, said that he had talked too long on important matters and begged now to be silent while the rest of the company

---

[1] Cf. *H.S.: A Memoir*, p. 293.

talked nonsense. He is certainly very interesting to meet, tho' one has to take him as he is, as a philosopher who is nothing but a philosopher. It is amusing to see him at billiards, standing with his cue in his hand, & with the aspect of a serious linen draper, while he explains the genesis of sentiment with reference to holing the white ball. Having demonstrated that to object to pocketing the white ball is a superstition unworthy of philosophers, he pockets it with a solemn triumph, & makes a miss into baulk.

Neither Myers' constant attempts to amuse and support Annie, nor the succession of health resorts to which Walter was taken, proved in the end of any avail. In April 1876 Annie went to stay with Myers' mother at Cheltenham; Myers walked with her through the woods of Leckhampton, and her company brought, as somehow it always did, peace to the restless sea of his emotions. He was not to enjoy such peace again for many years. When Annie returned to London Walter's trouble assumed an acute form. On the evening of 2nd May his behaviour became so excited that his brother George, and Annie's father, were telegraphed for. Walter was certified insane and taken to an asylum at Ticehurst in Sussex. There is a suggestion that this step was necessitated by the fact that he had been issuing cheques which he could not meet. On 3rd June 1875 Myers told Sidgwick: 'Gull has seen W. & expresses a very unfavourable opinion. Trewington tells me he thinks he will never leave Ticehurst. W. is now angry and complaining of plots etc. wh. much distresses A.'

Annie seems to have remained in London for most of June. There is a tradition in the Myers family that she and Myers agreed that under the circumstances it would be best if they stopped seeing each other; an entry in Myers' diary for 2nd July—'Miss Froude and A. on balcony. Farewell.'—marks their last meeting. A month later Myers set sail for Norway with his brother Arthur; their ship lay on the Humber through a moonlight night almost within view of the Yorkshire village where Annie was then staying.

Towards the end of August Annie found the strain of Walter's constant reproaches no longer bearable and begged to have the responsibility for decisions about him taken from her. A family conference held at Derwent Island, Keswick, from 19th August, decided that a council of five persons should act on her behalf. She offered to take charge of Walter if it was thought right, but the suggestion was set aside, and it was agreed that he should be taken from Ticehurst and put into the care of a Dr. Hall of Brighton, as was his wish. On Monday, 1st September, Annie drove from Keswick to Old Church with Myers' mother. A few days afterwards the latter wrote to Myers:

> I had been very anxious—we all had—at the fixed stony look in her face. She grew silent towards me, after having been *quite* frank & loving— & I could not with all my entreaties get her to speak of what was in her mind, after she had once said that she saw she had been quite wrong in everything—in this last step for W. (the certif.) & altogether about religion—in rejecting Xtianity—. I hoped she wd. pass thro' this crisis—& get a fuller happier faith—she was continually praying & getting me to read T. a Kempis to her—We came together on Monday & she brightened up during the drive & talked more like herself. I left her at O. Ch. at 7 p.m. thinking the children would cheer her. Next morning she was missing—a shawl by the lake—and in deep water she was found.

She had tried to cut her throat with a pair of scissors and, failing to inflict a fatal wound, had drowned herself in Ullswater. 'Indeed, indeed,' said Mrs. Myers, 'we must try and think that she has found the rest and peace which have been so sadly wanting to her lot.' Years of constant anxiety and ill-health, culminating in the stresses and the anguished vacillations of the past few weeks, had reduced Annie to a state of complete nervous exhaustion. Death had for long seemed to her the gateway to perfect peace; and now, in her extremity, she chose to pass through that gateway. A letter which she had written to Mrs. Myers from an hotel in Switzerland some five years previously tells us as much, perhaps, as we shall ever know of the thoughts which led her to the shores of Ullswater on that September night.[1]

[1] Mr. A. Jarman, 'Failure of a Quest', *Tomorrow* 12 (1964), pp. 17–29, has suggested that in the spring of 1876 Myers got Annie pregnant. Walter lost his reason when he learned what had happened, Myers deserted her for fear of jeopardising his career and, in despair, she committed suicide. There does not seem to me to be a shred of evidence for this theory, and there is a good deal of evidence against it. See my comments *J.S.P.R.* XLII (1964), pp. 316–23, and *J.S.P.R.* XLIII (1966), pp. 277–81. Another story which at one time had some circulation (I think I have discovered its source) was that Myers and Annie conspired to have Walter

Poor Mr. Seller's death has made a great impression on me,—he was exactly my age—to within a month, and I had so often wished to die not realising before what it would be to feel one's work neglected and undone. I had not known him very intimately before he was taken ill, but it always seemed to me that his disposition[s] of mind were good and pure, & *spiritual* as a man's could be—and his face and form were beautiful—with the beauty the old masters give to Christ. Before he was taken ill—when he looked at me— I used to feel it was more a spirit from another world than an earthly man. I could not understand his look then but now I do. The terrible weakness took away all power of thought & almost of speech & consciousness. I cannot explain why—but this death made me *fully*, I think, realize what it would be to die—it seemed as if it were I.— The end was perfect peace, though he had seemed anxious & troubled before. An hour before he died thinking he had almost lost consciousness, I took his hand and said 'Fear thou not—for I am with thee, be not afraid—for I am thy God.' He pressed my hand—a beautiful smile came over his face & he said 'no.' He never spoke again—he died with his hand in mine & I could not tell when his spirit fled.

Myers learned of her death on 7th September. Later the same year he described in verse the effect which the news had upon him:

> Then came the news that, on me hurled,
>   At once my youth within me slew,
> Made dim with woe the reeling world,
>   And hid the heaven that shone therethrough.
> Far off a soulless music sang;
>   Red-gold the glittering Baltic lay;
> What message on my spirit rang
>   From that ensanguined end of day!
> All night I journeyed, on and on,
>   Through Swedish forest silver-clear;
> All night a ghostly lumour shone
>   From many a Swedish moss and mere;
> And strangely to myself I seemed
>   A shade by shadowy Hermes led,
> With eyes that waked not, nay, nor dreamed,
>   Through void dominion of the dead.

certified so that they could prosecute an affair unhindered. This story too is entirely without foundation; the facts of what happened are quite clear from surviving correspondence.

And still I roam, with shades a shade,
  Their mourning pathways to and fro;
I wait till this confusion fade,
  These dreary phantoms melt and go;
Till out of gloom a star shall glow,
  A stillness gather in the stir,
And longing eyes her eyes shall know,
  And wounded heart be whole with her.[1]

In the late summer of 1876 Sidgwick and some of his friends had sittings with yet another visiting American, 'Dr.' Henry Slade. Slade was, I believe the first medium, at least in this country, to raise what was known as 'slate-writing' to something like a fine art.[2] Instances of supposed 'psychography'—the direct production of spirit writing upon paper, slate or even human skin—had indeed been common enough. But Slade seemed able to effect such feats whenever he wished and it should be noted, almost always in a well-lit room. The writing was commonly obtained in the following manner. An ordinary slate with a piece of slate pencil on it, would be pressed tightly against the under surface of a table; it would generally be pressed by both sitter and medium, but sometimes only by one or the other. After a while the sound of writing would be heard, and a message, usually of a trivial or nondescript character, would be found written on the upper surface of the slate. Sometimes a message would appear on the hidden side of a slate placed on top of the table; sometimes even inside a closed double slate held there. There were many variations on these themes; and the slate-writing was often accompanied by other curious physical effects—raps, touches, and movements of furniture.

Slade's phenomena attracted a good deal of notice in the press, and especially of course the Spiritualist press. The Sidgwicks had some ten sittings with him during July, August and early September 1876. Some at least of these sittings were held

[1] *Fragments*, p. 22.
[2] Many accounts of Slade's performances will be found in Stainton Moses' *Psychography*, 2nd edn., London, 1882. Cf. R. G. Medhurst, 'Stainton Moses and Contemporary Physical Mediums: 16. Henry Slade', *Light* LXXXVI (1966), pp. 165–70. On Slade see also J. C. F. Zöllner's *Transcendental Physics*, tr. C. C. Massey, London, 1880.

at Carlton Gardens, and not at Slade's rooms; but the Sidgwicks none the less strongly suspected him of trickery. Mrs. Sidgwick was inclined to doubt whether even the best of observers could watch the slate continuously enough to prevent Slade from surreptitiously writing upon it or from replacing it with a prepared slate. The touches and object movements could, she thought, have been produced by the Doctor's lean and supple legs; and she noticed various actual indications of fraud—for instance Slade's conjuror-like way of trying to distract the attention; his habit of sitting so that his right hand could manipulate the slate; his forcing his sitters to place their hands in a position which made it difficult for them to look under the table; his only allowing two sitters at a time; the vague and trivial nature of the communications.[1]

Myers had four sittings with Slade; the physical phenomena which had accompanied the slate-writing were rather more curious than any which the Sidgwicks witnessed. At his first sitting, on 26th July 1876, he was accompanied by Richard Jebb. Jebb held a slate closely against the underside of the table between Myers and himself. Slade's hands were on the table-top, and his legs were not under the table but parallel to it. Under these conditions the slate gave a violent jump, banging itself against the table, and alarming Jebb not a little.

At his third sitting, on 21st September 1876, Myers brought with him a friend named Hellis. Hellis was initially confident that he could 'explain all Slade's dodges'. But he changed his mind during the course of the sitting, and emerged 'very much shaken'. He now saw 'strong reason to suppose that there was something more than conjuring'.

Of the phenomena which had so struck Hellis, the oddest was one which Myers described as follows, in a letter to Sidgwick dated 21st September 1876:

> Slade put a large handbell on floor under table While Slade's hands & feet were visible to Hellis, (one hand held slate, one was on table: feet were outside table, close to Hellis,) the bell leapt up from under table, came round the edge of the table & settled on the table close to me,—at the other side from Slade— I saw it in the air. Hellis said that Slade cd. not move bell as he

---

[1] Mrs. Sidgwick, *loc. cit.*, p. 59.

(Hellis) had all Slade's person well in view, nor could confederate shoot it upwards from carpet because it did not go straight but flew out from under table & then backwards again *over* table, to settle before me . . .

Myers and Hellis visited Slade again the following day. They were sitting with their hands on the table, when it quickly rose up in the air, turned over, and stood itself upside down on Hellis' and Slade's heads. In a letter written the same day Myers told Sidgwick:

Hellis thinks Slade might have given table a jerk with his knees, but inasmuch as his arms were close to Hellis on the *wrong* side of the table, i.e. the side *towards* wh. it rose (&, in fact, not touching it as it rose,) he cannot conceive how it was got up high in air & placed on his head. I saw it rising thro' the air,— apparently untouched by anyone,—but of course the thing passed in a moment.

Myers planned a series of sittings, but these plans were upset when Professor Edwin Ray Lankester and Dr. Charles Donkin initiated legal proceedings against Slade for obtaining money under false pretences. After one sitting with Slade Lankester had come to the conclusion that he wrote the messages on his slates beforehand, exhibiting them only after he had made the sound of writing. Accordingly at a second seance Lankester seized and examined the slate before he had heard the sound of writing, and he discovered that words had already been written upon it. Slade's explanation was that he had heard the sound of writing and was about to present the slate to the sitters when it was seized.

This explanation, and the favourable testimony of various eminent witnesses, including A. R. Wallace, proved of no avail at his trial on 1st October, and Slade was sentenced to three months' hard labour. However, the conviction was quashed upon a technicality, and he fled the country.[1]

There does not seem to be any reason for regarding Slade's slate-writing performances as anything other than clever conjuring, especially in view of the fact that many of his sittings were held at his own rooms, where it would have been easy for him to make use of a confederate.[2] He had many imitators; one of

---

[1] See *Podmore* II, pp. 89–91.　　[2] Cf. Truesdell, *op. cit.*, p. 143–59.

them will be discussed in detail later, and so I will not here go into the question of his methods of trickery. The object movements witnessed by Myers and Hellis are certainly odd, but a discussion of them would take us too far afield at this point. Slade was undoubtedly detected at various times in the fraudulent production of such phenomena.[1]

In November 1876 the Sidgwick group decided that Miss Wood and Miss Fairlamb deserved one more trial. Myers went up to Newcastle on 7th December 1876 to arrange the sittings.

By this time the two girls had quarrelled and were sitting separately; Myers heard exciting reports from the local Spiritualists, especially about Miss Fairlamb. Blake and Armstrong and Mould said that now, whilst Miss Fairlamb sat outside the cabinet, figures would emerge from its interior; or else would grow up from Miss Fairlamb, leave her, and move about the room. At a seance which Myers attended on Friday, 8th December, Miss Fairlamb sat outside the cabinet 'in a very fair light' and a white form grew up from her. It could not, however, detach itself entirely. Myers still entertained high hopes of the medium, and wrote to Sidgwick on 8th December 1876:

> Miss F. is supposed to be somewhat distraite at present on account of an *amoureux* with whom she often wants to be going out instead of sitting:— but thus small, thus natural, thus transparent, seem to be the workings of the Mediums' hearts and minds!
> And when one hears Mould bawling out
> 'O Jeanneretta don't stay away!'
> with precisely the same calm and constancy as 2 years ago, & reflects that he has been doing it ever since, it is hard to believe that so persistent a worship has been fed upon nothing but drapery & delusions.

Sittings were held in Newcastle with the two mediums separately during the period 2nd–15th January 1877; nearly all were complete failures. In the case of Miss Wood there was on at least one occasion a strong suggestion of fraud. A figure draped in gauzy material emerged from the cabinet and moved about the seance room; but the tape which had secured Miss Wood's ankles (she had had the one round her neck cut on the

---

[1] See Fodor, *op. cit.*, *s.v.* 'Slade, Dr. Henry'.

plea that it was choking her) bore obvious signs of having been forced over her foot.¹

As far as I have discovered these were the last sustained investigations which the Sidgwick group carried out at this time, with the exception of some sittings which they had in March 1878 with a materialising medium named Haxby. Haxby's guides, 'Toby' and 'Abdulla', were quite manifestly the medium wrapped in, or simply holding, white gauzy material, and their gradual growth out of, and disappearance into, the floor (the *pièce de résistance* of the show) were quite visibly produced by the medium rising from the floor and shaking out his drapery, and then descending to the floor again, hiding away the muslin as he went. Not the least alarming feature of these sittings was the fact that a prominent Spiritualist present felt that 'all our doubts must now be removed' and declared that the sittings were even better than certain ones celebrated in Spiritualistic literature at which he had also been present.²

By the time of their final sittings with Miss Wood and Miss Fairlamb the Sidgwicks were very much disillusioned. They had witnessed no phenomena whatsoever of which it seemed impossible to give a normal explanation; on the other hand they had themselves detected fraud on one or two occasions (which I have not described above) and, even worse, had learned all too much about the evidential standards and critical abilities of the ordinary contributors to Spiritualist literature. The sittings which they had attended had often been extremely tedious, and they felt (no doubt justly) that even though there might possibly be a residuum of phenomena difficult to explain further investigations would probably prove a waste of time, trouble and money.

¹ Miss Fairlamb married and became Mrs. J. B. Mellon. For an account of some seances with her in 1885 see H. A. Garrat, *An Account of Four Spiritualistic Seances*, Chichester, n.d. She later went to Australia, where one of her materialisations was seized and found to be none other than herself. See T. Shekleton Henry, *Spookland*, Sydney, 1894. A reply by 'Psyche', *A Counterblast to Spookland*, Sydney, 1895, describes how, to vindicate herself, she allowed herself to be fastened inside a cage. Materialisations appeared outside it. Perhaps she got the idea from Miss Wood, who had done the same thing years before. See W. P. Adshead, *Miss Wood in Derbyshire*, London, 1879. Miss Wood had been 'seized' in 1877, see Podmore II, p. 108. She was caught out again in 1882—Podmore II, p. 113.

² Mrs. Sidgwick, *loc. cit.*, p. 62.

Only Myers seems to have felt it worth continuing his enquiries. He did not believe that *all* the phenomena he had witnessed were completely fraudulent—for instance he continued to think even many years later that Miss Wood and Miss Fairlamb may not have been entirely bogus. He now had, of course, a new and particularly urgent reason for wishing to assure himself of survival. Some might well say that the mere fact that he thought the investigations worth pursuing shows that intense grief had completely overthrown what little judgment he had left. And he was certainly prone to accept phenomena with too uncritical an eagerness; only on reflection would doubts, often instilled by the Sidgwicks, begin to trouble him. But on the other hand one must remember that he had witnessed phenomena more striking than any which the Sidgwicks had seen, and that it was another dozen years or so before he was prepared to avow that he had at last found evidence which could completely justify his conviction of survival.

As soon as the final series of sittings with the Newcastle mediums was over Myers went to Liverpool, where he met Dr. Hitchman[1] of the 'Liverpool Psychological Society', who told him of divers remarkable phenomena. These phenomena, Myers wrote to Sidgwick on 17th January 1877, laboured

> ... only under the defect wh. seems widely to permeate phenomena,—that of having occurred in the presence of *somebody else*.
> I found Hitchman to be a big old man with long white hair with a general look of being a character out of Dickens, but by no means so foolish as I expected. He said that he had seen almost all known mediums & put Banks immeasurably first, & a Miss Clark next...
> [Miss Clark's and a Miss Parry's] trifling phenomena however are hardly worth the attention of those who are privileged to sit with BANKS thro' whose mediumship Hitchman says he has seen no less than SEVEN materialised forms & the medium all together. He gave me in fact the idea that he had been jammed up among all these ghosts in a way that was almost oppressive. The greatest stranger present is allowed to sit in the cabinet and hold Banks's hands. Hitchman deposed that he had

---

[1] There is a biographical sketch of Hitchman (with portrait) in the *Spiritual Magazine* for 1875, pp. 4–10.

done so once,—had felt the ghost thickening about him till the ghost bad him get out of the cabinet & stepped out after him—drawing the curtain back & showing Banks on his chair. The ghost sometimes forms *outside* the cabinet, either growing *up* or growing *down*, sometimes beginning with a loose head in the air. Loose fingers are also frequently observed to dart about.

Myers met Banks, and offered him money for his services. Banks refused the money, promising Myers his services for nothing when he resumed sitting. Banks said that he valued his mediumship chiefly as having convinced himself; he thought Spiritualists often none the better for their knowledge, and 'the scum of the sects'. Unfortunately the proposed sitting does not seem to have taken place; the few accounts which remain suggest that Banks must indeed have been among the most interesting mediums of his time.[1]

Most of the mediums with whom Myers did succeed in having sittings during the years 1877, 1878 and 1879 proved disappointing. He had for instance a number of sittings with the famous 'Dr.' Monck, whose behaviour he thought 'very delicate and upright'. On one occasion Monck returned a £5 note which Myers sent him, stating that he was not fit to sit. He impressed Myers as a sincere though very vain man. Nothing of interest however seems to have happened at the sittings. Nor did anything of interest emerge from the thirteen sittings which Myers had in November and December 1878 and January 1879, with the famous Florence Cook, by then Mrs. Edward Corner; or from three sittings with her sister Kate, also a noted medium, in October 1878, and five more in the autumn of 1879.

Indeed, so far as I can discover, the only sittings of any interest which Myers had during these years were with two Parisian mediums whom he visited in July and August 1877. On 30th July 1877 he sat with a certain Mme Rohart; through her, for the first time, he received messages which purported to come from Annie Marshall. Parts of his notes on this seance run as follows; the names were given by tilts of the table, indicating that he had closed a series of tilts. Sentences were given 'clairaudiently' to Mme Rohart.

---

[1] See e.g. A. Aksakov, *Animisme et Spiritisme*, Paris, 1906, pp. 218–29; E. Louisa Thompson Nosworthy, 'Reminiscences of George Thompson', *Psychological Review* I (1879), pp. 348–62.

1. Name and father's name? Annie Hil/[l]
2. Month in which I saw you last? Jui/[llet]
3. Mme. Rohart asked relation to me? Co/[usine]
4. Initial of surname of friend present at last interview? F [roude]

Merci de l'affection que tu m'as donnée, merci du souvenire que tu accordes à ma mémoire. Depuis que je suis complètement dégagée de la matière je me sens heureuse, surtout de pouvoir t'assurer que je veille auprès de toi et sur toi-même. Plus je vais aller plus je vais me dégager, et alors ma lucidité, secondée par mon ancienne affection, sera toute à bon service, et tu verras bien que je t'aimais par les efforts multiples que je ferai pour me communiquer à toi. Courage, ami, la vie a des moments difficiles, mais ces moments-là tu les passeras vite, car tu possèdes en toi la philosophie du sage et du croyant, et elle t'aidera à traverser sans succomber les crises nécessaires à ton avancement et à ton bonheur terrestre. Chaque fois que tu m'appelleras je t'entendrai et te répondrai. Rappelle-moi au souvenir de notre bonne F. (Miss Froude) et dis-lui qu'elle ait, elle aussi, bon courage, et qu'elle ne se tourmente point du présent. Quant à moi, ma situation là-haut est bonne; je n'ai plus de souffrances, je sens que je m'élève chaque jour vers mon Dieu, et que je deviens meilleure. Aussi suis-je toute joyeuse de t'annoncer cette félicité dont je jouis et que calmera tes regrets, car il n'est pas de plus douce consolation que de savoir les êtres pleurés et aimés bienheureux auprès de leur Dieu.

Je désire aussi que tu me recommandes à Su[san] [Myers—note in margin that Christian name was asked for] et à Edw[ard] He/[slop][1], deux êtres que j'aimais tant, et qui tous deux m'ont donné içi-bas des preuves de leur touchante amitié. Aussi te prierais-je de leur dire à'tous deux non seulement que je me souviens de leur bonne et franche affection, mais que je désire leur souvenir et leur appel. Puis encore a Wal/[ter]; je désire pour lui qu'il soit instruit de ma visite d'outretombe et que tes raisonnements, autant que les preuves que je te donne aujourd'hui de ma présence, le convainquent que je puis me manifester. Ce serait pour lui une grande consolation, et pour moi un véritable bonheur de pouvoir me dire; je l'ai persuadé . . .

In what state of mind did you write your last letter to me?

Sous une inspiration de découragement (État tout àfait maladif)

---

[1] Brother-in-law of Annie's father.

I hope you did not suffer on account of the circumstances connected with your death.

Si, j'ai souffert beaucoup, mais cette souffrance n'a pas durée, car l'état de mon esprit était tel que Dieu l'a pris en considération et en pitié.

Do you know where I am going, in memory of you?

Ve/[vey].

Myers was very impressed by some features of this sitting. He wrote to Sidgwick: 'It is at least a case of thought-reading . . . Gurney will sit also.' He asked Sidgwick to send him a list of test questions to which Sidgwick and Annie would know the answers, but he would not; however subsequent sittings with Mme Rohart degenerated so much that the questions were never put. Myers did, however, obtain some further curious material from a certain Mme Redière. He described the sitting to Sidgwick in a letter of 16th August.

I had a curious sitting with an old woman in the Faubourg S. Antoine who got *raps* when letters of alphabet were touched by me. I despaired of getting a high spirit thro' this low woman & amused myself by laying traps,—i.e. *thinking* of the right words but pausing & trembling at *wrong* letters.

What came out was this:

AD HEMAR ADM AMR MARIEGAM ANNE ELISE MARSEH PAR MARESHELL

then I said MAR is right—try after that:

MARSHALL
HARRI
MON FRERE ME REND MAL

In this case I cannot doubt the thought-reading. It is I think absurd to suppose that while I had no *wishes* in the matter at all, & was giving my whole intelligence to giving *wrong* clues, the old hag nevertheless guessed the letters by the movement of my hand.

Evidence for thought-transference, however, was just what Myers did *not* wish to find; it would undermine whatever reasons he might have for believing that the messages came from Annie. All in all the outcome of his three further years of investigation was depressingly slight. Yet he seemed to himself to have at least grounds for hope. He would not perhaps have asserted that the grounds were very substantial; but the hope was substantial,[1] and his yearning and enthusiasm were such that even a little hope could inspire him to enormous efforts.

Despite Myers' continued (if not unwavering) optimism, his practical enquiries into Spiritualistic and related phenomena gradually lost momentum, and by the end of 1879 had almost petered out. Perhaps he could no longer obtain any support from the disillusioned Sidgwicks and felt that there was no point in prosecuting such enquiries on his own; perhaps too the rash of exposures of prominent mediums in the mid-eighteen-seventies had made him less sanguine as to what might immediately be achieved. At any rate the years following the death of Annie Marshall were for Myers a period of lessening practical endeavour and of 'a sinking into myself from thought to thought, a steady remonstrance, and a high resolve'. He gave himself a good deal to literary work, producing in 1880 a little monograph on Wordsworth which has been frequently reprinted; in 1882 a new long poem, *The Renewal of Youth*; and at various times a number of literary and critical essays, reprinted in 1883 as *Essays Modern* and *Essays Classical*. It is interesting to notice that he toys, in some of these works, with ideas which he was later to develop in greater detail. Here, for instance, is his account of Wordsworth's views on pre-existence:

> And Wordsworth, as is well known, has followed Plato in advancing for the child a much bolder claim. The child's soul, in this view, has existed before it entered the body—has existed in a world superior to ours, but connected, by the immanence of the same pervading spirit, with the material universe before our eyes. The child begins by feeling this material world strange to him. But he sees in it, as it were, what he has been accustomed to see; he discerns in it its kinship with the spiritual world which he dimly remembers; it is to him 'an unsubstantial fairy place'— a scene at once brighter and more unreal than it will appear in his eyes when he has become acclimatized to earth. And even when this freshness of insight has passed away, it occasionally happens that sights or sounds of unusual beauty or carrying

---

[1] On 28th Dec. 1880 he wrote to J. W. Cross (on the occasion of George Eliot's death): '. . . I trust, with a confidence which approaches belief, and on evidence which cannot easily be communicated, nor must lightly be set aside, that there is a reunion of soul and soul' (Letter in Yale University Library).

deep associations—a rainbow, a cuckoo's cry, a sunset of extraordinary splendour—will renew for a while this sense of vision and nearness to the spiritual world—a sense which never loses its reality, though with advancing years its presence grows briefer and more rare.[1]

His hopes at this time are well expressed in the concluding paragraph of his essay on *Greek Oracles*:

> And even now, in the face of philosophies of materialism and of negation so far more powerful than any which Sophocles had to meet, there are yet some minds into which, after all, a doubt may steal,—whether we have indeed so fully explained away the beliefs of the world's past, whether we can indeed so assuredly define the beliefs of its future,—or whether it may not still befit us to track with fresh feet the ancient mazes, to renew the world-old desire, and to set no despairing limit to the knowledge or the hopes of man.

When Myers' first bitter grief at the death of Annie Marshall had declined a little, he began once again to think of marriage and a settled home. Whether he dimly hoped to find someone who could take Annie's place in his affections, or whether he merely wished to follow Sidgwick's advice to give Cupid a sop to hold his noise, I do not know. But his endeavours attracted the notice of the gossips. On 20th June 1878 Mrs. Jebb wrote to her sister:

> Fred Myers is a goose, and we can't help all looking on his affair as a sort of comedy. He is very companionable and with an insidious nature. Fanny Butcher says her mother is so afraid of him that she believes if there were no other way of keeping Eleanor, another sister, from his influence, she would leave London altogether. Thus far he has had small chance of seeing Eleanor alone, and can hardly have made much impression on her affections.[2]

---

[1] *Wordsworth*, p. 135.

[2] Bobbitt, *op. cit.*, p. 141. T. H. Hall, 'The Mourning Years of F. W. H. Myers', *Tomorrow* 12 (1964), p. 210, says that Miss Helen Gurney, Edmund Gurney's daughter, told him that Myers 'hotly but unsuccessfully pursued' Miss Kate Sibley before her marriage to Gurney. This sounds like a symptom of the same unrest. However, either Miss Gurney's memory or her mother's does not seem to have been altogether reliable. Several of the stories she told—such as that Gurney said that no witnesses of 'crisis' apparitions had made notes immediately after the event, and that Myers accompanied Gurney and his wife on their honeymoon—are undoubted errors or exaggerations.

The next year Myers paid a visit to America, and Mrs. Jebb, herself an American, imagined that he had designs on her countrywomen. '*He* does not see,' she observed scornfully to her sister, 'that his girth is wide, his hair thin, his thirty-five years fully painted on face and figure, and that the only kind of person fitted to *attract* him, would scorn him.'[1] I have little doubt that Myers could see his growing deficiencies only too well, and that his quest for a wife was correspondingly anxious. Mrs. Jebb's letters to her sister make even the most feline of Jane Austen's to Cassandra seem positively charitable. Early in 1880, after a whirlwind courtship in Paris, Myers became engaged to Eveleen Tennant, then twenty-two years old, from a wealthy family, and without doubt one of the most beautiful girls of her time; Mrs. Jebb, I am sorry to say, regarded her healthy good looks as those of a 'barmaid beauty'; but the portrait of her by Millais is most striking. She and Myers were married at Westminster Abbey in March 1880.

Some of Myers' friends fancied that they could see in Eveleen a resemblance to Annie, especially about the eyes; Myers himself may have thought that there was a resemblance, and that under his influence Eveleen could become such another as Annie. He could not have been more mistaken. Eveleen was in her way a profoundly affectionate person, but she was, and always remained, a spoiled and emotional child. She could never work up any serious interest in any intellectual question. She had however great social and artistic gifts and was an exceptionally skilled portrait photographer—there were not many men who could look stony in her presence. Poor Evie! It was not too long before she began obscurely to feel that her husband hoped for more from her than she was able to give. 'Fred my king and my love,' she wrote to him in July 1884, 'I will try & be worthy of you but *do not* want me to be like your dear mother or Mrs. Sidgwick, I can't. I love you more and more and will be your idial' [*sic*]; and again, in an undated letter, 'You can do without me but I *cannot* live without your love—& yet I feel *sometimes* I don't have it and darkness incompasses me your poor Evie.' I do not think however that the marriage could be called an unhappy one. Different though their outlooks and aims may have been, they lived so to speak,

---

[1] Bobbitt, *op. cit.*, p. 153.

on the same tempestuous emotional plane; 'to you,' Evie once wrote to him somewhat desperately when she was cooped up in his mother's house, 'to you I can rush & talk *loud* & say all the things that come into my head & hug my baby & be my natural wild self.' There were occasional ructions; but at times, and especially in the early years of their marriage, they were extremely happy. Myers showed little interest in ghosts for nearly two years.

VI The Foundation of the Society for Psychical Research 1882

THE FOUNDATION of the Society for Psychical Research was not primarily the work of those who afterwards became its leaders.[1] Those chiefly responsible were Professor W. F. Barrett and certain prominent Spiritualists. Barrett had for many years been interested in the question of thought-transference, and in 1876 he had offered the British Association a paper on his experiments. The paper was accepted by the Anthropological sub-section, by the casting vote of its Chairman, Alfred Russel Wallace, but it was not published.[2] It was none the less reported in detail in the Press and caused much talk. Barrett was also interested in the phenomena of Spiritualism, and during the eighteen-seventies had become acquainted with Myers and Gurney, who assisted him in some of his later experiments on thought-transference.[3] He conceived the idea that if a group of Spiritualists, who would have the confidence of mediums and sensitives, would join forces in dispassionate investigation with a group of scientists and scholars, who would possess the funds and the training to conduct proper experiments, the phenomena might perhaps be elucidated. Accordingly he convened a conference of persons likely to be interested. The conference met in London at 38 Great Russell Street on 5th and 6th

---

[1] On the foundation of the S.P.R. see G. Wyld, *Notes of My Life*, London, 1903, pp. 78–9; E. D. Rogers, *Life and Experiences of Edmund Dawson Rogers*, London, n.d., pp. 46–7; Salter, *op. cit.*, pp. 5–12; Balfour Stewart's Presidential Address to the S.P.R., *P.S.P.R.* III (1885), pp. 64–68.

[2] It was eventually published by the S.P.R. See 'On some Phenomena Associated with Abnormal Conditions of Mind', *P.S.P.R.* I (1883), pp. 238–44.

[3] The term 'telepathy' was coined by Myers in 1882.

January 1882. The foundation of a Society was proposed, and a committee (of which Myers, Gurney and Sidgwick were members) was set up to consider the question. The committee met at Hensleigh Wedgwood's house on 7th and again on 9th January. Myers and Gurney were not hopeful about the prospects of such a Society, and made their support conditional upon Sidgwick's accepting the Presidency. Sidgwick, remembering the many dreary hours which he had already passed to no avail in psychical investigations, was likewise pessimistic; but he felt that recent experiments in thought-transference gave fresh grounds for hope, and he agreed to become President. The conference met again on 20th February, and the Society for Psychical Research was formally constituted. Its stated aim was 'to investigate that large body of debateable phenomena designated by such terms as mesmeric, psychical and spiritualistic', and to do so 'without prejudice or prepossession of any kind, and in the same spirit of exact and unimpassioned enquiry which has enabled Science to solve so many problems, once not less obscure nor less hotly debated'.

The subscription for full membership was fixed at two guineas a year (at which it remained for over eighty years). The Society took rooms at 14 Dean's Yard; later it moved to 19 Buckingham Place. Sidgwick presented it with 180 books to form the nucleus of a library. Edward T. Bennett became its first paid secretary. It issued *Proceedings* from July 1882, and a *Journal* from February 1884.

The Society was run by a President and a Council of about twenty. For the few first years the Council contained both the unconvinced, like Gurney, Myers and Rayleigh, and Spiritualists and neo-Spiritualists, such as Stainton Moses and C. C. Massey. But in 1886 internal dissensions developed. The Spiritualist wing took offence at certain of Mrs Sidgwick's comments on W. Eglinton's slate-writing feats; whilst the hard-headed wing felt that the Spiritualists had not been pulling their weight in the way of procuring phenomena. In the latter part of 1886 and the beginning of 1887 many Spiritualists resigned both from the Council and the Society, and Sidgwick and his friends were thereafter completely predominant.

The choice of Sidgwick as President was a most fortunate one. Unlike his wife, he was not himself an outstanding investigator or experimenter; but his services to the new Society were in many ways of inestimable value. First, and perhaps foremost, his reputation throughout the country was such that no one would think that a Society of which he was the head could be composed mainly of cranks or of knaves. He was, too, himself so well connected, and so influential in the university world (he became professor of moral philosophy at Cambridge in 1883, and his wife became Principal of Newnham in 1892), that he was able to draw a number of distinguished people into the Society. Again, he had, through his work on behalf of women's education and other unpopular causes, gained certain political skills of use in maintaining what would nowadays be called the Society's 'public image'.[1] Above everything else, Sidgwick was dogged. Once he had decided that a subject was worth enquiring into, or a movement worth support, he would not lightly desist from his efforts, and no amount of hostility would halt him.

Sidgwick's influence on the public image of the Society, and on the general tenor of its work, was increased by the fact that he stood almost in a tutorial relation to several of its most active workers. They submitted their ideas and their papers to him as they might have done to a tutor, and since either he or one of them was usually editor of the *Proceedings* and the *Journal* he saw and criticised all important articles before they were published. At Council or Committee meetings his opinion carried a weight which perhaps only the opinion of his wife later came to match; and their opinions did not often diverge.

As President of the S.P.R. for nine of its first eighteen years, Sidgwick was thus able to exercise over it a degree of control very unusual in the President of a learned Society; but a firm control was essential to the development of a body which could in its early years well have been ruined by its more credulous members. Few people could have exercised such control better than Sidgwick. No one was less prone than he to be influenced by the ignorant criticism which not infrequently appeared in newspapers and periodicals; and there was no one under whose sway all shades of opinion would have been more likely to receive a patient and a fair hearing. Not that he did not have his limitations. The Spiritualist wing of the Society was at times

[1] See the extract from his Journal quoted below, p. 161.

inclined to feel that the caution with which he and his wife regarded reports of physical phenomena amounted almost to a kind of censorship; and indeed one could hardly expect a moral philosopher of high principles to linger lovingly in a region where the possibly paranormal was so much interwoven with the pathological or even with the criminal. But in general Sidgwick's government of the Society was a model of sobriety and balance; and sobriety and balance are the qualities which Psychical Research above all requires.

There is no doubt that the S.P.R. answered a need of the times. This is evidenced not so much by the growth in its membership (membership rose from 150 at the beginning of 1883, to 707 in January 1890, and 946 in January 1900) as by the quality of those who joined. Among its early supporters were persons of outstanding eminence from nearly every field. In 1887 its Council Members and Honorary Members included a past Prime Minister (Gladstone—elected on Myers' proposal, the latter says in an unpublished note, 'before his lamentable adoption of a Home Rule policy'), and a future Prime Minister (Arthur Balfour); eight F.R.S.s—Wallace, Couch Adams, Lord Rayleigh, Oliver Lodge, A. Macalister, J. Venn, Balfour Stewart and J. J. Thomson; two bishops; and Tennyson and Ruskin,[1] two of the outstanding literary figures of the day. There were also a number of celebrities amongst the ordinary members—for instance, 'Lewis Carroll', J. A. Symonds and William Bateson—together with a surprising number of titled persons, some of whom were perhaps more decorative than distinguished.

It will be noted how many of the people named were keenly aware of the anti-religious tendencies of the day; and there is no doubt that several of them saw in psychical research a possible antidote to contemporary materialism. Gladstone called psychical research 'The most important work, which is being done in the world. By far the most important.'[2] And the driving force of the S.P.R. came very largely from the group of younger Trinity men of the eighteen-seventies mentioned previously (p. 64) as having turned, often with reluctance, towards

---

[1] Ruskin once wrote to Myers complaining about the ugly drawings which the S.P.R. had published in connection with some telepathic experiments.
[2] *J.S.P.R.* VIII (1898), p. 260.

agnosticism. Among the eleven who were named, six—Sidgwick, Myers, Gurney, the two Balfours, and Walter Leaf—became not merely members of the S.P.R., but its principal organisers, its very engine room. Closely linked with them was Sidgwick's wife, Nora, and one of his former students, Richard Hodgson.

Of the group of people, centring on Sidgwick, who were the S.P.R.'s most active workers, all had come from religious, and even deeply religious, households; all had been driven some distance away from the faiths in which they had been reared, and several had moved into agnosticism. A simple explanation of why they turned to psychical research would be that having been brought up with a religious orientation to life, and finding themselves as a result of recent developments in science and scholarship now, so to speak, cast adrift, they hoped that these new studies would in some way provide them with a substitute for the beliefs which they had lost.

But this explanation is, except perhaps in the case of Myers, rather too simple. Few if any of the Sidgwick group believed, or indeed hoped, that the Spiritualistic and related phenomena which they studied would prove the direct source of an actual religious revelation. It was more that as a result of their upbringings and of the circles they had come to move in most of them were intensely interested in religious and philosophical questions and were very much disposed to hope that it would in the end prove possible to give what might be called optimistic answers to them. Psychical research seemed in a number of different ways possibly relevant to such problems and for that reason alone well worth prosecuting; and they felt it just possible that in the course of their investigations they might run across facts which would justify them in leaning towards the optimistic answers. Even that may be putting it too strongly. Myers indeed continued to cherish hopes that some actual religious creed might as a result of psychical investigations be put, so to speak, on a sound scientific basis. In the course of time Hodgson came to share his hopes; but most of the others, I think, had only a more limited ambition, an ambition shared of course also by Myers and Hodgson—viz., simply to find some grounds for rejecting the pessimistic answers which the intellectual tendencies of the previous two decades seemed in a fair way to forcing upon them. This would not, to their way of thinking, have been a merely negative result. It would have opened the door to further developments—a door which had at times seemed in danger of being barred for ever—and the fact that the door was not closed might by itself have beneficial effects. Both Myers and Sidgwick feared that the ultimate victory of materialism might have disastrous social effects, and they felt that if psychical research could at least uncover some weapon with which the noisy and dangerous giant might be decisively despatched it would have performed a signal service. To J. A. Symonds Myers wrote on 28th August 1883:

> But the kind of adversary present to my mind is a man like Dr. Maudsley;—a man for whose private character I can well believe that I should feel much respect, but who represents a school of thought which, if it prevails, will bring the world to the nihilism of the brutes of the field. I want to snatch our young Ray-Lankesters as brands from the burning, to save the men whose minds associate religion & the mad house, psychology & the vivisection-table, Love & the Strand.[1]

Even those of the S.P.R.'s keenest workers who were not members of the Sidgwick group had often what might be described as near-religious reasons for their interest. There was for instance Oliver Lodge (later Sir Oliver). Lodge (born 1851) was professor of physics at Liverpool University and, though he became a close friend of Myers', he was never a member of the immediate Sidgwick entourage. In the eighteen-seventies he had come somewhat under the influence of Huxley and his kindred, but later on he managed to combine a belief in communication with the dead with the Broad Christianity in which he had been brought up, and wrote a considerable number of works on religious and philosophical matters. Another example is Frank Podmore (born 1856). Podmore, the son of a clergyman, had done well at Oxford in both Classics and Natural Sciences, but instead of pursuing a scientific or academic career, he became a civil servant, working in the General

---

[1] Bristol University Library. Perhaps Myers had been putting forward similar arguments when he wrote rather less pompously to Oliver Lodge on 26th January 1896: 'I have been jawing about religion and S.P.R.;—have defined the orthodox scientific religion as neo-Phallicism;—should like to explain this to you:—it is not meant to be insulting! but if you don't know what a phallus is, don't ask!'

Post Office in London. Though he was closely associated with Myers and Gurney during the eighteen-eighties and was joint Hon. Secretary of the S.P.R. from 1888 to 1896, he does not seem to have been on terms of close friendship with any of the Society's leaders.[1] None the less his aspirations were not very different from theirs. In his early youth, indeed, he had been a convinced Spiritualist; but he swung almost to the opposite extreme, writing a series of books and articles of the most sceptical tendency (his *Modern Spiritualism* has been frequently referred to above). Even so he always retained some glimmering of his early hopes.[2]

It may indeed not always have been entirely for the best that the study of this very tricky subject should have been largely prosecuted by people whose interest in it was to a considerable extent sustained by religious feeling and philosophical perplexity. On the other hand it might with justice be pointed out that these people were very powerfully restrained from excessive credulity and from excessive optimism about their results by a keen sense of the momentousness of the issues which they believed were at stake. In his obituary of Henry Sidgwick Myers wrote:

> ... we must remember that our very *raison d'etre* is the extension of the scientific method, of intellectual virtues—of curiosity, candour, care,—into regions where many a current of old tradition, of heated emotion, even of pseudo-scientific prejudice, deflects the bark which should steer only towards the cold, unreachable pole of absolute truth. We must recognise that we have more in common with those who may criticise or attack our work with competent diligence than with those who may acclaim and exaggerate it without adding thereto any careful work of their own. We must experiment unweariedly; we must continue to demolish fiction as well as to accumulate truth; we must make no terms with any hollow mysticism, any half-conscious deceit.[3]

There can in any case be little doubt that only persons with religious and near-religious interests and enthusiasms would have

---

[1] It seems possible that Podmore was a practising homosexual. See T. H. Hall, *The Strange Case of Edmund Gurney*, London, 1964, pp. 200–6.
[2] Cf. the letter quoted below, p. 316.
[3] *P.S.P.R.* XV (1900), pp. 459–60.

carried through the enormous programme of work which the early leaders of the S.P.R. set themselves. One doubts if wealthy or educated private persons have these days sufficient *concern* over the sorts of problems which worried and intrigued Sidgwick and his circle to launch a comparable undertaking. And one very much doubts whether the money for such an undertaking would be forthcoming from any public source. Most governments find the problems of this world a sufficient drain on their exchequers, and politicians perhaps do not much like the notion of thought-reading.

Sidgwick and his friends came from a class of people to which there is now hardly any equivalent, but whose contribution to science and thought has often been remarked upon. Most of them were wealthy, at least by the standards of today; most of them derived their wealth from a grandfather or great-grandfather who had made money in business or a profession. The founder of the fortunes was often a man of pious or Evangelical tendencies, who bequeathed his piety to his descendants along with his wealth. Sidgwick's grandfather was a self-made man, a wealthy cotton-spinner; his father (who had died in 1841) was a clergyman and became headmaster of a grammar school. Sidgwick himself did not inherit any very great wealth, but he was economical with money and, despite very considerable benefactions to various good causes, left £12,000 when he died in 1900. His wife came from a very wealthy family, which owed a good part of its substance to a nabob grandfather. In her childhood she had been much influenced by her Evangelical mother; and although at her death in 1936 she left only £10,000, she was said to have given over £30,000 to Newnham College at various times.[1] When Myers married in 1880 he had an income of somewhat over £500 a year as a school inspector, plus rather over £700 from investments; in 1899 his income as a school inspector was £879, and he obtained £3,180 from investments. He left £37,000; most of this money, of course, derived from his Marshall grandfather. Gurney's grandfather had been a baron of the exchequer, and his father was a clergyman. He left £17,000—a sum then sufficient to enable him to live fairly comfortably. Walter Leaf's father was an Evangelical merchant banker of immense wealth.

[1] *Dictionary of National Biography 1931–48*, s.v. 'Sidgwick, Eleanor Mildred'.

There are of course not a few people today who inherit wealth from businessmen forbears; but not many of them, I imagine, inherit along with it, as did the members of the Sidgwick group, if not piety exactly, or Evangelicalism, at any rate the sense that wealth is in some way a trust and ought to be put to good uses rather than dissipated in enjoyment and frivolity. In his bachelor days Sidgwick had, as an experiment, lived for a while on the minimum possible outlay; however with his usual moderation he usually stopped short of extreme austerity. Thus he is said at one time to have cut expensive wines out of his dinner-parties as an unbecoming luxury; but he felt that he had to make up the deficit to his guests by extra brilliant conversation, and after a while he found this so much strain that he reverted to the wines. His wife's austerity and absence of display became in her later years almost legendary. Myers was certainly not austere in his way of life. He appeared to A. C. Benson 'something utterly different from a wealthy and cultivated inspector of schools. I thought of him rather as something mediaeval and lordly—a Venetian merchant-prince, perhaps, with an outlook upon art and letters, and with none of the limitations in life, nothing of the timidity of dealing with its fulness, that my own more puritanical bringing-up had imposed on me.'[1] But even Myers had had inscribed over the door of his house—a house modelled by its architect, his cousin William Cecil Marshall, on a Cotswold manor—the lines:

> Aude, hospes, contemnere opes et te quoque dignum
> Finge Deo.

Only people with both wealth and a sense of the obligations entailed by wealth would have been likely to spend large sums on studies which could bring them neither advancement nor a cash return, or would have been likely to have the time to carry out the necessary extended investigations. And the sums which the Sidgwick group spent on psychical research were very far from negligible. On 31st October 1889 Myers complained in a letter to William James that the Sidgwick group had between them been subsidising the S.P.R. to the extent of £600 or £700 a year and were now having to subsidise the American branch as well. Sidgwick was the most frequent

[1] A. C. Benson, *The Leaves of the Tree*, London, 1911, p. 178.

contributor, but Myers also gave a great deal. On one occasion Myers sent the American Society a cheque for £120, saying that he would partially recoup from Sidgwick and Leaf. In February 1900 he offered the S.P.R. Council up to £250 to pay for the publication of a long paper (by the American J. H. Hyslop) of which he personally thought ill; and after his death his widow implemented the promise to the tune of £92.

Although those who were most active in the S.P.R. were generally speaking very much aware of the possible bearing, direct or indirect, which their studies might have upon religious and philosophical, or even social and moral, issues, they mostly felt that, for the time being at least, they were not likely to profit from further direct investigation of the phenomena of Spiritualism. They saw however various other possibilities for bringing to light weaknesses in the crude Büchnerian and Huxleian doctrines which had held the ascendant in the eighteen-seventies. They determined to examine simultaneously and in detail as many kinds of supposedly paranormal phenomena as they could, quite irrespective of whether or not these phenomena had any Spiritualistic or religious flavour.

Thus Spiritualistic phenomena formed only a small part of the terrain to be scrutinised by the six special working committees set up at the Society's foundation. Committees were set up for each of the following purposes:

1. An examination of the nature and extent of any influence which may be exerted by one mind upon another, apart from any generally recognised mode of perception. [Committee on thought-reading.]

2. The study of hypnotism, and the forms of so-called mesmeric trance, with its alleged insensibility to pain; clairvoyance and other allied phenomena. [Committee on mesmerism.]

3. A critical revision of Reichenbach's researches with certain organisations called 'sensitive', and an inquiry whether such organisations possess any power of perception beyond a highly exalted sensibility of the recognised sensory organs. [Committee on Reichenbach's experiments.]

4. A careful investigation of any reports, resting on strong testimony, regarding apparitions at the moment of death, or otherwise, or regarding disturbances in houses reputed to be haunted. [Committee on Apparitions, haunted houses, etc.]

5. An inquiry into the various physical phenomena com-

monly called Spiritualistic; with an attempt to discover their causes and general laws. [Committee on Physical Phenomena.]

6. The collection and collation of existing materials bearing on the history of these subjects. [Literary Committee.][1]

Considerable endeavours were also made to link up the Society's work with more orthodox but possibly related branches of study. Leading members of the S.P.R. played prominent parts in several International Congresses of psychology (Paris 1889, London 1892, Munich 1896, Paris 1900), and also brought the Society's work as much as possible to the notice of the educated world in general through letters in *The Times* and articles in leading Reviews.[2]

Professor W. F. Barrett, who was largely responsible for the foundation of the English Society for Psychical Research, was also instrumental in the foundation of a comparable Society in the United States. During a tour of that country in 1884 he succeeded in rousing the interest of various *savants*, especially in Unitarian Boston, and a Society was formed in January 1885, under the Presidency of Simon Newcomb. However, William James (b. 1842), the psychologist and philosopher, speedily became its leading light. James had met Gurney in England in 1882,

[1] *P.S.P.R.* I (1881), pp. 3-4.
[2] The more important articles were:
Barrett, Myers and Gurney, 'Thought Reading', *Nineteenth Century Review* XI (1882), pp. 890–900;
Gurney and Myers, 'Apparitions', *The Nineteenth Century* XV (1884), pp. 791–815;
Gurney and Myers, 'Visible Apparitions', *Nineteenth Century Review* XVI (1884), pp. 68–95, 851–2.
Gurney, 'Nature of Evidence in Matters Extraordinary', *National Review* IV (1884), pp. 472–91.
Gurney and Myers, 'Some Higher Aspects of Mesmerism', *National Review* V (1885), pp. 681–703;
Myers, 'Automatic Writing, or the Rationale of Planchette', *Contemporary Review* XLVII (1885), pp. 233–49;
Myers, 'Multiplex Personality', *Nineteenth Century Review* XX (1886), pp. 648–666;
Myers, 'Science and a Future Life', *Nineteenth Century Review* XXIX (1891), pp. 628–47;
Myers, 'The Drift of Psychical Research', *National Review* XXIV (1894), pp. 190–209;
Myers, 'On Some Fresh Facts indicating Man's Survival of Death', *National Review* XXXII (1898), pp. 230–42.

and they had struck up a close friendship; later James became a close friend of Myers'. In 1887 a young and energetic pupil of Sidgwick's, Richard Hodgson, went out to take over management of the American Society. It ran into considerable financial difficulties, and in December 1889 amalgamated with the British Society. The latter had periodically to subsidise it somewhat heavily, which led to a certain amount of ill-feeling since the American branch had in fact a number of distinctly wealthy members.

Barrett, to whose initiative the S.P.R. owed its foundation, was never quite one of its ruling clique; indeed, he came to be increasingly at loggerheads with that clique. The immediate cause of dissension was several series of experiments in thought-transference which Barrett and others conducted with the five daughters of the Rev. A. M. Creery of Bath;[1] Barrett had been the first to experiment with these girls, and they were his especial protégées. The early experiments gave results certainly very difficult to explain. In a later series of experiments the girls were caught using a rather primitive code, and the Sidgwick group at once excised both earlier and later experiments from their case for telepathy. Barrett would never agree that the later and crude cheating invalidated all the earlier results; he considered that his 1876 experiments, together with his experiments on the Creerys, had established his claim to be the discoverer of thought-transference, and he remained bitter towards the Sidgwicks for the rest of his life. Who was right in the matter I shall not try to say; but the Sidgwicks and their friends found Barrett a vain and querulous colleague and thought him lamentably deficient in critical standards. The friction grew greater rather than less with the passage of time.

The sheer quantity of work done by the S.P.R., and especially by the Sidgwick group, during its first twenty years was quite remarkable, and some at least of the evidence for the paranormal which was unearthed cannot be lightly or easily dismissed. Certain of those most closely concerned in the work came, as this evidence accumulated, to take a very high view of the importance of their task, to feel, in Myers' phrase, 'The

[1] See Appendix A.

consciousness that the hour at last had come; that the world-old secret was opening out to mortal view; that the first carrier pigeon had swooped into this fastness of beleagurred men.'[1] Even the cautious Sidgwick was, according to Myers, convinced of the unique importance of the undertaking:

> And thus, while renewing this toilsome quest in no sanguine spirit, he renewed it at least with the conviction that there was nothing else of equal moment to be done; that if, where religion and philosophy had failed in establishing certainty, Science were to fail also, 'the human race,' as he once said to me, 'had better think about these matters' (the basis of morals, the government of the universe) 'as little as they possibly can.'[2]

Sidgwick always retained doubts as to the interpretation which should be put on the evidence. Myers however had in his later years no doubts at all, and his happiness and his excitement were intense. 'Beneath a strange disguising', he wrote to William James on 3rd February 1897, 'these are mighty days; remember them well! for we shall be called upon to tell their story long hence in an unimaginable world.'

Many people would no doubt see something merely pathetic in the fact that these earnest *savants* should find, in such bizarre phenomena, answers, or hints of answers, to questions about the inmost nature of the Cosmos. Some would even allege that the questions themselves are absurd, or even meaningless. But the exhilaration which some of Sidgwick's friends felt at the seeming success of their endeavours is, I think, entirely comprehensible in the light of their personal histories and of the intellectual tendencies of their time. Myers once said that the most important question one could ask was 'Is the Universe friendly?' and with this view several of his colleagues would in one way or another have concurred. There had lately been much to suggest to them that the Universe was neither friendly to mankind nor yet unfriendly; it was just blankly indifferent. Psychical research seemed to offer a touch of warmth and hope in face of this chilling prospect. It was at least a candle in the darkness which was beginning to loom on every side.

[1] *Fragments*, p. 16.   [2] *P.S.P.R.* XV (1900), p. 458.

Part Two

THE WORK OF THE EARLY PSYCHICAL RESEARCHERS

VII Edmund Gurney and Phantasms of the Living

THE ENSUING CHAPTERS will give some account of the work which the Sidgwick group carried out between the foundation of the S.P.R. in 1882 and the death of Frederic Myers in 1901. I shall not have space to deal with all of this work and shall therefore confine myself to describing the parts of it which seem most directly related to those questions (touched on in the last chapter) which the members of the group had most at heart. The principal omissions are the experimental investigations of telepathy, and the experimental investigation of certain hypnotic phenomena. The most important experiments in telepathy published by the S.P.R. between 1882 and 1901 are briefly described in Appendix A. A list of Edmund Gurney's papers on hypnosis will be found below on p. 159n.

Of the six committees set up at the time of the S.P.R.'s foundation, the Literary Committee (whose purpose was the collection and collation of existing materials) did incomparably the most work. Just how considerable its labours were can perhaps be fully appreciated only by those who have looked through the forty-two boxes in which the results are now filed. In the year 1883 alone the six members of the Committee wrote more than 10,000 letters, and correspondence was only part of their activities. They had also often to travel in order to interview crucial witnesses, and to visit libraries and Record Offices. The quantity of material which they obtained, both through private enquiries and through advertisement in *The Times* and other periodicals, soon became so great that the more interesting cases were printed on slips (at Sidgwick's expense) to make it easier for students to examine them. The largest amount of work was carried out by the Committee's two Hon. Secretaries, Gurney and Myers, and especially by Gurney, who also shortly became the Society's first Hon. Secretary and the editor of its *Proceedings*. He devoted, in fact, nearly all his time to the work and was probably the most important figure in the early S.P.R. It is time to give a fuller account of him.[1]

It is often supposed that Edmund Gurney came from the famous Quaker banking family, the Gurneys of Earlham; but in fact his relationship to them was only collateral, and his own family was predominantly a legal one—his grandfather had been a baron of the exchequer, and his uncle, Russell Gurney, was Recorder of London. However, his father, John Hampden Gurney, had gone into the Church, becoming Rector of St. Mary's, Bryanston Square, and a Prebendary of St. Paul's. Edmund, who was born in 1847, was the fifth child in a family of eight. He seems to have been somewhat delicate and was educated privately; though by the time that he went up to Trinity in 1866, as a minor scholar in classics, he had developed a tall lean frame and a considerable aptitude for athletic sports.

His chief interests, however, were neither athletic nor scholarly, but artistic and above all musical. The consuming ambition of his early years was to achieve proficiency both as a performer and a composer of music; and his striking successes as a classic (the Porson Prize in 1870; fourth in the first class of the Classical Tripos in 1871) were achieved, as Myers put it, almost in the intervals of practice on the piano. In 1872 Gurney was elected to a Trinity Fellowship; and for the next three years he devoted himself chiefly to music, studying at Harrow under the famous teacher, John Farmer.

That a University man, especially a College Fellow, should contemplate a musical career, seemed to many at that time

---

[1] Materials on Gurney are scanty. The only MS. source of interest which I have been able to discover is his letters to William James in the Houghton Library, Harvard University. Croom Robertson's article in the *Dictionary of National Biography* and Myers' obituary notice, *P.S.P.R.* V (1888), pp. 359–73, are the chief sources. There is a little about him in various biographies, books of reminiscences, etc., see e.g. Leaf, *op. cit.*, pp. 95–7. See also Hall, *op. cit.* In what follows I am much indebted to an essay, as yet unpublished, by Prof. C. D. Broad, on 'The Life, Work and Death of Edmund Gurney'.

most unsuitable. When Gurney told the Master of Trinity, W. H. Thompson, of his ambitions, the latter remarked: 'Well, I suppose that is better than dancing.' Even within music Gurney's tastes were very wide; he could listen with pleasure and interest not merely to accepted 'musician's music' but to the latest *Opéra Bouffe* or to the Zulu drummers at the Westminster Aquarium. And his readiness to explore the musically unusual was paralleled by a general love of speculation and enquiry, and a complete disrespect for conventional lines of thought. His open-mindedness and his speculative capacities were combined, however, with a cool judgment and quick humour which kept him from extravagances; he would climb other people's Pisgahs, but he would fail to glimpse their Promised Lands.

Gurney's unconventional thinking and his dialectic skill made him prominent amongst the younger and abler Trinity men; and his gaiety, his wit, and above all, perhaps, the profound sympathy with which his sensitive nature would respond to the troubles and afflictions of others, greatly endeared him to them as a human being. There could be no more delightful companion than Gurney at his best; 'On a good day,' said F. W. Maitland, who had walked with him once in the Tyrol, 'it was a joy to hear him laugh.'[1] But good days were far from common in Gurney's life. A strain of melancholy in his character was even then sufficiently pronounced to be a frequent source of worry to his friends. No one could apply himself to a subject with greater industry or with greater enthusiasm than Gurney; but his bursts of energy were liable to be succeeded by periods of lassitude and of the most profound depression. Even as an undergraduate his studies had been interrupted for a year by what would now be called a nervous breakdown; and despondency grew upon him as it gradually became apparent that his musical hopes and ambitions would never be fulfilled. He could attain neither skill as a player nor originality in composition. He was endowed, it seemed, with every kind of analytic and scholarly gift; yet the artistic gifts for which he would cheerfully have traded all the others were largely denied him.

At the end of 1875 Gurney's life was overshadowed by a frightful tragedy. Three of his sisters, his closest sympathisers in

[1] H. A. L. Fisher, *Frederic William Maitland*, Cambridge, 1910, p. 22.

his musical aspirations, and the youngest of them especially beloved, were drowned in a boating accident on the Nile.[1] His speculations and cast of mind became thereafter almost obsessively sombre, and a few years later he told William James that 'the mystery of the Universe and the indefensibility of human suffering' were never far from him.

Gurney was not, by the standards of his time, a wealthy man, but he possessed a competence and had no pressing need to increase his income. Sometime in 1875 he moved to London, where he took houses first in Clarges Street, and later in Montpelier Square. He may have had some lingering hopes of musical fulfilment, but if so they quickly faded. In 1877 he met and married Kate Sibley, a girl who came from an impoverished family but who was outstandingly beautiful and also, seemingly, clever and talkative to a degree which less intense souls were apt to find tiresome. Perhaps it was marriage which turned Gurney to thoughts of a career; perhaps also it was simply a wish to do something useful in the world. In October 1877 he embarked on a course of medical studies at University College, London; next year he took up his studies at Cambridge, and in 1880, after working with his usual thoroughness, obtained his Second M.B. He then went to St. George's Hospital to start the clinical part of a physician's training; but he could not endure the sights and sounds of the dressing room,[2] and had to abandon the notion of a medical career. He turned almost at once to the law and read first with a special pleader and then with a conveyancer. For a while his industry was immense; but very soon his interest began to flag, and with it his labours.

The failure of his endeavours to become a musician had not lessened his love of music, nor his consuming interest in it. He managed to combine his medical course with the preparation of a theoretical book, *The Power of Sound*, which was published in 1880. The few people competent to judge rated it amongst the outstanding treatises on aesthetics of their generation; it displays a rare combination of artistic appreciation with logi-

---

[1] See *The Times*, 31st Dec. 1875 and 10th Jan. 1876. Cf. Hall, *op. cit.*, p. 21.

[2] It is hard to realise what hospitals were then like—cf. Sir Frederick Treves' reminiscences of the London Hospital in *The Elephant Man and Other Reminiscences*, London, 1923. Treves says (p. 57) that all the wounds in a ward would be washed with the same sponge and in the same bowl of water.

cal analysis and psychological insight.[1] Unfortunately most musicians found it too philosophical, and most philosophers too technical, for their comprehension. It brought him no great or immediate fame; but the work which had gone into it, reacting perhaps upon his growing despondency at the bleakness of the human situation, turned him increasingly towards the philosophical and psychological problems which were to occupy him for much of the rest of his life. He became a member of a philosophical dining and discussion group calling itself 'The Scratch Eight' (the other members were Shadworth Hodgson, F. W. Maitland, G. Croom Robertson, F. Pollock, Leslie Stephen, Carveth Read and James Sully); and he began to contribute philosophical papers to *Mind* and other periodicals. Several of the essays which he collected together in the first volume of *Tertium Quid* (1887) can still be read with interest today. He makes many acute remarks and is never prepared to accept the easy solutions popular amongst some of his contemporaries.

From the views and the attitudes which Gurney expresses in *Tertium Quid* it is fairly obvious how his interest in psychical research arose, and why he should have come to think the work of the S.P.R. of such importance. A leading—one might almost say the leading—feature of his personality was his extreme sensitivity to pain; not just to physical pain, but to grief and suffering of all kinds. This sensitivity however did not lead him —as it might have led another—to a brooding self-centredness; instead it made him vividly and excruciatingly aware of the predicaments of his fellow-men.[2] What oppressed him most was not his own suffering, but the untold suffering which everywhere surrounded him; and above all the fact that there was generally so little he or anyone else could do to set it right. Suffering seemed so often the by-product of a vast and blind Machine over whose workings we have, and are likely to have, only the slightest control; our utmost efforts can halt the

---

[1] Some of Gurney's literary criticism, e.g. the essay on 'Poets, Critics and Class-lists' (*Tertium Quid* II, pp. 119-90), seems to me quite as discerning as, say, Bagehot's well-known essay on 'Wordsworth, Tennyson and Browning'.

[2] Indeed of his fellow-creatures. His two articles on vivisection, 'A Chapter in the Ethics of Pain', *Fortnightly Review* XXXVI (1881), pp. 778-96, and 'An Epilogue on Vivisection', *Cornhill Magazine* XLV (1882), pp. 191-9, seem to me still worth reading. Darwin is said to have approved of them. They are reprinted *Tertium Quid* I, pp. 151-203, 204-26. Gurney says (p. 173): 'The presentation of

Juggernaut only for a second, and there will always be a victim in anguish beneath its wheels.

Many people have found a refuge from such thoughts in religious belief; but this refuge was denied to Gurney. Indeed the widespread occurrence of cases of permanent, and above all undeserved, suffering was amongst his chief reasons for doubting the existence of a benevolent Deity. Nor was he able to draw comfort from any of the surrogate religions in vogue at the time—from the positivist 'religion of humanity', say, or from the idealisation of science. They too are quite unable to accommodate cases of permanent suffering. Great pain is *incommensurable* with great pleasure. The two cannot (as utilitarians would like to think) balance each other out in the final reckoning. If there is in the world *one person* whose lot is irredeemably painful, the world is an evil place. The happiness of a thousand million others cannot make it otherwise.

The worst of all possible kinds of suffering, Gurney felt, is *hopeless* suffering, the suffering of those who are absolutely certain that never, under any circumstances, will they know anything but pain. The thought of such suffering appalled him:

> If for the worst and most permanent suffering there were no possible assuagement of hope, if I found in myself and all around me an absolute conviction that the individual existence ceased with the death of the body, and that the present iniquitous distribution of good and evil was therefore final, I should . . . desire the immediate extinction of the race.[1]

There are many whose sufferings can never in this world be remedied; the best we can do for such persons is to persuade them that they may find some measure of compensation after death. Now the general trend of modern science is, of course, against the possibility of survival; still the notion of survival is at any rate quite comprehensible, and we would not necessarily have to present a sufferer with absolute proof of it. Merely to give him hope would brighten his outlook enormously, for 'the

---

science *per se*—of a knowledge whose sole use would be to titillate the brains of an infinitesimal fraction of mankind—as not merely a fetish with an inherent mysterious claim on us for worship, but a Moloch with a similar claim on us for victims, is simple credulity and superstition.'

[1] *Tertium Quid* I, p. 133.

sense of possibilities that can never be disproved is capable of exercising a pervading effect on the human mind which is absolutely irrelevant to any numerical estimate of odds'.[1] A doubter may be saved from despair so long as his doubts are not converted into negative certainty—the vilest prison-camp in the world may prove just endurable to a prisoner who has not completely lost hope that a better life may somewhere await him.

It is, I think, fairly clear from this why Gurney was prepared to join Myers and Sidgwick in the investigations of Spiritualism which I have already described, and why in 1882 he gave his support to the newly founded S.P.R. The following year he was persuaded by his friends to abandon further thought of a career and to devote all his time to the new subject. He became the Society's first Honorary Secretary and held the position until his death, working with enormous industry on a variety of questions. Some parts of his work we are about to deal with; but other parts will have to be passed over—most notably his extensive theoretical and practical investigations of hypnosis, investigations which, though perhaps in some ways defective, were far in advance of any others of their kind then being carried out in England.[2]

When Gurney became Hon. Secretary of the S.P.R. in October 1883 he was thirty-six years old. He must have been keenly aware that his considerable abilities had not hitherto been usefully deployed. Not merely was he academically gifted; he had a commanding presence, and as a conversationalist and wit was compared with F. W. Maitland and Arthur Balfour (the latter of whom he somewhat resembled in appearance). He was as high-minded and as intellectual as any of the 'Souls', and he had many friends and admirers. Now at last he had

---

[1] *Tertium Quid* I, pp. 46–7.
[2] Gurney's principal papers on hypnotism in *P.S.P.R.* are:

'The Stages of Hypnotism', *P.S.P.R.* II (1884), pp. 61–72;
'The Problems of Hypnotism', *P.S.P.R.* II (1884), pp. 265–92;
'Peculiarities of Certain Post-Hypnotic States', *P.S.P.R.* IV (1887), pp. 268–323;
'Stages of Hypnotic Memory', *P.S.P.R.* IV (1887), pp. 515–31;
'Hypnotism and Telepathy', *P.S.P.R.* V (1888), pp. 215–59.

Much of the material concerned was also published in *Mind*. Cf. also the references given in Appendix A below; and see T. W. Mitchell, 'The Contributions of Psychical Research to Psychotherapeutics', *P.S.P.R.* XLV (1938), pp. 175–86.

found an occupation which not merely allowed him to exercise his unusual talents to the full, but seemed to give him a real chance of benefiting humankind. Three years later, on 16th April 1886, he wrote to William James concerning his own work for the S.P.R. 'I am glad I have done it, and feel sure that the time, being *my* time, could not have been better spent.'

Among the many curious occurrences of which the Literary Committee obtained accounts, the largest single class was that of 'crisis apparitions'. The term is almost self-explanatory. At a given time a certain person, the *percipient*, sees the figure, or hears the voice, of another person (in the majority of cases someone well known to him), whom we will call the *agent*. It transpires that at or about the time when the percipient thought he saw the agent, or thought he heard his voice, the agent was in a totally different place, and was undergoing some singular crisis in his affairs—generally death. These stories differed considerably from the ordinary run of popular ghost tales. There was nothing sensational about them, and they were, as the first *Report of the Literary Committee* (December 1882) put it 'far more likely to provoke sleep in the course of perusal than to banish it afterwards'.[1] The figures seen in most, though not all, cases appeared quite ordinary, apart at least from a tendency to vanish inexplicably. Indeed, the uniform dullness of the testimony was one of its most impressive features. Another was its sheer bulk. Even in December 1882 Myers and Gurney were able to write:

> Those who are used, as most of us have been all our lives, to hearing now and again a stray story at third or fourth hand, with the usual commentary of vague wonderment or shallow explanation, but without any suggestion of analysing or probing it, can scarcely imagine the effect on the mind of a sudden, large accumulation of direct, well-attested, and harmonious testimony. The similarities of unlooked-for detail which bind the phenomena together into distinct groups, the very similarities which make the accounts of them monotonous reading, give the strength of a faggot to the dispersed units which looked

---

[1] *P.S.P.R.* I (1882), pp. 117–18.

as if the mere dead weight of uninquiring incredulity might easily break them.[1]

Faced with such an amount of testimony—by now 400 cases bearing upon these 'Phantasms of the Living' had been collected—the Literary Committee held a series of meetings at Sidgwick's house (20th–27th August 1883) to decide what ought to be done. A resolution was passed entrusting to Gurney, Myers and Podmore the preparation of a book on crisis apparitions. Its title was to be *Phantasms of the Living*. Fifteen months later there was something of a rearrangement of plan. Sidgwick wrote in his Journal for 4th January 1885:

> Had a rather agitating discussion at Massey's about the book on 'Phantasms of the Living.' Hitherto we have agreed that Myers & Gurney are to write it jointly; but I have come to the conclusion that all our appearances in print ought to be conducted on the principle of individualizing responsibility. In this obscure and treacherous region, girt about with foes watching eagerly for some bad blunder, it is needlessly increasing our risks to run the danger of *two* reputations being exploded by one blunder: it is two heads on one neck: 'hoc Ithacus velit.' Let us have the freest and fullest mutual criticism—so that if possible each of us may feel himself *morally* responsible for our friend's blunders—but let the responsibility *before the world* be always attached to *one*, that we may sell our reputations as dearly as possible. I urged this view, but did not prevail: it was a delicate matter as I was palpably aiming at ousting FM. and leaving EG. as sole author: estimating the superior trustworthiness of the latter in scientific reasoning as more important than his literary inferiority. I could see that M. was annoyed; but he bore it admirably. Ultimately we compromised thus. M. to write a long introduction and G. the body of the book.

And so it was left. Myers wrote an Introduction, giving the historical background to the investigation and indicating its supposed importance for psychology and for religion; Gurney wrote the bulk of the book; Podmore's role was simply that of investigator of a large number of cases.

The amount of work which Myers and Podmore put in on *Phantasms of the Living* was not small; but Gurney's efforts were

[1] *P.S.P.R.* I (1882), p. 118.

prodigious. In the course of following up cases he would not infrequently write fifty or sixty letters in one day and in his own hand. He had also not merely to verify the cases, but to sort them, classify them and think about them. Sir Oliver Lodge, who visited him at this time, found the sitting-room of his house in Montpelier Square completely covered with little piles of the printed slips to which the case histories had been transferred.

Phantasms of the Living was published a little more than three years after it was projected. Its two volumes contain over 1,300 pages, the great majority of which were written by Gurney. The 702 cases which he deals with are carefully classified and analysed; and the book contains in addition long, and often highly original, discussions of such matters as experimental investigations of telepathy, hallucinations among the sane, the canons of evidence to be applied in assessing cases and (in connection with the latter), the alleged evidence for the paranormal powers of witches. When one remembers that during these three years Gurney also carried out some arduous experimental and theoretical work on hypnotism, as well as his duties as the S.P.R.'s Hon. Secretary and editor, his industry and application become staggering. He had certainly found his *métier*; but there is some reason to believe that at times his health suffered.

The central thesis of *Phantasms of the Living* (first propounded by Gurney and Myers in 1884.)[1] is this: crisis apparitions of the kind described earlier are best interpreted as *hallucinations* generated in the percipient by the receipt of a *telepathic* 'message' from the dying agent. That ghosts are *hallucinatory* is suggested by their complete or almost complete failure to leave any physical traces behind them,[2] and by the fact that they occasionally behave in ways impossible to physical objects. They disappear instantaneously in locked rooms; and even walk through walls in the traditional manner. That crisis apparitions are caused by the receipt of a telepathic 'message' from the dying person is strongly suggested by the fact that they can be placed at the end of an unbroken series of cases, a series of

[1] 'Third Report of the Literary Committee: A Theory of Apparitions, Part I', *P.S.P.R.* II (1884), pp. 109–36; 'Fourth Report of the Literary Committee: A Theory of Apparitions, Part II', *P.S.P.R.* II (1884), pp. 157–86.

[2] In one case the figure seen appeared to extinguish a night-light; see *Phantasms* II, pp. 202–3.

which cases of experimental and spontaneous telepathy form the early and middle terms. First of all come the instances of experimental telepathy in which, let us say, a percipient in one place is able to reproduce a drawing held before the eyes of an agent in another place. Then come cases of spontaneous telepathy, which most commonly occur when the agent is undergoing some shock or strong emotion; thus a lady lying in bed early one morning felt a pain in her mouth at the moment when her husband was struck painfully in the mouth by the tiller of his yacht.[1] Next we have more complex cases of spontaneous telepathy, where the percipient's experience is not, so to speak, a reproduction of that of the agent, but is rather *founded* upon it, the details coming from the percipient's mind. An example would perhaps be that of 'arrival' cases,[2] in which a person about to arrive at a given spot is actually seen there in advance of his arrival by someone not expecting him; here what the percipient sees—the agent as he appears to people other than himself—is most unlikely to correspond closely with what is in the agent's mind, so that the *details* of the picture must presumably be in some way supplied by the percipient. Finally come crisis apparitions themselves, in which the details of the phantom, which often behaves normally and is normally clad, would seem necessarily to have come from the percipient's mind; for the agent may be at the bottom of the sea, or lying in night clothes upon his death-bed. Here is an example of a crisis case, not, I think, either above or below average in evidential quality and dramatic interest; the narrator is Ellen M. Greany, described as 'a trusted and valued servant in the family of Miss Porter, at 16 Russell Square, W.C.'

> May 20th, 1884.
>
> I sat one evening reading, when on looking up from my book, I distinctly saw a school-friend of mine, to whom I was very much attached, standing near the door. I was about to exclaim at the strangeness of her visit when, to my horror, there were no signs of anyone in the room but my mother. I related what I had seen to her, knowing she could not have seen, as she was sitting with her back towards the door, nor did she hear anything unusual, and was greatly amused at my scare, suggesting I had read too much or been dreaming.

---

[1] *Phantasms* I, pp. 188–9.   [2] See *Phantasms* I, pp. 251–4; II, pp. 96–100.

A day or so after this strange event, I had news to say my friend was no more. The strange part was that I did not even know she was ill, much less in danger, so could not have felt anxious at the time on her account, but may have been thinking of her; that I cannot testify. Her illness was short, and death very unexpected. Her mother told me she spoke of me not long before she died . . . She died the same evening and about the same time that I saw her vision, which was the end of October, 1874.

ELLEN M. GREANY

In answer to an inquiry, Ellen Greany adds that this hallucination is the only one she has ever experienced. She tells Miss Porter that she went to see her dead friend before the funeral, which accords with her statement that she heard the news of the death very soon after it occurred; and there is no reason to doubt that, at the time when she heard the news, she was able correctly to identify the day of her vision.[1]

[Gurney adds the corroborative testimony of Miss Greany's mother and gives a short account of his interview with Miss Greany, who impressed him as a 'superior and intelligent person'.]

It is quite impossible to convey by a sketchy summary and solitary example the full impressiveness of the argument from continuity with which Gurney supports the telepathic theory of crisis apparitions. Since Gurney's time every serious discussion of crisis apparitions has taken its start from his classification and arrangement of them. To pass from even the ablest of previous works to *Phantasms of the Living* is like passing from a mediaeval bestiary or herbal to Linnaeus' *Systema Naturae*.

It is true, of course, that few of the cases which Gurney cites are evidentially quite perfect. In some the incident antedates the description of it by ten years or even more; in others occasional details may be vague; sometimes witnesses whose corroboratory testimony would have been valuable have died; and so on. On the other hand, in no case is the evidence negligible; in all the cases treated in the main part of the book (with a small and specified class of exceptions) the evidence given is first-hand. It is almost always backed by corroboratory evidence; and in almost all cases the witnesses were interviewed and appraised

[1] *Phantasms* II, pp. 54–5.

by a responsible member of the S.P.R., usually one of the three authors. Gurney was firmly of the view that the cases strengthened each other like the sticks of a faggot. Some few of the sticks might be weak; but since they were not to be made into a *chain* of evidence, that did not matter.

It is certainly far from easy to dismiss the supposed correlation between deaths and crisis apparitions as the product of defective testimony. Gurney's analysis of the possible sources of error is lucid and exhaustive; and he shows quite conclusively that in order to get rid of our bundle of crisis cases we should have to press our sceptical arguments with an almost paranoid persistency:

> Not only have we to assume such an extent of forgetfulness and inaccuracy, about simple and striking facts of the immediate past, as is totally unexampled in any other range of experience. Not only have we to assume that distressing or exciting news about another person produces a havoc in the memory which has never been noted in connection with distress or excitement in any other form. We must leave this merely general ground, and make suppositions as detailed as the evidence itself. We must suppose that some people have a way of dating their letters in indifference to the calendar, or making entries in their diaries on the wrong page and never discovering the error; and that whole families have been struck by the collective hallucination that one of their members had made a particular remark, the substance of which had never even entered that member's head; and that it is a recognised custom to write mournful letters about bereavements which have never occurred; and that when A describes to a friend how he has distinctly heard the voice of B, it is not infrequently a slip of the tongue for C; and that when D says he is not subject to hallucinations of vision, it is through momentary forgetfulness of the fact that he has a spectral illusion once a week; and that when a wife interrupts a husband's slumbers with words of distress or alarm, it is only her fun, or a sudden morbid craving for undeserved sympathy; and that when people assert that they were in sound health, in good spirits, and wide awake, at a particular time which they had occasion to note, it is a safe conclusion that they were having a nightmare, or were the prostrate victims of nervous hypochondria. Every one of these improbabilities is, perhaps, in itself a possibility; but as the narratives drive us from one desperate expedient to another, when time after time

we are compelled to own that deliberate falsification is less unlikely than the assumptions we are making, and then again when we submit the theory of deliberate falsification to the cumulative test, and see what is involved in the supposition that hundreds of persons of established character, known to us for the most part and unknown to one another, have simultaneously formed a plot to deceive us—there comes a point where the reason rebels. Common-sense persists in recognising that when phenomena, which are united by a fundamental characteristic and have every appearance of forming a single natural group, are presented to be explained, an explanation which multiplies causes is improbable, and an explanation which multiplies improbable causes becomes, at a certain point, incredible.[1]

It was furthermore (Gurney felt) quite impossible to convey in print the full impression which personal contact with the witnesses had made upon him. On 20th January 1887 he wrote to William James:

> I cannot describe to you the effect on my own mind which my hundreds of personal interviews have had. It has only been in a very small number of cases . . . that a case which seemed genuine and sound on paper has not been *strengthened* by the impression (& often by the details) which conversation and careful cross-questioning added. I have again & again & again come away with a real feeling of irritation & discontent at having been the only outsider who was present, & the only one who had had a chance of getting the impression which *deserved* to be got; & which I have almost entirely refrained from even trying to express in the book, as it seemed to me undesirable to give testimonials & to weary the reader's patience & put his back up by forcing on him my view of the character of my witnesses, which he had no chance of confirming or refuting. The most frequent features of the favourable impression have been (1) the realisation as to most of the evidence given of its independence of any silly supernatural notions—this has constantly been the rule rather than the exception; and (2) the realisation, especially in the sensorial cases, of the *uniqueness* of the experience. The viva voce account has constantly struck me as just what you or I might give of a singular experience, which *did happen*, but which was wholly isolated & inexplicable.

---

[1] *Phantasms* I, pp. 163–4.

But even if we agree (as I for one would agree) that the coincidences between deaths and apparitions cannot readily be dismissed on evidential grounds, it would still not follow that anything 'paranormal' is involved in them. We might argue as follows: The labours of the Literary Committee have shown that waking hallucinations are much commoner than we might have supposed even among sane people. Now given this fact—interesting no doubt, but hardly paranormal—we should of course expect that occasionally A will see the 'apparition' of B at or around the time when B chances to die. A may well suppose that the apparition was in some way caused by B's death. He will, of course, be mistaken, the relation between the two being quite fortuitous (and very possibly exaggerated in retrospect).

Gurney dealt with the chance coincidence explanation in one of the most interesting parts of *Phantasms of the Living*. He conducted a census, in which the following question was put to a sample of 5,705 persons:

> Since January 1, 1874, have you—when in good health, free from anxiety, and completely awake—had a vivid impression of seeing or being touched by a human being, or of hearing a voice or sound which suggested a human presence, when no one was there? Yes or no?[1]

Twenty-one persons reported that they had in the period concerned had a visual hallucination of someone they knew; these twenty-one persons had between them had twenty-three hallucinations.

Amongst the cases obtained by the Literary Committee through personal contacts and appeals in periodicals were thirty-two well-attested visual crisis apparitions which had occurred within the last twelve years; they are all printed in *Phantasms of the Living*. An apparition was considered to be a 'crisis' apparition if it coincided to within twelve hours either way with the death of the presumed agent. Gurney estimated that the number of persons who might have seen or heard of the Committee's appeals for cases would at the outside have been 300,000. He then argued as follows. His census sample of 5,705 persons had between them had over the last twelve years 23

[1] *Phantasms* II, p. 7.

visual hallucinations of recognised persons, or one hallucination to every 248 people. The death rate *per diem* of the country's population was at that time 1 in 16,590. Therefore if upon one and only one occasion A has a visual hallucination of B, a living or hitherto living person, the chances that the day of its occurrence will also be the day of B's death will likewise be 1 in 16,590. Now during the last twelve years 1 person in 248 has had such a recognised hallucination. The probability that any one person taken at random will have had a coincidental visual hallucination during the last twelve years should therefore according to chance expectation be 1 in (16,590 x 248), or about 1 in 4,000,000. The odds against finding in a field of 300,000 32 persons who have had coincidental hallucinations will be roughly a trillion of trillion of trillions to one.

Gurney also made similar, though somewhat less startling, calculations in respect of auditory hallucinations; and it is hard indeed to see how the theory of chance coincidence can be sustained. Gurney's arguments however present difficulties which will be touched on later.

Although it is hard to sustain the theory that the correlations between recognised visual hallucinations and the deaths of the persons recognised in the hallucinations are purely accidental, it is not altogether easy to accept the rival view, that the correlations may be set down to telepathy. For even if we disregard the thorny question of whether or not there is any sound evidence for telepathy, the telepathic theory still faces some awkward problems over the fact that apparitions, including crisis apparitions, are sometimes *collectively* perceived, that is, are simultaneously seen in the same place by more than one percipient. The mere fact that an hallucination can be shared itself requires an explanation (and also, of course, raises some tricky ontological problems). As regards collective crisis apparitions, Gurney argued as follows: it is very difficult to suppose that in collective cases the two percipients B and C are separately and independently affected by telepathic impressions from the agent A. For in view of the fact, noted above, that the details of a crisis apparition seem generally to be supplied by the percipient rather than the agent, it would seem most unlikely that B and C would each create similar phantasms of A, and even more unlikely that (as sometimes happens) B would create a figure standing face on to him, whilst C, at right angles to B, creates a complementary profile version. And again there would on this hypothesis be no reason why the percipients should in the great majority of cases be *together* when they see the apparition.

An alternative idea would be that B receives a telepathic impression from A, and then passes it to C by a further process of thought-transference—of 'telepathic infection' as it were. On this theory we would expect to find cases in which hallucinations *not* originating from a distant agent have been passed from one person to another. Little, if any, evidence of this kind had (and has) come to light. But perhaps, Gurney felt, our best bet might be to try an amalgamation of the two hypotheses. The fact that in most of the collective cases the several percipients were at the same spot might suggest that simple community of scene can establish conditions favourable to thought-transference. And we might then suppose further that A might telepathically affect both B and C, but that C's hallucination may derive its character in some way from B's; or that, if C is unknown to A, and therefore unlikely to receive a telepathic impression from him, a rapport may be established between A and C through the rapport of both of them with B; or that the rapport between B and C may in fact be established through their joint rapport with A.

Myers dissented from these somewhat complicated and cumbrous speculations, which certainly far outrun the known facts; and he propounded a theory of his own in a note which concludes the main portion of *Phantasms*. The clue to the understanding of apparitions in general, and of collective apparitions in particular, might, he thought, be found in cases of *clairvoyance*—especially of 'independent clairvoyance' (often called 'travelling' clairvoyance), in which 'the clairvoyant seems to visit scenes, or to discern objects, without needing that those scenes or objects should form part of the perception or memory of any known mind'.[1] The evidence for independent clairvoyance was indeed, Myers conceded, not strong, being mostly scattered, and not of an experimental kind. But there is a little evidence that such clairvoyance can be initiated by someone (a mesmerist) with whom the percipient might be supposed to

[1] *Phantasms* II, p. 286.

be in rapport. There is also some suggestion that the clairvoyant faculty is at its keenest when the percipient is in a coma or a trance or even dangerously ill. Now the S.P.R. had amongst its records a few, a very few, first-hand accounts of 'reciprocal' cases; cases, that is, in which a person who imagines himself to be viewing (as if from an appropriate point of view) some distant scene, had in fact been perceived at that scene by a person present there. As Myers expressed it: 'Correspondently with clairvoyant perception there may be phantasmogenetic efficiency.'[1] It would of course be possible to explain many such cases in terms of reciprocal telepathy; but Myers preferred to put a different interpretation upon them:

> I treat the respective hallucinations of each member of the affected group as each and all directly generated by a conception in a distant mind—a conception which presents itself to that mind as though its centre of activity were translated to the scene where the group are sitting, and which presents itself to each member of that group as though their hallucinations did not come to them incoherently or independently, but were diffused from a 'radiant point,' or phantasmogenetic focus, corresponding with that region of space where the distant agent conceives himself to be exercising his supernormal perception.[2]

Myers thinks that what happens in collective crisis cases is that the dying man's conception of himself as at a certain scene or with a particular person presents itself in a fully externalised fashion to persons who are present at the scene in question, and who are endowed with a certain idiosyncratic sensitivity. That it actually is the dying man's conception of himself that in some obscure way *externalises* itself at a particular point in space is suggested by various considerations. For instance the details of an apparition's appearance, its clothing etc., are almost always such as *could* have originated from the dying man; and are sometimes such as *must* have come from him (for instance when the apparition wears clothes which the percipient did not know the agent possessed). Again the fact that there are various cases of purely *local* apparitions rather suggests that a percipient may simply witness a phantasm generated by causes external to himself. It may be that it is to reciprocal cases that we should

---

[1] *Phantasms* II, p. 289.   [2] *Phantasms* II, p. 291.

turn for a fuller understanding of how a man's conception of himself may be externalised in these ways.

In a letter to William James of 16th January 1887, Gurney said of Myers' theory: 'Myers's note seems to me a hopeless attempt to present a frankly material view of ghosts with elimination of the material element, & I don't see how my objections to it ... Vol II pp 269–70 can be answered.' But Gurney's own theory is so complex and invokes so many unknowns (such as 'rapport' between percipients, and the 'channeling' of the agent's telepathic message through percipient B to percipient C) that one wonders whether the ingenuity he devotes to expounding it might not have been equally well employed in dismissing the phenomena, or at any rate collective apparitions, altogether. Nor is it clear (at least to me) how his blending of two totally unsatisfactory kinds of telepathic theory can produce a satisfactory one. However, Gurney was himself fully aware of the difficulties. The letter to William James, quoted above, goes on:

> But I am not happy as to my own view. All I would say is that one must use the words & ideas that already exist; and that the phenomenon of collective percipience is *more like* what we call hallucination than what we call perception of the external world. But I cannot help supposing that the *community* of percipience implies objectivity, of a sort, of whose basis & limits we know nothing.

In this decidedly unsatisfactory state theorising about crisis and collective cases has rested ever since; the phenomena remain as puzzling as ever.

Phantasms of the Living was published in October 1886; it had been delayed for some months by a fire at the printers'. It did not at first attract a great deal of notice from the world at large. The *Westminster* gave it a reasonable notice, *Mind* a short but polite one. *The Times* devoted a leader to it on 30th October. Several reviews attempted to be humorous, with a marked lack of success. However, the following year a number of extended attacks on it appeared. The one which attracted most attention in this country was A. T. Innes' 'Where are the Letters?' in *The Nineteenth Century* for August 1887. Innes remarked that

Phantasms provides us with plenty of good evidence about the deaths involved in the crisis cases. But 'the real question is on the other side, What evidence do the editors adduce that the "percipients" at a distance felt or perceived at the time what they now tell the editors they did?' The most conclusive kind of evidence would be a contemporary letter of the percipient's describing his experience, and immediately posted to a third party. Of much less value, though still not valueless, would be a contemporary memorandum retained by the percipient.

To despatch a letter or to make such a memorandum would be a natural thing for the percipient of an apparition to do, and indeed many percipients (some forty of them) allege that they in fact wrote such documents. None the less, the authors of *Phantasms* have not seen the crucial letter in a single case; and they have seen memoranda only in nine cases. Even these memoranda are in most instances either too brief to be of service, or else not quoted verbatim by the authors.

Now we cannot expect that percipients will always write letters or make memoranda about their experiences, though we should expect them to do so in many cases. But where a percipient claims that he did indeed write such a letter or make such a memorandum, or where it seems very likely that he would have written or made one, and where he now states that the letter or memorandum concerned has been lost or destoryed, we have good grounds for suspicion. People simply would not lose or destroy such letters or memoranda—rather they would preserve them carefully. Yet cases in which contemporary documents have allegedly been lost or destroyed figure amongst those to which the authors of *Phantasms* attach most weight.

In his reply Gurney, as well as disagreeing with Innes' treatment of various individual cases, suggested that his arguments were based upon three false assumptions.

(*a*) *That the percipients of apparitions would immediately write letters describing their experiences.* What of their very probable fear of being thought superstitious, and of the likelihood that they have no confidential correspondents?

(*b*) *That if such letters were written they would be preserved.* After all, most people have never given thought to the problems of telepathy, and could not be expected to see the importance of preserving evidence. Why should they retain a letter or memorandum once they had verified the coincidence to their own satisfaction? And the cases in which memoranda *have* been preserved can hardly just be set aside as Innes sets them aside, unless we are prepared to regard them all as instances of fraud.

(*c*) *That a flaw in a record in respect of a detail at once vitiates the whole thing.* 'Our experience of human testimony does not support the sweeping assertion that a narrative must be substantially and fundamentally false, because it has followed a certain common and natural law of growth in respect of details inessential to its central incidents.'

I am myself inclined to think that Gurney's view of human nature is, so far as the preservation of records is concerned, a truer one than Innes'. After all, Gurney could back his assertions with the experience he had gained in the course of interviewing and corresponding with hundreds of percipients.

Very much less courteous than Innes' article was a critique of *Phantasms* by the American philosopher C. S. Peirce which appeared the following December in the *Proceedings* of the American S.P.R. Peirce suggested, in tones which did not hide a consciousness of superior wisdom, that each single one of the visual crisis cases published in *Phantasms* violated one or more of the eighteen conditions which they should have fulfilled to be acceptable as evidence. Among those conditions were: that the percipient should not have had any other hallucination than the one concerned; that he should have been in good health; that he should not have been suffering from anxiety; that his testimony should not be loose or inaccurate; that he should have confided the story to a third party before news of the agent's death arrived; that the apparition should have been clearly and immediately recognised; and that it should undoubtedly have occurred within the twelve-hour limit. Unfortunately Peirce's study of the cases in question had not been sufficiently careful, and Gurney was able to point out in his reply that Peirce had time and again misunderstood, misrepresented and even misquoted them. Peirce's rejoinder was lengthy and querulous, and Gurney was able to deal with it much as before. None the less Peirce did light upon two serious objections to Gurney's arguments against the theory of chance coincidence. The first objection was that people are more likely to forget hallucinations which do not coincide with deaths than hallucinations which do; this would of course have meant that the odds against the thirty-two coincidental cases in *Phantasms* being the results of chance-coincidence were much less than Gurney had suggested. The second of Peirce's objections was that in assessing at 300,000 the number of people likely to have come within range of the Literary Committee's appeals for cases Gurney was very considerably underestimating the extent to which stories of apparitions get around. Gurney's figure had been based largely upon the circulation of the periodicals in which notices had appeared; but of course anyone at all who had seen a ghost might well have told the story to one of several friends each of whom might have seen the appeal and mentioned it to him.

It was, on the data then available, quite impossible to say quite definitely that Peirce was wrong on these points, though Gurney contested them in various ways. But a few years later the 'Census of Hallucinations' drew the sting from both of Peirce's arguments.[1]

The last of Gurney's replies to Peirce was published posthumously, and was completed by a note from Myers. Gurney himself had died in a Brighton hotel, alone and tragically, on 23rd June 1888, seemingly of an overdose of chloroform. His death at the early age of forty-one was perhaps the greatest single blow that psychical research has ever suffered; and it was not, I think, a light one to psychology in general. His work in psychical research had come to absorb him completely, and he was in many ways uniquely gifted for it. He was deeply versed in relevant literature of all kinds—psychological, physiological, philosophical, mesmeric—and when the working fit was upon him his industry was prodigious. The powers of analysis and classification which he displayed in handling the enormous mass of refractory material comprised in *Phantasms of the Living* are of the highest order, and his powers of theorising and of perceiving fresh avenues of investigation did not lag behind. In controversy he was at his best, relishing the stimulus, conscious of his powers, master of the facts. He was always polite and frequently humorous, and his cool intelligence usually enabled

[1] See below, pp. 182–5.

him to cut just that much deeper than his opponent. No one however could have been more prompt in acknowledging mistakes. To William James he wrote on 31st March 1885:

> I think our case is *really* strong enough to show that the subject ought to be earnestly prosecuted, & it is a great mistake to discount the result by the slightest exaggeration of its strength. I feel that every sentence written on these matters ought absolutely to *reek* with candour.

It has sometimes been suggested, and most especially by Mr. Trevor Hall, that Gurney was so naïve a person, and himself so absolutely honest, that he was incapable of supposing others likely to deceive him, and was hence liable to be taken in by charlatans. And it is indeed true that his belief in the goodness and the good faith of his friends was unfailing. But he was well acquainted with divers kinds of Spiritualistic frauds and with all sorts of possible sources of mistaken testimony and of experimental error, and I can detect no signs of excess credulity in *Phantasms* or in his other writings. 'That Gurney was credulous and easily imposed upon,' observed Andrew Lang, 'those who knew him, and knew his penetrating humour, cannot admit; nor is the theory likely to be maintained by those whom bias does not prevent from studying with care his writings.'[1]

Gurney's intellectual gifts will be obvious to anyone who gives serious attention just to *Phantasms of the Living*; but his personality remains a little obscure. His many friends liked and admired him intensely, not just for his brilliant conversation and his intellectual gifts, but for his humour, his kindliness, the penetration with which he would divine their troubles, the sympathy with which he would share in them. Jane Harrison recollected him as perhaps 'the most lovable and beautiful human being I ever met'.[2] During a visit to Cambridge in May 1873 George Eliot was so struck with his good looks that for several days she could think of nothing else, and 'she afterwards discovered that his mind was as beautiful as his face'.[3]

---

[1] *Encyclopaedia Britannica*, 11th edn., Cambridge, 1911, s.v. 'Gurney, Edmund'.
[2] Jane Harrison, *Reminiscences of a Student's Life*, London, 1925, p. 55.
[3] O. Browning, *Life of George Eliot*, London, 1890, p. 116. The famous occasion on which George Eliot walked with Myers in the Fellows' Garden at Trinity (see Myers' *Essays Modern*, pp. 268–9) seems to have been in May or June 1877. See *The George Eliot Letters*, ed. G. S. Haight, London, 1954, VI, p. 380. George Eliot is said to have founded the character of Daniel Deronda in part on Gurney. In

'Nothing was wanting,' said Myers in an unpublished fragment of autobiography, 'from the deep earnest loving utterances—ingots from the treasure-house of his heart;—to the ironic mockery which places one outside a trouble, and shows flashingly its transitoriness in the sum of things.'

On the other hand some people seem to have found Gurney cold and aloof, and his conversation, however brilliant, impersonal and sarcastic. Even those who genuinely liked and admired him were sometimes disconcerted by his manner. Lady Battersea noted in her diary for 2nd September 1881: 'Mr. Gurney talks too much of humanity really to care for it.'[1] Myers, in a letter to his wife dated 5th July 1884, mentions: '... a moonlight walk with the Coon [sc. Gurney] who feels sadly that he does not get people to feel how much he cares for them and sympathises with them,—owing to something in his manner which they think sarcastic'. Perhaps the answer may be that only highly educated and perceptive persons could even begin to appreciate Gurney. If one could neither grasp the nature of his intellectual perplexities nor sense the despair which they too often occasioned him, one might well suspect that his continual talk about the human predicament was a pose, and take literally the mockery and self-mockery with which he would partially hide his feelings.

Those who understood Gurney found him a most lovable person; and in their affection, and in a sense of common endeavour with them in some worthwhile undertaking, he found the chief source of the little happiness which life brought him. In December 1887 he wrote to Myers:

> Your letter was an *immense* comfort. I had divined that you had also been at a low water mark in another way. I am glad *you* can do, what I believe *no one* else could do,—perceive how little my appearance of agnostic & gloomy isolation answers to my real inside. The difference between us is that I cannot *make*

---

this connection an entry in the diaries of Lady Battersea (wife of Cyril Flower, later Lord Battersea, a College friend of Myers') for 3rd June 1879 may be of interest. 'Mr. Gurney is a fine, good creature. We talked of George Eliot and of Daniel Deronda. Mr. G. thinks it the most remarkable of her works, as it contains a grand idea: How one fine nature can become the salvation of a narrow egotistical one, how it can open the gates of heaven to a poor *earth bound* soul' (B.M. Add. MS. 47932).

[1] B.M. Add. MS. 47934.

definite the issues which—could we know them—might reconcile us to our fates. Meanwhile the *one* thing I can cleave to is the sense of union in the depths—& in the heights if there are any.

Gurney would not, I think, have been a happy man in any age, and his nature and the circumstances of his death made some people fear or suspect that he might have committed suicide. According to his daughter's account of what her mother told her, Gurney received on the Thursday before his death a letter asking him to go to Brighton.[1] He left for Brighton on the Friday. On the afternoon of the following day, Saturday, 23rd June, the door of his room in the Royal Albion Hotel was found to be still locked, and was broken in. Gurney was dead in his bed. He lay on his left side, his right hand holding over his nose and mouth some cotton wool covered by a sponge bag. A small empty bottle stood nearby.

An inquest was held on the Monday. A slight suggestion of suicide was raised, but it was overborne by other testimony. Gurney's brother Alfred, vicar of St. Barnabas, Pimlico, and author of various devotional works, stated that Gurney had been accustomed to use narcotics to relieve persistent neuralgia and insomnia. Myers' brother Arthur, a physician and an old friend of Gurney's, testified similarly, and added that he had often discussed with Gurney the use of chloroform as an analgesic or narcotic, but had no certain knowledge that he had ever tried it.[2] Evidence was produced that shortly before his

---

[1] Hall, *op. cit.*, p. 5.

[2] Hall, *op. cit.*, pp. 1–26, suggests that Arthur and Frederic Myers, together presumably with the Rev. Alfred Gurney, conspired to invent the story about the neuralgia to deceive the jury into recording a verdict of death by misadventure. No doubt they would have done their best, both for Gurney's sake and the S.P.R.'s, to present a favourable picture to the court; but the supposition that a respectable physician and a clergyman of high repute and outstanding piety would conspire together to commit perjury in this way seems to me quite fantastic. I have commented on Mr. Hall's arguments, *J.S.P.R.* XLIII (1965), pp. 57–9. That Gurney did in fact suffer from neuralgia is, as Broad remarks (*loc. cit.*), at least strongly suggested by some passages in *Tertium Quid*. 'Even the most confident view of the desirability of mundane existence may be considerably modified in the course of a night's neuralgia' (I, p. 33); 'To any person who would choose . . . that all the human race should suffer this night from face-ache, rather than that one . . . should pass it on the rack, the distinction is essential' (I, pp. 181–2). 'Thus anyone might fairly choose that B should have a very bad face-ache sooner than that a thousand other people should have a rather bad one' (I, p. 185). In one of his letters to William James, Gurney remarks that he was once much troubled by insomnia, and in another he describes a visit to a dentist and some experiences

death Gurney had been actively planning his future, and the jury returned a verdict of 'accidentally suffocated by an overdose of chloroform taken probably for the relief of pain'.

None the less, some people had doubts. Henry James wrote to William James on 26th June 1888[1] that 'suicide is *suspected* I gather—from the strangeness of the form of his death. But he was only *generally* unhappy, and was even "cheerful" up to the last. Therefore it seems improbable.' Sidgwick confessed in his Journal that he had 'painful doubts'. At least one member of the Sidgwick circle seems to have become convinced that Gurney's death was suicidal. The 'third case C.', whom Richard Hodgson cites (*P.S.P.R.* XIII, p. 350) among his instances of communicators supposedly confused because their 'passings' had been suicidal, was in fact Gurney (as may be seen by comparing the passage with *P.S.P.R.* XXVIII, p. 303). However, it appears from a letter written by Mrs. Sidgwick to Sir Oliver Lodge on 25th July 1915[2] that Hodgson's belief probably originated from his hearing something of the contents of some extremely private 'communications' which a *soi-disant* Gurney gave to Myers and Lodge in 1889 and 1890 through the American medium, Mrs. Piper.[3] Since Mrs. Sidgwick says she

---

under nitrous oxide. Arthur Myers wrote a long letter to his brother Frederic on the day of the Inquest, and I can find no hint of any conspiracy in it.

[1] Houghton Library, Harvard University.

[2] Mrs. Sidgwick's own views on Gurney's death do not appear very clearly from the letter. She says: 'Re Gurney—I cannot of course mention the possibility of suicide [in her forthcoming paper on Mrs. Piper] and cannot therefore say what I feel hardly any doubt is the real explanation of the "balled-up"-ness in America namely that Hodgson had made up his mind by the time Mrs. P. returned to America that it was suicide and had a theory that suicides were confused for a long time after death. He discusses this theory in his second report Vol. XIII, p. 350 and compare p. 377. "The third case C." was Gurney [footnote omitted] (as by the way it will be possible for a detective to discover after my paper is published, for I quote the sentence at the end of the paragraph on p. 350. However it is most unlikely that anyone will put two and two together and it would not much matter perhaps if they did).

'Hodgson must have known what you said about Gurney in Vol. VI as soon as that was published (1890 or 91) but I do not know how much more he knew. It is very unlikely that anyone wrote to him about the evidential communications, they were so extremely private. None of us ever saw the records I think unless it was Myers. When Hodgson's second report was published he evidently knew something, but where he learnt it I do not know. It might have been told him while the proofs were being revised.'

[3] See *P.S.P.R.* VI, pp. 493, 516, 524, 552, 645; XXIII, pp. 140–62; XXVIII, pp. 300–5.

thinks that only Myers saw the seance records, it seems *possible* that it was from Myers that Hodgson received the information concerned.[1] But the relevant parts of the records were destroyed, and one can hardly even contemplate attaching any weight to secondhand accounts of evidence from beyond the grave; except perhaps in so far as the reception of that evidence shows that some of those who were well acquainted with Gurney and with his circumstances did not find it inconceivable that he might have committed suicide.

Could something have happened to Gurney on 22nd June 1888 to precipitate a particularly severe attack of depression? Mr. Trevor Hall has lately suggested that it might have done.[2] In 1882 and 1883 Gurney and Myers had conducted in Brighton and London some experiments in the telepathic transference of drawings and other material. The subjects were G. A. Smith, a young Brightonian, and Douglas Blackburn, a local journalist. The experiments were seemingly successful. Smith was a talented young man and was, *inter alia*, a very gifted hypnotist (he had been giving stage demonstrations of hypnosis and thought-reading). After the experiments Gurney employed Smith as a secretary, and his hypnotic abilities proved very useful in subsequent experimental work. Smith acted as hypnotist both in straightforward hypnotic experiments, and in experiments in telepathy under hypnosis; he continued to help with such experiments for several years after Gurney's death (see Appendix A). Many years later, in 1908 and again in 1911, Blackburn confessed in print[3] that he and Smith (who was now doing well in the new field of cine-photography) had deceived Gurney and Myers in 1882 and 1883 by the successful operation of a code. Smith strongly denied the charge. None the less Mr. Hall thinks it probable that Smith deceived Gurney not merely in 1882–3, but also in the later experiments; he often provided subjects for them from among his own acquaintances at Brighton. Now at the time of Gurney's death, Smith was away on his honeymoon, and this makes Gurney's visit to Brighton

[1] Myers, however, wrote to William James on 28th Feb. 1890 that the principal secret revealed by the Gurney communicator was 'nothing about his *death*, nor about his *wife*—but a matter wh. cd. not be guessed at, rightly or wrongly'. But more than one 'secret' seems to have been revealed.
[2] *Op. cit.*, pp. 174–99.
[3] In *John Bull*, Dec. 1908 and Jan. 1909; and the *Daily News*, 1st Sept. 1911.

hard to explain, for he usually went down there to carry out experiments with Smith's assistance. Mr. Hall suggests that during Smith's absence someone (perhaps his sister) anxious to extricate him from his life of deception, wrote to Gurney and, upon his arrival at Brighton, presented him with complete evidence of Smith's duplicity. Gurney had recently been upset by Innes' and Peirce's criticisms of *Phantasms* (Mr. Hall believes that these were shattering), and by the detection in fraud of the Creery sisters, the experiments with whom had figured prominently in *Phantasms*. The unmasking of Smith finally brought home to Gurney the fact that all his work lay in ruins and, in despair, he chloroformed himself.

There is however no reason for scenting a mystery in the fact that Gurney paid a visit to Brighton without Smith. It has lately been pointed out that Gurney had recently become interested in a haunted house there.[1] He had interviewed the chief witness, apparently at Brighton, on 13th June 1888,[2] the very day on which Smith was married at Ramsgate. It is of course at least conceivable that Gurney made away with himself in a sudden fit of depression occasioned by learning something about Smith, perhaps from an accidental meeting with one of their subjects. But there are some obvious objections. It is very difficult to see why Mr. Hall thinks the discovery of Smith's duplicity would have been the complete ruination of Gurney's work; many of his most interesting hypnotic experiments did not depend in any way on Smith's integrity; and his main work, *Phantasms of the Living*, was, I venture to think, very little damaged by Innes and Peirce, and in Gurney's eyes hardly damaged at all.

Again it seems very odd that Smith should have risked a comfortable berth by continued cheating (if indeed he had cheated in the first place);[3] experiments in telepathy were only

---

[1] See *P.S.P.R.* VI (1889), pp. 256–70.
[2] *P.S.P.R.* VI, p. 264. Gurney may have stayed at Brighton for some days. *The Brighton Gazette and Fashionable Visitors List* for Thursday, 14th June 1888, says that a 'Mr. Gurney' had arrived at 56 Middle Street, presumably a lodging-house. But the name Gurney is too common for one to be sure that it was Edmund. Gurney's memorandum of his visit of 13th June is headed '18 Prestonville Road'. It is preserved in the S.P.R. archives.
[3] Blackburn's career and character are obscure, but they do not seem to have

a small part of his duties, and it is extremely unlikely that his livelihood in any way depended on his obtaining positive results. He was often employed by the S.P.R. to investigate mediums and haunted houses, and his reports are generally quite level-headed.[1] There are however two definite hints that he may have practised deception in the later experiments in which he was involved.[2] The first is an entry in Sidgwick's Journal for 5th July 1885, concerning experiments at Brighton for which Smith was the hypnotist-agent and a lad named Conway the subject-percipient. Sidgwick fancied that Smith might have given Conway hints by slight sounds: but Gurney was absolutely convinced of Smith's honesty. The second is the following extract from a letter of Myers to his wife, dated 6th April 1891: 'I have had a long talk about *Brighton* [where Smith had been acting as hypnotist for some experiments on telepathy under hypnosis] at Hillside. Mrs. Sidgwick will go very soon, meantime *nothing is to be said to anyone* about suspicious circumstances. Most important that *nothing* should leak out—you won't tell *Arthur* or *anyone*, I am sure.' But in both these cases the suspicions aroused seem to have been allayed.

If Gurney indeed committed suicide as a result of learning that Smith had been deceiving him, it would not, I am sure, have been because he felt his work had been destroyed, but for a personal reason—that Smith had now become a close friend. Something of the relation between the two may perhaps be gathered from a letter which Gurney wrote to William James on 16th April 1886:

> Smith's *bona fides* is quite beyond all doubt to anyone who knows him. I know him, I believe, quite completely. He has been acting as my private secretary for more than a year—with me for hours a day, & I believe I know his character as well as, say, you have known that of any one of your pupils. He has been my pupil in a sense. He is blameless & acute, perfectly steady and self-respecting, devoted to the work, & excellent at tracing impostures.

---

been such as to inspire complete confidence in his 'confessions', see *J.S.P.R.* XLIII (1965), pp. 222–3.
[1] See e.g. *J.S.P.R.* I (1885), pp. 313–17; *P.S.P.R.* XI (1895), pp. 225–8.
[2] Mr. Hall's criticisms of these experiments, *op. cit.*, pp. 159–68, have themselves been subjected to criticism.

As to whether or not Gurney did indeed commit suicide I can express no firm opinion. In a person of his depressive tendencies there would probably have been no need for a specific incident to have tipped the scales; nor would there have been perhaps any clear dividing line between the deliberate use of too much chloroform and a carelessness engendered by despair.

Sidgwick and his friends were dismayed—even shattered by Gurney's death. Myers felt the blow particularly. 'For fifteen years', he wrote to Lady Battersea on 4th July 1888, 'we had been as intimate and as attached to each other as men can be;—every part of our respective natures found response by comprehension in the other. But I will not say more of that.'

The remaining members of the group divided up Gurney's work amongst them as best they could. Myers and Podmore became joint Honorary Secretaries of the S.P.R., and Sidgwick took on the editorship of the Society's publications. In the spring of 1889 work was begun on a project which Gurney had long had in mind—a 'Census of Hallucinations' which would finally answer arguments like those put forward by C. S. Peirce (see above, pp. 173–4). The Census was conducted in connection with the International Congresses of Psychology referred to above (p. 147). There were parallel censuses in France, Germany, Russia and Brazil; however, the English census was much the most extensive, and I shall not deal with the others.

The committee which was responsible for the tremendous task of obtaining, analysing and writing up the returns consisted of Mrs. Sidgwick, Miss Alice Johnson and Sidgwick himself, together with Frank Podmore and Dr. A. T. Myers, though the two first named carried out most of the work. The 'Census Question' was this:

> Have you ever, when believing yourself to be completely awake, had a vivid impression of seeing or being touched by a living being or inanimate object, or of hearing a voice; which impression, so far as you could discover, was not due to any external physical cause?

There were 410 volunteer collectors, mostly members of the S.P.R. or their friends; each collector was requested to put the census question to twenty-five persons, or a multiple thereof, over the age of twenty-one. There was of course a possibility that collectors (although instructed not to do so) might be inclined to seek out persons whom they already knew to have experienced an hallucination. As a control against this, the Census question was also put to whole groups of people—all the guests at a given dinner-party, all the workers at a given factory, and so forth—who could not have been specially selected in this way.

Answers were obtained from 17,000 people (the original target of 50,000 proving quite impracticable). Of these persons 2,272 answered in the affirmative; but when obvious instances of dream and delirium were ruled out, the number was reduced to 1,684. These 1,684 persons had had between them 1,942 hallucinations. The 1,942 hallucinations included rather over 300 recognised visual hallucinations of persons known to the percipient; and of these 80 coincided within twelve hours either way with the deaths of the supposed agents.

However, there were complications. For it was quite clear from the returns that people were much more liable to forget hallucinations which did not coincide with deaths than to forget ones which did—this, it will be remembered, was one of Peirce's objections to Gurney's claim that the number of coincidental hallucinations greatly exceeded chance. The Census Committee calculated from a comparison of the most recent hallucinations with more distant ones that this effect would be offset if the number of non-coincidental hallucinations was assumed to be four times as great as the number actually reported. This left 80 coincidental cases out of a presumed 1,300.

The Committee then examined these 80 cases, and for one reason or another eliminated 48 of them (including almost all those which the collector might have known about beforehand). This left 32 cases better evidenced than the rest. In the majority of these cases there was independent testimony of one kind or another that the percipient had mentioned the apparition before hearing of the agent's death; in at least 10 of them the percipient had not the slightest reason to expect the death of the agent. Now calculation from the Registrar-General's tables of the time showed that the chances of any one person taken at random dying on a given day were 1 in 19,000; and the chance that any given single event, such as a non-recurrent recognised hallucination of a certain person, would occur on the same day as the death of any person taken at random was therefore also 1 in 19,000. One recognised visual hallucination out of 19,000 should by chance alone be a death coincidence. The actual number of death coincidences, 32 out of 1,300, is 440 times the chance expectation.

It might of course be observed at this point that the statistical reasoning here is suspect. It talks of the chances of a person taken at random dying on a given day; but on a given day all people are not equally likely to die. If, as seems not impossible, one is more likely to have an hallucination of a person who is elderly or sick than of a person who is young and fit, then of course hallucinations will coincide with deaths more frequently than chance would at first sight suggest. However, this point was taken up by Miss Alice Johnson in reply to the criticisms of Herr Edmund Parish; and she was able to show that in the 32 crisis cases which the Census Report finally left standing the ages of the decedents were distributed amongst all age groups roughly as the Registrar-General's tables would lead one to predict.[1] There was no especial loading with elderly people. And the Census Committee had already pointed out that in at least 10 of the crucial 32 cases the percipient had no apprehension whatever that any misfortune was likely to befall the decedent.

The methods by which the Census was conducted were of course antiquated and would certainly not be regarded as satisfactory today. None the less it was a work on a considerable scale, and one cannot easily point to any conclusions drawn by the Census Committee which the data do not justify. The *Report on the Census of Hallucinations*[2] without doubt threw the onus on the critic. It was no longer up to psychical researchers to give reasons for supposing that there is a correlation between deaths and crisis apparitions. It was up to whoever disputed this to find stratagems ingenious enough to explain away the evidence.[3]

---

[1] *P.S.P.R.* XI (1895), pp. 170–1.

[2] *P.S.P.R.* X (1894), pp. 25–422.

[3] The criticisms of Herr Edmund Parish, referred to above, seem to me not worth summarising. See his *Ueber die Trugwahrnehmung*, Leipzig, 1894, and an

English version, *Hallucinations and Illusions*, London, 1897; and cf. the very amusing attack on him by Andrew Lang, *The Making of Religion*, 2nd edn., London, 1900, pp. 307–23. Of greater interest is N. Vaschide's *Les Hallucinations Télépathiques*, Paris, 1908. Vaschide collected from 34 experiments 1,374 cases of subjective 'Hallucinations'. Of these 1,325 were thought by the subjects of them to be 'veridical'. But investigation showed that only 48 cases were in fact veridical. Vaschide seems to think that this finding invalidates the results of the *Census of Hallucinations* and of *Phantasms of the Living*; but he seems to use the term 'hallucination' to cover a far wider variety of subjective experiences than Gurney or the Census Committee did (so that e.g. vivid mental images are included), and his results do not appear to me to be in the least comparable to theirs. Ivor Ll. Tuckett, *The Evidence for the Supernatural*, London, 1911, pp. 297–305, repeats the arguments of Innes, Parish and Vaschide.

Several critics of the evidence for 'crisis' apparitions have relied heavily on the one or two cases published by the S.P.R. in which flaws have subsequently been found. Material (so far unpublished) has lately come to hand suggesting that in the most popular of such cases—that of the 'Hornby' apparition—the percipient may not after all have been mistaken (cf. *J.S.P.R.* XLIII (1965), pp. 61–2); but one of the cases (not a crisis case) printed in *Phantasms* later turned out to have been a hoax. The usual assumption seems to be that if we can once show that some case which was thought well-evidenced enough for publication was in fact unsound, no accumulation of other cases of similar evidential standard will provide us with satisfactory evidence for the phenomenon, for we can now see that evidence such as that presented in each case is in fact not foolproof. The cases cannot 'add up'. This seems to me quite fallacious; good evidence does not become bad evidence because evidence of *that* standard has sometimes been faulted. Good evidence is simply evidence of a kind which in the great majority of cases has proved trustworthy. The most able attempt to apply such arguments which I know is D. J. West's 'The Investigation of Spontaneous Cases', *P.S.P.R.* XLVIII (1948), pp. 264–305. But Dr. West stops short of extremes.

VIII Phantasms of the Dead

Phantasms of the Living did not touch on the apparitions of persons who had been dead for more than twelve hours. The *Report on the Census of Hallucinations* dealt with them to some extent but did not gather an especially rich harvest. However, the problem of 'post-mortem' apparitions was taken up in the S.P.R.'s *Proceedings* by several members of the Sidgwick group. The first was Mrs. Sidgwick, who published a lengthy paper on the subject in 1885.[1]

This was the first occasion on which Mrs. Sidgwick made use, at least in psychical research, of her remarkable gifts for assimilating and analysing large masses of intractable material (it will be remembered that she was later on the chief author of the *Report on the Census of Hallucinations*). Her husband rightly felt that she was uniquely gifted for such work; work of a kind that was necessarily predominant in the early days of psychical research. She carried it out not from any strong personal wish to establish human survival of bodily death (she did not herself break away from the Church), but as a duty, because she felt, as her husband did and for much the same reasons, that the subject was of high importance to the world at large. She was correspondingly cautious in assessing the phenomena; she was always slow to make up her mind on a question, and equally slow in changing it. Myers in especial was deeply impressed by her methodical and utterly unemotional approach. In an unpublished autobiographical fragment he wrote that she 'not only without ostentation but even without enthusiasm, gently and calmly does all she can—she would do it in the same way if

---

[1] 'Notes on the Evidence, Collected by the Society, for Phantasms of the Dead', *P.S.P.R.* III (1885), pp. 69-150.

her name were never to be mentioned. Not only this—but she would do it, I believe, in the same way if she were working only for the joy and strengthening of other souls.' Such detachment was so remote from Myers' own feelings that to him she must have seemed already half-way to the angels.

The Society had in its files, Mrs. Sidgwick said, some 370 cases (the residue of a larger number actually sent in or obtained) which 'believers in ghosts would be apt to attribute to the agency of deceased human beings'. The majority of these cases, she felt, could probably be set aside as just ordinary illusions or hallucinations. There were however four classes of cases of post-mortem apparitions in which some further kind of explanation seemed necessary.

1. Cases in which the phantasm had conveyed to the percipient correct information previously unknown to him. The Literary Committee had come across five or six such cases, none of them very strong; in fact in several the information conveyed, or rather inferred, was simply that the (supposed) agent had died.

2. Cases in which the manifestation seemed to aim at some clearly defined objective. Of such cases only two had come in; one was a dream, and the other (a delightful story of a deceased lady who haunted her husband until he consented to their daughter's marriage) was probably the outcome of grief and worry on the part of the percipient.

3. Cases in which the apparition closely resembled a deceased person unknown to the percipient, and the percipient had afterwards been able to recognise the apparition from a portrait; and cases in which the apparition presented some characteristic peculiar to the deceased, a characteristic not at the time known to the percipient. The Society had at this time two such cases in its collection, and neither was of a very convincing kind.

4. Cases in which two or more people had seen, independently of each other and at different times, closely similar apparitions. A traditional haunting ghost, appearing several times in the same locality, would belong to this category; Mrs. Sidgwick deals in her article with 18 such cases, adding that there were perhaps another half-dozen in the files. Since the fourth class of post-mortem apparitions was decidedly the

largest, a slightly more extended account of it seems called for.

Most of the cases of haunting ghosts for which the Society obtained first-hand and seemingly reputable testimony ran pretty much to a type. And this type was distinctly different from the blood-curdling apparitions of fiction and folklore; the stories were not on the whole of a kind which one would suppose people likely either to invent or to frighten themselves into believing. A real-life haunting ghost (if one can properly use such a phrase) tends (with occasional exceptions) to be life-like in aspect, and to be glimpsed around a building like a spare member of the household. Not infrequently it is seen by someone seemingly ignorant of previous sightings, and occasionally by more than one person at a time. The most obvious difference between a haunting phantom and a real person is the tendency of the former to disappear inexplicably—usually (though not always) after a stay not longer than a minute. Quite commonly the figure looks out of sorts; but it rarely speaks to, or otherwise notices, those who observe it, and it rarely appears intelligent or otherwise purposeful. Sometimes there is a strong hint that it resembles a certain deceased person who formerly occupied, and indeed suffered in, the locality concerned; but it is uncommon for such a link to be firmly established. Though haunting ghosts do not often speak, articulate voices are sometimes heard about the house in places where there is at any rate no living person. Commonly enough, though by no means invariably, the house concerned is troubled by miscellaneous peculiar noises—especially inexplicable footsteps, raps and cracks—a fact which has made some writers suggest that a structural or situational peculiarity of the house may cause the noises, and the noises lead in turn, via the nerves of the occupants, to the hallucinatory figures. However, in these old stories the commonest reaction of the occupants of the house is not alarm (though that is a common reaction) but the fear that if the servants get to hear of the phenomena they will at once decamp.

An example which illustrates some, though not all, of these features, is one collected by Gurney in 1885 and printed in Mrs. Sidgwick's paper.[1] It has the merit, for present purposes, of being short as such things go. There are some better-attested

[1] *Loc. cit.*, pp. 102–5.

cases in print, and also not a few worse. The events narrated were not too distant, and the percipients are stated to have been level-headed and free from nervousness. The first account is 'Mrs. W.'s'.

February 19th, 1885.

In June, 1881, we went to live in a detached villa just out of the town of C—. Our household consisted of my husband and myself, my step-daughter, and two little boys, aged 9 and 6, and two female servants. The house was between 10 and 20 years old. We had been there about three weeks, when, about 11 o'clock one morning, as I was playing the piano in the drawing-room, I had the following experience:—I was suddenly aware of a figure peeping round the corner of the folding-doors to my left; thinking it must be a visitor, I jumped up and went into the passage, but no one was there, and the hall door, which was half glass, was shut. I only saw the upper half of the figure, which was that of a tall man, with a very pale face and dark hair and moustache. The impression lasted only a second or two, but I saw the face so distinctly that to this day I should recognise it if I met it in a crowd. It had a sorrowful expression. It was impossible for anyone to come into the house without being seen or heard. I was startled, but not the least frightened. I had heard no report whatever as to the house being haunted; and am certainly not given to superstitious fancies. I did not mention my experience to anyone at the time, and formed no theory about it. In the following August, one evening about 8.30, I had occasion to go into the drawing-room to get something out of the cupboard, when, on turning round, I saw the same face in the bay-window, in front of the shutters, which were closed. I again saw only the upper part of the figure, which seemed to be in a somewhat crouching posture. The light on this occasion came from the hall and the dining-room, and did not shine directly on the window; but I was able perfectly to distinguish the face and the expression of the eyes. This time I *was* frightened, and mentioned the matter to my husband the same evening. I then also told him of my first experience. On each of these occasions I was from 8 to 10 feet distant from the figure.

Later in the same month I was playing cricket in the garden with my little boys. From my position at the wickets I could see right into the house through an open door, down a passage, and through the hall as far as the front door. The kitchen door opened into the passage. I distinctly saw the same face peeping round at me out of the kitchen door. I again only saw the upper half of the figure. I threw down the bat and ran in. No one was in the kitchen. One servant was out, and I found that the other was up in her bedroom. I mentioned this incident at once to my husband, who also examined the kitchen without any result.

A little later in the year, about 8 o'clock one evening, I was coming down stairs alone, when I heard a voice from the direction, apparently, of my little boys' bedroom, the door of which was open. It distinctly said, in a deep sorrowful tone, 'I can't find it.' I called out to my little boys, but they did not reply, and I have not the slightest doubt that they were asleep; they always called out if they heard me upstairs. My step-daughter, who was downstairs in the dining-room with the door open, also heard the voice, and thinking it was me calling, cried out, 'What are you looking for?' We were extremely puzzled. The voice could not by any possibility have belonged to any member of the household. The servants were in the kitchen, and my husband was out.

A short time after I was again coming downstairs after dark in the evening when I felt a sharp slap on the back. It startled but did not hurt me. There was no one near me, and I ran downstairs and told my husband and my step-daughter.

I have never in my life, on any other occasion, had any hallucination of sight, hearing or touch.

The following is Miss W.'s account:

In July, 1881, I was sitting playing the piano in our house in C—, about 11.30 in the morning, when I saw the head and shoulders of a man peeping round the folding-doors, in just the same way as they had appeared to my mother, but I had not at that time heard of her experience. I jumped up, and advanced, thinking it was an acquaintance from a few yards off. This impression, however, lasted only for a second; the face disappeared, but recalling it, I perceived at once that it was certainly not that of the gentleman whom I had for a second thought of. The resemblance was only that they were both dark. The face was pale and melancholy, and the hair very dark. I at once went to Mrs. W. in the dining-room, and asked if anyone had called. She said, 'No'; and I then told her what I had seen. I then for the first time heard from her what *she* had seen, and our descriptions completely agreed. We had even both noticed that the hair was parted in the middle, and that a good deal of shirt-front showed.

A few weeks later, about 11 p.m., Mrs. W. and I were playing bezique in the dining-room. Mr. W. was out, and the servants had gone to bed. The door of the room was open, and I was facing it. I suddenly had an impression that someone was looking at me, and I looked up. There was the same face, and the upper half of the figure, peeping round into the room from the hall. I said, 'There's the man again!' Mrs. W. rushed to the door, but there was no one in the hall or passage; the front door was locked, and the green baize door which communicated with the back part of the house was shut. The figure had been on the side of the dining-room door, nearest to the front door, and could not have got to the green baize door without passing well in our sight. We were a good deal frightened, and we mentioned the occurrence to Mr. W. on his return. He went all over the house, as usual before going to bed, and all windows were fastened, and everything in order.

A few weeks after this, about 11.30 a.m., I was upstairs playing battledore and shuttlecock with my eldest brother in his bedroom. The door was open. Stepping back in the course of the game, I got out on to the landing; I looked sideways over my shoulder, in order to strike the shuttlecock, and suddenly saw the same face as before, and my brother called out at the same moment, 'There's a man on the landing.' I was startled myself, but to reassure the child I said there was no one—that he had made a mistake—and shut the door and went on with the game. I told my father and Mrs. W. of this as soon as I saw them.

Later in the autumn, I was sitting alone in the dining-room one evening, with the door open. Mrs. W. had been upstairs, and I heard her coming down. Suddenly I heard a deep melancholy voice say, 'I can't find it.' I called out, 'What are you looking for?' At the same time the voice was not the least like Mrs. W.'s. She then came in and told me she had heard exactly the same thing. My father was out at the time, but we told him of the circumstance on his return.

In September of 1882, I was for a week in the house with only the two children and the servants. It was about 7.30 on Sunday evening, and nearly dark. The others were all out in the garden. I was standing at the dining-room window, when I caught a glimpse of a tall man's figure slipping into the porch. I must have seen if anybody had approached the porch by the path from the front gate, and I should certainly have heard the latch of the gate, which used to make a considerable noise, and I should also have heard footsteps on the gravel-path. The figure appeared quite suddenly; it had on a tall hat. I was very much astonished, but ran to the door, thinking it might possibly be my father. No one was there; I went to the gate, and looked up and down the road. No one was in sight, and there was no possibility that anybody could have got so suddenly out of view.

I have never at any other time in my life had any hallucination whatever, either of sight or hearing.

I remember Mrs. W. telling me of her experience of the slap as soon as she came downstairs.

I ought to add that at the time when we were negotiating about the house, the landlady of the lodgings where my father and I were staying told me that all the villas of the row in which our house was situated, ten in number, were haunted. I was with my father when I heard this. Mrs. W. was not with us. I am certain that the remark made no impression whatever on me, and that it did not even recur to my mind till I saw what I have described. I did not even mention the remark to Mrs. W.

Mrs. Sidgwick's conclusion, after reviewing these cases, was:

I can only say that having made every effort—as my paper will, I hope, have shown—to exercise a reasonable scepticism, I yet do not feel equal to the degree of unbelief in human testimony necessary to avoid accepting at least provisionally the conclusion that there are, in a certain sense, haunted houses, *i.e.*, that there are houses in which similar quasi-human apparitions have occurred at different times to different inhabitants, under circumstances which exclude the hypothesis of suggestion or expectation.

But Mrs. Sidgwick was quite unable to advance any satisfactory theory to explain the phenomena. The popular view, that ghosts are the spirits of deceased persons, though tempting in some ways, was, she felt, untenable in view of the fact that ghosts almost always appear clothed, and may be accompanied by other phantasmal objects. It is hard indeed to conceive of the spirits of handkerchiefs or of coaches. There are also few cases, if any, in which the haunting figure can be positively identified with some deceased person. Another suggestion might be that haunting ghosts are the result of a deceased person feeling an intense interest in a certain locality, and by this interest being put in telepathic rapport with living persons in that locality. But this theory too would lead us to expect some definite similarity between the haunting figure and some deceased person (and would in some cases also land us in exactly the problems over collective percipience which so exercised the authors of *Phantasms of the Living*). For two other possible theories—that the first appearance of the ghost is a straightforward hallucination on the part of the percipient, subsequent percipients being, so to speak, telepathically infected by him; and that ghosts are the result of the reactions of percipients to some sort of subtle influence which a person may impress on a locality during his lifetime—there were at any rate no telling indications. The upshot of Mrs. Sidgwick's discussion was that there was as yet no very clear evidence pointing towards the operation of a 'post-mortem agency'.

During the next few years there came in both some new cases of haunting ghosts, and a certain number of further cases of Mrs. Sidgwick's classes 1–3 (that is, cases of apparitions conveying to the percipient information previously unknown to him; cases of purposive apparitions; and cases of apparitions subsequently recognised from pictures). This new material brought Gurney to feel more strongly the difficulties of explaining cases of local apparitions, and also certain cases of post-mortem apparitions, in terms of the agency of living persons; and it brought Myers to the belief that post-mortem agency was definitely indicated. Here is an example of a post-mortem apparition recognised from a picture:[1]

September 15th, 1886.

Dear Sir,—The facts are simply these. I was sleeping in a hotel in Madeira in January 1885. It was a bright moonlight night. The windows were open and the blinds up. I felt some one was in my room. On opening my eyes, I saw a young fellow about 25, dressed in flannels, standing at the side of my bed and pointing with the first finger of his right hand to the place I was lying. I lay for some seconds to convince myself of some one being really there. I then sat up and looked at him. I saw his features so plainly that I recognised them in a photograph which was shown me some days after. I asked him what he wanted; he did not speak, but his eyes and hand seemed to tell me I was in his place. As he did not answer, I struck out at him with my fist as I sat up, but did not reach him, and as I was

---

[1] From pp. 416–17 of Gurney and Myers, 'On Apparitions occurring soon after Death', *P.S.P.R.* V (1889), pp. 403–85.

going to spring out of bed he slowly vanished through the door, which was shut, keeping his eyes upon me all the time . . .

JOHN E. HUSBANDS.

[The following letters are from a Miss Falkner, who was a resident at the hotel when the incident occurred.]

October 8th, 1886

The figure that Mr. Husbands saw while in Madeira was that of a young fellow who died unexpectedly months previously, in the room which Mr. Husbands was occupying. Curiously enough, Mr. H. had never heard of him or his death. He told me the story the morning after he had seen the figure, and I recognised the young fellow from the description. It impressed me very much, but I did not mention it to him or anyone. I loitered about until I heard Mr. Husbands tell the same tale to my brother; we left Mr. H. and said simultaneously 'He has seen Mr. D.'

No more was said on the subject for days; then I abruptly showed the photograph.

Mr. Husbands said at once, 'That is the young fellow who appeared to me the other night, but he was dressed differently' —describing a dress he often wore—'cricket suit (or tennis) fastened at the neck with sailor knot.' I must say that Mr. Husbands is a most practical man, and the very last one would expect 'a spirit' to visit.

K. FALKNER.

October 20th, 1886

I enclose you photograph and an extract from my sister-in-law's letter which I received this morning, as it will verify my statement. Mr. Husbands saw the figure either the 3rd or 4th of February, 1885.

The people who had occupied the rooms had never told us if they had seen anything, so we may conclude they had not.

K. FALKNER.

If this case stood alone it would no doubt be easy enough to find plausible reasons for dismissing it; backed as it is by other, comparable, cases it is at least curious. As mentioned above, Myers was by the end of the eighteen-eighties beginning to think that a fair number of the post-mortem cases could best be interpreted as 'manifestations of persistent personal energy'; though by this phrase he appears to have meant no more than that the manifestations have some connection with a person once alive.¹ He seems to have thought that it was upon such an assumption that the phenomena in question could be most sensibly classified; they could be arranged in a series from crisis cases, in some of which the decedent's purposes were clearly evident, through apparitions post-dating death by weeks or months (which were generally, though not always, less clearly purposeful), to haunting ghosts, which might best be regarded as corresponding in some way to the dreams of deceased persons.

Myers was cautious in expressing these views in public; but even so his belief in post-mortem agency was strongly attacked by Frank Podmore, in the *Proceedings* of the S.P.R. for November 1889. The vast majority of post-mortem apparitions do not, Podmore remarked, suggest the operations of anything which could be called a personality. In cases of haunting ghosts there is rarely any evidence worth the name to link the figure seen with some particular deceased person. The witnesses have not infrequently been persons who have had other hallucinations, and who are therefore presumably liable to such experiences; and often there has been a deplorable lapse of time between the apparition and the setting down of an account of it. The possible influence of the expectancy and the anxiety induced by odd noises of natural origin has been much underestimated. And the supposed similarities of the figures seen in the same locality by different percipients seem often to rest simply upon the absence of recorded differences. In some cases of hauntings all sorts of quite different figures have been seen at different times by different people.

Even in cases which cannot readily be dismissed upon considerations such as these, it is simpler to suppose that the later apparitions occur because the original (hallucinated) percipient telepathically affects the later ones. Such a view, in contrast to the survivalist one, invokes no new principles of explanation.

In his reply, 'A Defence of Phantasms of the Dead', published in the S.P.R. *Proceedings* in January 1890, Myers stressed the need for further evidence, but declined to accept Podmore's arguments. The fact, for instance, that some of the percipients in these cases had had other hallucinations does not necessarily

---

[1] p. 15 of Myers' 'On Recognised Apparitions occurring more than a year after Death', *P.S.P.R.* VI (1889), pp. 13–65.

tell against the genuineness of their experiences. Podmore does not point out that a proportion of these other hallucinations had been *veridical*, that is, had been crisis cases, collective apparitions, and so forth; their veridicality might be held in some sense to establish the percipients' credentials. The theory of telepathic contagion is quite unsupported by any evidence that ordinary hallucinations are contagious; and it is absurd to suppose that (say) a year or so after the victim of an hallucination has left the scene of his alarms his retrospective panic can cause the new occupants of the house to glimpse phantasmal figures or hear throaty but throatless whispers. The theory of post-mortem agency does not really invoke any new principles, such as the independence of mind from matter. We already have good evidence for its independence. Telepathic communication is often most successful when the agent is in a coma or otherwise enfeebled, i.e. when the physical activities of his brain are likely to be at a low ebb.

The collection of stories of apparitions went on actively for some while longer, and it culminated of course in the Census of 1889–94 already referred to. Members of the S.P.R. made attempts to witness apparitions for themselves; but ghosts are kittle cattle, and so far as I am aware the nearest any member of the Society got to encountering a ghost was to hear odd raps and other minor noises in the Brighton house occupied on behalf of the S.P.R. in 1888–9 by Mr. G. A. Smith.[1]

The most entertaining ghost,[2] I think, ever directly investigated by any member of the Sidgwick group, or indeed of the S.P.R., was the phantom warrior which troubled Handschuchsheim Castle, near Heidelberg. This castle was occupied by a Mr. Graham, a friend of Myers'. Graham gave the most alluring accounts of the warrior's gigantic size, fearsome expression and blood-curdling groans, and Myers proposed to Lodge that he should accompany him on an expedition. '. . . as

[1] Cf. *P.S.P.R.* VI (1889), pp. 309–13.
[2] There is an intriguing hint of what may have been an even more entertaining case in a letter from Myers to Mrs. Dugdale, dated 9th Jan. 1892: 'Our national Hero and our national Beauty (if I may so term them) little expected that light wd. be thrown on the vexed question of their mutual relationship by the incautious appearance of a ghost *en déshabille*. The movements of these two historic personages are so well known that it ought to be possible even now to determine whether or not Lady Hamilton (& her legitimate ghost) can prove an *alibi*, or whether these appearances are fatally against her.'

the ghost is *almost your size'*, he wrote to Lodge on 25th June 1890, 'you wd. be a good person to tackle him. He is *phosphorescent*, too, which wd. please & interest you.'

However, Lodge was engaged elsewhere, and Myers went on his own. That nothing transpired may no doubt be set down to the fact that he kept a candle burning during his vigil whilst he played piquet with his host.[1]

Among the ghosts whose habitats members of the Sidgwick group had the chance of inspecting personally was the most famous ghost of all, the so-called 'Morton' ghost. This case is far too long to quote, but the original account[2] is readily accessible in various places.[3] The ghost frequented 'Garden Reach', a house built in 1860 (and now named 'St Anne's Home') in Pittvill Circus Road, Cheltenham. The figure was that of a tall lady in widow's weeds, who generally held a handkerchief over her face. Its footsteps were often heard, not infrequently without its visible presence; and the house was afflicted with various other peculiar noises. The ghost was generally supposed to resemble a certain Imogen Swinhoe, the second wife of the original owner of the house. Her husband had been a drunkard, and she had herself taken to drink. She was widowed in 1876 and died in 1878 and was the only widow connected with the house. However, she had left husband and house *before* she was widowed—though she was reported to covet her husband's first wife's jewels, which had been secreted in the building. The ghost, whether or not that of the late Mrs. Swinhoe, was first reliably reported in 1882. It continued to be seen at intervals for several years. Appearances became most frequent in 1884, the figure literally fading away thereafter. It was seen, generally briefly, occasionally for half-an-hour or more, in various different parts of the house and garden, sometimes in broad daylight. It was seen on different occasions

[1] On the Handschuchsheim ghost see *The Reminiscences of Lady Dorothy Nevill*, London, 1906, pp. 269–71. M. Grant Duff, *A Victorian Vintage*, London, 1930, p. 126, says that Myers said the Handschuchsheim ghost was the result of 'a remarkable number of unrelated circumstances, well calculated to excite the imagination'.

[2] 'Record of a Haunted House' by Miss 'R. C. Morton', *P.S.P.R.* VIII (1892), pp. 311–32.

[3] e.g. B. Abdy Collins, *The Cheltenham Ghost*, London, 1948; *Human Personality* II, pp. 388–96; Sir E. Bennett, *Apparitions and Haunted Houses*, London, 1939, pp. 185–209.

by at least twenty people and was sometimes seen by more than one person at a time. The chief witness was a Miss Rose Despard, a young lady seemingly in her twenties, the eldest unmarried daughter of the tenant, Captain Despard. Rose Despard, who was preparing for a medical career, seems to have been a singularly intrepid person, and wrote a careful account of the case, based in part on a contemporary Journal. She stretched strings across the ghost's path (and saw it walk through them); she cornered it and tried to touch it (but it eluded her); she tried to photograph it (but never caught it in sufficiently good light); she spoke to it (without receiving a reply); and upon hearing its footsteps outside her door at night would go out and follow it. The fact that sometimes the hearing of noises preceded the appearance might suggest that imagination played a part; but there does not seem to be much doubt that on various occasions the ghost was collectively perceived, and that it was seen by several witnesses who had not previously heard stories about it. To Miss Despard's account of the case is added the signed testimony of six other witnesses, mostly interviewed by Myers, who was able to keep a close watch on the case through his Cheltenham connections. By 1891 the appearances had died away completely, and Captain Despard, who had feared for the value of the house, which belonged to a friend of his, gave permission for his daughter's narrative to be published (though under an assumed name). It is without doubt the most curious case of its kind ever printed.

After the publication of Miss Despard's paper, and of the *Report on the Census of Hallucinations*, in 1892 and 1894 respectively, there was a general and gradual waning of interest in the collection of stories of apparitions. The S.P.R. published no major paper on the subject between 1894 and 1923. And this decline of interest, though perhaps regrettable, is very easy to understand. For the S.P.R.'s leaders, the Sidgwick group, were all of them keenly interested in looking for evidence of human survival of bodily death; and, though their investigations of stories of apparitions had unearthed a good many sets of facts hard to reconcile with any ordinary hypothesis, it had not produced any very compelling evidence for survival. If so striking a case as the Despard ghost, and so enormous a labour as that involved in the Census of Hallucinations, had not provided such evidence, well might one despair of ever obtaining it from the study of apparitions. Furthermore, the S.P.R. had now, in Mrs. Piper, for the first time found a medium who looked like providing substantial and repeatable evidence pointing in the direction of survival. The Piper case absorbed more and more of the thoughts and energies of the S.P.R.'s leaders. Even Myers began to feel the routine chore of investigating ghost stories very tiresome by comparison with the far more exciting prospects that were opening up before him. But before we deal with Mrs. Piper some other matters must be examined.

IX The Physical Phenomena

THE INVESTIGATIONS of physical mediums which Myers, Gurney and the Sidgwicks had carried out in the eighteen-seventies had made them question the utility of pursuing that line of enquiry any further. Gurney and the Sidgwicks were convinced that all, or almost all, of the materialisations and other obscure physical effects which they had witnessed were fraudulently produced; and even Myers, who believed that on some occasions he had met with genuine phenomena, seems to have doubted whether continued experimentation, at least with paid mediums, would yield much profit. Such experimentation could besides not have been altogether the most congenial of tasks to a group of what Myers would probably have called 'high souls'. The conversation of a Pocky or a Benny had little save its allegedly supernatural origin to recommend it to seekers after Truth.

None of the Sidgwick group was a member of the Physical Phenomena Committee set up at the foundation of the S.P.R. This committee had felt itself bound to avoid paid mediums, but had achieved no fully convincing results with amateurs—even with Mrs. Everitt, who produced some raps and table levitations for it. It seems to have petered out fairly quickly, I suspect because of dissensions amongst its members.[1] It was not until 1885 and 1886 that any further extended examination of the physical phenomena of mediumship was undertaken; and even then the phenomenon chiefly investigated was not materialisation but slate-writing.[2] Slate-writing had come into

[1] See letter of F. S. Hughes, *J.S.P.R.* II (1885), pp. 80–1; and letter of E. D. Rogers, *J.S.P.R.* II (1885), pp. 114–15.
[2] Attempts by the Sidgwick group in the early eighteen-eighties to mount a serious investigation of Kate Fox-Jencken were thwarted by her alcoholism.

vogue after Slade's exhibitions in 1876 (see pp. 124–7 above), and among the various mediums who practised it the most successful was probably William Eglinton.[1] Eglinton could produce some very pretty effects and had succeeded in convincing a number of eminent people of his genuineness—for instance, the Hon. Roden Noel, the poet, Hensleigh Wedgwood, and three M.P.s—Sir Baldwin Leighton, the Hon. Percy Wyndham and even, allegedly, W. E. Gladstone.

Amongst the phenomena which reputable witnesses said they had obtained through Eglinton's mediumship, generally in good light, and sometimes in their own houses, were these: writing on the upper surface of a slate held below the extended leaf of a folding table and pressed tightly upwards against it; writing on the hidden surface of one of two slates held firmly together above the table; writing inside a closed and locked folding-slate laid upon the table; writing underneath a tumbler placed mouth downwards on a slate and forced against a table-leaf from below. The slates were generally, though not always, held by both medium and sitter. Many witnesses were prepared to state that the fragment of slate pencil which was always placed upon or between the slates immediately prior to an experiment had been worn down during the writing, and perhaps that it had adhered to the end of the message; almost all alleged that they had heard the pencil moving across the slate whilst the message was being written; a few claimed that they had seen the chalk beneath a tumbler moving as it completed the message. Some witnesses testified that the messages which they had received were 'evidential'; some that the messages had been written by whichever of three or four differently coloured fragments of pencil they had requested. Occasionally sitters were favoured with the celebrated 'book test'. One sitter would take a book at random from a bookshelf; another sitter would choose a page number, another the number of a line. They would then write page and line upon a slate, concealing them from the medium. A second slate would be placed on top of this, and both held together on top of the table; or else a

[1] On Eglinton in general, see J. S. Farmer, *'Twixt Two Worlds: A Narrative of the Life and Work of William Eglinton*, London, 1886; H. Cholmondeley-Pennell, *'Bringing it to Book': Facts of Slate-writing through Mr. W. Eglinton*, London, 1884. A list of occasions on which he was detected in fraud will be found *J.S.P.R.* II (1886), pp. 467–9.

folding-slate would be used, locked, and laid on top of the table. The book itself was meanwhile guarded in some way. After a time the appropriate line would be found written underneath the note of the page and line.

A very considerable portion of those who witnessed these remarkable occurrences were quite definite that they had at no time lost sight of the medium, or loosened their grip upon the crucial slates.

The Sidgwick group's most active investigators of physical phenomena in general, and of slate-writing in particular, were Mrs. Sidgwick and a newcomer to the Cambridge scene, Richard Hodgson (b. 1855). Hodgson was Australian by birth; and Henry James (the son of William James) used as a boy to wonder 'whether he was not a typical Australian, thinking of Australians as frontiersmen and bushrangers'.[1] Certainly his breeziness of manner and stubborn individualism prevented him from fitting easily into genteel drawing-rooms, whilst he gloried in fresh air and healthy exercise, both for their own sakes and as instruments for subduing the riotous flesh. Hodgson had taken a doctorate in law at Melbourne University, but his interests had shifted towards philosophy and the sciences, especially, it seems, through reading a symposium on life after death which appeared in *The Nineteenth Century* for 1877. In 1878, at the age of twenty-three, he went to Cambridge to study Moral Sciences. In early youth he had been known to 'testify' at Methodist meetings; and although his belief was soon dissipated by a study of Spencer and evolutionary philosophy (while still an undergraduate he published in the *Contemporary Review* an article defending Spencer against T. H. Green),[2] he retained all his life a burning interest in all moral and religious questions. Perhaps it was also from the days when he had borne public witness to the truth that he derived a habit of expressing, in his booming voice, opinions upon all subjects with a studied frankness which even the many friends whom his natural kindliness had won him sometimes found extremely trying.

During his days as a student at St. John's Hodgson, no doubt under Sidgwick's influence, had taken an active part in an

---

[1] A. Baird, *The Life of Richard Hodgson*, London, 1949, p. 282.
[2] 'Professor Green as a Critic', *Contemporary Review* XXXVIII (1880), pp. 898–912. Its tone is characteristically denunciatory.

undergraduate Society for Psychical Research; and when the S.P.R. was founded in 1882 he joined it immediately. In 1884 he procured a position as University Extension Lecturer. He had barely taken up this appointment, however, when he was despatched to India (at Sidgwick's expense) to investigate the alleged theosophical marvels said to have been taking place at Adyar, whither Madame Blavatsky had repaired a few years previously.[1] His experiences on this trip together with the interest in, and knowledge of, conjuring methods which they led him to acquire, seemed to make him the most suitable person to join Mrs. Sidgwick in an investigation of 'physical phenomena', an investigation for which the more Spiritualistic members of the S.P.R. were beginning to clamour.

In the S.P.R.'s *Journal* for June 1886 Mrs. Sidgwick published and commented upon the somewhat numerous reports on seances with Eglinton which members of the Society had sent in. These members had witnessed a fair cross-section of the kinds of slate-writing phenomena described above, together with a number of variations and of other effects. Most of the witnesses (though not Hodgson) were impressed by Eglinton's performances, and many explicitly stated that they had maintained a continuous check upon both medium and slates at the crucial times. Mrs. Sidgwick however, basing herself (one suspects) especially upon Hodgson's experiences and her own, had 'no hesitation in attributing the performances to clever conjuring'. She felt that the witnesses had greatly overestimated their powers of maintaining close and continuous observation of the medium and his paraphernalia. 'Moreover,' she said, 'not only observation, but memory often fails;—we are liable not only to allow our attention to be distracted, but to forget immediately that it has been distracted, or that the event which distracted it ever occurred, the very intensity of our interest in the evidence we are seeking helping in this.' These remarks are certainly borne out by Hodgson's report. Hodgson noted, as most witnesses did not, that Eglinton tried to distract his sitters, and that he carried out various manœuvres—such as dropping the slate or changing his hands on the plea of fatigue—which,

---

[1] The Sidgwick group had at first been rather impressed by Madame Blavatsky. Hodgson's report, *P.S.P.R.* III (1885), pp. 207–380, accused her of wholesale fraud and imposture. It has been strongly attacked by theosophists.

though seemingly natural, might have served to disguise acts of legerdemain. Hodgson also suggested (a suggestion in which Mrs. Sidgwick concurred) that the writing was in fact executed before it was heard to be executed; that Eglinton having successfully but silently written something or substituted a prepared slate, then imitated the sound of a slate pencil (perhaps by scratching with his fingernail on slate or table), and immediately exhibited the 'message'.

The publication of this paper caused a great outcry. Subsequent issues of the *Journal* were deluged with attacks on Mrs Sidgwick and with accounts of Eglinton's psychographic feats. Mr. George Herschell, an 'expert in conjuring', asserted that at best conjuring could produce 'only a mild parody of the very simplest phenomena'.[1] Hensleigh Wedgwood cited as irrefutable evidence of the genuineness of the phenomena various occasions upon which Eglinton and other mediums had obtained writing on the inner surface of two slates screwed or nailed together.[2] A considerable number of the more Spiritualistically inclined S.P.R. members were so incensed by what they considered the unjust disparagement of their favourite medium that they resigned from the Society. However, events were soon to suggest that their action had been precipitate.

One of the persons who had sent accounts of sittings with Eglinton to the S.P.R. was a frail and bespectacled young man named S. J. Davey. Davey was at first extremely impressed by the phenomena. Furthermore, the spirits had told him that he had 'developed his own powers to an appreciable extent',[3] a hint which induced him to try some sittings by himself. To his amazement writing appeared on his own slates between sittings. He was naturally much excited, and his unwise revelation of his gifts to a correspondent led to persistent later rumours that he was himself a medium.[4] Unfortunately he soon discovered that he had been taken in by practical jokers. This discovery, together with some further and less satisfactory experiences with Eglinton, led him to experiment in the production of slate-

---

[1] *J.S.P.R.* II (1886), p. 355.
[2] *J.S.P.R.* II (1886), pp. 455–60.
[3] *J.S.P.R.* III (1887), p. 10.
[4] Even so late as 1925. See Campbell Holms, *The Facts of Psychic Science and Philosophy*, London, 1925, p. 190.

writing by means of conjuring. Poor health gave him leisure for practice, and he soon became so adept that in the autumn of 1886, and with the collaboration of Hodgson, he was able to 'come out' as an amateur medium. The papers which he and Hodgson wrote about his seances are of considerable importance both to the psychologist interested in conjuring and illusion, and to the psychical researcher anxious to detect possible flaws in testimony concerning paranormal events.[1]

Davey was able by conjuring to reproduce or approximate all the kinds of slate-writing phenomena which I have so far mentioned as occurring in Eglinton's presence, including the production of writing inside slates screwed together. This is not to say that he was able to duplicate *all* of Eglinton's phenomena, or to copy all of the latter's refinements; Davey never, for instance, carried out a successful 'book test' with a book brought to the seance by a sitter, or obtained actual writing (as distinct from chalk marks) beneath an upturned tumbler. But the main outlines of the principal feats he undoubtedly did reproduce; and his sitters, many of whom were obviously intelligent, and some of whom knew that he was a conjurer, were often as dumbfounded as any of Eglinton's. The statements of these witnesses are revealing documents indeed. A comparison of their statements with accounts of how the tricks were actually performed makes it quite apparent that by various ruses Davey could almost at will distract a sitter long enough for the execution of some piece of legerdemain; and that he could distract him so simply and so naturally that he would not merely fail to note the legerdemain, but also fail even to note what had distracted him. The point will perhaps be best illustrated if I give a sitter's account of some of Davey's performances, together with the explanations of how the tricks in question were accomplished. The explanations are given in square brackets. Three tricks are described and, since Davey ran them concurrently, the better to distract his sitter (a certain Mr. S.), I have indicated which portion of the text is related to which trick by inserting the signs (i), (ii) and (iii).

[1] R. Hodgson and S. J. Davey, 'The Possibilities of Malobservation and Lapse of Memory from a Practical Point of View', *P.S.P.R.* IV (1887), pp. 381–495; R. Hodgson, 'Mr. Davey's Imitations by Conjuring of Phenomena sometimes attributed to Spirit Agency', *P.S.P.R.* VIII (1892), pp. 253–310.

(i) After I had finished examining the slate, Mr. Davey asked me to write in the slate any question I liked while he was absent from the room. Picking up a piece of grey crayon, I wrote the following question: 'What is the specific gravity of platinum?' and then having locked the slate and retained the key, I placed the former on the table and the latter in my pocket.

[(i) When Davey returned to the room he asked Mr. S. to examine the table. Whilst Mr. S. was thus occupied, Davey removed the locked slate, probably under cover of a duster which was used for cleaning the slates, and substituted a precisely similar slate (both slates were his own property). He then gave Mr. S. some ordinary slates to wash and dry. During this interval Davey left the room, opened the slates, answered the question, and returned and exchanged the slates once again. (ii) Davey now took three slates. On one of them, which had not been in the hands of the sitter, and on the under surface of which was a prepared message, he placed a fragment of red crayon. He then covered up this slate with another, and left them on the table in full view. (The third slate he held under the table flap for a while, obtaining writing on its upper surface by the simple expedient of writing on the lower surface with a crumb of pencil attached to a thimble, taking the slate out to show the blank upper surface, and turning it upside down as he replaced it. Mr. S. simply forgot to report this trick.) (i) Davey and Mr. S. then both put their hands on the locked slate on top of the table.]

(i) After the lapse of a few minutes I heard a distinct sound as of writing, and on being requested to unlock the slate I there discovered to my great surprise the answer of my question: 'We don't know the specific gravity, Joey.' The pencil with which it was written was a little piece which we had enclosed, and which would just rattle between the sides of the folded slate.

Having had my hands on the slate above the table, I can certify that the slate was not touched or tampered with during the time the writing was going on.

(iii) Then, again, Mr. Davey requested me to place a small fragment of slate-pencil in the lock slate, which latter had been previously cleansed with sponge by *me*. Respecting the method of closing the slate, &c., everything was done as in the *first* instance; the slate was locked, and I retained the key.

[(ii) In the meantime Davey lifted the top slate of the two on the table, but there was no writing there. He reversed the positions of the two slates so that the slate with the message on the under surface was now on top. He then took these two slates and placed them under the flap of the table, reversing them together, as he did so.]

(ii) I held one side with my hand as before. I then heard the same sound as previously, and when the slate was placed on the table I found the following short address distinctly written: 'Dear Mr. S.—,—The substitution dodge is good; the chemical is better, but you see by the writing the spirits know a trick worth two of that. The medium is honest, and I am the only true Joey.' The writing was in red crayon, and was in regular parallel straight lines.

[(iii) While Mr. S. was examining this message, Davey exchanged the locked slates as before. The spare locked slate had all along had a prepared message inside it. Davey then put his hands on this slate and by means of a slate pencil attached to his knee imitated the sound of writing.]

(iii) As soon as the sound of writing was over, I picked the slate from off the table, where it had been lying right under my eyes, unlocked it, and read as follows: 'We are very pleased to be able to give you this writing under these conditions, because with your special knowledge upon the subject you can negative the theory of antecedent preparation of this slate as advanced by certain wiseacres to explain the mystery.—"Joey".' The fact that the pencil when removed from the interior of the slate had diminished in size and showed distinct traces of friction convinces me that it was the pencil and nothing else which produced the caligraphy [*sic*]. If the particles taken from the pencil by friction did not go on the surface of the slate, where could they go?[1]

If witnesses' testimony concerning events which took place before their very eyes in Hodgson's or Davey's commonplace apartments is so exceedingly unreliable, how much more unreliable may be their testimony about events taking place in the emotion-charged surroundings of a darkened seance room? Evidence that under such conditions the most astounding misperceptions might occur soon began to come in. Mrs. Sidgwick quoted the following confession from an exposed medium:

> The first séance I held after it became known to the Rochester people that I was a medium, a gentleman from Chicago recognised his daughter Lizzie in me after I had covered my small

---

[1] Modified from *P.S.P.R.* VIII (1892), pp. 288–9.

moustache with a piece of flesh-coloured cloth, and reduced the size of my face with a shawl I had purposely hung up in the back of the cabinet. From this sitting my fame commenced to spread.[1]

An example which became famous is the statement made in 1887 by Dr. H. H. Furness of the University of Pennsylvania to the Seybert Commission on Spiritualism:

> Again, at another séance, a woman, a visitor, led from the Cabinet to me a Materialized Spirit, whom she introduced to me as 'her daughter, her dear darling daughter', while nothing could be clearer to me than the features of the medium in every line and lineament. Again and again, men have led round the circles the Materialized Spirits of their wives, and introduced them to each visitor in turn; fathers have taken round their daughters, and I have seen widows sob in the arms of their dead husbands. Testimony such as this staggers me. Have I been smitten with color-blindness? Before me, as far as I can detect, stands the very medium herself, in shape, size, form and feature true to a line, and yet, one after another, honest men and women at my side, within ten minutes of each other, assert that she is the absolute counterpart of their nearest and dearest friends, nay, that she *is* that friend.[2]

The cumulative evidence that sitters at seances for physical phenomena are liable not merely to fail to notice crucial manœuvres by the medium, but also, at least under the handicap of strong emotions or dim lighting, to be entirely deluded about the very nature of events which they actually witness, became so strong that it seemed to many as though even the most astonishing phenomenon ever reported—the growth in moderate light out of a medium's body of a full-form materialisation capable of independent movement and speech (cf. p. 82 above)—might be explained away as an ingenious piece of jugglery. Certainly there does not seem to be the slightest

---

[1] *P.S.P.R.* IV (1886), p. 63.

[2] *Preliminary Report of the Commission appointed by the University of Pennsylvania to investigate Modern Spiritualism in accordance with the Request of the late Henry Seybert*, Philadelphia, 1887, pp. 150-1. The most extreme example of this kind of thing that I have come across is that of a medium whose foot, covered with a handkerchief, was lovingly kissed in the darkness by an emotional sitter, who subsequently said she had known it was her deceased relation because it smelt as her 'dear dead body' had done. See [Julia E. Garrett], *Mediums Unmasked*, Los Angeles, 1892, p. 50.

reason for supposing that the vast majority of the spectacular physical phenomena reported in the eighteen-seventies and eighteen-eighties were anything other than fraudulent. Whether or not there was, or is, a residue of genuine phenomena is a question indeed. Some leading members of the S.P.R.—for instance Hodgson, Podmore and Miss Alice Johnson[1]—were so forcibly struck by the unreliability of even the best witnesses that they always remained reluctant to consider even the possibility that there might be genuine phenomena as well as fraudulent. In this I think that they were going too far; but it is easy to understand how they were led to such views.[2]

There were, however, several prominent members of the S.P.R. who did not altogether relinquish their belief in some at least of the physical phenomena of Spiritualism. In 1887 a committee on physical phenomena was once again established; its members were Myers, Barrett, Crookes, Lodge, Sidgwick and Angelo Lewis ('Professor Hoffman' of Hoffman's *Modern Magic*). The revitalised committee met regularly until at least the summer of 1890, but unfortunately it could by no means light upon any current phenomena. The most it was able to do was to discuss accounts of cases already over and done with. Various of these accounts—ones in which a professional medium did not figure—were published by Myers in Vol. VII of the S.P.R.'s *Proceedings* (1891–2). Some of them are certainly curious. For instance a young army officer, named H. G. Gore Graham, described how, some two or three years prior to the time of writing, he and his mother, sister and younger brother, had taken to whiling away 'the dusk of the winter afternoons' by 'turning the table' (the table concerned being a small round work-table). The table would tip out intelligent messages, and

[1] Miss Alice Johnson, of Newnham College, took a first class in Natural Sciences in 1881, and was Demonstrator in animal morphology at the newly founded Balfour laboratory from 1884 to 1890. She became Mrs. Sidgwick's private secretary, and, later, organising secretary and research officer of the Society for Psychical Research.

[2] On the methods of trick mediums see for instance: Truesdell, *op. cit.* (a most entertaining work); Garrett, *op. cit.*, Anon., *Revelations of a Spirit Medium*, ed. (with useful bibliography) by H. Price and E. J. Dingwall, London, 1922 (facsimile of the rare original, St. Paul, Minn., 1891); Anon.; *Confessions of a Medium*, London, 1882; Anon., *Some Account of the Vampires of Onset*, Boston, 1892; H. R. Evans, *Hours with the Ghosts*, Chicago, 1897; 'A Life-long Spiritualist', *Mysteries of the Séance and Tricks and Traps of Bogus Mediums*, Boston, 1903; J. Jastrow, *Fact and Fable in Psychology*, New York, 1901; H. Carrington, *The Physical Phenomena of Spiritualism*, Boston, 1907; D. P. Abbott, *Behind the Scenes with the Mediums*, Chicago, 1908.

occasionally its movements became quite violent. One evening after they had finished a seance

> lights were brought and we sat down to read. There were three of us only in the room, my mother, young brother, and myself ... My brother was sitting near the fire with his eyes closed. My mother and myself were reading at the large table. All at once I heard a scraping sound upon the carpet as if something was being dragged over it. My mother and I looked up and we immediately asked each other if it could possibly be our table moving of its own accord. We both then recommenced reading. Presently the sound was heard again. I looked quickly at the small table, and saw it distinctly move for about six inches ... My brother also looked up and started from his chair somewhat alarmed. My mother also saw it, and I must confess we all felt to a certain degree startled by what we had seen, and not wishing to see any more just then, we removed it from the room.[1]

A week or so later Mr. Graham was alone in the room after a very violent seance. The table was left standing a few feet from the fire, which was burning brightly, and was the only light in the room:

> It occurred to me to try if I could make the table move by subjecting it to a certain amount of indignity, as it had always proved particularly violent when treated in any way unceremoniously.
>
> I then picked up a small terrier which was lying on the rug and held it towards the table as if to place the animal on the top. To my intense astonishment the table jumped towards me, rising off the ground, and so alarmed the dog that he squeaked and ran away. The table moved laterally quite six inches and rose in the air about the same distance.

It is not easy to see what this young serving officer and his family could have gained by concocting such a story and then endorsing it with their signatures. Much the same might be said of some of the other narratives in the collection; they are however mostly too complex to be set down here.

Of the more spectacular stories which the committee was able to examine, a good many concerned the phenomena which had centred around D. D. Home. Home, after years of ill-

[1] *P.S.P.R.* VII (1891), pp. 157–8.

health, had died in 1886, and the publication in 1888 of Mme Home's book *D. D. Home: His Life and Mission* led the committee to institute an energetic drive to obtain further information about the remarkable events said to have occurred in his presence. In January 1889 Myers visited Home's widow in Paris, and was allowed to inspect the originals of more than a hundred documents and letters cited or quoted in the biography.[1] The committee unearthed a certain amount of new testimony as to the phenomena, but it was quite unable to track to their sources various allegations that Home had been detected in trickery. These assorted materials were published in, or appended to, a lengthy review of Mme Home's book which Myers and Barrett contributed to the S.P.R. *Journal* for July 1889. Of the new accounts, those of General Boldero were perhaps the most interesting. I will quote here a letter which the General (at that time a colonel) wrote to his wife in February 1870 immediately after attending a sitting with Home at the house of a friend. Unfortunately he does not state what the conditions of lighting were during the first half of the seance; but the report is of value for present purposes, since it describes several of the kinds of phenomenon in which Home specialised.

> We had an excellent séance last night, although some of the manifestations were, they said, not so good as they had had there before. Now to relate what took place. I reached the house, a most excellent one, at about 20 minutes to eight, found the host and hostess old people:—he had been an army doctor and entered the service in 1809, was at the taking of the Cape, and at Waterloo in the Greys, and is a hale old gentleman of 86. His wife, an old lady, two nieces, Misses Jamieson, and another old lady whose name I did not catch, I will call her K., Home, and self, and a Mr. Maitland came later. The young ladies' Christian names were Susan and Elizabeth. We sat round a rosewood table (it was heavy and had one leg in the centre with three feet) in the following order:—Home, then on his left the hostess, next to her Elizabeth, then self, then Susan, then the host, then K., so back to Home. After about 10 minutes the trembling commenced and the table began to move, much cold air was felt. I forgot to mention that the table was covered with an ordinary drawing-room table cover, and on it rested a piece

---

[1] Home's papers are now in the archives of the S.P.R.

of paper and pencil and an accordion of a large size—raps then commenced; one or two simple questions were asked and answered. Then Home proposed to try the accordion, he held it in his right hand by the bottom, i.e., upside down under the table, and it began to play chords. By his desire I looked under the table, and distinctly saw it open and shut as if some one was playing upon it. It first played an air which no one knew, then 'Still so gently' was asked for and played. Also 'Home, sweet Home!' Elizabeth then held the instrument and it played some beautiful chords. Home again took it and held it out from under the table and music came from it. It then played an air of Moore's, and ended by a discordant chord. Home said that represented 'earthly music', the table gave three jumps. Accordion then played very softly and beautifully—'That is heavenly' —the accordion gave three deep notes. Five raps were then heard, which signified the desire for the alphabet. Susan took the pencil. Home repeated the alphabet, and as soon as he came to the letter required he was stopped by the 'spirits' who rapped three times, sometimes raps under the table, sometimes the table gave three raps on the floor, and sometimes the accordion played three notes. After a little I said something about fear to Susan, who had been writing; all of a sudden she said, 'My hand is paralysed, I cannot write.' 'Give me the pencil,' said I, and directly five thumps took place, meaning alphabet. The following was then spelt out, I writing it down:—

'Fear not, Susan, trust in God.'
'Your father is near.'

There was a question about her father, and I said perhaps they mean the Heavenly Father. Instantly there was a great commotion in the table, and this was then spelt out, I still writing:—

'He is the Great Father.'

Elizabeth's pocket-handkerchief was on her lap; I saw it move, and it was gently drawn under the table and placed upon the doctor's knees, who sat opposite to her. Susan's pocket-handkerchief and gloves were also lifted up and down.

Home's chair was moved about the room, and the screen which was placed in front of the fire moved at least a yard by itself. The ladies' dresses were constantly pulled, and they said, or at least two of them said, that they saw hands. I myself saw something, but cannot exactly describe what it was. Home was most visibly effected [sic], but was struggling against it, as the host and hostess did not want to see him in a trance. Presently he roused himself, and said to Susan, K., and myself: 'Will you come into the library, and see what will happen there?' The library opened into the landing, where there was a bright gaslight, but the room itself had no light. The door was, however, left wide open; we were round a little table, the rest seated, and I on my knees. In an instant the table began to rock, and a very weird sound was heard in the corner of the room. An immense shifting bookcase, that would at least require four men to move, began slowly to come towards us. This rather frightened Susan, who was very plucky notwithstanding and she gave a little start. In a few minutes Home went off into a trance. He got up and walked about a little, and then came to me and took me by the hand, saying, 'Will you look at Dan's feet and see that he does not move them off the ground, and tell the others to look at his head?' I watched, and saw his whole body elongated as much as nine inches or a foot. I went and felt his feet, and found them on the ground. I must tell you he was standing where the light of the gas on the landing fell upon him. It was an extraordinary sight. He then said, 'Come here,' so I went back to him. He was still of prolonged stature. He took both my hands and placed them on each side of his waist above his hips; there was a vacuum between his waistcoat and trousers. 'Feel Dan, that you may be satisfied'; and surely enough he came back to his own size, and I could feel the flesh shrink. He again was elongated, and I could feel his flesh stretch and again shrink. It was most extraordinary to see him gradually lengthen. He then walked about a little and went up to his bedroom. I followed and saw him put his hand into the fire and take out a burning coal. I foolishly perhaps called the ladies, not wishing them to lose the sight, but they seemed to have a bad effect, for as they were coming up he told them not to come and put back the coal he had been carrying into the grate, and said something was wanting on the part of the ladies,—that they were afraid he would be hurt. He then returned to the library . . .[1]

The committee also induced Sir William Crookes to publish his original notes of some of the sittings which he had with D. D. Home between May 1871 and April 1872.[2] These sittings had previously been touched upon in Crookes' article in the *Quarterly Journal of Science* for January 1874 (reprinted in his *Researches*). He described eleven sittings in all. At some time or

[1] *J.S.P.R.* IV (1889), pp. 124–6.
[2] 'Notes of séances with D. D. Home', *P.S.P.R.* VI (1889), pp. 98–127.

another during those sittings many of Home's most characteristic phenomena were exhibited, often in light—for instance movements and levitations of the table and of other objects; the appearance of materialised hands and figures; the handling of red-hot coals; mysterious playing of an accordion; and the rapping out of messages ostensibly from dead persons. Some of the phenomena were instrumentally recorded. Crookes' notes upon them constitute what is, *prima facie*, the most puzzling evidence for the reality of the physical phenomena of Spiritualism which the S.P.R. published before the year 1909; I shall accordingly reproduce some passages from a specimen seance.

MONDAY, May 22nd, 1871.—Sitting at 81, South Audley Street, the residence of Miss Douglas. From 9.45 to 11 p.m.

Present:—Mr. D. D. Home (medium), Miss Douglas, Mr. B., Mr. Alfred Russel Wallace, Mrs. Wm. Crookes, Mr. Wm. Crookes.

In the front drawing room, at a low table, supported on centre pillar and three feet. Lighted with candles the whole of the evening . . .

In a few minutes a slight tremor of the table was felt. Mr. A. R. Wallace was touched. Then Mrs. Crookes felt her knee touched and her dress pulled. Miss Douglas's dress was pulled, and I was touched on my right knee as by a heavy hand firmly placed on it.

The table tilted up on two and sometimes on one leg several times, rising at the side opposite each person successively, whilst all who wished took the candle and examined underneath to see that no one of the party was doing it with the feet. Granting that Mr. Home might have been able, if he so desired, to influence mechanically the movement of the table, it is evident that he could only have done so in two directions, but here the table moved successively in six directions.

The table now rose completely off the ground several times, whilst the gentlemen present took a candle, and kneeling down, deliberately examined the position of Mr. Home's feet and knees, and saw the three feet of the table quite off the ground. This was repeated, until each observer expressed himself satisfied that the levitation was not produced by mechanical means on the part of the medium or any one else present.

[Crookes next carried out a series of experiments in which a balance was hooked under the edge of the table, and the force required to tilt the table measured. The table was told 'be light', 'be heavy', etc., and responded as shown. Its weight was 32 lbs, and the force normally required to tilt it was 8 lbs. Unfortunately Crookes does not make it clear at what point the balance was attached to the table. Presumably it was attached by Crookes himself; he was sitting, according to his diagram, perhaps 110° round the circular table from Home. When the command 'be heavy' was given all sitters put their hands under the table.]

Experiment 1.—'Be light.' The table tilted, when the balance showed a weight of scarcely half a pound.

Experiment 2.—'Be heavy.' The table now bore a pull of 20 lb. before it tilted up on one side, all hands being placed under the top edge of the table, thumbs visible.

Experiment 3.—I now asked if the opposing force could be so applied as to cause the table to rise up off the ground quite horizontally when I was pulling. Immediately the table rose up completely off the ground, the top keeping quite horizontal, and the spring balance showing a pull of 23 lb. During this experiment Mr. Home's hands were put *on* the table, the others being under as at first.

Experiment 4.—'Be heavy.' All hands beneath the table top. It required a pull of 43 lb. to lift the table from the floor this time.

Experiment 5.—'Be heavy.' This time Mr. B. took a lighted candle and looked under the table to assure himself that the additional weight was not produced by anyone's feet or otherwise. Whilst he was there observing I tried with the balance and found that a pull of 27 lb. was required to lift the table up. Mr. Home, Mr. A. R. Wallace, and the two ladies had their fingers fairly under the top of the table, and Mr. B. said that no one was touching the table beneath to cause the increase of weight.

At the end of this seance Home held an accordion under the table with one hand, keeping his other hand on the table. Alfred Russel Wallace then looked under the table and perceived a supernumerary hand moving the instrument up and down and playing upon it.[1]

What is so astonishing (one is almost tempted to say appalling) about D. D. Home is the sheer *number* of seemingly disinterested persons who were prepared to testify that he had in good or passable light produced startling phenomena before

---

[1] *P.S.P.R.* VI (1889), pp. 104–5. Wallace describes what appears to be the same seance in his *My Life: A Record of Events and Opinions*, London, 1905, II, pp. 286–7.

their very eyes. If the phenomena in question—let us say movements or levitations of heavy objects in houses which the medium could certainly not have equipped with off-stage machinery—occurred as reported, they could hardly have been the work of conjuring; and yet the hypothesis that Home was a sort of super-Svengali whose hypnotic powers enabled him to inflict whatever hallucinations he liked upon his willing victims cannot cover more than a fraction of the phenomena.[1] It is true that not infrequently a phantom hand or a phantom figure would be visible only to some of the sitters, which rather suggests hallucination; but so many of the other phenomena were observed on so many different occasions by so many different witnesses that the question of hallucination can in most cases hardly be raised. No hypnotist so far discovered has infallibly been able to hypnotise all the members of his audience, and hypnotise them so deeply that every single one of them will at command perceive hallucinatory object-movements. And this is to say nothing of the physical traces which the manifestations sometimes left behind them, or of the fact that, so far as I am aware, not one of the supposed hypnotic subjects afterwards recalled that he had been influenced.

Unfortunately the same arguments cannot be applied with similar force in the only other case of past physical phenomena of which a member of the physical phenomena committee was able to obtain extended records. This was the case of the phenomena associated with William Stainton Moses. It will be remembered that in 1872 Moses, having recently removed to London, joined his close friends, Dr. and Mrs. Stanhope Speer, in forming a 'home circle'. They very shortly obtained remarkable physical phenomena; and in the following year Moses began to produce the famous automatic writings to which reference has already been made. Records of the sittings were kept by Moses himself and (independently) by each of the Speers. After Moses' death in 1892 the records were passed to Myers, who devoted the first of his two long articles on 'The Experiences of W. Stainton Moses'[2] especially to the physical

[1] For attempts to explain Home's phenomena as the results of hallucination see *Podmore* II, pp. 244–69; Count Perovsky-Petrovo-Solovovo, 'Hallucination Theory of Physical Phenomena', *P.S.P.R.* XXI (1909), pp. 436–82; Miss A. Johnson, 'The Education of the Sitter', *P.S.P.R.* XXI (1909), pp. 483–511.
[2] *P.S.P.R.* IX (1894), pp. 245–353.

phenomena. These phenomena were very striking and bore a marked resemblance to those which occurred in Home's presence. They included raps, sometimes conveying 'evidential' messages; independent movements of objects; levitation of the medium; 'materialised' hands and figures; strange luminous effects of various kinds; mysterious musical sounds; direct writing; and the drenching of medium and sitters with various liquid scents. Evidentially however the case of Stainton Moses is for a number of reasons much less impressive than that of Home. Moses sat for the most part only with his close friends, Dr. and Mrs. Speer, and external testimony to the phenomena is far from abundant; the crucial accounts of the sittings—those by Dr. and Mrs. Speer—are far too exiguous to unsettle a disbeliever; and a considerable proportion of the events in question took place in total darkness, so that fraud can only be ruled out on moral grounds. Moral considerations were, indeed, sufficient to convince Myers that Stainton Moses would not have cheated. Myers, an old friend of Moses', found it inconceivable that a man whose massive probity was attested by all who knew him could possibly stoop to deliberate deception. He found it equally inconceivable that Moses could have cheated whilst in a dissociated state, for the tricks concerned would have required elaborate and calculated prior preparation. And furthermore there was about the ordinary Moses hardly a hint of morbid tendency or of want of self-control.

Podmore also was acquainted with Stainton Moses and felt the force of these arguments. His chapter on Moses in his *Modern Spiritualism* displays symptoms of a certain embarrassment. He concludes, indeed, that the clue to the enigma of Moses' life 'must be sought in the annals of morbid psychology',[1] but his attempts to follow up the clue are not entirely happy. He says:

> It is more in accordance with known analogies to suppose that the medium in such cases yields, perhaps, innocently at first to the promptings of an impulse which may come to him as from a higher power, or that he is moved by an instinctive compulsion to aid in the development of his automatic romance; that, like a child of larger growth, he plays his part in a self-suggested drama with something of the freedom from moral and rational

[1] *Podmore* II, p. 288.

limitations which characterises our nightly dreams, but with something also of that double consciousness which warns us, even in dreams, that we are playing a part. In any case, if he continues to abet and encourage this automatic prompting, it is not likely that he can long retain both honesty and sanity unimpaired.[1]

It could I think fairly be pointed out that Moses filled 32 notebooks (31 of them still extant) with records of, and reflections upon, his dealings with the spirits, and that nowhere amongst the results (so far as I can ascertain) is there the slightest hint of any impulses from the higher powers prompting him to help out the development of his 'automatic romance' by trickery.

Podmore does indeed scent traces of trickery in the actual phenomena, but his arguments do not always seem to the point. He spends a fair amount of time in showing that phenomena (such as lights or 'apports' appearing in the dark) which are obviously capable of being produced by fraud *could* have been so produced, and passes cursorily over the rappings and object-movements as unworthy of serious consideration. Yet in so far as there is evidence for the genuineness of Moses' phenomena not dependent upon the assumption that he was honest, it comes chiefly from the rappings and object-movements. The Speers' dining-room table was 'an extremely weighty dining-table made of solid Honduras mahogany', and yet it was from time to time reported to carry out extraordinary antics in the light. Here, for example, is Dr. Speer's account of the sitting of 15th January 1873:

> Séance in red light. Great movements of the table. It was repeatedly lifted up to the level of our faces, even without touching it. Subdued light, quite sufficient to see the table and our hands. The table was moved and floated several times; we could watch in light its every movement.[2]

Mrs. Speer's account of the same sitting goes:

> We commenced this evening sitting in subdued light, quite sufficient to see the table and our hands. After sitting a few minutes, the table was moved and floated several times; we could watch in the light its every movement. After seeing it tilted from side to side, and lifted two feet from the ground . . .[3]

[1] *Podmore* II, p. 326.   [2] *P.S.P.R.* IX (1894), p. 301.   [3] *Light*, 1892, p. 151.

Dr. and Mrs. Speer made (separate) notes of many of their sittings with Moses; but unfortunately these notes, doubtless because of the Speers' complete faith, rarely give sufficient details of the phenomena and the conditions of lighting in which they took place. However, the following somewhat fuller account, furnished by a witness outside the Speers' home circle (Serjeant E. W. Cox), is certainly most curious.

> On Tuesday, June 2nd, 1873, a personal friend [Moses] came to my residence in Russell Square to dress for a dinner party to which we were invited. He had previously exhibited considerable power as a Psychic. Having half an hour to spare, we went into the dining-room. It was just six o'clock, and of course broad daylight. I was opening letters; he was reading the *Times*. My dining-table is of mahogany, very heavy, old-fashioned, six feet wide, nine feet long. It stands on a Turkey carpet, which much increases the difficulty of moving it. A subsequent trial showed that the united efforts of two strong men were required to move it one inch. There was no cloth upon it, and the light fell full under it. No person was in the room but my friend and myself. Suddenly, as we were sitting thus, frequent and loud rappings came upon the table. My friend was then sitting holding the newspaper with both hands, one arm resting on the table, the other on the back of chair, and turned sideways from the table, so that his legs and feet were not under the table, but at the side of it. Presently the solid table quivered as if with an ague fit. Then it swayed to and fro so violently as almost to dislocate the big pillar-like legs, of which there were eight. Then it moved forward about three inches. I looked under it to be sure that it was not touched: but still it moved, and still the blows were loud upon it.
>
> ... I then suggested that it would be an invaluable opportunity, with so great a power in action, to make trial of *motion without contact*, the presence of two persons only, the daylight, the place, the size and weight of the table, making the experiment a crucial one. Accordingly we stood upright, he on one side of the table, I on the other side of it. We stood two feet from it, and held our hands eight inches above it. In one minute it rocked violently. Then it moved over the carpet a distance of seven inches. Then it rose three inches from the floor on the side on which my friend was standing. Then it rose equally on my side. Finally my friend held his hands four inches over the end of the table, and asked that it would rise and touch his hand three times. It did so; and then, in accordance with the like request,

it rose to my hand held at the other end to the same height above it and in the same manner.[1]

Perhaps the most that can be said of the case of Stainton Moses is that whilst a rational man could hardly found a belief in paranormal phenomena upon it, it is in some respects supplementary and in others complementary to the far more puzzling case of D. D. Home. Moses' phenomena, if less well attested than Home's, are strikingly similar to them; and whereas Home, though not exactly a professional medium, owed his social successes largely to his mediumship, Stainton Moses was a private citizen who 'went very little into Society', and at first published under a pseudonym. However, these two cases, whether or not they buttressed each other were, merely on account of their pastness, likely to carry conviction only to the convinced. What was needed, if any firm and positive conclusions were to be reached, was a case currently active, a case whose genuineness could be incontrovertibly established by competent observers and scientific methods.

[1] *P.S.P.R.* IX (1894), pp. 259-60.

X Eusapia

EGLINTON SEEMS TO HAVE BEEN the only physical medium of whom the Sidgwick group organised an extensive investigation between 1878 and 1894. There were of course occasional flashes in the pan; but none which led to any conflagration. The most curious was a gentleman who figures in the correspondence as 'Mr. D. of Barton-on-Humber'.[1] Some time in 1890 Sidgwick learned that a near relation of a friend of his had discovered himself to be a physical medium, and could lift up and carry around a table with his hands touching the upper surface only. This gentleman was a professional man of good social status and a well-known amateur *savant* in the directions of philology, anthropology and ancient astronomy. In November 1890 Myers went up to Barton-on-Humber to observe the marvels, and was shortly joined there by Mrs. Sidgwick. Sidgwick himself also paid a visit to Mr. D. at some period. Mr. D.'s *pièce de résistance* was to walk around in subdued light carrying a table apparently suspended from his finger-tips; once he held it up for fifteen seconds by the light of a duplex lamp and two candles, being the while within four feet of Myers and Mrs. Sidgwick. There were other phenomena: movement of the table without contact; removal of paper from a closed box; and alleged direct writing and drawing upon the paper.

Myers and Mrs. Sidgwick were impressed; the authenticity of the phenomena depended entirely upon Mr. D.'s word; but Mr. D. was, as Myers put it in a letter to Lodge, 'quite of our own standing socially, morally & intellectually'. An issue of *Proceedings* dealing with Mr. D.'s phenomena was contemplated.

[1] I am almost certain that 'Mr. D.' was Mr. Robert Brown, Jr., F.S.A., a solicitor of Barton-on-Humber.

But early in 1891 Mrs. Sidgwick received a letter from a lady who had been present at some of the sittings. During a seance this lady had twice glimpsed a rod concealed under Mr. D.'s wrist, and 'His right hand was not raised as completely from the table as the left hand was . . . also two of the middle fingers were kept close together on the table . . . On both occasions of the table going up the cuff was tightly strained to the arm.'

Mr. D.'s position was such that it was hardly possible to condemn him on the basis of one such doubtful piece of information; and furthermore he succeeded in demonstrating the phenomenon with bared arms. However, in the autumn of 1891 another lady sitter informed Mrs. Sidgwick that Mr. D. had told her that he wished to test Mrs. Sidgwick's powers of observation, and had asked her to assist him in levitating the table by fraudulent means. She complied; but when she heard that Mr. D. had signed a declaration that the phenomena had not been produced by normal means she felt obliged to reveal what she knew.

The Sidgwicks, out of regard for others, determined not to publish Mr. D.'s name but, in Sidgwick's ominous phrase, 'took effectual means to prevent a repetition of his trickery'. Sidgwick told the story at a general meeting of the S.P.R. on 13th July 1894, and concluded with the following words:

> The experience that I have narrated certainly shows that a professional man of good social position and intellectual interests may carry on systematic deception for years, with no apparent motive except (I suppose) the pleasure of exciting the wonder of his deceived friends, and the pleasure of laughing in his sleeve at their credulity. But here the resemblance ends. Mr.[D.](1) never professed to regard his 'phenomena' as a possible basis for religious or philosophical conclusions, or to take a serious interest in the scientific investigation of them: and (2) he consistently refused to publish any account of them in his own name. How entirely different Mr. Stainton Moses' behaviour was in both respects has been amply shown in Mr. Myers' article.[1]

Perhaps it was because of the sad affair of Mr. D., and of the further cases of 'disinterested deception' at which Podmore darkly hints,[2] that nothing found its way into print concerning

---

[1] *J.S.P.R.* VI (1894), p. 278.   [2] *Podmore* II, p. 292.

the curious physical phenomena which, during the eighteen-nineties, Myers thought he had found among his own friends. He briefly mentions these phenomena in various letters. For instance, on 8th October 1892 he wrote to Charles Richet:[1]

> I have lately had table go up in air—in dark—but with only trusted friends present—viz. (1) Hon. A. Yorke, whom I think you know—a friend of 20 years' standing, Equerry to the Queen,—through whose mediumship I think the thing took place (2) Lady Kenmore (3) Miss Wingfield (4) Miss M. Wingfield—(5) FWHM. Also lots of intelligent raps & several very good *diagnoses*.

Again on 8th December 1892 he wrote to Richet:

> There have been some physical phenomena obtained at Lord Radnor's place, Longford Castle, by Miss Wingfield and the Hon. *Alec Yorke*. I forget whether you know him—he is a very old friend of mine, & I have always known that he had *gifts*; but he is a *courtier* by profession—being Equerry to the Queen, —so he has been unwilling to take the thing up or to be connected with it . . .
> They had a luminous matchbox (i.e. painted with luminous paint) carried about the room, & similar physical phenomena.

Myers continued to sit with Miss Wingfield at intervals for the rest of his life; though as far as I know he never published any of his results.[2]

Of all the physical mediums or alleged physical mediums who came the way of the Sidgwick group before the year 1900 the most interesting was undoubtedly a Neapolitan lady named Eusapia Palladino.[3] Eusapia's origins are very obscure—there are various conflicting and even romantic accounts of them. By

---

[1] Professor of physiology in the Faculty of Medicine at Paris. Gurney and Myers had met Richet during visits to the Continent to study hypnosis, in which Richet was interested.

[2] He mentions the raps which he witnessed in Miss Wingfield's presence, *Human Personality* II, p. 208.

[3] The best short account of Eusapia is by E. J. Dingwall, *Very Peculiar People*, London, n.d., pp. 178–217, which has a very useful bibliography. See also H. Carrington, *Eusapia Palladino and Her Phenomena*, London, 1909. The most extended work on her is E. Morselli, *Psicologia e 'Spiritismo'*, 2 vols., Turin, 1908. On her early days see G. Damiani in *Human Nature* VI (1872), pp. 272–4; and the same writer's letter in *The Spiritualist*, 15th March 1873.

1872, under the patronage of a certain Signor Damiani, she was beginning to obtain celebrity as a medium in the Naples district. The phenomena which took place in her presence, so Damiani said, included table levitations, the breakage of crockery, the appearance of mysterious lights, and detonations like pistol shots. Unfortunately these spiritual manifestations were not matched by any corresponding spirituality in Eusapia's character. She was vulgar, earthy, and addicted to bad company. There are even hints that during the seances sitters' purses and other valuables were rather too liable to dematerialise. It was clear that she was afflicted by a band of evil spirits, and British Spiritualists offered their advice to Signor Damiani in the columns of *The Spiritualist*. Miss Florence Cook of Hackney undertook a clairvoyant diagnosis of Eusapia's condition.[1] Miss Cook perceived that Eusapia kept low company, and was followed by an undesirable man; and there is every indication that Miss Cook was right.

For the next sixteen years or so Eusapia seems to have operated for the most part in and around Naples. She then came rather suddenly to the notice of the learned world as a result of two seances which Lombroso, the noted alienist, had with her in 1890. A somewhat remarkable incident occurred at the end of the second seance after the lights had been turned up. Eusapia, tied to her chair with strips of linen, was sitting in front of a curtained-off alcove. Inside the alcove, about one metre distant from the medium, was a small table. While the observers were discussing the seance, a noise was heard in the alcove, and from it there emerged the little table moving slowly towards Eusapia. An instant search revealed neither strings nor confederate.

Lombroso had long been known as a determined sceptic, and as a result of his conversion to belief in the phenomena a number of scientists held a series of seventeen sittings with Eusapia in Milan late in 1892.[2] The sitters included Lombroso himself; Schiaparelli, the astronomer; and Charles Richet.

[1] *Spiritualist*, 1st Aug. 1873.
[2] See summaries by F. Podmore, *P.S.P.R.* IX (1893–4), pp. 218–25; G. and C. Bell, *Bulletin of the Psychological Section of the Medico-Legal Society*, New York, 1893, pp. 18–29. Richet's accounts are in *Annales des Sciences Psychiques* III (1893), pp. 1–31. I have not seen the original report which was published in Supplement No. 883 of the *Italia del Popolo* (Dingwall, *op. cit.*, p. 215).

They witnessed a number of curious events. For instance, one side of a small table (weighing 20 lb.), the side nearest Eusapia, was tilted up in light which clearly illuminated the regions above and below it; it remained tilted for several minutes, whilst Eusapia's hands, her sleeves rolled up to the elbow, were visibly clear of it, and her feet were beating time against each other. Some photographs were taken. However, the conditions under which most of the phenomena took place were not very satisfactory (though they satisfied all the sitters except Richet); and it was noticed that levitations of the table occurred only if Eusapia's skirt puffed out to meet the table and she held her hands above it. The most interesting things took place during the later sittings, at which the seance room was divided into two halves by curtains. Eusapia was placed facing the sitters on a chair at the junction of the curtains, which were then joined over her head. Her front was dimly illuminated by a lantern with red glass slides, and her hands and feet were visibly held. Under these conditions the sitters obtained occasional tantalising glimpses of extra hands which were thrust out between the curtains. Sitters were also touched or grasped through the curtains; and one sitter, Aksakov, put his hand through the curtains above the medium's head, where it was touched by another hand. It was then seized and pulled inside, and a chair from behind the curtain was pushed into it.

Richet was the only member of the Milan committee who did not sign the report endorsing the genuineness of the phenomena. He felt that too many possibilities of fraud remained. None the less he was immensely intrigued, and in 1894 he arranged that Eusapia should visit him at an island which he owned off the south coast of France—the Île Roubaud, near Hyères. The only house on the island was Richet's own; and at least it seemed impossible that Eusapia could introduce a confederate.

Richet invited Myers and Lodge to join the party, and they arrived on 21st July 1894. Lodge has left an extended description of their stay.[1] They seemed to have had a delightful time—at least if one sets aside some trifling inconvenience from mosquitoes and flies. The heat was such that during the day Myers and Lodge roamed the island in pyjamas, swimming periodically; Richet spent his mornings fishing from a small boat to

[1] *Past Years*, London, 1931, pp. 292–306.

obtain food for the party. In the evenings they held seances in a sitting-room on the ground floor. During the seances the door of this room was normally locked, and the shutters of its two windows were fastened without being quite closed. A note-taker (either Richet's secretary, M. Bellier, or a Polish investigator, J. Ochorowicz) sat outside a window and took down all that those in the room called out to him. The sitters, including Eusapia, would group themselves round a table; at the beginning of a seance they would sit by lamp-light, later in the dim light that came through the shutters from the note-taker's lamp and from the moon. They witnessed a fair cross-section of Eusapia's phenomena—table levitations, grasps, touches, lights; materialised hands, billowing of curtains, raps, the movements of objects, the playing of musical instruments, the precipitation of scents, and supposed direct writing—all, it should be emphasised, when the medium seemed to be well controlled. As illustrations I shall now quote extracts from the published accounts of the first sitting, and the fourth and last sitting, those of 21st and 26th July 1894.[1] It was not thought necessary to print the accounts of later sittings in such detail as that of the first.

First Sitting, July 21st, 1894

... 12.35—Sittings at the small table were now resumed, with a change of position. The table was moved considerably further from the window and positions were as shewn. The shutter was more widely opened so as to admit light from the bright moon outside. The candle of the recorder also gave some little light, but the lamp inside the room was not lighted. R. held both arms and one hand of E., while M. held both feet and her other arm. R. then felt a hand move over his head and rest on his mouth for some seconds, during which he spoke to us with his voice muffled. The round table now approached. R.'s head was stroked behind. R. held both E.'s knees, still retaining one hand while M. held the other, and the round table continued to approach in violent jerks.

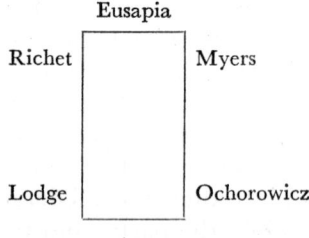

---

[1] From J.S.P.R. VI (1894), pp. 350-1, 355-7.

12.49.—A small cigar box fell on our table, and a sound was heard in the air as of something rattling. R. was holding head and right hand; M., holding left hand, raised it in the air holding it lightly by the tips of its fingers, but with part of his own hand free. A saucer containing small shot (from another part of the room), was then put into this hand of M. in the air. A covered wire of the electric battery came on to the table and wrapped itself round R.'s and E.'s heads, and was pulled till E. called out. Henceforth R. held her head and body, M. kept one hand and both feet, while L. held the other hand, and in this position E. made several spasmodic movements, each of which was accompanied or followed by violent movements of the neighbouring round table.

12.57.—The accordion which was on the round table got on to the floor somehow, and began to play single notes. Bellier counted 26 of them and then ceased counting. While the accordion played, E.'s fingers made movements in the hands of both M. and L. in accord with the notes as if she were playing them at a distance with difficulty. The lightly-touched quick notes were also thus felt by L. with singular precision. Sometimes the touch failed to elicit a response, and this failure was usually succeeded by an interval of silence and rest.

1.5.—E. being well held, M. heard a noise on the round table at his side, and turning to look saw a white object detach itself, from the table and move slowly through the clear space between his own head and E.'s, visibly crossing the painted stripes of colour on the wall of the room. L. now saw the object coming past M.'s head and settling on the table. It was the lamp-shade coming white side first.

1.10.—The round table was moved further off and blows came upon it. L. was touched on the back, while R. saw both E.'s hands (which were still, as always, being held), and her body was also visible.

1.17.—The 'châlet', [musical-box] which was on the round table, now began to play, and then visibly approached, being seen both by M. and L. coming through the air, and settled on our table against M.'s chest. Shortly afterwards it moved away from M.'s chest on to the middle of our table and played there. Then it got on the floor between R. and E., and R. said 'enough of that music.' It stopped, probably because run down. M. was repeatedly and vigorously pushed on the back while L. was trying to see what was touching him [changing places with O. for the purpose]. L. could see M.'s back readily, but could not see anything upon it, though M. kept on calling out that he was being pushed, and that things which pushed like that must be visible. Soon afterwards the sitting was suspended and E. came out of the trance. During the latter half of the sitting, E. had taken one of M.'s fingers and drawn some scrawls with it outside R.'s flannel jacket, which was buttoned up to his neck. M. said 'She is using me to write on you', and it was thought no more of. But after the séance, when undressing, R. found on his shirt front, underneath both flannel jacket and high white waistcoat, a clear blue scrawl; and he came at once to bedrooms to shew it.

Fourth Sitting, July 26th

On 26th July a sitting was held in which Ochorowicz took notes outside the window, Bellier having left the island; and the observers were Richet, Myers and Lodge. The room was again arranged and guarded by Lodge, who again locked the door when the other two observers had entered with Eusapia. The first incident of note was some extremely loud and dangerous-sounding bangs on the square table and on the small table at which they sat. These bangs were louder than could be made with hand blows [and were sufficient to cause alarm for the safety of the hands among which they sometimes occurred]. L. and M. distinctly and simultaneously saw a small bright light rapidly moving in front of them above the table, like a spark or a firefly. The small table rose high into the air in fair light, and remained there barely touched by E. on the top, while eleven was counted.

An arm chair in the window, four feet of clear space intervening between it and the back of Eusapia, now began to move. It was very visible to Lodge and to all; the shutters being open and sky-light glinting on the back of the chair. It was seen to approach and otherwise move a few inches several times, it also made intelligent visible tilts in reply to questions. Eusapia was well held, and all conditions perfect. No one was near the chair. . . .

Noise as of key being fumbled in the door, and Ochorowicz from outside asked who was unlocking the door. Eusapia's hands were well held and no one was near the door. The clear space of several feet near door was plainly visible. Blows occurred on the door. The key then arrived on the table, [and was felt there by L.] It disappeared again, and was heard to be replacing itself in the door with a sound as of the door being locked (or unlocked); then the key came again on to the table into Richet's hand and stayed there. (At the beginning of the séance the door had been locked, and at the end it was still locked; judging by sound, it had *probably* been unlocked and locked again during this episode. The door certainly remained shut all the time.) Richet saw an indistinct black square-looking object which seemed to prolong the key when it was brought towards his head.

There was light enough to see the position of everybody's normal hands all the time on this occasion, and we were sitting some four or five feet distant from the door. [It was a perfectly distinct phenomenon.]

Richet next saw something detached, like a bird in the air, going to M.'s head. At the instant he saw it touch, M. called out that he was touched on the head.

L., R., and M. then all saw the curious imitation-hand or feather fingers stretching horizontally over the vertical gap between the half-open shutters: a thing which L. had several times seen before.

M. was seized from behind while standing, and vigorously pulled and shaken about; while all four were standing holding hands round the table. L. saw him moving and felt a transmitted pull . . .

Medium now conducted the standing group to near the writing desk in the corner, and made three little movements with her held hand. They seemed to take effect and tilt the desk backwards, after a very short but appreciable interval. Then she moved further away and repeated the action; the same movement of the bureau occurred, but with more delay. Then once more, this time two metres from the desk; and the interval elapsing before the response was now greater, perhaps as much as two seconds.

Myers and Lodge were quite convinced of the genuineness of the phenomena. 'There is *no doubt* as to this business,' wrote Myers to William James on 1st August 1894, '& we are all plunged into the grossest superstition, John King[1] and all. The stubborn sceptic may still say if he likes, like the German of Homer, that the phenomena are not attributable to "John King" but to "some other person of the same name"!—or the double of Eusapia, etc.'

Myers and Lodge immediately requested the Sidgwicks to come out and see for themselves which, somewhat reluctantly,

---

[1] Like so many other physical mediums, Eusapia, claimed 'John King' as one of her 'guides'. Cf. above, p. 17.

they agreed to do. To James Bryce Sidgwick wrote on 8th August 1894:

> ... the call of duty has descended on us in connexion with the S.P.R.— in whose affairs a crisis is impending. Three chief members of our group of investigators: F. Myers, O. J. Lodge, and Richet, (Professor of Physiology in Paris) have convinced themselves of the truth of the physical phenomena of Spiritualism ... we have read the notes taken from day to day of the experiments, and it is certainly difficult to see how the results recorded can have been produced by ordinary physical means.
>
> At the same time as the S.P.R. has now for some years acquired a reputation for *comparative* sanity and intelligence by detecting and exposing the frauds of mediums; and as Eusapia's 'phenomena' are similar [in] kind to the frauds we have exposed, it will be a rather sharp turn in our public career if our most representative men come forward as believers. Consequently we both feel bound to accept Richet's invitation and go for ten days or a fortnight to the 'Île Roubaud', and if possible, obtain personal experience. It will be rather a bore, and, I fear, tiring to my wife: but we both feel that it has to be done.[1]

The Sidgwicks' reluctance to investigate further instances of supposed physical phenomena is quite understandable in view of their previous unhappy and uncomfortable experiences; and equally understandable is their concern for the public reputation of the Society of which they were the principal representatives. None the less their distaste for physical phenomena and their tenderness for the S.P.R.'s public image were leading causes of the unfortunate *Affaire Eusapia*.

For the time being however all seemed to go well. Towards the end of August Lodge and the Sidgwicks set off for the south of France. Eusapia was now at Richet's château at Carqueiranne, near Toulon. They had half a dozen sittings in a cosmopolitan assembly which for part of the time included Ochorowicz, Schrenck-Notzing of Munich, and Dr. Ségard, chief medical officer of the French Mediterranean fleet. (Lodge was most impressed by Mrs. Sidgwick's ability to speak alternately French with most of the company, English with himself, German with Schrenck-Notzing, and Italian with Eusapia.) Phenomena took place mostly in the dark, or in very dim light,

[1] Bodleian, MS Bryce 15 fol. 83.

and were hence not so impressive as those which Lodge and Myers had witnessed in July. None the less at their very first sitting, Sunday, 19th August 1894, the Sidgwicks obtained phenomena which they regarded at the time, and in the discussion afterwards, as conclusively supernormal. Mrs. Sidgwick controlled Eusapia's left hand, constantly verifying that there had been no substitution; Sidgwick similarly controlled the right hand. Ochorowicz lay underneath the table and held Eusapia's feet. Under these conditions Mrs. Sidgwick felt mysterious touches and pushes and was embraced by an unaccountable hand and arm; and Sidgwick felt a hand placed on his head. Later seances followed much the same pattern. Whilst Eusapia was supposedly well controlled, sitters would be touched, grasped or prodded as if by hands; sometimes hands would actually be seen. There were occasional movements of objects in the room. For instance, at the Sidgwick's final sitting, on 4th September, during which—according to Mrs. Sidgwick—'it was never completely dark, and sometimes the light was very fair', a melon and a small wicker table were brought from behind the medium and placed on the table round which the company sat. The most curious phenomenon was perhaps the occasional sounding of notes on a piano behind Eusapia and seemingly out of her reach. Mrs. Sidgwick's unpublished notes (still in the S.P.R. archives) of one such incident at the seance of 21st August go as follows:

> The final sounding of notes occurred at the end of séance and when the light had been partially turned up so that key board of piano could be seen. R. had both E.'s hands—her arms stretched across the table to him. I had my left foot without shoe on her right foot and my right foot more or less in contact with her left foot, but the foot moved a good deal and I could not answer for contact all the time. If E. did the piano at all it must have been with her *right* foot and it would almost certainly have been seen.

At a meeting of the S.P.R. on 26th October 1894 Lodge gave an account of his experiences. He stated his definite conclusion that some at any rate of the phenomena were undisputably genuine. He averred that the sitters were perfectly calm and cool, not susceptible to hypnosis, and well aware of the necessity for careful control of the medium—control which they aided by 'continually calling out to each other as to the security or otherwise of that portion of the body of the medium which they had in trust'. Collusion on the part of the sitters was unthinkable. The remote and uninhabited nature of the island would have rendered the introduction of a confederate impossible, even apart from the fact that Lodge himself had prepared the seance room beforehand and locked it during sittings. Lodge was particularly struck by the fact that when effects were produced upon a distant object Eusapia would often make sympathetic movements:

> When the accordion is being played, the fingers of the medium are moving in a thoroughly appropriate manner, and the process reminds one of the twitching of a dog's legs when he is supposed to be dreaming that he is chasing a hare. It is as if Eusapia were dreaming that she was fingering an instrument, and dreaming it so vividly that the instrument is actually played. It is as if a dog dreamt of the chase with such energy that a distant hare was really captured and killed, as by a phantom dog.[1]

At the same meeting of the Society Mrs. Sidgwick gave a short account of her own and her husband's experiences at Carqueiranne, and Sidgwick said that 'although he kept his mind open to suggestions as to methods of producing an illusory belief that a medium's hand was being held when it was in fact free, he felt bound to say that none of the methods of this kind that were known to him appeared to him to afford an admissible explanation in the present case'.[2]

Hodgson however was not similarly convinced of the authenticity even of the most striking phenomena. When he read Lodge's account in manuscript he cabled to Myers (23rd November 1894) in an attempt to prevent its publication. Myers said to Lodge in a letter of the same date that he felt inclined to reply to Hodgson as the Delphic Apollo did to the Locrians: 'If you who have never seen the cattle-bearing Libya know it better than I who have, I greatly admire your cleverness.' Hodgson did not succeed in preventing publication, but in the April 1895 S.P.R. *Journal* he printed a strong criticism of the sittings on the island. His principal points were these:

1. The accounts of the seances are not sufficiently specific as

[1] *J.S.P.R.* VI (1894), p. 333.   [2] *J.S.P.R.* VI (1894), p. 345.

to the exact way in which the hands and feet of the medium were secured. Previous records showed that during sittings Eusapia habitually indulged in violent spasmodic movements, as a result of which she might manage to persuade both controllers to hold the same hand, or might even be able to replace a hand or a foot with a dummy. We are entitled to assume that the same movements occurred at the island; and also that Eusapia as usual managed to dictate the conditions of holding so that, e.g., her hand or foot rested on top of that of the person 'controlling' her. In no case is it clear that one investigator was controlling *both* hands at a crucial juncture, thus ensuring that one hand was not doing duty for two. One freed hand would be sufficient to produce most of the phenomena reported.

2. Various table levitations might be explained if Eusapia had had a strap looped round her chest and shoulders under her blouse, with a hook hanging down from it at the front. She could have attached the hook to the table, and then have raised the table by leaning backwards, even keeping it level by pressing against a leg.

3. The cases of observed movements, and of appearance of hands, at a distance from the medium can be accounted for on the supposition that she had a rod concealed about her, perhaps with a dummy hand at its end, or had rigged up secret cords or threads in the seance room beforehand. She was not searched before sittings, and slender cords or rods would have escaped the notice of the investigators in dim light.

In private Hodgson expressed himself even more strongly. In a letter to Mrs. Sidgwick dated 1st February 189[5] he announced that Richet, in common with all previous investigators of Eusapia, was entirely ignorant of methods of trickery.

> Lodge's conviction [Hodgson went on] I do not regard as of special value, partly because, as I recall (rightly or wrongly) [wrongly—see *J.S.P.R.* II, p. 290] he was impressed by Eglinton, but chiefly because of the *detailed notes*, wh., *pace* Myers & Lodge—I cannot think of without a shudder. *Myers* (bless his dear soul!) *can* be as sceptical as anyone about some individual person or thing, but if he once gets his sympathies enlisted,— his evidence isn't worth 2 straws. This is part and parcel of his big, poetic divine genuine soul, & he can't help it!

Myers, Lodge, Richet and Ochorowicz were not convinced by Hodgson's arguments, and each of them wrote a reply.[1] Hodgson, they remarked, had made unjustified inferences about the inadequacy of their hand and foot controls by trading on the fact that details are not given in the reports, and even by interpreting words pedantically. Three of the investigators were very experienced sitters—Myers observed that he had had 367 seances before the S.P.R. was founded, and that if, after so much practice, he could not be certain of his hand-holds, he had better stop sitting or else take a back seat. All were fully aware of the stock ways in which fraudulent mediums could free a hand. They held Eusapia's hands right across the palms and fingers, frequently the thumbs too, and there was no *room* for another sitter's hand to grasp it as well. Myers remarked that furthermore it would have been impossible for him to mistake Lodge's massive and muscular hand for Eusapia's small one, or to mistake the quivering and perspiring hand of Eusapia for a stuffed glove. Eusapia did not writhe spasmodically or appear to be trying to free herself; during some phenomena she was visibly held; sometimes both her hands *were* held by one person. There were on some occasions even phenomena when both hands were held by one person and both feet by another. Once a large table (48 lb.), visible to the sitters, was raised, moved and overturned when Myers was between Eusapia and it. It was four feet from Myers' back, and Eusapia was tightly wedged between Lodge and Myers. Her movements, or rather lack of them, could be distinctly seen.

It could, I think, not be said that Hodgson emerged clearly victorious from these arguments; though he certainly emerged undaunted. It was arranged that the matter should be put to further test in the summer. Eusapia was invited for a protracted stay at Myers' house in Cambridge. Careful preparations were made for her reception and investigation. A practice sitting was held at which, to Myers' amusement, Sidgwick threw himself under the table, his long white beard trailing on the floor, to practise holding Eusapia's legs. Eusapia arrived at Cambridge on 30th July 1895, and at first things seemed promising. At 7.30 p.m. on the evening of the next day, Wednesday, 31st July, while it was still daylight, she gave an

[1] *J.S.P.R.* VII (1895), pp. 55–79.

impromptu sitting to Myers and his wife. Myers' contemporary notes (now in the S.P.R. archives) are as follows:

> After getting raps at two deal tables in turn, we sat at a small deal table, and EM secured Eusapia as follows, at Eusapia's request. E's foot on Eusapia's two feet—steadily kept there throughout what follows—E's right hand on Eusapia's knees [and again steadily kept there]. Eusapia's two hands fully in sight, during some of the levitations resting on EM's left hand & arm, wh. lay on the table, in daylight, about 18 inches from my eyes. During other levitations I held Eu's right hand well up in the air & E held her left hand on top of or an inch or two above the table—no thumb or part of hand of Eu's under table—
>
> From my position I cd. always see Eu's body to waist & her arms & hands, & when table was up in air I cd. see her whole body, knees with EM's hand on, & feet with EM's foot on; thin plain deal leg of table being an insignificant obstacle to my view.
>
> Under these circumstances the table rose in the air with all feet off the ground five or six times during about ten minutes. We had time between the elevations to discuss our *positions*, wh. we decided that we could not improve. Table rose about six or eight inches, & remained in the air from one to four seconds. We were of course on the look out especially for this phenomenon, & each rise was preluded by swaying and agitation of the table, so that our attention was each time fully on the alert. The séance being impromptu, we had no note-paper & cannot be certain as to the *number* of elevations. On each occasion it appeared to us that no known force cd. have raised & sustained the table as we in fact saw it raised & sustained.

Unfortunately the remaining twenty sittings were of nothing like this level of interest, the phenomena being, on the whole, distinctly less impressive than those witnessed at Carqueiranne by the Sidgwicks. This was all the more unfortunate because various famous scientists—Lord Rayleigh, J. J. Thomson, Francis Darwin—were persuaded to attend some of the sittings; to say nothing of the Maskelynes, father and son, and of Richet and Lodge, all of whom attended at least once. The conditions under which most of the sittings were held were these. The party sat round a table in the spacious drawing-room of Leckhampton House, Eusapia's hands being controlled by the sitters on either side of her and her feet either by those sitters or by someone lying under the table. One of the sitters (usually Miss Alice Johnson) sat at a separate table, often in a part of the room separated from the rest by curtains, and took down the sitters' comments by the light of a shaded lamp or candle.[1] Eusapia's staple phenomena—table levitations, touches and grasps of the sitters, and movements of small articles or pieces of furniture not too far from her—were fairly frequent. The light was generally dim or non-existent, but those who held Eusapia's hands and feet felt, on the whole, comparatively certain that they had not lost control. However, some suspicious circumstances were noticed quite early on. Eusapia was very difficult over the controls she would permit. She would generally not allow one sitter to control both hands (which would, of course, have made substitution of one hand for two difficult) and she frequently insisted on laying her hand on top of the controller's. She refused to be tied in any way and sometimes objected to her legs being held. At the second sitting, on 3rd August, Mrs. H. M. Stanley (Myers' sister-in-law and wife of the explorer), who had Eusapia's right hand resting on hers, noted that during phenomena the hand seemed to be narrowed or partially withdrawn. After this sitting Mrs. Sidgwick recorded her conviction that Eusapia executed the touches with a freed hand; a view which she found grounds for expressing again after various subsequent sittings.

However, not all the phenomena which occurred could be explained on any such simple hypothesis. There were, for instance, the curious protuberances from Eusapia's body which some sitters occasionally observed. At one point the third sitting, 4th August 1895, Eusapia was standing up; one of her hands was held by Myers, the other by Miss Johnson. Mrs. Myers sat on the floor and held the feet. Under these conditions Myers and Miss Johnson were touched. They raised Eusapia's hands in the air, and again Miss Johnson was pushed from behind, and a nearby chair was moved a number of times. Looking upwards, Mrs. Myers could see against the ceiling, which was illuminated by light from the note-taker's candle, several kinds of protrusion from Eusapia's body. She listed them as follows, in a statement preserved in the S.P.R. archives:

[1] These notes are in the S.P.R. archives and I have drawn upon them in what follows.

1. An arm exactly like Eusapia's in which I saw even the place where the sleeve ends with the thickening of the outline & wrinkles of the sleeve & edge of under cuff (which is white). This projection had hand & fingers and held the chair. II. Two long simultaneous prolongations—like neck of swan; one of which I saw prod Mr. Myers on the back three times with force—but without visible hand—the other went round to Miss Johnson & was lost to my view—III. A kind of stump linked to the body by a narrower neck coming from about the hips or flank which struck Mr. Myers in the lower ribs (he says). This I think also struck me—I was struck on the thigh—but I could not see in the low shadow what it *was* that struck me. No bending of the medium's body visible to me—no movement of legs or feet.

Mrs. Myers and Mrs. Stanley changed places, and Mrs. Stanley saw a hand growing out of Eusapia's back and touching Myers' back. After the sitting Mrs. Myers helped Eusapia to undress, and folded up her clothes for her. There was no sign of any machinery. Other sitters, for instance Lord Rayleigh, perceived similar, though somewhat less spectacular, effects at later sittings.

Another extremely curious phenomenon which took place in several sittings was a billowing out of the window curtains. Thus at the end of the fourth sitting, when Eusapia was no longer held, Miss Alice Johnson brought in the photographic lamp and put it on the table, unshaded, but with its back to Eusapia. Eusapia was now sitting at a little distance from the table, with her back towards, but clear of, the curtains of a large window. Richet was sitting on her left, Rayleigh on her right. A curtain (not one in front of an open pane) swelled out behind Lord Rayleigh several times, on some occasions as much as $2\frac{1}{2}$ feet, Professor Thomson thought. Eusapia was clearly visible to all, and so were the curtain movements. Lord Rayleigh put his head up against the curtain and felt it pressing against him several times as it moved. He put his hand between Eusapia's back and the curtain and felt along the floor between her and it, but found nothing. The movement was as if the curtain were blown out by a wind. It did not, however, bulge out from the top, but from some distance down.

The situation after the series of sittings had progressed some way was thus ambiguous. There were on the one hand clear hints of hand-substitution; but on the other hand there were such very odd things as the blunt yet seemingly living protuberances from Eusapia's body, and the movements of the curtains. After the fifth sitting, on 7th August, Sidgwick and Myers sent £40 to Hodgson to enable him to cross the Atlantic and try to resolve the issue. Hodgson arrived at Cambridge on Thursday, 29th August. He took part in the thirteenth sitting, the next evening, and in all subsequent sittings.

Hodgson thought that the established practice of guarding Eusapia's hands and feet as carefully as possible, and of calling out the conditions of control to the note-taker, simply helped Eusapia by informing her when it was unsafe for her to execute some fraudulent manœuvre. Accordingly he made his own control as lax as possible, passing himself off as an amiable imbecile. He found that Eusapia was working her hands close together, and then by a deft move inducing both controllers to accept the same hand, thus freeing the other hand for mischief. She would also free a foot in a similar way. Practically all the phenomena at the last sittings were undoubtedly fraudulent, and all the regular sitters were able to observe the fraud in action. They came to the conclusion, in the light of the insight gained into Eusapia's methods, and making due allowance for imperfect observation, that 'nothing but trickery had been at work in the Cambridge series of experiments'.[1] On Monday, 16th September, Eusapia left Cambridge, accompanied by Hodgson. She had not as yet been fully informed of her exposure.[2]

There were however not a few people, especially among continental investigators, who felt that all the trickery had not been on Eusapia's side. Criticism of the Cambridge sittings[3] grew over the next few years, and resolved itself under the following heads.

[1] *J.S.P.R.* VII (1895), p. 159.
[2] The Maskelynes, father and son, attended one sitting, but failed to detect the trickery which they suspected and whose *modus operandi* they suggested. When the S.P.R. account, which made no mention of them, came out, J. N. Maskelyne wrote a long account of their sitting, which was published in the *Daily Chronicle* for 29th Oct. 1895. A somewhat acrimonious correspondence followed, and the matter was taken up in other papers. The *British Medical Journal*, 9th Nov. 1895, had a scoffing leader, to which Sidgwick replied on 16th Nov.
[3] See e.g. J. Maxwell, *Metapsychical Phenomena*, London, 1905, pp. 405–17; A. de Rochas, *L'Extériorisation de la Motricité*, Paris, 1906, pp. 201–64; C. Richet, *Thirty Years of Psychical Research*, London, 1923, p. 456; Carrington, *op. cit.*, pp. 51–7; Dingwall, *op. cit.*, pp. 187–92; J. Page Hopps, *J.S.P.R.* VII (1895), p. 164.

(*a*) Eusapia was not happy at Cambridge, and therefore could not have been in good form. She disliked the English climate and English food. She was an unlettered peasant, with tastes only for *pasta* and for naughty Neapolitan stories, and she would have been completely at sea in the cultivated surroundings of Leckhampton House.

(*b*) It had always been known that when in a state of trance or of dissociation Eusapia would, if not properly controlled, cheat in the crude ways discovered by Hodgson. She was especially liable to do so when her powers were low. Hodgson's relaxation of control would therefore have produced the cheating which it was designed to detect. If he had been properly conversant with the previous literature on Eusapia he would have been aware of this fact.

The S.P.R.'s defence against such criticism (the defenders being Sidgwick, Mrs. Sidgwick and Miss Alice Johnson) seems to have been as follows.[1]

(*a*) Eusapia was perfectly happy at Cambridge. Her smallest whim was indulged. She was taken out shopping at her hosts' expense, and taken on other excursions. People played croquet and other games with her—she cheated at these too. She was allowed to cook her own Italian meals in the kitchen. Professor Sidgwick even flirted with her (a fact not made available to the impious) and she was photographed wearing his academic robes.

(*b*) Hodgson laid his trap for Eusapia only *after* it seemed pretty certain that she was indulging in trickery. His aim was simply to get details of her methods. The continental observers who rushed to claim that they had known all along about Eusapia's propensity to cheat if not properly controlled had not committed their knowledge to print until after Hodgson's exposé. Eusapia's trickery was of a skilful and practised kind, and could not be attributed simply to her being in trance and not responsible for her acts.

It appears to me that Hodgson's critics have something of a

[1] See Mrs. Sidgwick's review of Morselli, *P.S.P.R.* XXI (1909), pp. 516–25; Miss A. Johnson's Note on Maxwell's Criticisms, *P.S.P.R.* XVIII (1904), p. 501; pp. 67–9 and 77–8 of her 'Mrs. Henry Sidgwick's Work in Psychical Research' *P.S.P.R.* XLIV (1936), pp. 53–93; a MS. fragment, 'Eusapia Palladino', by Miss Johnson, in the S.P.R. archives (the first draft of a projected account and defence of the Cambridge sittings).

case. No doubt Eusapia *was* kindly treated at Cambridge, and no doubt she hugely enjoyed the croquet, shopping and other fuss. But that she found the investigators congenial as persons I find it hard to believe; for what points of contact could there possibly have been between the ignorant and earthy Eusapia, who was liable upon awakening from her trances to throw herself into the arms of the nearest male sitter with unmistakable intent, and a group of earnest and highly educated enquirers into the inmost secrets of the Cosmos? And it is certainly not true that Hodgson was the first to describe Eusapia's methods of trickery; nor is it true that it was only after Hodgson's discoveries that continental investigators noted Eusapia's propensity to cheat if she could when power was low. As a matter of fact this had been pointed out by Ochorowicz (from personal experience) in the S.P.R. *Journal* for April 1895.[1] It would of course have been quite reasonable for Hodgson to have relaxed control had his intention simply been to find what modes of trickery Eusapia generally employed and to improve control at later sittings. But Eusapia's trickery, which was of a simple and well-known kind, and certainly not such as could have produced more than a fraction of the phenomena at the Île Roubaud, was in fact used to brand all her phenomena as imposture, and herself as merely a vulgar cheat. Lodge 'did not see eye to eye with Hodgson in the matter':[2] and I am inclined to see eye to eye with Lodge.

In the S.P.R. *Journal* for April 1896 Sidgwick wrote sternly that a full account of the Cambridge sittings had not been printed because

> ... it has not been the practice of the S.P.R. to direct attention to the performances of any so-called 'medium' who has been proved guilty of systematic fraud ... In accordance, therefore, with our established custom, I propose to ignore her performances for the future, as I ignore those of other persons engaged in the same mischievous trade.

And when, a year or two later, Myers wished to re-open investigations because of startling reports from the continent, Sidgwick squashed him by remarking: 'I cannot see any reason

---

[1] *J.S.P.R.* VII (1895), p. 77.
[2] Letter to Lord Rayleigh (the younger) 14th Nov. 1924 in the S.P.R. archives.

for departing from our deliberate decision to have nothing further to do with any medium whom we might find guilty of intentional and systematic fraud.'[1]

Richet however did not accept Sidgwick's and Hodgson's view of the matter. He continued to experiment with Eusapia and became absolutely convinced that at times she produced genuine phenomena. He wrote to Lodge on 28th October 1898 that he had seen extra hands in half-light whilst Eusapia's hands were visibly held. He had once grasped and held one of these supernumerary hands for 25 seconds. Late in 1898 he persuaded Myers who, though disgusted with Eusapia, had, like Lodge, never completely lost faith in the phenomena, to come to his house at Paris where Eusapia had been giving some remarkable sittings. Myers attended two sittings, on 1st and 3rd December 1898; the other sitters were Richet, Th. Flournoy (a distinguished Swiss psychologist), the Duc and Duchesse de Montebello (the French Ambassador at St. Petersburg and his wife), Emil Boirac (present at the second sitting only), and Mme Richet, who acted as note-taker.[2] In the first sitting the light was better than Myers had ever seen it with Eusapia—a duplex lamp, unscreened though turned low, a fire, and moonlight coming through a window. It was 'light enough to see every finger of Eusapia; every feature; every detail of her dress'. Eusapia's hands were always far apart, and during all important phenomena both were visible; both her feet were held at all important times by an observer underneath the table. She made no attempt to juggle her hands or her feet. Under these conditions a zither, which had been placed in a curtained-off window recess behind the medium (the window being shuttered and bolted) was moved and played. It was then taken from the recess, brought round behind the sitters (so that they were between it and Eusapia), played again, and brought over Myers' shoulder on to the table. An amorphous and cloudy-looking projection emerged from behind the window curtains, raised the zither, struck eight or ten notes upon it, and then disappeared. While both of Eusapia's hands were visibly held,

[1] *P.S.P.R.* XLV (1938), p. 165.
[2] Flournoy's account of the first sitting will be found in his *Esprits et Médiums*, Geneva, 1911, pp. 405-6; Boirac's account of the second sitting in his *Psychic Science*, London, 1918, pp. 311-14. Madame Richet's Notes, seemingly edited and translated by Myers, are in the S.P.R. archives.

Myers put his hand inside the curtains; it was there grasped by another hand. Amongst other phenomena which occurred were billowing of the heavy window curtains and touchings of the sitters.

At the second sitting similar phenomena took place. The light was somewhat lower, but Eusapia was still visibly controlled. One of the sitters held the zither behind the curtain. It was seized, played upon, and carried to the table. Myers was grasped through the curtain by a strong hand.

Myers was fully convinced, and when he returned to England he proposed to publish an account of his experiences. Hodgson was at that time editor of the S.P.R.'s *Journal* and *Proceedings*. He seems to have felt it his duty to prosecute a sort of Holy War against fraudulent mediums, and had been planning to sponsor an article by J. G. Smith which should constitute 'some definite classing' of Eusapia 'amongst the ranks of tricksters'. He was distinctly put out by Myers' reconversion. 'All my plans would have gone smoothly as a bell,' he wrote on 17th January 1899, perhaps to Miss Alice Johnson, 'and would have redounded to the credit of the S.P.R. so far as I can see, but I am quite open to call for criticisms of my intentions. Now however . . . the situation has changed.' Myers' notes(or Mme Richet's notes, rather) he described as 'worthless' (and they are indeed on the abbreviated side); he was himself 'absolutely convinced that Eusapia is a trickster from beginning to end'. In the upshot all that was published was a letter from Myers stating that as a result of recent experiences he had once again been converted to belief in Eusapia's phenomena.[1] No further action was taken. This was, it seems to me, a very great pity. By the time that the S.P.R., in consequence of further reports from the continent, at last got round to publishing a lengthy paper about Eusapia[2] she was almost at the end of her career, and ten years had been lost in which the experimental ingenuity of Lodge or Rayleigh might just possibly have resolved some puzzles which still remain. Though, indeed I very much doubt whether the Sidgwick group's

---

[1] *J.S.P.R.* IX (1899), p. 35.
[2] The Hon. Everard Feilding, W. W. Baggally, and Hereward Carrington, 'Report on a Series of Sittings with Eusapia Palladino', *P.S.P.R.* XXIII (1909), pp. 309–569.

otherworldly interests would have been furthered by the investigations.

That there are very considerable puzzles about these phenomena appears to me undoubted, even on the basis of such tiny portions of the evidence as I have been able to mention. And in the particular case of Eusapia the puzzles were highlighted by the 1909 paper mentioned above. The principal sitters—the Hon. Everard Feilding, Hereward Carrington, and W.W. Baggally—had as thorough a knowledge and experience of trick methods as any trio of investigators ever assembled; they visited Eusapia at Naples on her home terrain; and as persons they were far more congenial to her than the Cambridge intellectuals. In eleven sittings held in the middle one of the three adjacent hotel rooms which they occupied they obtained the most astounding phenomena, sometimes in good light, almost always in a light sufficient for adequate visual checking. The minute by minute account of phenomena and conditions of control which they dictated to a stenographer is without doubt the most interesting record of its kind ever published. Objects were moved, and an accordion played, inside a cabinet (a corner of the room which had been curtained off) while the medium was visibly and securely held outside it; objects were carried out of the cabinet and placed on the table; the sitters were touched and gripped by hands visible and invisible which sometimes melted away in their grasp; amorphous heads, things like primitive cabbages on stalks, and other knobbly excrescences were extruded between the curtains of the cabinet; the table round which the sitters were grouped was completely levitated many times; and a small footstool in the room was several times moved along the floor in clear view and certainly not attached to any strings.

These sittings took place outside the period with which this book is concerned, and I cannot give a full account of them. The following year, after a disastrous visit to the United States, Eusapia's powers, whatever they were, seem to have faded completely. She died in 1918.

It would be unwise to generalise too widely on the basis of the career of this somewhat doubtful character. None the less my own feeling is that those who might be called the die-hard members of the Sidgwick group—especially Richard Hodgson and Miss Alice Johnson—were unduly impressed by the early demonstrations of the possibilities of malobservations and errors of memory in reports of seances.

The early demonstrations and illustrations of malobservation and errors of memory seemed to establish these points:

1. That even in good light, and under conditions favourable to observation, an intelligent sitter can be so distracted and misled that a piece of legerdemain which will lead to the subsequent production of a *fait accompli* (let us say some writing on a slate) can be carried out under his very eyes.

2. That in darkness it is similarly almost impossible even for an intelligent and alert sitter to maintain continuous tactual observation of a medium's hands, etc., and so assure himself that the phenomena (which he does not *see* in progress) are not fraudulent.

3. That in dim light, emotional or credulous sitters may grossly misinterpret phenomena which they actually witness; may, e.g., mistake a mask and some muslin drapery for a deceased person known to them.

In the case of Eusapia Palladino (not to mention that of Home) phenomena—and ones which I do not think that any conjurer has ever duplicated under comparable conditions—were at times actually *seen in progress* in fair light by competent and seemingly balanced observers; and it is not at all obvious (at least to me) that it is reasonable to set these phenomena unceremoniously aside (which Hodgson and Miss Johnson wanted to do) on the pretext that the witnesses of them are bound to have been hopelessly misled. In 1908 Everard Feilding became so exasperated by Miss Alice Johnson's armchair scepticism about the Naples sittings that he exclaimed in a letter to her dated 6th December 1908: 'I wish to goodness you had come out when I wired so that instead of sniffing at us when we return you might be sniffed at yourself by Podmore.'[1]

The rectitude of those not exposed to temptation can be very annoying. However, in fairness to Miss Johnson it must be added that she was as willing to impugn her own powers of observation as those of others. Nothing in the whole Eusapia story is odder than the document[2] in which Miss Johnson, writing about the Cambridge sittings some years after their

[1] S.P.R. archives. [2] See p. 239n above.

occurrence, tries to convince herself that on the occasion when Mrs. Myers had seen protrusions from Eusapia's body, whilst Myers controlled Eusapia's right arm and Miss Johnson her left, she (Miss Johnson) had lost control of herself in the excitement of the moment and suffered from an hallucination.

I believe that at an early stage of the sitting I let Eusapia's left arm go without knowing it, and that my impression of holding it the rest of the time was what may be described as a hallucinatory after-image of my actual holding at the beginning. It is possible that she substituted some other object, which produced on me the illusion of an arm, but I am more inclined to think that it was an actual hallucination on my part.

There is a certain appealing humility about this statement. Had Hodgson been in Miss Johnson's place he would almost certainly have alleged that it was Myers who was led astray.[1]

---

[1] The case of Eusapia Palladino affords, of course, splendid opportunities to *esprits forts*; their usual approach to the 1908 sittings is to recount her well-known methods of eluding control (which have already been mentioned), and to suppose that such was the investigators' 'will to believe' that they allowed her to put them into practice. See, e.g., D. H. Rawcliffe, *Illusions and Delusions of the Supernatural and the Occult*, New York, 1959, pp. 320-32. But the 1908 trio of investigators, as is quite apparent from their report, were well aware of Eusapia's little ways and, if they suffered from a 'will to believe', they had at any rate managed to suppress it until 1908.

Podmore suggested (*J.S.P.R.* XIV (1909), pp. 172-6, and *The Newer Spiritualism*, London, 1910, pp. 114-44) that most of the phenomena in the more exciting 1908 sittings could be explained if one assumed that Eusapia had deceived Baggally into letting go of the hand or foot which he was controlling; Baggally's reply (*J.S.P.R.* XIV (1909), pp. 213-38) is to the effect that Podmore simply ignores phenomena which do not fit into his theory. Baggally appears to me to be right. C.E.M. Hansel, *E.S.P.: A Scientific Evaluation*, New York, 1966, p. 212, gives several reasons why the conditions under which Eusapia sat in Naples were 'highly favourable' to illusion; but they stray almost as far from the facts as his criticism of Mrs. Piper (see below, Appendix B).

XI The Mental Mediums

'IT IS PLEASANT', said William James as he passed from a discussion of Eusapia Palladino to consider Myers' views about automatic writing and kindred topics, 'to turn from phenomena of the dark-sitting and rat-hole type (with their tragicomic suggestion that the whole order of nature might possibly be overturned in one's own head, by the way in which one imagined oneself, on a certain occasion, to be holding a tricky peasant woman's feet) to the "calm air of delightful studies".'[1] James is here reflecting the view of the majority of the S.P.R.'s leaders. For it rapidly became the firm belief of several of them that there are two kinds of medium, 'mental' mediums, who write or speak automatically or see visions, and 'physical' mediums, who are responsible for curious physical effects like those discussed in the last chapter. The two kinds of mediumship (so it was held) are quite distinct, and do not often occur in the same individual; and this is fortunate, for the 'physical' phenomena are almost always fraudulent, and hardly anybody who claims to produce them can be relied upon. If mental mediums (who provide the chief evidence for survival) also commonly produced physical phenomena, we should have the best of reasons for distrusting them and for looking askance at the putative evidence for survival. The fact, for instance, that physical phenomena were said to have occurred in the presence of Stainton Moses is in itself enough to make us justifiably suspicious of him.

I am however rather inclined to doubt that Stainton Moses really is an exceptional case. The two kinds of mediumship go together much more commonly than has been supposed.[2] It is

[1] In his Presidential Address, *P.S.P.R.* XII (1896), p. 6.
[2] Cf. Podmore, *The Newer Spiritualism*, London, 1910, p. 157.

true that Mrs. Piper, the first outstanding mental medium with whom the Sidgwick group was able to conduct extensive experiments, never produced physical phenomena; nor, so far as I am aware, did any of the automatists who figured so prominently in S.P.R. publications in and after the turn of the century. But Mrs. Thompson and Mrs. Leonard, two other outstanding mental mediums, obtained 'physical' as well as 'mental' phenomena; so too did three automatists who were among the first to provide members of the Sidgwick group with *prima facie* evidence for survival.

The first of these was a lady known in the literature as 'Miss A.' Her real name was Kate Wingfield.[1] Myers became acquainted with her in the spring of 1884. Miss Wingfield began experimenting in automatic writing in the mid-eighteen-eighties and speedily developed the faculty; she obtained many lengthy communications allegedly from deceased persons. These communications were not always very illuminating, but occasionally they contained 'evidential' materials, and more frequently diagnosed and prescribed for the ailments of sitters with some accuracy. After a while Miss Wingfield discovered that she had also the power of seeing persons and scenes in a crystal; sometimes she would even see writing. In the course of time she became able to perceive the scenes and figures and writing without a crystal. Eventually, towards the end of the century, she developed actual trance mediumship. And all these varieties of 'mental' mediumship were regularly accompanied by paranormal raps, which would themselves spell out messages; occasionally there were more violent physical manifestations, such as table levitations. Now the 'mental' phenomena were certainly very curious, and were confirmed by the testimony of independent witnesses. For instance, Miss Wingfield's crystal visions seemed sometimes to give her unaccountable knowledge of the present activities of distant persons; occasionally she would even 'witness' scenes long past. In a short, but by no means exceptionally good, case of the former sort, Miss

[1] On Miss Wingfield see esp. pp. 498–516 of Myers' 'The Subliminal Consciousness', *P.S.P.R.* VIII (1892), pp. 436–535; pp. 73–92 of his 'The Subliminal Consciousness', *P.S.P.R.* IX (1893), pp. 26–128; and Sir Lawrence J. Jones' Presidential Address, *P.S.P.R.* XXXVIII (1928), pp. 17–48. Selections from her automatic writing were later published under her own name (*Guidance from Beyond*, London, 1923, and *More Guidance from Beyond*, London, 1925).

Wingfield's own statement, and a confirmatory statement by Lady Radnor, go as follows:

> Some time ago I was looking in my crystal and saw Lady Radnor sitting in a room I had never seen, in a big red chair; and a lady in a black dress and white cap whom I had never seen came in and put her hand upon Lady R.'s shoulder. It was about 7.30, I think. I immediately, that same evening, wrote to Lady R. to ask her to write down what she was doing at 7.30, as I had seen her in the crystal. Shortly afterwards I saw Lady R., and she said she had done as I asked her, and told me to tell her what I saw. It was quite right; she had been sitting in a red armchair, and Lady Jane E., dressed as I described her, had come in and put her hand on her shoulder. Afterwards, when I met Lady Jane E., I recognised her, without knowing who she was, as the lady I had seen. Also, when I went to the house, I recognised the chair.
>
> [This is perfectly correct. Miss A. had never been to Longford when she described my room, which was right in every particular, even to the fact that my chair was quite touching the corner of the high fender.—H. M. RADNOR.][1]

Again, Miss Wingfield's automatic writing sometimes gave quite accurate information about its purported originators, deceased persons of whom it seemed very unlikely that she could have had any normal knowledge. And, in a number of cases, crystal or clairvoyant visions, automatic writing and raps were quite inextricably intermixed, the whole sometimes adding up to the most curious miniature dramas in which fact conceivably known to the medium, fact not likely to be known to the medium, and sheer fantasy were inseparably blended. A fairly short example, one of the 'historical' cases, is this:

> On February 23rd, 1890, Miss A. and I [Lady Radnor] were in the 'Cage' [in Salisbury Cathedral] and she told me she saw a grand ceremonial taking place. There appeared to be a tall chair which obstructed the view down the choir, and gradually the place appeared filled with clericals and others dressed in their best attire. Then she saw a tall big man, slowly walking up, dressed in red with white and lace over it, something that hung round his neck and down to his feet of broad gold embroidery, and a broad sort of mitre (but not peaked) more like a biretta, of beautiful embroidery.

[1] *P.S.P.R.* VIII (1892), pp. 501–2.

Then there were three or four dressed very much like him, gorgeously dressed, and lots of little boys about in red and white and lace—holding candles, books, &c. The whole place was very full of people, and it was evidently a great occasion. After the principal figure had knelt in front of the chair—looking to the west for some little time—he stood up and ten little boys lifted up the chair and carried it higher up and placed it in front of the altar, still facing west. Then the principal figure walked up two steps and faced the east. (The whole of the arrangements of the altar, &c., as Miss A. saw them, are quite different from what they are now.)

[It is here meant that Miss A.'s description was correct for that past date; as Lord Radnor explicitly told me was the case.] He had nothing on his head now. He knelt some little time, and then the most gorgeously dressed of the other figures placed something like a mitre on his head and retired, and the principal figure walked up to the chair, and sat down on it facing the congregation. Miss A said she saw him later dead in a coffin, with the Winchester Cross over him. She says he was tall, big, clean-shaven, a little curling hair, and blue-grey eyes.

Miss A. asked what she was seeing, and the answer came by raps.

A.: The induction of Briant Uppa.

Then Miss A. said: There can't be such a name; it must be wrong.

She tried again, and got—

A.: You are wrong. It was Duppa, not Uppa. Brian Duppa.

Q. Who was Brian Duppa?   A.: Chister.

Q. What was he?   A.: Bishop here.

Q. When? or what was his date?   A.: 44–16. His researches would help you. Manuscripts should lay at Winchester.

On returning home, we were talking after tea, and I casually took up [Brennan's *History of Wiltshire*, and said to Miss A, laughing: 'Now I will look for your Bishop.' . . . The pages where the Bishops' names were were uncut, sides and top. I cut them, and to our delight we found on p. 149:—'Brian Duppa or De Uphaugh, D.D. . . . tutor to Prince Charles . . . translated to the See of Chichester (Chister?) . . . Bishop of 1641 . . . (deposed soon after by Parliament) . . . preferred soon after to the See of Winchester.' He was at Carisbrook with Charles I, and is supposed to have assisted him in the writing of the *Eikon Basilike*, which book Miss A. had been looking at in my boudoir a few days previously, but which contains no mention of him nor his name.[1]

It is very difficult to know what to say of such cases. So far as I am aware no one ever supposed that Miss Wingfield was a conscious cheat. The most plausible explanation of the veridical information received in this case, and in other, somewhat comparable cases, is of course that the medium or sensitive had read the information in some book or periodical and then forgotten about it, and that when she later on fell into a state of slight dissociation it came to the fore again. On the other hand Miss Wingfield certainly did at times seem to have veridical crystal visions in which it was seemingly impossible for her to cheat; and even in the rather scanty records which have been published there are a surprising number of accurate communications from or concerning deceased persons whom it seems most unlikely that she could have known. But then again, what of the raps, so suspect to psychical researchers? It is at least amusing to think of paranormal raps disturbing the quiet of Salisbury Cathedral.

One might make rather similar comments upon another set of cases, those connected with two automatists called Mrs. Everett and Mrs. Turner.[2] Myers, who knew them, regarded their integrity as beyond question; so did Hensleigh Wedgwood, who discovered the case. Mrs. Turner, the younger sister, but a widow, was according to Hensleigh Wedgwood, 'far the stronger influence' in producing the writing; however, in most of the cases actually published, Mrs. Everett and Wedgwood himself operated a 'planchette' board. Again we have an admixture of inexplicable physical phenomena; again we have a number of cases of veridical communications from communicators ostensibly unknown to the operators; again we cannot discount the awkward possibility that the medium had somewhere read or heard the information concerned and had stored it at a subconscious level. For instance, to take one of the more dramatic (and perhaps therefore less plausible) cases: Hensleigh Wedgwood and Mrs. Everett on one occasion obtained some osten-

[1] *P.S.P.R.* VIII (1892), pp. 508-9.
[2] They figure in *P.S.P.R.* IX (1893), pp. 92-106, as 'Mrs. R.' and 'Mrs. V.' Mrs. Everett's diaries are preserved in the S.P.R. archives. She is not to be confused with the Mrs. Everitt mentioned above, pp. 73, 200.

sible communications from a lady called Alice Grimbold, who gave a very detailed account of the circumstances surrounding a murder in which she had been involved in 1605, and of her own subsequent execution. These particulars were eventually verified from a decidedly recondite book, James Thompson's *History of Leicester* (1849). Both operators averred that they had never heard of this book in their lives; and yet it is quite impossible to show that one or other of them had not run across it but forgotten it. Mediums *might* be, not people with the faculty of communicating with deceased persons, or even with clairvoyant gifts, but simply people with unusually sticky subconscious memories.

What of course was needed to overset such arguments was a medium who could produce veridical communications to order; who could, that is, regularly produce 'communications' from the deceased friends and relatives of persons brought, preferably without advance notice or even under pseudonyms, to see her. If a medium did this sufficiently often, and with sufficient details, it could not possibly be claimed that she was serving up only information which she had previously acquired and forgotten about. These conditions were met, at times more than amply, by an American medium, Mrs. Leonora E. Piper.[1] Mrs. Piper was, if we forget an alleged ability to shrivel flowers, innocent of the shady physical phenomena.

Mrs. Piper lived in Boston, Massachusetts, where her husband was employed in a large store. She possessed considerable good looks and, in sharp contrast to the vulgar physical mediums, was an undoubted lady. Her range of information and of conversation however seems to have been decidedly limited; so much so that Myers, in a letter to William James, unkindly referred to her as 'that insipid prophetess'. Her intellectual limitations were however an advantage when it came to the question whether she might have obtained her results fraudulently for, as will I think become clear later, to have done so she would have needed to have practised fraud of the most

---

[1] Mrs. Piper's biography has been written by her daughter. See Alta L. Piper, *The Life and Work of Mrs. Piper*, London, 1929; see also M. Sage, *Mrs. Piper and the Society for Psychical Research*, London, 1903.

ingenious kind. And her means, even when supplemented by her earnings as a medium, would certainly not have enabled her to employ agents.

Her career as a medium began more or less accidentally in 1884. In anxiety as to her own health, she visited a blind healing medium named J. R. Cocke. At her first visit she lost consciousness for a few minutes; at her second she passed into a trance and wrote on a piece of paper a message for one of the sitters, Judge Frost of Cambridge, Mass. Judge Frost, though a Spiritualist for thirty years, described it as the most remarkable he had ever received.

Mrs. Piper then began to hold sittings at her home for her family and friends. She spoke in trance and was at first purportedly controlled by, among others, such distinguished persons as Bach and Longfellow. However, after a while a *soi-disant* French doctor, who gave the name of Phinuit (Cocke's guide had been called 'Finney'), became chief 'control'. Phinuit spoke in a gruff male voice, in a curious mixture of Frenchisms, negro patois, and Yankee slang, sometimes swearing vulgarly. His diagnoses and prescriptions were often successful in a rough and ready way. He would give sitters accounts of the doings of living relatives and would transmit messages (often with appropriate gestures) from deceased ones, whom he would describe as being beside him. Very much more rarely, a deceased person would speak himself.

Rumours about these sittings reached the ears of William James' mother-in-law, Mrs. Gibbens, who managed to obtain a sitting for herself, and another for her daughter, James' sister-in-law. They returned with remarkable tales of the medium's knowledge of their family concerns. James, though he 'played the *esprit fort*' before his female relations, was sufficiently interested to go anonymously to a sitting. He was distinctly startled by what he heard.

> The medium . . . repeated most of the names of 'spirits' whom she had announced on the two former occasions and added others. The names came with difficulty, and were only gradually made perfect. My wife's father's name of Gibbens was announced first as Niblin, then as Giblin. A child Herman (whom we had lost the previous year) had his name spelled out as Herrin. I think that in no case were both Christian and sur-

names given on this visit. But the *facts predicated* of the persons named made it in many instances impossible not to recognise the particular individuals who were talked about.[1]

James was sufficiently struck to continue his own sittings with Mrs. Piper during 1885 and to send some twenty-five other persons to her under pseudonyms. In the spring of 1886 he gave a brief account of the results in the *Proceedings* of the American S.P.R. Fifteen of the persons who had had sittings with her received at the first sitting 'names and facts ... which it seemed improbable should have been known to the medium in a normal way'. The remainder got nothing but unknown names and trivial talk. Unfortunately only five of the sittings were stenographically reported in full. None the less 'My own conviction', said James, 'is not evidence, but it seems fitting to record it. I am persuaded of the medium's honesty, and of the genuineness of her trance; and although at first disposed to think that the "hits" she made were either lucky coincidences, or the result of knowledge on her part of who the sitter was and of his or her family affairs, I now believe her to be in possession of a power as yet unexplained.'

Pressure of work forced James to give up the enquiry into Mrs. Piper at this point. But in May of the following year (1887) Richard Hodgson arrived in Boston to become secretary of the American S.P.R. He found the openness of American manners, even of Boston manners, far more to his taste than the restrained conventions of England; and in the intellectual yet sporting circles of Boston's Tavern Club he found, perhaps for the first time in his life, a society in which he felt perfectly at home. His appointment had been especially urged by Mr. R. Pearsall Smith, a pronounced sceptic, who hoped that Hodgson's skill in detecting fraud would soon demolish the villainous Mrs. Piper.[2] This may well have been Hodgson's hope too, for he later confessed that his *amour propre* had never quite recovered from his failure to expose her.

The damage to Hodgson's *amour propre* began with the anonymous sittings which he had himself during the course of 1887. It seemed most unlikely that Mrs. Piper, in Boston, could by any device get to know intimate details about Hodgson's friends

[1] *P.S.P.R.* VI (1890), p. 652.　　　　[2] Baird, *op. cit.*, pp. 32–3.

and relatives in Australia; yet such details were given at her sittings. Here is an extract from his notes on his first sitting.

> Phinuit began, after the usual introduction, by describing members of my family.
> 'Mother living, father dead, little brother dead.' [True.] Father and mother described correctly, though not with much detail. In connection with the enumeration of the members of our family, Phinuit tried to get a name beginning with 'R', but failed. [A little sister of mine, named Rebecca, died when I was very young, I think less than eighteen months old.]
> 'Four of you living besides mother.' [True.]
> Phinuit mentioned the name 'Fred.' I said that it might be my cousin. 'He says you went to school together. He goes on jumping-frogs, and laughs. He says he used to get the better of you. He had convulsive movements before his death, struggles. He went off in a sort of spasm. You were not there.' [My cousin Fred far excelled any other person that I have seen in the games of leap-frog, fly the garter, &c. He took very long flying jumps, and whenever he played, the game was lined by crowds of schoolmates to watch him. He injured his spine in a gymnasium in Melbourne, Australia, in 1871, and was carried to the hospital, where he lingered for a fortnight, with occasional spasmodic convulsions, in one of which he died.]
> Phinuit described a lady, in general terms, dark hair, dark eyes, slim figure, &c., and said that she was much closer to me than any other person: that she 'died slowly. Too bad you weren't with her. You were at a distance. It was a great pain to both of you that you weren't there. She would have sent you a message, if she had known she was going. She had two rings; one was buried with her body; the other ought to have gone to you. The second part of her first name is—sie.' [True, with the exception of the statement about the rings, which may or may not be true . . .][1]

During 1888 and 1889 Hodgson continued to sit with Mrs. Piper himself, and to arrange sittings for others and collect reports from them. Unfortunately shortage of funds prevented full stenographic records being made of more than a few sittings. However, quite a number of sitters were able to make full notes, and sometimes too Hodgson himself acted as note-taker, and was able to keep virtually a complete record. Some

[1] p. 60 of R. Hodgson, 'A Record of Certain Phenomena of Trance', *P.S.P.R.* VIII (1892), pp. 1–167.

of the sittings were very remarkable; and, as a check upon Mrs. Piper's honesty, she and her family were shadowed for some weeks by detectives. No evidence was discovered that she went around enquiring into the affairs of possible sitters, or that she received letters from agents who might have done so. It then occurred to Hodgson and William James that a further valuable test would be to remove her to a totally new environment, where she could have neither talkative friends nor established agents. Accordingly Mrs. Piper was invited to England by a special committee consisting of Lodge, Myers and Walter Leaf. She set off in November 1889, accompanied by her two children, whom she refused to leave behind.

Mrs. Piper stayed twice in Liverpool with Lodge, twice in Cambridge with Myers and the Sidgwicks, and twice in London in lodgings chosen by the committee. Careful precautions were taken to prevent her from obtaining information about her hosts and about possible sitters. Almost all her sitters were introduced anonymously. Lodge's house contained (by chance) completely new servants, who could have known little about his concerns. He locked up the family Bible and photograph albums.[1] Mrs. Piper allowed him to examine her mail and to search her baggage, though the payment which she received—30 shillings a day—would hardly have enabled her to employ agents. Myers obtained for Mrs. Piper and her children a servant who could have known nothing of himself and his Cambridge friends; he chose sitters, he tells us 'in great measure by chance', sometimes introducing them only after the trance had begun. Of some sittings stenographic records were kept, of the majority full contemporary notes were taken; those made of the most successful sittings, the twenty-one held under Lodge's auspices, being in fact the fullest.[2]

The conclusions which the committee came to were substantially in agreement with those previously reached by James and Hodgson; the views of all five of these gentlemen, and also of the Sidgwicks, may be summarised as follows:

[1] None the less, C. A. Mercier, *Spiritualism and Sir Oliver Lodge*, London, 1917, p. 116, triumphantly demands to know if Lodge had not a family photograph album and a family Bible from which Mrs. Piper might have obtained her information.

[2] See 'A Record of Observations of Certain Phenomena of Trance' by Myers, Lodge, Leaf and James, *P.S.P.R.* VI (1890), pp. 436–659.

1. Mrs. Piper's behaviour in her normal state never gave the least ground for suspicion. No one ever detected her in a suspicious action. Indeed, her patience under the trying scrutiny to which she was subjected was most praiseworthy. Furthermore, her trance appeared to be geniuine—when she was entranced she could be pricked, cut, burned and even have an ammonia bottle held under her nose without being disturbed.

2. Mrs. Piper's chief 'control', Dr. Phinuit, though a distinctive 'character', gave no clear indication that he was anything other than a secondary personality of Mrs. Piper's. His accounts of his earth life were contradictory, and investigation did not confirm them. It was true that his diagnoses of the ailments of sitters and their friends were often shrewd, and his prescriptions successful; but he gave no serious indication of being able either to speak or to comprehend French, his supposed native tongue.

3. Worse than this; Phinuit's behaviour was at times altogether shady. On a bad day he would keep up a constant babble of inane conversation, interspersed with false assertions about the sitters and their deceased relatives. He would fish for information in a quite blatant manner, and if he got any he would serve it up again a few minutes later as though he had known it all along. Sitters who came only on bad days, or by their demeanour provoked bad days, might go away disgusted and suspect the whole performance of being a fraud.

4. But on a good day Phinuit might, with hardly any fishing, relay copious and very largely correct 'communications' from the deceased friends and relatives of sitters. Sitters who, for whatever reason, struck lucky in this way, might go away quite dumbfounded, feeling it quite inconceivable that Mrs. Piper could by any normal means have got access to the information which had been retailed to them.

Both Lodge and Myers received, purportedly from their own deceased friends and relations, information which greatly impressed them. To test the hypothesis that Mrs. Piper might have obtained this information, somehow, by surreptitious enquiries of her own, Lodge set an agent to see how much of the information summarised in this passage he could unearth by enquiries on the spot:

It happens that an uncle of mine in London, now quite an old man, and one of a surviving three out of a very large family, had a twin brother who died some twenty or more years ago. I interested him generally in the subject, and wrote to ask if he would lend me some relic of his brother. By morning post on a certain day I received a curious old gold watch, which this brother had worn and been fond of; and that same morning, no one in the house having seen it or knowing anything about it, I handed it to Mrs Piper when in a state of trance.

I was told almost immediately that it had belonged to one of my uncles—one that had been very fond of Uncle Robert, the name of the survivor—that the watch was now in possession of this same Uncle Robert, with whom he was anxious to communicate. After some difficulty and many wrong attempts Dr. Phinuit caught the name, Jerry, short for Jeremiah, and said emphatically, as if a third person was speaking, 'This is my watch, and Robert is my brother, and I am here. Uncle Jerry, my watch.' . . .

Having thus ostensibly got into communication through some means or other with what purported to be a deceased relative, whom I had indeed known slightly in his later years of blindness, but of whose early life I knew nothing, I pointed out to him that to make Uncle Robert aware of his presence it would be well to recall trivial details of their boyhood, all of which I would faithfully report.

He quite caught the idea, and proceeded during several successive sittings ostensibly to instruct Dr. Phinuit to mention a number of little things such as would enable his brother to recognise him. . . .

'Uncle Jerry' recalled episodes such as swimming the creek when they were boys together, and running some risk of getting drowned; killing a cat in Smith's field; the possession of a small rifle, and of a long peculiar skin, like a snake-skin, which he thought was not in the possession of Uncle Robert.

All these facts have been more or less completely verified. . .[1]

Two things may be noted in passing about this material. Firstly the summary of it does not mention a number of erroneous statements and of statements likely to be true of anyone, which Uncle Jerry, or Phinuit, made (the full records, with annotations, are printed at the end of Lodge's report). Secondly the hypothesis of telepathy from the sitters seems completely

[1] *P.S.P.R.* VI (1890), pp. 458–9.

ruled out. If there was any thought-transference, it must have been from Uncle Jerry's surviving brothers, both of whom lived hundreds of miles away.

Lodge's agent, Mr. G. A. Smith, who was certainly a very able man, spent several days in and around Barking, quizzing oldest inhabitants, looking up records, and so on; but he was unable to get further than establishing the probable location of 'Smith's Field'.

Mrs. Piper returned to the United States in February 1890. Despite the strain of being thrown among and scrutinised by total strangers, she had achieved some striking successes. After her return she entered with the American branch of the S.P.R. into an agreement which gave Richard Hodgson a large measure of control over her sittings in the next few years. In return she was to receive about £200 a year. Hodgson himself devoted much of the rest of his life to studying her, often in the face of considerable hardship and financial difficulty. He lived in one room and his slender salary was irregularly paid. This last was a cause of considerable friction between the English and the American branches of the S.P.R. To save Hodgson from actual starvation Myers and Sidgwick had frequently to subsidise him; yet the American branch had members much wealthier than they.

The result of Hodgson's self-sacrifice, the Sidgwick group's generosity, and Mrs. Piper's co-operation, was the accumulation of a detailed and at that time unique set of seance records, which extended over a good part of the next fifteen years. Sitters were introduced anonymously and with great precaution; full notes were generally taken either by Hodgson or by Miss Edmunds, his secretary; and the sittings were subsequently annotated by the sitters. 'Evidential material' continued to flow in. S.P.R. members watched the spectacle, many with acute interest, a few with irritation, and some with a growing and exhilarating hope that these experiments marked the dawn of a new era in man's knowledge of the Universe.

For some years Phinuit remained the chief communicator, and things went on much as before. Hodgson was convinced that Mrs. Piper possessed supernormal powers, but in his first paper on her[1] he was not disposed to accept that her 'com-

[1] *P.S.P.R.* VIII (1892), *loc. cit.*

municators' really were the deceased persons they purported to be. He found their personalities too fragmentary to be convincing. He inclined instead to believe that in her trances Mrs. Piper could obtain, telepathically or by clairvoyance, information which she would then serve up as though from a deceased person. But new developments in the Piper phenomena, especially the emergence of at least one communicator whose personality was more than fragmentary, caused him to alter his opinions and to accept the communicators almost at face value.[1]

During a sitting on 22nd March 1892, there appeared as a control a young man named George Pellew. Pellew came from a well-known Washington family and had been killed in a riding accident a few weeks earlier. He had had literary and philosophical interests and was known, though not intimately, to Hodgson. Five years previously he had anonymously had one and only one sitting with Mrs. Piper; there was however no reason to suppose that she could then have learned anything about him. Pellew gradually replaced Phinuit as chief control, and as the principal intermediary between sitters and their deceased friends. The 'G.P.' communicator, unlike Phinuit, was very realistic; he bore, Hodgson suggested, the same sort of relation to the real G.P. as a very good pen-and-ink sketch bears to a portrait in oils. He showed a most intimate knowledge of the affairs of the living G.P. and recognised and commented upon objects which had belonged to him. Out of 150 sitters who were introduced to him, G.P. recognised the thirty and only the thirty with whom the living Pellew had been acquainted. He appropriately adjusted the topics and the style of his conversation to each of these friends and often showed a close knowledge of their concerns. Only occasionally did the personation slip up badly; it did so, for instance, in a rather comic way when a sitter began to discuss with G.P. Chauncey Wright's views about 'Cosmical weather'. The point would have been well understood by the living G.P.

> Sitter: Well, now that you have got into that world, George, have you got any new light upon the character of natural law? Do you now find that law is . . .

---

[1] See his 'A Further Record of Observations of Certain Phenomena of Trance', *P.S.P.R.* XIII (1898), pp. 284–582.

G.P. Yes, law is thought.
Sitter: Do you now find that law is permanent?
G.P. Cause is thought.
Sitter: That doesn't answer.
G.P. Ask it.
Sitter: Is law permanent, or is it only transitory result?
G.P. It is permanent.
Sitter: Then do you agree with Chauncey Wright?
G.P. And everlasting.
Sitter: Then do you agree with Chauncey Wright?
G.P. Most certainly on that point.
Another Sitter: What do you think of his views on cosmical weather?
G.P. He knows nothing, his theory is ludicrous.
Sitter: He just said he agreed with him. That was the point I was asking about, the permanency of law.[1]

The emergence of the G.P. communicator was accompanied by the development of another method of communication, that of automatic writing. Mrs. Piper had occasionally written in trance before, but the vast majority of communications during the Phinuit regime had been by voice. Writing had two advantages over speaking: a full record was automatically made; and a greater number of communicators found it possible to manipulate the hand than had been able to use the voice. Now that Phinuit could be by-passed there was a general betterment in the tone of the communications, and Phinuit himself improved. It was sometimes possible to obtain communications by voice and hand simultaneously. Persons talking to the communicator who used the hand had to speak to the hand and not to the ear!

G.P. remained the master of ceremonies on the 'other side' until early in 1897. Fortunately Hodgson had almost complete control over Mrs. Piper's sittings and sitters during the period 1892–7, and very full records were kept. However, G.P. too was gradually displaced. In 1895 there appeared a communicator claiming to be W. Stainton Moses. The next year Moses introduced controls who purported to be the members of the 'Imperator Band' which had inspired his own automatic writings (see above, p. 78). The Imperator Band gradually assumed charge of Mrs. Piper. Mrs. Piper had recently had a

[1] *P.S.P.R.* XV (1900), pp. 26–7.

serious operation, and the controls insisted that the numbers both of her seances and sitters should be kept down. The remainder of Mrs. Piper's career is of little concern to us. The Imperator Band were never able to establish their identities with the Imperator Band which had inspired Stainton Moses. Some people—especially Hodgson, but also James—were impressed by the Band's teachings; though the mistakes made in e.g. Biblical chronology or scientific fact are sometimes ludicrous. Hodgson's early death prevented him from completing a projected paper about this phase of Mrs. Piper's mediumship.

Nearly everyone who had extensive dealings with Mrs. Piper became convinced that she possessed supernormal powers; even Frank Podmore, the S.P.R.'s severest sceptic (who had not had extensive first-hand dealings with her), became so convinced. He gave his reasons in a paper which he read to the S.P.R. in March 1899.[1]

He compares the Piper case with that of other sensitives who had been famous in the past, and concludes that it is unique in the fullness of the records and the abundance of the material. 'Our choice now seems clearly defined between deliberate and systematic fraud on the one hand and supernormal faculty on the other.' But he felt that the arguments against fraud were overwhelming. Mrs. Piper had never once in almost thirteen years been detected in a dishonest action; nor had wind been got of the activities of any agents employed by her. And even apart from such considerations, the arrangements which had been made to preserve the anonymity of sitters and to ensure that Mrs. Piper could by no means obtain surreptitious information about them—arrangements made not just by Hodgson, but at various times by a number of other persons who had had charge of her—seemed to preclude the possibility of fraud. Nor was the information which Mrs. Piper's communicators commonly served up generally of a kind which seemed likely to have come from public records, servants, gravestones, and the like. Names came through only with difficulty; dates were rarely given exactly; material relating to different persons was hardly ever mixed up. In delineation of character Mrs. Piper far outreached anything which could have been achieved as a result

[1] 'Discussion of the Trance-Phenomena of Mrs. Piper', *P.S.P.R.* XIV (1898), pp. 50–78.

of an agent's enquiries; successful communicators would commonly address sitters in exactly the right tone, and might refer to private and intimate matters, or to personal possessions of a trivial but significant kind.

Perhaps it is time to give some examples of the communications which thus impressed even the most hard-headed. Unfortunately it is quite impossible to give here anything like adequate examples of good and of indifferent communications, and it is certainly not possible to bring out their relative frequency.

The following is an example of Mrs. Piper (or Phinuit) in a successful vein. The sitting is dated 8th December 1893. The sitters (it was their first sitting) were the Rev. and Mrs. S. W. Sutton, who had lost their little daughter Katherine (Kakie) some six weeks previously. The note-taker was Mrs. Howard, a friend of Hodgson's and a very rapid writer. Mrs. Sutton's annotations are given in square brackets.

> Mrs. Howard held Mrs. Piper's hands. She became immediately entranced under the control of Dr. Phinuit. After a brief communication to Mrs. Howard I took Mrs. Piper's hands and Phinuit said: This is a lovely lady,—she has done much good,—has helped so many poor souls. A little child is coming to you. This is the dearest lady I have met for a long time—the most light I have seen while in Mrs. Piper's body. He reaches out his hands as to a child, and says coaxingly: come here, dear. Don't be afraid. Come, darling, here is your mother. He describes the child and her 'lovely curls.' Where is Papa? Want papa. [He takes from the table a silver medal.] I want this—want to bite it. [She used to bite it.] [Reaches for a string of buttons.] Quick! I want to put them in my mouth. [The buttons also. To bite the buttons was forbidden. He exactly imitated her arch manner.] I will get her to talk to you in a minute. Who is Frank in the body? [We do not know.] [My uncle Frank had died a few years before. We were much attached. Possibly Phinuit was confused and my uncle was trying to communicate.] A lady is here who passed out of the body with tumour in the bowels. [My friend, Mrs. C., died of ovarian tumour.] She has the child—she is bringing it to me. Who is Dodo? [Her name for her brother George.] Speak to me quickly. I want you to call Dodo. Tell Dodo I am happy. Cry for me no more. [Puts hands to throat.] No sore throat any more. [She had pain and distress of the

throat and tongue.] Papa, speak to me. Can not you see me? I am not dead, I am living. I am happy with Grandma. [My mother had been dead many years.] Phinuit says: Here are two more. One, two, three here,— one older and one younger than Kakie. [Correct.] That is a boy, the one that came first. [Both were boys] . . .

The little one calls the lady, Auntie. [Not her aunt.] I wish you could see these children. Phinuit turns to Mr. Sutton and says: You do a great deal of good in the body. [To me] He is a *dear* man! Was this little one's tongue very dry? She keeps showing me her tongue. [Her tongue was paralysed, and she suffered much with it to the end.] Her name is Katherine. [Correct.] She calls herself Kakie. She passed out last. [Correct.] Tell Dodo Kakie is in a spiritual body. Where is horsey? [I gave him a little horse.] Big horsey, not this little one. [Probably refers to a toy cart-horse she used to like.] Dear Papa, take me wide. [To ride.] Do you miss your Kakie? Do you see Kakie? The pretty white flowers you put on me I have here. I took their little souls out and kept them with me. Phinuit describes lilies of the valley, which were the flowers we placed in her casket.

Papa, want to go wide horsey. [She plead this all through her illness.] Every day I go to see horsey. I like that horsey. I go to ride. I am with you every day. [We had just come from Mr. Sutton's parents, where we drove frequently, and I had seen Kakie with us. (This means that Mrs. Sutton had seen the 'apparition' of Kakie.—R. H.) Margaret (her sister) is still there driving daily.] [I asked if she remembered anything after she was brought downstairs.] I was so hot, my head was so hot. [Correct.] [I asked if she knew who was caring for her, if it was any comfort to have us with her.] Oh, yes,—oh, yes. [I asked if she suffered in dying.] I saw the light and followed it to this pretty lady. You will love me always? You will let me come to you at home. I will come to you every day, and I will put my hand on you, when you go to sleep. Do not cry for me,— that makes me sad. Eleanor. I want Eleanor. [Her little sister. She called her much during her last illness.] I want my buttons. Row, Row,—my song,—sing it now. I sing with you. [We sing, and a soft child voice sings with us.]

> Lightly row, lightly row,
> O'er the merry waves we go,
> Smoothly glide, smoothly glide,
> With the ebbing tide.

[Phinuit hushes us, and Kakie finishes alone.]
> Let the winds and waters be
> Mingled with our melody,
> Sing and float, sing and float,
> In our little boat.

Papa sing. I hear your voice, but it is so heavy. [Papa and Kakie sing. Phinuit exclaims: see her little curls fly!] [Her curls were not long enough to fly at death, six weeks before.] Kakie sings: Bye, bye, ba bye, bye, bye, O baby bye. Sing that with me, papa. [Papa and Kakie sing. These two songs were the ones she used to sing.] [She sang slight snatches of others in life not at the sitting.] Where is Dinah? I want Dinah. [Dinah was an old black rag-doll, not with us.] I want Bagie [her name for her sister Margaret]. I want Bagie to bring me my Dinah. I want to go to Bagie. I want Bagie. I see Bagie all the time. Tell Dodo when you see him that I love him. Dear Dodo. He used to march with me, he put me way up. [Correct.] Dodo did sing to me. That was a horrid body. I have a pretty body now. Tell Grandma I love her. I want her to know I live. Grandma does know it, Marmie—Great—grandma, Marmie. [We called her Great Grandmother *Marmie*, but *she* always called her *Grammie*. Both Grandmother and Great Grandmother were then living.][1]

Of course thought-transference from the sitters (at least if one is satisfied that thought-transference occurs) is a very plausible explanation of such communications. But it cannot be the explanation of cases where, as in the example of 'Uncle Jerry' quoted above, information unknown to any of the sitters is given. Quite a number of such cases occurred in the English and other early sittings, and they were even more frequent during the G.P. period. A curious example is summarised as follows by Hodgson. The 'Madame Elisa' referred to was a lady, known in life both to Hodgson and to Myers; she had died some while before. 'F.' was her uncle, who survived her.

> The notice of his ['F.'s'] death was in a Boston morning paper, and I happened to see it on my way to the sitting. The first writing of the sitting came from Madame Elisa, without my expecting it. She wrote clearly and strongly, explaining that F. was there with her, but unable to speak directly, that she

---
[1] *P.S.P.R.* XIII (1897), pp. 485-6.

wished to give me an account of how she had helped F. to reach her. She said that she had been present at his death-bed, and had spoken to him, and she repeated what she had said, an unusual form of expression, and indicated that he had heard and recognised her. This was confirmed in detail in the only way possible at that time, by a very intimate friend of Madame Elisa and myself, and also of the nearest surviving relative of F. I showed my friend the account of the sitting, and to this friend, a day or two later, the relative, who was present at the death-bed, stated spontaneously that F. when dying said that he saw Madame Elisa who was speaking to him, and he repeated what she was saying. The expression so repeated, which the relative quoted to my friend, was that which I had received from Madame Elisa through Mrs. Piper's trance, when the death-bed incident was of course entirely unknown to me.[1]

It was no doubt the strain which such cases threw on the telepathic hypothesis that in part induced Hodgson to move over in his second paper on Mrs. Piper (written in 1897–8 after a long study of the G.P. case) to the view that the communicators were indeed the surviving spirits of deceased persons. But various other considerations also weighed heavily with him. These may be summarized as follows:[2]

1. The fragmentariness and disjointedness of many communications may reasonably be accounted for in terms of the difficulties which communicators might be expected to encounter in controlling the medium's organism. And the incompleteness and fragmentariness in question are of a kind which supports the spiritualistic rather than the telepathic hypothesis. For

2. The knowledge of sitters and their affairs displayed by communicating entities is characteristically limited; it is limited to the knowledge which the *communicators themselves* might be expected to possess. Accounting for this on the telepathic hypothesis would be very difficult; it would involve crediting the medium with a remarkable power of *selecting* from among the innumerable items of information about the sitters which she *could* have reached only those which in fact a given deceased person might be expected to possess.

3. Again, one communicator will be good, another bad, with

[1] *P.S.P.R.* XIII (1898), p. 378n.   [2] *P.S.P.R.* XIII (1898), pp. 351–406.

the same sitter; some communicators, like G.P., were uniformly, or almost uniformly, good with a great variety of sitters. This surely supports the spiritistic explanation. It can hardly be supposed that all G.P.'s friends just happened to be gifted telepathic agents.

4. More than this, there are not a few cases of communicators who first of all communicate in the presence of their friends and relatives, and later return at sittings when those friends and relatives are not present and deliver further, and appropriate, messages for them. This naturally weakens the force of the telepathic explanation; as also do the various cases of communicators who give correct but quite unexpected answers to sitters' questions.

5. Hodgson was also particularly impressed by cases of communications from suicides and from persons who had died in a state of mental distress. Such persons can, generally speaking, for some while after their deaths communicate only in a confused fashion; and this despite the presence as sitters of intimate friends whose knowledge of them the medium should be able to ransack by telepathy.

How far Hodgson, in addition to favouring some form of the spirit hypothesis, at this time actually accepted the teachings delivered by the spirits, I do not know. (Mrs. Piper's controls seem in the main to have expounded doctrines of a fairly orthodox Spiritualist kind.[1]) Hodgson came in the end to believe implicitly in the Imperator controls, and to mould his whole way of life on their teachings.

Hodgson read parts of his second paper on Mrs. Piper at a General Meeting of the S.P.R. on 11th March 1898. Sidgwick said in discussion that he was impressed by the evidence that Mrs. Piper possessed telepathic powers. But as for the spirit hypothesis 'he could not say more than that a *prima facie* case had been established for further investigation, keeping this hypothesis in view'.[2] He commented upon Phinuit's low moral tone and shiftiness, and thought that G.P. exhibited some of the same characteristics. G.P. resembled Phinuit also in desiring to appear to know more than he did; yet he exhibited the most lamentable lack of understanding of philosophy (of which the living G.P. had been a keen student). Hodgson replied that

[1] Cf. Sage, *op. cit.*, pp. 99–110. [2] *J.S.P.R.* VIII (1898), p. 220.

other communicators referred to Phinuit's weaknesses without exhibiting them themselves. In regard to G.P.'s ignorance of philosophy Hodgson pointed out that 'the conditions of communication must be kept before the mind, and that if Professor Sidgwick were compelled to discourse philosophy through Mrs. Piper's organism, the result would be a very different thing from his lectures at Cambridge'.[1]

Views in part resembling Sidgwick's were developed at some length by Mrs. Sidgwick in a paper in the S.P.R. *Proceedings* for 1900[2] (a paper which she afterwards amplified to book length in *P.S.P.R.* XXVIII). In this paper she accepts, for the sake of argument, that the spirits of deceased persons are in some way involved in at least some of the communications, and asks the subsidiary question, is the actual communicating intelligence other than Mrs. Piper's? Hodgson, of course, had argued that deceased persons really could gain control of Mrs. Piper's organism. Mrs. Sidgwick came to the conclusion that departed spirits could influence Mrs. Piper's mind only telepathically, and that the 'communications' were hence of an indirect or mediated kind. She admitted that the communicating personalities often gave the impression of being quite distinct from Mrs. Piper; but this, she pointed out, can also hold true in cases of secondary personality. And in some ways the communicating personalities are apt to resemble secondary personalities—they are suggestible and given to childish rationalisations to cover up mistakes. They are indeed perhaps not as rounded and complete as some secondary personalities. They get involved in incoherences, prevarications and self-contradictions of a most awkward kind. They will not admit ignorance, but instead tell all sorts of complicated lies to back up or excuse their own *gaffes*. Phinuit is particularly bad in these respects, and it is quite clear that neither he nor the 'Imperator' group of controls can possibly be what they claim to be. Yet the most impressive control of all, G.P., the one for whose separate individuality there would seem to be the strongest evidence, guarantees the credentials of both Phinuit and the Imperator controls, and so stands or falls with them. And the moral and

[1] *J.S.P.R.* VIII (1898), p. 221.
[2] 'Discussion of the Trance Phenomena of Mrs. Piper', *P.S.P.R.* XV (1900), pp. 16-38.

intellectual standards of the communicators are frequently well below those which they had when alive. The instance of G.P.'s confusion over 'cosmical weather' has already been quoted. Another example is the *soi-disant* George Eliot who claimed that she had met in the next world Chaucer, the only and original author of the Canterbury Tales, a Bacon who said he was Shakespeare, and Adam Bede. Mrs. Piper's own personality crops out in many places, and can be seen in the communicators' interests in clothes and hats, and in their ignorance of science—one communicator said that the etheric body was made of 'vacium'.

I have cited Mrs. Sidgwick's paper at length, not because I feel that the controversy between her and Hodgson is important or even capable of solution, but in order to provide further examples of Mrs. Piper at her worst to set against the more favourable examples cited before.[1] However, something which sitters frequently insisted upon should perhaps also be borne in mind, namely that very often no printed record of a sitting can possibly convey a proper idea of the verisimilitude of Mrs. Piper's personation. To the recipient of the messages the very manner in which they were delivered might convey a certainty which could neither be resisted nor yet communicated.

It was not until 1898 that in Mrs. Edmond Thompson, the wife of a prosperous merchant, a trance medium was found in England whose powers seemed at all comparable to Mrs. Piper's, and who was prepared to submit to prolonged investigation in the same way. Mrs. Thompson's mediumship had begun in 1897, when she was aged twenty-nine, and accounts of its early development may be found in *Light* for that and the following year (she is there known as 'Mrs. T.'). Her chief 'control' was Nelly, a deceased daughter. Her early phenomena were often physical—raps, lights, occasional 'apports', movements and even levitations of chairs and tables, and the billowing of curtains in true Eusapian style. She even supposedly materialised spirit hands and spirit drapery; these were however for the

---

[1] See also the rather querulous 'Discussion of the Trance Phenomena of Mrs. Piper' by A. Lang, *P.S.P.R.* XV (1900), pp. 39–52; and, for some examples of wholly hostile (but also often wholly erroneous) criticism, Appendix B, below.

most part heard and felt rather than seen. Mrs. Thompson was not, at any time, paid for her services.

The reports about Mrs. Thompson in *Light* attracted Myers' attention, and on 2nd September 1898 he went by arrangement to call upon her. He was much impressed by the apparent sincerity and candour of Mr. and Mrs. Thompson, and he struck up a close friendship with them. He was able to exercise over Mrs. Thompson's sittings the sort of complete control which Hodgson had had over Mrs. Piper's. He had himself upwards of 150 sittings with her, the records of which have unfortunately disappeared, and during the period 1898–1900 he introduced a fair range of other sitters, mostly anonymously.

Under Myers' influence Mrs. Thompson ceased to try for physical phenomena (that Myers should wish to steer clear of them was quite understandable in view of his brushes with Hodgson). However, the other modes in which she might obtain 'messages' were quite numerous; in this respect she somewhat resembled Miss Wingfield. She might see pictures or writing in a crystal or on a wall, or even see spirits standing in the room with her. She wrote automatically, both in trance and in a waking state. Most commonly however communications through her were by voice. Her chief control, Nelly, generally relayed (as Phinuit had done) information and messages from deceased persons whom she said she had with her; and she often gave information about the supposed present activities and whereabouts of living friends or relations of the communicator or of the sitters. Only rarely did a communicator other than Nelly control Mrs. Thompson directly.

Much the longest, and seemingly much the most successful, series of sittings was Myers' own; it convinced him completely that he was at last in touch with Annie Marshall. Unfortunately he did not live to write an account of them. A number of sitters did however write accounts of their sittings, and these were printed in the *Proceedings* of the S.P.R. for June 1902.

The most interesting sittings were perhaps the seven had by a Dutchman, Dr. F. van Eeden, during two visits to England in 1899 and 1900. At his early visits (his name being, of course, kept from Mrs. Thompson) he received from Nelly a good deal of detailed and accurate information about his family and background in Holland; so accurate was some of this information that he was at first inclined to believe that he really had been put in touch with deceased persons. However, reflection inclined him to accept the telepathic view instead, for mistakes were made which the supposed communicators would not have made. But some striking communications received during his second series of sittings induced him to change his mind again, and to conclude 'it is impossible for me to abstain from the conviction that I have really been a witness, were it only for a few minutes, of the voluntary manifestation of a deceased person'.[1] These communications came from a young Dutchman who had made two attempts to commit suicide, the second of them successful. In the first he had cut his throat: but had recovered; in the second he had shot himself. At the sitting of 2nd June 1900, Nelly was handed a parcel containing a piece of the dead man's clothing. Van Eeden states[2] that no one in the world knew that he had it, or that he had brought it to England.

> *Nelly.* . . . 'I am frightened. I feel as if I want to run away.' (To van E.) 'That lady won't be cross.' (To Lady Battersea) 'Don't go away. I feel rather frightened. What's Marfa, Martha? She's got a lot of people belonging to her.'
> *Van E.* 'That's my wife.'
> *Nelly.* 'She was not very well. It is better now. She went to lie down. [Doubtful.] Old gentleman sends his love to Martha. He says: "My love, Martha."
> 'This' (pointing to parcel) 'is a much younger gentleman. Very studified, fond of study.' [Right.]
> *Van E.* 'Why were you frightened?'
> *Nelly.* 'Because something seemed like a shock to me. He's not a rich gentleman. If he lived a bit longer he would have had more. He wanted to make some.' [Right.]
> *Van E.* 'How do you know?'
> *Nelly.* 'Mrs. Cartwright tells me.'
> *Van E.* 'Ask her why you were frightened.'
> *Nelly.* 'She says because I was afraid of making faults.' [Obviously wrong.]
> 'Gentleman used to have headache at the back of his head. He used to take tablets to make his head go better.' [Doubtful.]
> [Some remarks about an unidentified 'Stout William' are omitted.]

---

[1] *P.S.P.R.* XVII (1902), p. 84. [2] *P.S.P.R.* XVII (1902), pp. 77-8.

Van E. 'You have not told me the principal thing about this man' (parcel).

Nelly. 'The principal thing is his sudden death.' [Right.] 'I can tell you better when she (Lady Battersea) is not there. It frightens me. Everybody was frightened, seeming to say "O dear! Good gracious!" . . .

'This gentleman could shoot. He was rather an out-of-doors man. What a funny hat he used to wear. Round with a cord around. He had a velvet jacket. You have a velvet jacket too, but not real velvet, and like trousers. [Right.] But that gentleman had real velvet jacket.' [References to dress—Doubtful.] 'I can't see any blood about this gentleman, but a horrible sore place: somebody wiped it all up. It looks black.' [The bullet wound probably.] 'I am happy because that man is happy now. He was in a state of muddle, and when he realised what he had done, he said it is better to make amends and be happy.'

Van E. 'How did he make amends?'

Nelly. 'When any people want to kill themselves he goes behind them and stops their hands, saying, "just wait." He stops their hands from cutting their throats. He says, "Don't do that: you will wake up and find yourselves in another world haunted with the facts, and that's a greater punishment." He's got such a horror that anybody would do the same thing, and he asks them to stop, and it makes him so happy.' [He cut his own throat, but recovered; and afterwards shot himself.]

(To van E.) 'You don't seem to have any whiskers. I don't see your head properly. Some one covers up your head. He covers up your head to show how his own head was covered up. O dear, isn't it funny? You must not cut off your head when you die.' [The suicide's head was covered up when he was found dead.] . . .[1]

At the next sitting, that of 5th June, Nelly gave some more information about the young man of the parcel.

'This person (of the parcel) talks foreign language. [Right.] Has got something about the throat' [i.e. the wound resulting from the unsuccessful attempt at suicide.] 'Talks not very distinctly. [Right.] He can talk English a bit, but not many. [Right.] He is standing before a desk with white knobs on it. [Doubtful.] He was very disappointed and got depressed and got a headache. Worried much. [Right.]

'Very friendly, and used to go about a good deal with a tall,

---

[1] *P.S.P.R.* XVII (1902), pp. 104–5.

fair man, fair complexion.' [He was intimate with a tall, fair man, who in turn committed suicide two days after him.] 'They had a good quarrel.' [Probably Right.] 'I don't like that fair man. I don't believe in him, don't trust him. It was a shock to him (parcel-man) to find this out about his friend. [Doubtful.]

. . . 'He was alive when your Queen was crowned. [Right.] He had a way, used to be like that (swaying her hand). [Right.] I do love him, really I do. It was a great shock to your wife. She said she could not have thought it of him. [Right.]

'Something very peculiar happened to his uncle.' [Statement about uncle found to be true on subsequent enquiry.]

'Ought I to like the strange gentleman?

'This gentleman wore ring with a dark stone in it. [Doubtful.] He wrote some letters that you read. [Right.] You looked at them and said: "How could a man do such a thing that could write like that?" ' [This was my sentiment, though I do not recollect having said the words.—*Note by van E.*] (Coughing) 'Could he not make the people have what he wrote?'

Van E. 'But he got his writings printed.'

Nelly. 'Yes, but it gave him no satisfaction. [Right.] He thought great things of those things. [Right.] You wrote a book, he admired it very much. [Right.] But he criticised it nevertheless. [Right.] He does not seem to have had a wife. [Right.] I see him sleeping alone. Do you like that tall friend?'

At the sitting of 7th June the suicide himself appeared to control Mrs. Thompson. Van Eeden spoke to him in Dutch, and got immediate and appropriate answers, in English, but with many correct Dutch names and a few Dutch phrases. A curious thing was that on waking briefly during the sitting Mrs. Thompson complained of a taste like chloroform in her mouth. The young suicide's wounded trachea had been dressed with iodoform.

Another sitter, Mrs. A. W. Verrall, was also impressed. She had twenty-two sittings with Mrs. Thompson. Out of 238 definite statements made by Nelly about present or past matters, 33 were false, 64 uncertain, and 141 true. Of the 141 true statements, 51 could have been obtained from obvious normal sources—reference books and public records. In the remaining 90 cases Mrs. Thompson's possession of the information could not be accounted for. Certainly an impressive performance.

A sitter who was not impressed was Richard Hodgson. Hodgson had six sittings with Mrs. Thompson, but obtained nothing of any value. On the contrary, he thought that there were indications that she might have surreptitiously gleaned information from some letters which had been accessible to her during a seance. His unfavourable view of her was no doubt strengthened by his knowledge of her early physical phenomena; and perhaps, as J. G. Piddington later suggested, by the fact that her trances were so unlike Mrs. Piper's that he might not have thought them genuine.

Mrs. Thompson was strongly (and I think correctly) defended against Hodgson by Frank Podmore[1]—a case of diamond cut diamond, if ever there was one. Podmore pointed out that the evidence which sitters other than Hodgson had obtained for Mrs. Thompson's possessing supernormal powers was really quite considerable; and that the facts of psychopathology suggested that if a sensitive cheated in a state of dissociation it should not be regarded as a mark of moral culpability or as grounds for setting aside the evidence obtained when she is properly watched. There is at least no doubt that Mrs. Thompson courted investigation in the fullest and frankest way, expressing the view that the most stringent precautions ought to be taken.[2]

The interpretation of Mrs. Thompson's phenomena presents difficulties somewhat analogous to, but even greater than, those which arise in the interpretation of Mrs. Piper's. I shall not pursue the case further, since the most important paper on it, that by J. G. Piddington,[3] lies outside the period with which we are concerned. Piddington, indeed, though convinced that Mrs. Thompson possessed paranormal powers, was unable to come to any positive conclusions as to their nature. His view, he said, could only be stated negatively

> ... by confessing that after repeated revisions of what I had written, I have given up the attempt to define my opinions in despair. I do not halt between two opinions, but I shilly-shally

---

[1] *The Newer Spiritualism*, pp. 157–8.
[2] *J.S.P.R.* X (1901), p. 144.
[3] J. G. Piddington, 'On the Types of Phenomena Displayed in Mrs. Thompson's Trance', *P.S.P.R.* XVIII (1904), pp. 104–307.

between many: so much so that I hesitate to dignify such vacillation with the name of 'suspense of judgment.'[1]

Both Mrs. Thompson and Mrs. Piper continued active as mediums for some years more; and both played some part in the 'Cross-Correspondences', the series of parallel or interlinked communications obtained through different mediums and automatists, and allegedly devised by the spirits of deceased members of the Sidgwick group for the benefit of their colleagues still in the flesh. But all this, though fascinating, lies outside the period we have to deal with.[2] Later on however I shall say a little about the Piper material and the question of survival.

---

[1] *P.S.P.R.* XVIII (1904), p. 111.
[2] I have also left out of consideration the lengthy accounts of sittings with Mrs. Piper by two Americans, Professor W. R. Newbold and Professor J. H. Hyslop. See *P.S.P.R.* XIV (1898), pp. 6-49; and *P.S.P.R.* XVI (1901), pp. 1-649.

XII Myers' Theory of the Subliminal Self

THERE WERE CONSIDERABLE DIFFERENCES within the Sidgwick group on the question of whether or not the phenomena which they had unearthed pointed towards human survival of bodily death. Sidgwick had doubts; so in a different way had Leaf; Gurney was never convinced. But Myers and Hodgson finally arrived at a full belief in survival; and Mrs. Sidgwick very much more slowly and cautiously trod the same road. These differences seem on the surface to be quite considerable; and no doubt from a practical point of view they *are* considerable. But they did not involve the members of the Sidgwick group in quite the theoretical differences one might expect, for believers and non-believers alike came in greater or in less measure to accept much the same sort of theoretical framework or at any rate theoretical terminology. This framework was principally developed by Myers; and it is a framework which has also been accepted by not a few subsequent writers on similar topics—including some who have hesitated to take the extra step of believing in survival. No account of the Sidgwick group would be complete without an examination of it.

Myers' theory of the 'subliminal self' was set forth in a series of articles in the S.P.R. *Proceedings* from 1892 onwards, and in his large and unfinished posthumous book, *Human Personality and its Survival of Bodily Death* (1903), which incorporates substantial chunks of the articles. No doubt someone who had known Myers at the time of the S.P.R.'s foundation—who had known his religious history, and his admiration for Plato and

Wordsworth—could have predicted the general nature of his theory. But by its details such a person might well have been surprised. Myers had, of course, always had an interest in science, and had made abortive attempts to be allowed to sit the Natural Sciences Tripos in his fifth year at Cambridge; but his main interests and specialisms had been literary and classical. He had however of late years begun to read widely, and by no means superficially, in almost every branch of science. The speed with which he could grasp a subject was remarkable—Gurney once said that Myers could master a literature whilst he was reading a book. His memory was prodigious. There was no subject which he felt might not conceivably be of relevance to his central line of study. His reading was limited only by an imperfect knowledge of mathematics—a defect for which he tried to compensate by constant questioning of scientists known to him. Lodge was his most frequent target and was decidedly impressed with his grasp of scientific issues; he said that amongst other things Myers had anticipated the 'solar system' model of atomic structure,[1] and had shown an interest in wireless telegraphy which had in turn stimulated Lodge himself to some of his discoveries.[2] Myers was especially well versed in psychological literature, including branches of it then very little known in England. He was, I think, the first in this country to draw attention to some of Janet's writings, and also to the work of Breuer and Freud.[3] All this reading Myers put to account in developing his theory; and it enabled him to illustrate his arguments with a large number of curious analogies, some of them, I am afraid, more misleading than helpful.

The worst feature of Myers' *Human Personality* is probably the style in which it is written. Myers' workaday prose is sometimes masterly—clear and classical, with occasional delicate ingrainings of humour. But when he comes to touch on religion and the soul, his prose too often dissolves into a kind of Cosmic chant:

> . . . far hence, beyond Orion and Andromeda, the cosmic process works and shall work for ever through unbegotten

---

[1] J. A. Hill, ed., *Letters from Sir Oliver Lodge*, London, 1932, p. 220.
[2] See *J.S.P.R.* XV (1911), p. 74.
[3] In 1893—see *P.S.P.R.* IX, p. 12.

souls. And even as it was not in truth the great ghost of Hector only, but the whole nascent race of Rome, which bore from the Trojan altar the hallowing fire, so is it not one Saviour only, but the whole nascent race of man—nay, all the immeasurable progeny and population of the heavens—which issues continually from behind the veil of Being, and forth from the Sanctuary of the Universe carries the ever-burning flame: *Aeternumque adytis effert penetralibus ignem.*[1]

Whatever one may think of Myers' sonorous style, or for that matter of his theory of the subliminal self, his *Human Personality* is still a work of very considerable value. It is of value partly because of its extensive coverage of the evidence for 'psychical' phenomena which had been gathered up to the year 1900—and even then the quantity of such evidence was by no means slight. But it is especially valuable because of its detailed and exhaustive classification of cases, and for its arrangement of them in what might be called natural series. William James said that Myers possessed '... a genius not unlike that of Charles Darwin for discovering shadings and transitions, and grading down discontinuities in his argument'.[2] The phenomena with which psychical research deals are presented not as isolated outcrops, as dubious sports, freaks or miracles; but as facts which have natural affinities to phenomena whose occurrence no one disputes. There is a continuous set of gradations between facts which everyone accepts and facts which might be called 'paranormal'; and it is hard indeed to find a logical halting-place anywhere along the line. Thus Myers presents the case of Mrs. Piper as the terminal point of a series of which hysterical anaesthesiae; tics; automatic writing; automatic writing with indications of telepathy; somnambulism; fugues; cases of multiple personality; cases of pseudopossession; cases of pseudopossession with hints of telepathy; and hypnotic parallels for many of these phenomena; form the earlier steps. Similarly apparitions of the dead are described only after images; the telepathic transmission of images; dreams; telepathy and clairvoyance in dreams; hallucinations; hypnotic hallucinations; crystal visions; and crisis apparitions; have all been dealt with.

The arrangement of cases in series is not merely valuable in

[1] *Human Personality* II, p. 292.   [2] *P.S.P.R.* XVIII (1903), p. 30.

its own right, and as a means, if not for awakening sceptics from their dogmatic slumbers, at any rate for giving them bad dreams. I shall later argue that if evidence that human personality may survive the dissolution of the body is presented in a matrix of other curious facts about human personality, that evidence becomes more readily acceptable; for the other facts help to enlarge the very concept of personality in a way which makes survival seem a logical possibility.

Upon and around this array of facts Myers erects his famous theory of the subliminal self. The details and exact applications of the theory are not infrequently difficult to follow. This is partly, no doubt, because Myers was still working on it at the time of his death. But there are two other obvious sources of difficulty. The first is simply that, as one would perhaps expect, Myers' eyes continually wander from the path at his feet towards the distant and numinous heights which lie before him. The second is the abstruseness and complexity of the concepts central to his theory, such as consciousness, mind, soul, spirit, personality, psychical activity. Myers offers little elucidation of these terms, though his intentions may perhaps have been more obvious to his contemporaries than they are to us. Among present-day psychologists words like 'consciousness', 'mind', and so forth have become not merely unfashionable, but even faintly heterodox. Many psychologists have not wittingly used them in their professional moments these twenty years. Perhaps for this reason there has come about a rather common misconception of Myers' theory of the subliminal self—that it belongs among, and may be assimilated to, theories about 'The Unconscious'. It has often been expounded in a way which makes it appear as a sort of prototype of Jung's 'Analytic psychology'.[1] But this is quite wrong. Freud and Jung both held what might be described as the 'searchlight' or 'inner sense' view of consciousness.[2] 'Experiences' or 'mental

[1] I have been guilty of this error myself, *P.S.P.R.* LIII, (1961), pp. 230–1.
[2] 'We see the process of a thing becoming conscious as a specific psychical act, distinct from and independent of the process of the formation of a presentation or idea; and we regard consciousness as a sense organ which perceives data that arise elsewhere' (S. Freud, *The Interpretation of Dreams*, tr. J. Strachey, London, 1954, p. 144). '... we can readily compare consciousness with the rays of a search-light. Only those objects upon which the shaft of light falls enter the field of perception. An object that is by accident in darkness has not ceased to exist, it is merely not seen. So what is unconscious to me exists somewhere, and it is highly probable that

events' move into or out of the searchlight of consciousness (or the vision of the inward eye), but whether they are in it or out of it they remain mental events or entities.

Now Myers seems to have rejected the view that there can be such literally unconscious mental events. It is true that in his earlier writings he occasionally uses the adjective 'unconscious' almost as a pseudonym for 'subliminal';[1] but his general drift is pretty clear. He was much influenced by William James' *Principles of Psychology* (1890) and reviewed it at length in the S.P.R. *Proceedings*.[2] James devotes a dozen pages to exposing the logical errors involved in all 'proofs' that there can be literally unconscious mental states. He says (very reasonably, it seems to me) that postulating unconscious mental states is 'the sovereign means for believing what one likes in psychology, and of turning what might become a science into a tumbling-ground for whimsies'.[3] Of James' arguments Myers remarks:

> Professor James strikes the right note when, in reply to the argument that 'secondarily automatic' performances 'must consist of unconscious perceptions, inferences, and volitions,' he suggests that the consciousness of these actions exists, but is split off from the rest of the consciousness of the hemispheres.[4]

Not long afterwards he wrote of the 'threshold' of consciousness: 'For all which lies below that threshold *subliminal* seems the fittest word. "Unconscious", or even "subconscious", would be directly misleading.'[5]

I think that Myers not merely rejects the notion of unconscious mental events; as a natural consequence he probably also rejects the 'searchlight' view of consciousness.[6] When he

---

it has not changed essentially from what it was when I first saw it' (C. G. Jung, *Contributions to Analytical Psychology*, tr. H. G. and C. F. Baynes, London, 1928, p. 81).

[1] See, e.g., his 'Further Notes on the Unconscious Self', *J.S.P.R.* II (1885–6), pp. 122–31, 234–43.
[2] *P.S.P.R.* VII (1891), pp. 111–33.
[3] *Principles* II, p. 163.
[4] *P.S.P.R.* VII (1891), p. 117.
[5] *P.S.P.R.* VII (1892), p. 305.
[6] But he never quite rids himself of the 'searchlight' terminology; and, just occasionally, at least in his early days, he seems to toy with the notion that there might be several 'searchlights' rather than several streams of consciousness. Thus he says, *J.S.P.R.* II (1885), p. 129, 'Socrates' "mind" is capable of concentrating itself round more than one focus either simultaneously or successively.'

talks of 'consciousness', 'double consciousness' and so on, he seems usually to mean something very like what William James meant by 'the stream of thought'; an on-going and sensibly continuous flux of mental activity—of thinking, feeling, perceiving, hoping, intending, and so forth. In fact Myers sometimes uses the phrase 'stream of thought', and frequently the phrase 'stream of consciousness'. And when he asserts that all psychical actions are 'conscious',[1] I think he means not that they are all in fact caught in the beam of some searchlight or another, but that they are all events which could in principle figure in a 'stream of consciousness'. This at least seems to be the upshot of his curious contention[2] that consciousness is to be *defined* in terms of memorability. 'I cannot see how we can phrase our definition more simply than by saying that any act or condition must be regarded as conscious if it *is potentially memorable.*' Myers perhaps means here that memorability is a *criterion* of consciousness; only if an event is of a kind which *could* be remembered, is it of a kind which *could* also form part of a stream of consciousness. In other places[3] he does indeed talk of memorability as a 'test' of consciousness. But I do not think it would be easy to state even the 'criterion' view convincingly.

William James had been able to assert that every 'thought' (under which heading he includes most forms of mental activity) is part of a personal consciousness, and indeed that a 'personality' simply *is* a stream of thought. He expresses the point thus:

> A French writer, speaking of our ideas, says somewhere in a fit of anti-spiritualistic excitement that, misled by certain peculiarities which they display, we 'end by personifying' the procession which they make,—such personification being regarded by him as a great philosophic blunder on our part. It could only be a blunder if the notion of personality meant something essentially different from anything to be found in the mental procession. But if that procession be itself the very 'original' of the notion of personality, to personify it cannot possibly be wrong. It is already personified. There are no marks of personality to be gathered *aliunde*, and then found lacking in the train of thought. It has them all already . . .[4]

---

[1] *P.S.P.R.* VII (1892), p. 305.
[2] *Human Personality* I, pp. 36–7; *P.S.P.R.* VII (1892), p. 117.
[3] *P.S.P.R.* IV (1887), p. 257; *J.S.P.R.* II (1885), p. 123.
[4] *Principles* I, pp. 226–7.

Myers however was led by his studies in psychopathology to think it possible that there might be streams of consciousness too fragmentary or too impoverished to constitute a personality. He uses the term 'personality' only for streams of consciousness of a certain length and complexity:

> ... let us apply the word *personality*, as its etymology suggests, to something more external and transitory [than a possible principle of underlying psychical unity]—to each of those apparent characters, or chains of memory and desire, which may at any time mask at once and manifest a psychical existence deeper and more perdurable than their own.[1]

He uses the term 'self' in what seems to be a rather similar sense: 'I here use the word "self" as a brief descriptive term for any chain of memory sufficiently continuous, and embracing sufficient particulars, to acquire what is popularly called a "character" of its own.'

Myers also uses the word 'Self' (usually with a capital letter) in a much wider sense, so that a 'self' as defined above might be only a part of 'the Self', the total Self, which may include several co-existing 'selves' and even (as we shall later see) a 'soul', or unifying principle. He also uses the term 'Personality' as equivalent to 'Self' (as the title of *Human Personality* indicates).

There is one further point which perhaps needs to be brought out at this stage. Myers came gradually to hold the now unfashionable view that a stream of consciousness can have what is perhaps best described as causal efficacy in respect of external behaviour. He was not at first (it is worth noting) firmly of this opinion. At one time he thought it might even be feasible to explain telepathy in terms of 'brain-waves',[2] and in 1885 a correspondent complained in the S.P.R.'s *Journal* that Myers had 'raised Dr. Carpenter's theory [of cerebral automatism] to a higher and most dangerous power'.[3] But in 1890 came James' *Principles of Psychology*. James argued that consciousness has a selective and a regulative effect upon brain-functioning, and hence upon behaviour:

> Now let consciousness only be what it seems to itself, and it will help an instable brain to compass its proper ends. The move-

---
[1] *P.S.P.R.* VII (1892), p. 305.
[2] Cf. p. 28 of his 'Automatic Writing', *P.S.P.R.* III (1885), pp. 1–63.
[3] *J.S.P.R.* II (1885), p. 27.

ments of the brain *per se* yield the means of attaining these ends mechanically, but only out of a lot of other ends, if so they may be called, which are not the proper ones of the animal, but often quite opposed. The brain is an instrument of possibilities, but of no certainties. But the consciousness, with its own ends present to it, and knowing also well which possibilities lead thereto and which away, will, if endowed with causal efficacy, reinforce the favorable possibilities and repress the unfavourable or indifferent ones. The nerve-currents, coursing through the cells and fibres, must in this case be supposed strengthened by the fact of their awaking one consciousness and dampened by awaking another. *How* such reaction of the consciousness upon the currents may occur must remain at present unsolved: it is enough for my purpose to have shown that it may not uselessly exist, and that the matter is less simple than the brain-automatists hold.[1]

James holds that this view is supported by such considerations as these:

(*a*) Consciousness is at its most intense when the need for regulation of this kind is greatest.

(*b*) If part of a brain is scooped out, neighbouring parts will take over its functions. It seems plausible to suppose that in some way the notion of the missing duties must regulate the recovery of function.

(*c*) Pleasures are generally associated with events conducive to an organism's survival, pains with events detrimental to it. Why should this be so if pleasures and pains exert no causal efficacy?

In his review of the *Principles*, Myers expresses a cautious approval of argument (*b*),[2] and thereafter shows a progressively greater inclination to allow consciousness a causal efficacy. For instance, in his essay on *Science and a Future Life* (1891) he points to telepathy, especially cases of it which take place when bodily vitality is at a low ebb, as evidence that consciousness can be causally efficient in producing a result at a distance from the brain; and throughout *Human Personality* and his later *Proceedings* articles he constantly, though somewhat obscurely, hints that consciousness has a selective function,

[1] *Principles* I, pp. 141-2.
[2] *P.S.P.R.* VII (1891), p. 116.

and even that a spirit can use a brain 'as something between a typewriter and a calculating machine'.[1]

Myers thus seems to hold that one can explain someone's actions, at least in part, by reference to the stream of consciousness accompanying and originating them. Hence if one encountered someone whose actions were seemingly unaccompanied by any stream of consciousness—whose hand, for instance, wrote without his awareness replies to questions which he was not conscious of having heard—one might be able to *explain* those actions by reference to the functioning of an extra and 'submerged' stream of consciousness associated with his organism. Such an explanation would be an alternative, or at least a supplement, to one couched in terms of Carpenter's 'cerebral automatism'.

We are now in a position to state Myers' theory of the subliminal self in outline, which will best be done in his own words:

> I suggest, then, that the stream of consciousness in which we habitually live is not the only consciousness which exists in connection with our organism. Our habitual or empirical consciousness may consist of a mere selection from a multitude of thoughts and sensations, of which some at least are equally conscious with those that we empirically know. I accord no primacy to my ordinary waking self, except that among my potential selves this one has shown itself the fittest to meet the needs of common life. I hold that it has established no further claim, and that it is perfectly possible that other thoughts, feelings, and memories, either isolated or in continuous connection, may now be actively conscious, as we say, 'within me', —in some kind of co-ordination with my organism, and forming some part of my total individuality. I conceive it possible that at some future time, and under changed conditions, I may recollect all; I may assume these various personalities under one single consciousness, in which ultimate and complete consciousness the empirical consciousness which at this moment directs my hand may be only one element out of many.[2]

Those streams of consciousness, or isolated conscious events, which occur in connection with one's organism, but which

[1] *Human Personality* II, p. 201. [2] *P.S.P.R.* VII (1892), p. 301.

do not form part of one's 'habitual' (or supraliminal) consciousness, together comprise what Myers calls one's *subliminal self*. They are on his view a pretty mixed bag, ranging from recollections, discarded from the workaday consciousness, of trivial happenings or routine physiological processes, to glimpses of the workings of the World-Soul. In terms of the powers and activities of the subliminal self Myers attempts to treat a very wide range of psychological phenomena, including, of course, most of the distinctively paranormal ones. So the first question to ask is, what solid evidence does he bring forward that subliminal selves exist? The best starting point is perhaps cases of what are commonly called 'glove anaesthesias'.[1] These are anaesthesias affecting a circumscribed bodily area, say the hand and wrist; the area does not correspond to the region innervated by a particular nerve, but rather to the patient's own anatomical ideas. None the less the anaesthesias are not the results of conscious self-suggestion; very often patients remain unaware of them until told by a doctor. A particularly significant point is that the anaesthetic hand does not get itself into trouble, does not get burned or cut or bruised; whereas sufferers from anaesthesias due to nervous damage or decay may burn themselves badly and realize the fact only through their senses of vision or of smell. In 'glove anaesthesia' it is as though the hand were still being controlled by a supervisory consciousness. And this is what Myers suggests. Hysteria, he holds, is the result of a shrinkage or withdrawal of the empirical or everyday stream of consciousness, added perhaps to the existence of a somewhat more fluctuating boundary between the supraliminal and the subliminal than is commonly the case. In 'glove anaesthesias' the anaesthetic hand has been left, so to speak, high and dry by the recession of the main stream of consciousness; and some subliminal stream of consciousness has assumed supervision of it. Comparable hysterical blindnesses and deafnesses occur, and Myers interprets them similarly.

When the hand concerned, as sometimes happens, shows signs of developing a personality and an intelligence distinct from that of the rest of the organism; when it begins, for instance, to write messages of whose content its owner is unaware, and to hold conversations in its own right; an explanation in

[1] Cf. *Human Personality* I, pp. 43 ff.

terms of a submerged stream of consciousness begins to sound exceedingly plausible. Myers cites two of Janet's cases.[1] Janet found that certain hysterical patients could be brought under hypnosis to a condition in which they would carry on a lively conversation with some person present whilst quite unaware of the fact that one of their hands was conducting by means of signs or writing another and different 'conversation' with Janet himself. Furthermore, although the waking personality of these patients could never be brought to recollect the conversations which their hands had held with Janet, Janet was able, by hypnosis, to converse in at least one case with a personality which *recalled* the manual conversation and regarded the personality which had conducted the ordinary conversation as 'that other'. This Myers appears to feel gives us direct evidence for the existence of a submerged stream of consciousness.

Gurney obtained some very similar results, using ordinary persons under the influence of post-hypnotic suggestion.[2]

Between such cases and cases of ordinary 'automatic writing' there would appear to be no very clear dividing line. In cases of fully fledged automatic writing—and they have not been by any means rare—the intelligence which communicates through the hand may, without claiming to be a deceased human being, manifest a 'character' of its own, and express opinions and claim a history quite different from those of the hand's owner. Furthermore, the successive episodes in its career may be bound together into a coherent and consistent and (so far as can be ascertained) entirely accurate 'chain of memory' of the kind which Myers thought the distinctive hall-mark of a conscious and self-conscious 'personality'. Cases of automatic writing shade off without any obvious break into cases of 'multiple personality'. In some of these the various personalities 'co-exist' and may even manifest simultaneously. They may be aware of each other's doings, but regard those doings as totally alien to them. They may each claim an unbroken history going back many years and may produce evidence in support of their claims. And in some cases it may not be at all clear which, if any, is the main or 'true' personality. Under these circumstances it would seem absurd to suggest that only one of the apparently quite separate personalities is the expression of a stream of

[1] See *P.S.P.R.* IV (1887), pp. 237–51.   [2] Cf. *P.S.P.R.* IV (1887), pp. 292–323.

consciousness. The personalities are much of a muchness. If we are going to admit that one of them is originated or attended by a stream of consciousness, we cannot deny that each of the others has a similar basis.

Evidence of the kinds just cited had convinced Janet, and also William James, that secondary streams of consciousness might now and again come into being. But both had regarded the appearance of such secondary consciousnesses as a rare and pathological phenomenon, and the secondary consciousnesses themselves as generally feeble or childish. The big step which Myers took away from Janet's position was to assert that such streams of consciousness, far from being rare and essentially degenerative, are a normal, and furthermore a fundamental, part of everyone's mental constitution. There are many commonplace, or at any rate not infrequent, psychological phenomena which can only be understood and explained on the assumption that one's supraliminal stream of consciousness is continually being influenced and intruded upon by submerged or subliminal streams of consciousness.

Dreams and hypnosis provide simple examples. Myers holds that during sleep the supraliminal stream of consciousness is in abeyance; but that 'to some extent at least the abeyance of the supraliminal life must be the liberation of the subliminal'.[1] By this he possibly means that in sleep the empirical stream of consciousness is in a relaxed and perhaps a confused state, and that at such a time it is possible for items from another stream of consciousness to find their way into it more easily than usual. In so far as we can remember dreams in the waking state they would seem by definition to have entered the empirical stream of consciousness. The subliminal origin of dreams accounts for what one might describe as the *alien* character of many dream personages and dream scenes. One sees unfamiliar scenes without any conscious attempt to imagine them; dream personages act in ways one could not predict and indeed may actively dislike; and so on. It is as though the unusually vivid imaginings of a subliminal stream of consciousness pass into the empirical consciousness whilst the circumstances which brought them into being for the most part do not.[2]

[1] *Human Personality* I, p. 122.
[2] Gurney says, *Phantasms* I, p. 70n, that it had occurred to him at least once in a

Out of ordinary dreams there may develop somnambulic states in which a dream stratum of the subliminal takes control of the body. Such states may have their own chain of memory lying outside the primary memory; and between them and states of 'secondary personality' there is no clear dividing line.

Myers was very impressed by Gurney's experiments on 'The Stages of Hypnosis'.[1] These experiments seemed to show that a subject's memories of successive trances may form a memory-chain which is inaccessible during his waking hours, but can be immediately recaptured when he is again hypnotised. Furthermore, different memory-chains may even be established for states of light and of deep hypnosis.

Myers thinks that what happens in hypnosis is that some part of the subliminal self comes forward in response to an appeal sent, as it were, downwards from the supraliminal, and displaces the supraliminal self, or part of it. Deep hypnosis and light hypnosis may bring forward a different subliminal stream, and the two streams may have quite separate memory-chains. That the subliminal streams of consciousness revealed by hypnosis continue active even when the ordinary workaday stream of consciousness has resumed its rule is shown by a number of recorded observations; and especially by the observation that a post-hypnotic suggestion, completely forgotten by the subject but none the less requiring a calculation for its performance, may be correctly executed without the subject having the least awareness of having carried out any calculation.

In hysteria, dreams, hypnosis and somnambulism it seems to be the same, or pretty much the same, stratum of the subliminal self which comes forward; a layer characterised by a certain childishness, incoherence and dramatic tendency. Indeed, under hypnosis memories of somnambulic states or even of dreams, memories lost to the waking consciousness, may be recovered; this proves that the same stream of consciousness is involved in all three cases. Now amid the childishness which

---

dream to be asked a riddle, to give up, and to be told the answer. On waking he found the answer sufficiently pertinent to show that the question could not have been framed without distinct reference to it.

[1] See *Human Personality* I, pp. 448-55.

emerges from this layer of the Personality we also find indications of faculties superior to those of the empirical consciousness. There is ore as well as detritus in the subliminal. Dreamers and hypnotic subjects may solve problems refractory to their waking consciousness, may recover forgotten memories or show sensory hyperacuity. A genius is someone in frequent touch with his subliminal, though perhaps with a deeper layer of it than that commonly tapped by dreamers and hypnotic subjects. The inspirations of genius ('subliminal uprushes' as Myers terms them) may seem to him to be quite alien; as dream-scenes may appear to a dreamer. Among many literary examples Myers quotes De Musset's 'On ne travaille pas, on écoute, c'est comme un inconnu qui vous parle à l'oreille,' and R. L. Stevenson, who could actually dream the adventures which provided the plots for his novels. Musical works would emerge complete and unpremeditated into Mozart's mind. Arithmetical prodigies may find the answers to unsolved problems come into their minds without any conscious processes of ratiocination.

The emergence in dreams, hysteria, hypnosis and somnambulism of a subliminal stream of consciousness may bring with it hints not just of heightened faculties, but of quite novel faculties. Myers adduces a number of cases in which telepathy or clairvoyance or even precognition have seemingly been exercised in a dream, a somnambulic state or an hypnotic trance. Such faculties emerge into view, Myers seems to believe, only or chiefly when the subliminal is being tapped; and so they are essentially subliminal faculties. This suggests that the subliminal consciousness, far from being (as Janet had supposed) a symptom of degeneration and of disintegration, may in fact be evolutive, and may represent the most fundamental part of the Personality.

In the later parts of his book Myers tackles phenomena of the kind which Spiritualists would adduce as evidence for the activities of discarnate spirits; viz., apparitions of the dying and the dead, and the phenomena of 'mental' mediumship. He labels these phenomena respectively 'sensory automatisms', and 'motor automatisms'; massive emotional impulses coinciding perhaps with a death being, he thinks, a sort of intermediate case. These 'automatisms' are to be regarded as 'messages' sent to the supraliminal self by the subliminal self, whose superior faculties have obtained for it information which the supraliminal self ought to possess. In a sensory automatism—for instance, a crisis apparition—we have an intrusion of subliminal material into the supraliminal stream of consciousness; in motor automatism, for instance automatic writing, we have a partial displacement of supraliminal control of the organism, and the substitution of subliminal control—a kind of possession by the subliminal. The fact that automatisms are messages from the subliminal will account for their intrusive character, for the symbolism which they so often contain, and for the dramatic and supernormal powers which are sometimes manifested in them.

I find Myers' views about sensory automatisms decidedly obscure. What he says, for instance, about crystal-gazing is indeed pretty clear; gazing into a crystal is, for whatever reason, a means of bringing into the supraliminal stream of consciousness images which would otherwise remain in the subliminal. But when he moves on to talk about apparitions he is very difficult to follow. He was swayed by arguments similar to those which I ran through before (cf. above, pp. 168–71) into believing that the telepathic theory of crisis apparitions could not be sustained, and that *a fortiori* telepathy does not provide a satisfactory explanation of the other and rarer kinds of apparitions. The occurrence of collective apparitions suggests very strongly that when one sees a ghost there must in some sense really be something there. The most revealing cases are perhaps those of apparitions of persons neither dead nor undergoing a crisis. There are in the literature a number of 'arrival' cases, cases in which someone's 'fetch' or double has (without that person being himself aware that anything unusual was taking place) been seen at a certain spot a few minutes or hours prior to his (unexpected) arrival there. Such cases suggested to Myers that there could be an excursion of some part of the Personality (presumably a secondary self or stream of consciousness) away from the body. There are furthermore a number of somewhat similar cases in which the empirical consciousness has so to speak itself gone on the excursion; so that the 'travelling clairvoyant' has strongly believed himself to be at that precise point in space where his double is actually seen. This does not show, (Myers feels) that there was in any sense a *physical object* there; yet there perhaps was (in some very obscure fashion) an actual 'modification' of that portion of space. The perception of this modification must have been a matter not of external but of internal vision; vision related not to changes at the sense-organs, but to changes in the brain—changes possibly instigated by the subliminal consciousness, which became aware of the modification through clairvoyance. A post-mortem apparition can by analogy be regarded as, so to speak, a travelling clairvoyant who has been permanently cut off from his body.

What exactly it is that modifies space and is perceived at a certain point thereof remains obscure. Myers has a somewhat disconcerting habit of referring to it as the 'spirit', a term which he defines, not very helpfully, as 'that unknown fraction of a man's personality . . . which we discern as operating before or after death in the metetherial environment'.[1] One feels that what is seen cannot just *be* a personality if by 'personality' is meant simply a detached stream of consciousness of a certain complexity. To talk of literally 'perceiving' a stream of consciousness other than one's own would seem to be simply a logical error—by definition whatever experiences one has are one's own and not another person's; and in any case the percipient's consciousness in such cases cannot be supposed to resemble the stream of consciousness of the alleged travelling clairvoyant, who would presumably be seeing or imagining not his own form but the scene ahead of him. Myers must, I think, mean that whatever goes forth—be it stream of consciousness, soul or spirit—either possesses, or else somehow creates for itself, a kind of quasi-body. Thus he says of the case of Canon Bourne, whose groom and three daughters collectively saw his double together with that of his horse (he himself being alive, fit, and elsewhere at the time):

> Here I conceive that Canon Bourne, while riding in the hunting-field, was also subliminally dreaming of himself (imagining himself with some part of his submerged consciousness) as having had a fall, and as beckoning to his daughters—an incoherent dream indeed, but of a quite ordinary type. I go on to suppose that, Canon Bourne being born with the psychorrhagic diathesis [a tendency to such psychic excursions], a certain

---

[1] *Human Personality* I, p. 251.

psychical element so far detached itself from his organism as to affect a certain portion of space—near the daughters of whom he was thinking—to affect it, I say, not materially nor even optically, but yet in such a manner that to a certain kind of immaterial and non-optical sensitivity a phantasm of himself and his horse became discernible. His horse was of course as purely a part of the phantasmal picture as his hat.[1]

However, it would not be just to pursue criticism of Myers very far, as he is himself fully aware of the obscurity of his views. He says that his explanation 'suffers from the complexity and apparent absurdity inevitable in dealing with phenomena which greatly transcend known laws', a remark with which we may unreservedly agree.

Myers' treatment of motor automatisms is fairly straightforward. The simpler cases—for instance, automatic writing with no smack of telepathy about it—can be interpreted simply in terms of a subliminal stream of consciousness coming, for whatever reason, to exercise temporary control over some part of the organism. Sometimes automatic writing or trance speaking may come from some fictitious personality, in our society generally a *soi-disant* deceased person, but in others sometimes a god or a demon; here the superficial layer of the subliminal which is operative is simply giving evidence of the rather childish dramatic flair which characterises it, and also (probably) of its suggestibility. Now and then automatic writings will give hints or more than hints that the subliminal is exercising its supernormal powers in their composition. And sometimes one comes across cases which combine the appearance of coming from some definite deceased person, with the retailing about him of information unknown to the writers, or even to the others present. In such cases we must at least postulate that the subliminal is exercising its supernormal abilities to feed its own personations with correct information obtained telepathically or clairvoyantly. These cases in turn shade into ones where the information given is so copious and the personation so exact that we may eventually be tempted or even forced to say that the automatist's subliminal must at least have been influenced by some surviving portion of the deceased person concerned; and finally into those very rare cases in which the

[1] *Human Personality* I, p. 264.

personation is so nearly perfect that we may even be led to suppose that the deceased person himself is somehow directly controlling the nervous machinery of the automatist. This would, Myers feels, be quite comprehensible in the light of what has gone before. We have seen that a subliminal stream of consciousness can at times take over control of the nervous machinery normally worked by the supraliminal self; we have also found some reason for supposing that such a stream of consciousness can actually quit the organism; and there are one or two cases of a living person having (unconsciously and hence subliminally) 'controlled' a medium or automatist. If the subliminal self of a living person can influence and perhaps even operate upon a medium's nervous machinery, why should not the subliminal, or formerly subliminal, self of a deceased person do likewise?[1] We may at least be certain that if any portion of one's personality survives the dissolution of the body it is one's subliminal; for departed spirits give conclusive evidence of being able to exercise the supernormal powers which are the subliminal's special prerogative.

So far I have not mentioned Myers' views about the 'physical phenomena'—the raps and telekinesis (movement of objects at a distance) and materialisations so characteristic of Spiritualistic seances. Although Myers was rather more disposed to believe in such phenomena than were several of his colleagues, there is not a great deal about them in *Human Personality*,[2] and it is by no means entirely clear how he would have fitted them in to his explanatory scheme. In so far as I can elicit his views, they seem to be as follows.

Both supraliminal and subliminal selves may be supposed to operate the organism by producing appropriate changes in the molecules of the brain. Now some facts—for instance the increased control over bodily functions sometimes manifested under hypnosis—suggests that the subliminal self may be better at influencing molecules than is the supraliminal self. We might

---

[1] Myers makes the curious suggestion (*Human Personality* II, pp. 254-5) that the errors and confusions which deceased persons fall into when endeavouring to control a medium's brain sometimes resemble the aphasias and agraphias which may be produced by brain damage; he thinks that a study of these errors might elucidate the relations between mind and brain.

[2] The principal references are *Human Personality* II, pp. 92-3, 207-8, 521-2, 529-43, 544-9.

perhaps suppose that the subliminal self can influence the molecules of parts of the body other than the brain, or the molecules of someone else's brain. Such powers might even be extended to inorganic molecules, so making possible the raps and object-movements which occurred in the presence of such sensitives as Miss Wingfield.

As to how these effects might be produced—either by the subliminal self of a living person or by the spirit of a deceased one—Myers offers the following explanation. Spirits might be supposed, on account of their advanced state, to be capable of operating upon molecules, and even upon the most primitive of all particles, singly. Their powers would thus resemble those of 'Maxwell Demons'—imaginary creatures who are, for theoretical purposes, conceived as catching, sorting and redirecting molecules as we might catch, sort and redirect cricket balls or tennis balls. Entities with such powers would be able to draw phosphorus out of sitters to produce 'spirit lights'; to divert all the molecules in an object upwards, so causing it to levitate; to enable a medium to handle (as Home had done) hot coals by interposing a layer of cold air between the coal and the hand; even to draw substances forth from a medium out of which a materialised or ectoplasmic hand or arm or body might be created.

Myers himself regarded these speculations as tentative in the extreme, and they are inserted here only for the sake of completeness. I shall not discuss them, though they suggest (what would now be technically possible) an experiment to look for possible telekinetic effects on the electrical rhythms of a detached slab of cortical tissue.

Myers' *Human Personality* was published early in 1903. Its fame had preceded it and, when at last it appeared, it received a good deal of notice. Amongst those who wrote lengthy reviews of assessments of it were William James, Oliver Lodge, Theodore Flournoy, Walter Leaf, Frederic Harrison, W. H. Mallock, Andrew Lang, William McDougall, G. F. Stout and F. C. S. Schiller.[1] James, Lodge and Schiller praised it highly, and the

[1] James, *P.S.P.R.* XVIII (1903), pp. 22–33; Lodge, *ibid.*, pp. 39–41; Flournoy, *ibid*, 42–52; Leaf, *ibid.*, 53–61; A. Lang, *ibid.*, pp. 62–77; Frederic Harrison, *The*

two former were much influenced by it. Harrison and Mallock poured scorn on it, but would have been well advised to have read it first. Leaf, Flournoy, Lang and McDougall were in varying degrees appreciative, though the last-named was exceedingly critical of the notion of the 'subliminal self'. Stout shared McDougall's suspicions of the subliminal self but not, apparently, the admiration which he none the less felt for Myers. Stout's is the only one of the wholly critical accounts which is both polite and reasoned, and I shall take his remarks as the starting point for a brief examination of Myers' theory.

Stout observes that Myers' theory 'diverges in a startling way from all the various forms of the doctrine of subconscious or unconscious mental states and processes which have ever been current among psychologists'. The crucial difference lies in the fact that the subliminal self does not wholly derive its contents from the conscious experience of the ordinary self. It has 'its own separate system of mental traces and dispositions formed in the course of its own separate experience'. This means that the theory of the subliminal self 'has at least as much affinity with such conceptions as that of a tutelary genius or a guardian angel' as it has with notions about the subconscious mind. Myers' prime purpose in advancing the theory was, Stout believes, to show that all phases of mental life, both the normal and the paranormal, require the presence and operation of the subliminal self, and hence to supply a 'principle of continuity' which will lead his readers on from acceptance of the ordinary phenomena to acceptance of the extraordinary ones.

To thwart these intentions, Stout holds, it is only necessary to provide alternative explanations of the normal phenomena; if we can explain the normal cases without reference to the workings of the subliminal self this alone will suffice to destroy Myers' principle of continuity. Such alternative explanations are easy to supply. For instance, Stout approaches cases of multiple personality in the following way. It is a common enough ex-

---

Nineteenth Century and After LIII (1903), pp. 645–50; W. H. Mallock, *ibid.*, pp. 628–644; W. McDougall, *Mind*, N.S., XII (1903), pp. 513–28; G. F. Stout, *The Hibbert Journal* II (1903), pp. 44–64; Andrew Lang, *ibid.*, pp. 514–31; and cf. F. C. S. Schiller's 'The Progress of Psychical Research', *Fortnightly Review* LXXVII (1905), pp. 60–73.

perience to fail to recall a name, and then have it suddenly emerge into conciousness after an interval in which one has been occupied with other matters. The conscious effort to remember must have set going a subconscious process which continued after the conscious effort has ceased. This suggests that not all the traces of past experience which actually exist are at the ready disposal of the conscious self. It is quite conceivable that some of them can only be revived when the organism is in a certain state. And this is all we require to give us the possibility of alternating personalities. We do not need to have to resort to submerged streams of consciousness or extra selves. But if this is so, the subliminal self cannot constitute a principle of continuity in terms of which both normal and paranormal psychological phenomena must be explained, and in the light of which the latter may seem more easy to accept.

Some of Stout's detailed criticisms are undoubtedly telling. But he does not seem to me to have altogether grasped Myers' aims and views. The fault is probably as much on Myers' side as on his. It seems fairly clear that Myers does not regard the subliminal self as a unified entity like a guardian angel or tutelary genius. He defines it negatively—it is made up simply of those mental events, whatever their nature, which lie below the threshold of consciousness—and he is in several places quite explicit about its heterogeneity.[1] He looks upon it almost as a sort of ragbag into which certain celestial garments have in some obscure manner found their way. But it is easy to see how Stout's misconception arose. Myers is concerned with the subliminal self most especially in its supernormal aspects, and in consequence bestows upon it something of the admiration proper to a tutelary genius. He also thinks that there is a unifying principle—to wit, the soul—'behind' all mental phenomena. But the subliminal self, however elevated the language which he sometimes applies to it, is not the soul, and it is not in and of itself even unified. The concept of the 'subliminal self' is simply not qualified to act as a unifying theoretical principle.

Myers' theoretical claims are in fact exceedingly modest. He does not purport to be putting forward a developed explanatory system, like Freud's, say, or even Jung's. He would, I think, have said that in relating the various phenomena he discusses

[1] See, e.g., the second paragraph on p. 306 of *P.S.P.R.* VII (1892).

to the workings of submerged streams of consciousness he was not so much explaining them as indicating where an explanation of them is to be sought. In his first article on the subliminal consciousness he wrote:

> There must be a thicker harvest of facts, a freer communication between opposing schools, a wider basis for induction, before we can be sure of explaining rightly even the apparently simplest of subliminal phenomena. It must be enough if some notion has here been given at once of the variety and of the strange interrelations of the phenomena which are waiting to be explained.[1]

The truest success of his *Human Personality* would, he felt, lie in its rapid supersession.

The subliminal self is thus, in Myers' view, not a unitary concept, and to 'explain' something in terms of it is to take only the first step on the road to a full explanation. It does not seem likely that he would, as Stout alleged, have adopted it as a 'principle of continuity' to ease us from the normal to the paranormal. In fact I think he would have said that when the evidence is fully displayed a continuity between the normal and the paranormal is *obvious*, and that it is *because* of this obvious continuity that we are justified in hoping to explain the whole range of cases in the same kind of way.

None the less Stout's article prompts some disturbing reflections. Stout and McDougall both suggest alternative ways of looking at most of the kinds of phenomena in which Myers had been disposed to recognise the workings of subliminal streams of consciousness. And the mere fact that such alternative explanations can be made to look plausible raises another, and a more important, set of problems. For if we are even to contemplate accepting Myers' views about the pervasiveness of subliminal influence, the existence of subliminal streams of consciousness must in at least some cases be established beyond doubt. We cannot extrapolate our findings, as Myers does, to almost the whole range of psychological phenomena unless the findings themselves are unimpeachable; we must have, as Myers himself put it, a 'measured base' for our 'trigonometrical survey'. Now Myers found his 'measured base' in

---
[1] *P.S.P.R.* VII (1892), p. 326.

such phenomena as hysterical anaesthesias, automatic writing and multiple personality. And it is indeed extremely tempting to see in cases of these kinds direct evidence for the simultaneous existence of more than one stream of consciousness in connection with the same organism. But the evidence in the vast majority of such cases is simply not direct. In many instances of multiple personality the various personalities alternate with each other and appear more or less ignorant of each other's doings. That the personalities actually co-exist is an inference and, one might well add, an exceedingly doubtful one. For it is certainly simpler, and it is in many ways more satisfactory, to relate the changes of personality to periodic sharp alterations in a *single* stream of consciousness. Even in cases where the personalities claim to co-exist, and can give a fairly coherent account of what they were doing when 'submerged', such an interpretation, though superficially less plausible, could certainly not be ruled out. It is only when the different personalities simultaneously control different parts of the same organism that this view of things becomes strained. Cases in which fully developed personalities have manifested together in this fashion are very rare, and I do not know of any which have taken place outside the seance room; though in one or two instances a submerged personality has later claimed responsibility for small actions of which the controlling personality was unaware. Of course cases of automatic writing have been by no means uncommon, and would at first sight appear to provide us with evidence of the required type. But the personalities which manifest in these cases, though often quite different from the personality of the hand's owner, are hardly ever fully developed, and may themselves alternate. It is not obvious that a full explanation of them could not be given in terms of 'unconscious cerebration'; there would then be no need to invoke or imagine secondary streams of consciousness.

The only way in which it would seem possible even to make it seem likely that automatic writing is accompanied and originated by a subliminal stream of consciousness would be to rule out alternative explanations, in particular those cast in terms of unconscious cerebral processes. Now Myers was fully aware that the evidence for survival would to many people only begin to look even presentable if arguments could first of all be advanced to show that the mind is not wholly dependent on the brain. The problem is never far from him, though he rarely confronts it head-on. He tries instead to ease his readers around and beyond it, so that before they have braced up to meet the obstacle it is behind them. His own opinions had run a similar course. In the early and middle eighteen-eighties he had been quite prepared to explain automatic writing by reference to unconscious cerebration, and even to consider 'brain-wave' explanations of telepathy. After a while, perhaps under the influence of William James (see above. p. 282), he turned more decidedly against brain-automaton theories; and he also began to feel that telepathy and clairvoyance could not possibly be explained in terms of brain activities. His principal reasons for rejecting neural explanations of telepathy seem to have been five: 'Brain-waves' cannot explain the fairly numerous cases of clairvoyance (i.e. cases in which there is no 'agent'); telepathy, unlike all known forms of physical radiation, is unaffected by distance; it is impossible to give a physical explanation of precognition, of which he thought there were some authentic cases; the information transmitted is often received in a disguised or symbolic form; telepathy often takes place when the organism of the agent is in a very enfeebled state.[1] A good deal of evidence for telepathy comes from cases of automatic writing, and Myers was accordingly inclined to believe that in automatic writing there emerges a part of the Personality whose functioning cannot be fully explained in terms of cerebral activity. The only possibility left open (so long as we are not confronted with actual evidence for survival) would presumably be that automatic writing is a manifestation of a hidden stream of consciousness, a stream of consciousness in some way partially independent of the brain.

Myers thus provides, though he does not specifically deploy, materials upon which some sort of answer to the charge that he has no good grounds for assuming the existence of submerged streams of consciousness might be based. But even if the reply were valid, it would hardly provide us with a 'measured base' for any 'trigonometrical survey'. Cases of automatic writing constitute only a small part of the material with which we have to deal. How are we to justify extending the principles

[1] Cf. esp. *Human Personality* I, pp. 245–6.

derived from a study of them to a wide, an enormous, range of other phenomena? How could Myers answer Janet, who continued to regard the existence of a secondary stream of consciousness as an aberrant and pathological phenomenon? The only conclusive answer would be an empirical demonstration that everyone possesses a subliminal stream of consciousness, and that its operations can be traced in the sorts of phenomena which Myers indicates. And the only conclusive form which such a demonstration could take would be the bringing to light in a large number of people of a hidden stream of consciousness which could give a coherent and testable account of its own past history and actions. The emergent stream of consciousness might manifest alongside the old, operating, say, the hand or the vocal apparatus; but better still it might be united with the supraliminal consciousness so that the new, conjoint personality could 'recollect all' and give us its testimony that the two original personalities had indeed once co-existed. Now Myers can hardly be blamed for not himself providing the required demonstrations; but one would at least like to be shown some grounds for supposing that the demonstrations might one day be achieved. I can neither find such grounds in *Human Personality* nor think of any for myself, and I am therefore inclined to feel that Myers' theory of the subliminal self, at least in its *general* application, will never progress; though perhaps it is not *absolutely* inconceivable that developments in hypnotic or pharmacological techniques might one day make it seem a viable proposition.[1]

[1] See, for instance, some of the experiences described in R. E. L. Masters and Jean Houston, *The Varieties of Psychedelic Experience*, London, 1967. Also possibly relevant are recent findings on the results of surgical separation of the two hemispheres of the human brain, concerning which a recent writer remarks: 'All the evidence indicates that separation of the hemispheres creates two independent spheres of consciousness' (M. S. Gazzaniga, *Scientific American*, Aug. 1967, p. 29). Compare Myers's suggestion, *P.S.P.R.* III (1885), p. 63, 'that in graphic automatism the action of the right hemisphere is predominant, because the secondary self can appropriate its energies more readily than those of the left hemisphere, which is more immediately at the service of the waking mind'.

XIII Myers' Cosmology and Theory of the Soul

INTERMINGLED WITH MYERS' THEORY of the subliminal self, and tending to confuse matters not a little, is what is virtually a second theory or kind of explanatory principle. I refer to Myers' doctrines about the nature and functions of the soul. What he says in this connection is so often unclear that I shall expound his views to a large extent by quotation.

Myers regards 'each man as at once profoundly unitary and almost infinitely composite, as inheriting from earthly ancestors a multiplex and "colonial" organism—polyzoic and perhaps polypsychic in an extreme degree'.[1] From this it follows that what one needs to do in the first place is not (as Janet had supposed) to explain disintegrations of the psychic stream, but to account for how it is in the first place integrated. One possibility would be

> ... the discovery of laws affecting primarily that unseen or spiritual plane of being where I imagine the origin of life to lie. If we can suppose telepathy to be a first indication of a law of this type, and to occupy in the spiritual world some such place as gravitation occupies in the material world, we might imagine something analogous to the force of cohesion as operating in the psychical contexture of a human personality.[2]

Another possibility—and the one which Myers himself favours—is

> ... the ancient hypothesis of an indwelling soul, possessing and using the body as a whole, yet bearing a real, though obscure

---

[1] *Human Personality* I, p. 34.   [2] *Human Personality* I, p. 38.

relation to the various more or less apparently disparate conscious groupings manifested in connection with the organism and in connection with more or less localised groups of nerve-matter.[1]

What exactly Myers means by the term 'soul', beyond what is hinted at above, I am very far from certain; but we can at any rate amplify the quotation with some further extracts and references. These will best be arranged under two headings:

(a) *The soul as unifying continuum.* Myers seems to have thought 'the real though obscure relation' which the soul bears to the 'various conscious groupings' is that the 'conscious groupings' are in some not too clear sense modifications of a soul-substance (a view discussed at some length by William James in a celebrated passage of his *Principles of Psychology*).

> Such a personality, at any rate, as the development of higher from lower organisms shows, involves the aggregation of countless minor psychical entities, whose characteristics still persist, although in a manner consistent with the possibility that one larger psychical entity, whether pre-existent or otherwise, is the unifying continuum of which those smaller entities are fragments, and exercises over them a pervading, though an incomplete, control.[2]

In one place at least[3] Myers equates the term 'soul' with the phrase 'transcendental self', but I doubt if we should be justified in supposing therefore that he was influenced by Kant.

Matters are further complicated by the fact that Myers sometimes talks of the subliminal self, no doubt through enthusiasm for its alleged supernormal powers, as though it *were* the soul. For instance, he says that the remarkable faculties of the subliminal self make it 'at least an earthly soul, a provisional spirit'.[4] I am very far from clear what he is driving at here; but I feel fairly confident that his fundamental view is that the soul is a unifying continuum of which supraliminal and subliminal selves alike are modifications.

(b) *The soul as controlling agency.* In two of the quotations given above the soul is represented as not merely unifying, but controlling, the diverse conscious groupings. This control is in turn the means by which the soul can control the organism.

---

[1] *Human Personality* I, p. 35.
[2] *Human Personality* I, p. 38.
[3] *P.S.P.R.* IV (1887), p. 260.
[4] *Human Personality* II, p. 521.

For my part, I feel forced to fall back upon the old-world conception of a *soul* which exercises an imperfect and fluctuating control over the organism; and exercises that control, I would add, along two main channels, only partly coincident—that of ordinary consciousness, adapted to the maintenance of a guidance of earth-life; and that of subliminal consciousness, adapted to the maintenance of our larger spiritual life during our confinement in the flesh.[1]

This must not, of course, be taken to mean that the soul controls the organism indirectly, through the mediation of subliminal and supraliminal streams of consciousness, which are distinct from it. Different aspects or modifications of the soul (the 'subliminal' and the 'supraliminal') control different aspects of the organism. The actual nature of the mechanism by which the soul achieves its control of the organism Myers finds inexplicable; he talks of it in terms of the avowed metaphor of 'paying attention'. Thus he suggests at some length[2] that when the supraliminal consciousness is at a low ebb, as during sleep or hypnosis, the soul need no longer attend to the activity of the nervous centres correlated with the supraliminal activities; it is free either to pay more attention to the nervous centres correlated with subliminal activities, making possible the enhanced control over routine bodily activities often reported in hypnotised subjects, or else partially to quit the body, or otherwise exercise the exalted faculties which the necessity to concentrate upon workaday events normally inhibits.

Myers holds that the hypothesis of an 'indwelling soul' is 'conceivably provable'.[3] The phenomena which he regards as at any rate tending to prove it are of four principal kinds:

1. He seems to believe that evidence for survival is *ipso facto* evidence for the hypothesis of an indwelling soul.

> I claim . . . that it is conceivably provable,—I myself hold it as actually proved,—by direct observation. I hold that certain manifestations of central individualities, associated now or formerly with certain definite organisms, have been observed in operation apart from those organisms, both while the organisms were still living, and after they had decayed.[4]

---

[1] *Human Personality* I, p. 74.
[2] *Human Personality* I, pp. 217–18.
[3] *Human Personality* I, p. 35.
[4] *Human Personality* I, p. 35.

2. Myers was also much inclined to toy with the notion of pre-existence, which (he felt) would, like survival, necessarily require the existence of a soul. He was somewhat disposed to think[1] that the mere occurrence of telepathy suggests that we possess souls which originated elsewhere—for telepathy could not have developed in the course of a merely terrene evolution (why I am not sure). Some of the 'subliminal uprushes' characteristic of geniuses and of calculating boys seem also to point to pre-existence:

> I do not say that Dase himself learnt or divined the multiplication table in some ideal world. I only say that Dase and all the rest of us are the spawn or output of some unseen world in which the multiplication-table is, so to speak, in the air. Dase trailed it after him, as the poet says of the clouds of glory, when he 'descended into generation' in a humble position at Hamburg . . .[2]

3. Myers is also inclined to regard cases of 'travelling clairvoyance' or 'telepathic clairvoyance' as evidence that our bodies are animated by a separable spiritual principle or soul; though he admits that such cases are 'possibly purely subjective'.

> In 'telepathic clairvoyance,' the percipient seems to himself to be present at the scene where the so-called agent actually is at the time. And in reciprocal cases, not only is the percipient conscious of invading the agent's presence, but the latter is in some way aware of the invasion. Further the description of several cases of experimental self-projection concur in the impression felt of spiritual transportation, of tethering connection with the body, of return thereinto with a shock. And two narratives of animation suspended to the verge of death (Dr. Wiltse and M. Bertrand . . .), have dwelt on that crisis as an apparent escape of the spirit from the body, to which it is ultimately retracted by a remaining psychical link of attachment.[3]

Rather similar in Myers' view, are cases of

4. *Ecstasy*: a term which he used to denote supposed instances of 'actual excursion of the incarnate spirit from its organism' not just into this world, but into the spirit world. In the moments between awakening from trance and recovering

---
[1] Cf. *Human Personality* II, p. 523. [2] *Human Personality* I, p. 119.
[3] *Human Personality* II, p. 525.

full consciousness of their surroundings, both Mrs. Piper and Mrs. Thompson would retain a dreamlike awareness as of another, and more beautiful, world, and of conversations which they seemed to have held with deceased persons inhabiting it; conversations which sometimes turned out to have been 'evidential' in that the mediums received information which they could not have acquired by any normal means.

> To put the matter briefly, if a spirit from outside can enter the organism, the spirit from inside can go out, can change its centre of perception and action, in a way less complete and irrevocable than the change of death. Ecstasy would thus be simply the complementary or correlative aspect of spirit-control ... May there not be an extension of travelling clairvoyance to the spiritual world? A spontaneous transfer of the centre of perception into that region from whence discarnate spirits seem now to be able, on their side, to communicate with growing freedom?[1]

Myers thinks that comparable phenomena are to be found in almost all religions:

> From the medicine-man of the lowest savages up to St. John, St. Peter, St. Paul, with Buddha and Mahomet on the way, we find records which, though morally and intellectually much differing, are in psychological essence the same.
> At all stages alike we find that the spirit is conceived as quitting the body; or, if not quitting it, at least as greatly expanding its range of perception in some state resembling trance ...
> With our new insight we may correlate the highest and the lowest ecstatic phenomenon with no injury whatsoever to the highest. The shaman, the medicine-man—when he is not a mere impostor—enters as truly into the spiritual world as St. Peter or St. Paul. Only he enters a different region thereof; a confused and darkened picture terrifies instead of exalting him.[2]

For my part I am very far from clear why Myers feels that an examination of these various kinds of phenomena should turn one towards a soul-theory, instead of towards the view that, since the agglomeration of mental events which go to make up a human Personality can exist independently of a brain, those mental events must be, so to speak, self-cohesive and self-regulatory. Perhaps Myers is led into a soul-theory partly by

[1] *Human Personality* II, p. 259. [2] *Human Personality* II, p. 260.

the looseness of his own terminology. He uses the word 'spirit' both theoretically, as equivalent to 'soul', and, more neutrally, as meaning whatever portion of the personality may be supposed to survive death or otherwise function independently of the body. Having obtained what he believes to be evidence for the existence of 'spirits' in the second sense, he slips into treating it as evidence for the existence of 'spirits' in the first sense, that is to say of 'souls'. However, I shall excuse myself from discussing these questions further on the ground that it was Myers' theory of the subliminal self rather than his theory of the soul which had so great an influence both upon his colleagues and upon subsequent psychical researchers. My excuses may be cowardly; but the terrain hereabouts is so crumbling, so extensive and so shrouded in the smoke of ancient combat, that were I to set foot upon it I would no doubt be instantly swallowed up.

To complete this account of Myers' thought it is necessary to set his speculations about the soul in the perspective of his world-view (if that is not too narrow a term). In so doing I shall take the broadest interpretation of the words 'soul' and 'spirit'—so that a 'spirit' is simply the unknown fraction of a man's personality which is assumed to survive the dissolution of his body—and by-pass the awkward questions about the nature of the soul which have just been touched upon.

Myers' expressions of his religious and cosmological views are for the most part widely scattered amongst his miscellaneous writings, and often amongst the least known of them. However, in 1896 he was invited to join the Synthetic Society, a society for the discussion of religious and philosophical questions recently founded by Arthur Balfour and Wilfrid Ward. This society was modelled upon the earlier and more famous Metaphysical Society; but, in contrast to the latter, its membership was confined to those whose wish it was to 'contribute towards a working philosophy of religious belief'. Myers read two papers to the Synthetic Society, and in preparing them he was forced to work his ideas into more definite shape. Whence those ideas came it is not always possible to say. No doubt some emerged directly from the speculations about the subliminal self and its powers which he had carried on for over a decade and had already in part committed to print. But I rather suspect that others were based upon communications from the departed spirits with whom he was now convinced that he was in genuine contact.

Certain of the Synthetic Society's members were such advanced Hegelians that other members could hardly understand what they were talking about,[1] and beside their intricate sidesteps towards the Absolute, Myers' papers are quite down-to-earth.[2] None the less, I am sometimes far from certain what his exact views were, and in an attempt to impose clarity upon them I shall expound them in seven numbered sections. I must emphasise that sections (4) and (5) are partly my own guesswork and interpolations, though I believe them to represent Myers' views correctly.

(1) The 'preamble of all religions', the 'primary belief' from which they all begin, is that our workaday, material world is interpenetrated, and at least to an extent acted upon, by another order of things, an unseen spiritual world in which, in some very obscure sense, we are here and now already dwellers. If such an unseen world exists, it must have its own laws, and there must also be laws governing its interactions with this world. It should be possible for us to discover these laws, and so learn more of the unseen world, by the ordinary methods of scientific enquiry. Indeed, it is only if the existence and nature of such a world can be established scientifically that we may expect any *rapprochement* between the warring sects, or any widespread adoption of religious views amongst the modern, educated public. 'Without fresh facts none of us can get any further. There are simply not enough known determinants for any valid solution. What use in fondling hallowed traditions, or in juggling with metaphysical terminology? Unless the human race can find more facts, it may give up the problem of the Moral Universe altogether.'[3]

---

[1] The *Papers read before the Synthetic Society* were edited by Arthur Balfour and privately printed in 1909. The volume is exceedingly scarce. There is a copy in the S.P.R. Library.

[2] One is reprinted *in toto* in *Human Personality* II, pp. 284–92; the other is very largely embodied in Myers' Presidential Address to the S.P.R., 'The Function of a Society for Psychical Research', *P.S.P.R.* XV (1900), pp. 110–27, reprinted in *Human Personality* II, pp. 292–307.

[3] *P.S.P.R.* XV (1900), p. 456.

(2) In our search for laws relating to the unseen world we must beware of setting our sights too high at first.

> ... the founders of religions have hitherto dealt in the same way with the invisible world as Thales or Anaximander dealt with the visible. They have attempted to begin at once with the highest generalisations. Starting from the existence of a God,—the highest of all possible truths, and the least capable of being accurately conceived or defined,—they have proceeded downwards to explain or justify his dealings with man. They have assumed that the things which are of most importance to us are therefore the things which we are most likely to be enabled to know ...
>
> It is possible that in all this mankind have begun at the wrong end. The analogy of physical discovery, at any rate, suggests that the truths which we learn first are not the highest truths, nor the most attractive truths, nor the truths that most concern ourselves. The chemist begins with the production of fetid gases and not of gold; the physiologist must deal with bone and cartilage [sic] before he gets to nerve and brain ... We must learn first not what we are most eager to learn, but what fits on best to what we know already.[1]

(3) It is accordingly from quite trivial facts that we may expect to glean our first hints that we possess or are evolving capacities which transcend merely terrene laws, that we are beings in some way partaking of two worlds. Cases of telepathy, for instance, in themselves quite insignificant, suggest that our minds, at least the subliminal parts of them, can sometimes overcome the limitations of the material world and operate in some transphysical or 'metetherial' plane.

(4) The metetherial plane whose existence is revealed by telepathy may, for a variety of reasons, be identified with the unseen world in which departed spirits have their being. We now know (Myers believes) that departed spirits can communicate telepathically with those still incarnate, and from this we may conclude that both at least participate in the metetherial realm. There are also cases and considerations which suggest that telepathy is the normal and indeed only possible mode of communication between disembodied spirits and is hence, so to speak, not merely *part* of their world, but that which binds

[1] *Essays Modern*, London, 1883, pp. 226–7.

them into a common world in the first place. We can therefore obtain information about the metetherial plane by 'communicating' with the discarnate in the orthodox ways.

How literally Myers took the traditional descriptions of the spirit spheres and of the occupations of their inhabitants I do not know; but he certainly believed that if a communicating spirit could 'identify' himself convincingly, his account of his present situation and prospects ought to carry weight. With regard to the condition of departed souls Myers held that certain theses

> ... have been provisionally established ... First and chiefly, I at least see ground to believe that their state is one of endless evolution in wisdom and love. Their loves of earth persist; and most of all those highest loves which seek their outlet in adoration and worship. We do not find, indeed, that support is given by souls in bliss to any special scheme of terrene theology. Thereon they know less than we mortal men have often fancied that we knew. Yet from their step of vantage-ground in the Universe, at least, they see that it is good.[1]

(5) Some of Myers' speculations about the unseen world however are very confusing and seem almost in danger of being self-contradictory. At times he talks about the unseen world as though it were a kind of ultra-rarified luminiferous ether (the 'metetherial') extending throughout space and permeating all the physical universe. One half imagines him to believe that departed spirits somehow float in, or are concentrations of, this subtle fluid, and that telepathy is effected by the propagation of waves across it.

> And, moreover, if indeed as Tennyson has elsewhere suggested, and as many men now believe, there exist some power of communication between human minds without sensory agency—
>
> > Star to star vibrates light; may soul to soul
> > Strike thro' some finer element of her own?—
>
> then surely it would be in accordance with analogy that these centres of psychical perception should be immersed in a psychical *continuum,* and that their receptivity should extend to influences of larger than human scope.[2]

---

[1] *Human Personality* II, p. 287.
[2] *Science and a Future Life*, London, 1893, p. 160.

On the other hand Myers also talks about the metetherial realm as of a World-Soul from contact with which we can in a suitable frame of mind draw in a revitalising strength and Grace. To this way of thinking the metetherial is (to use one of Myers' cruder metaphors) a source of moral and even intellectual nourishment. Somewhere in it lies that ideal Platonic virtue which he once saw shine for a moment through the tragic form of Annie Marshall; there too are to be found the pre-existent mathematical truths of which the peasant Dase retained subliminal memories when he 'descended into generation'.

Now there would appear on the face of it to be an almost irreconcilable difference between these two notions of the unseen world. If the metetherial really is a quasi-physical fluid like the ether, it can hardly at the same time also be the Origin and Original of moral and intellectual ideas. To identify a moral idea with the eddyings of a fluid, even of a celestial fluid, would be a gross logical error. I do not for a moment suppose that Myers wished to make such an identification, though it may be that the difficulty was to some extent obscured for him by his own compelling 'sense of something far more deeply interfused' with our own material realm. And indeed his occasional references to a 'cosmic energy' flowing into us from the metetherial and vivifying our bodies as well as our minds are extremely puzzling.

I should be inclined to guess, from hints which Myers drops in various places, that he in fact held to some such scheme of things as this. Spirits may be able to *recognise* spatial relations (so that they can manifest at an agreed place) but they are themselves probably independent of space;[1] their interactions with each other are telepathic, and the laws of telepathy are non-spatial laws. All talk of ethers beyond the ether, and of spirits being immersed in a psychic continuum, is strictly metaphorical. To say that a departed spirit moves in a psychic continuum or metetherial realm is simply a way of expressing the fact that he is part of a network of telepathic affinities uniting spirit with spirit. The spirits of the recently dead may retain telepathic links with spirits still in the flesh and may endeavour to contact them, or to 'guide' their activities. Beyond and

[1] Cf. *Human Personality* I, pp. 30, 231.

behind such spirits, but still with affinities to them, are the spirits whose advancement in knowledge and understanding has linked them in fellowship to higher souls; and the higher souls in turn are linked to souls higher yet. And linked to all, in greater or in less degree, is a Universal Spirit and Source of Love and Wisdom so vast and (in one sense) so remote that we can hardly begin to comprehend it.

In prayer we attempt to put ourselves *en rapport* with, and to obtain benefits from, the occupants of the unseen world. If we succeed in contacting them, we may gain from them, by telepathy, what might indeed be called an influx of moral and intellectual energy—we may receive knowledge, strength, sympathy, guidance and, above all, love. And of course such benefits *may* come unsolicited, for there are always many in the next world anxious to help those still in this. Whether the benefits come directly from the World-Soul (as may perhaps sometimes happen to favoured mortals), or are so to speak channelled through spirits nearer to, but still above, us, is perhaps not a matter of importance.[1]

There may be some truth in the marvellous accounts which communicators so often give of the scenery of their metetherial home; but this does not show that the unseen world is in any sense a quasi-physical world. The explanation is no doubt that the spirits construct their own surroundings by the same strange mechanism which enables the agent in a crisis case or an arrival case to externalise a fully developed image of himself and even of his clothes and his surroundings.

(6) Acceptance of this simple creed can be of moral efficacy. We now have actual scientific evidence of 'another world which may develop the faculties, prolong the affections, redress the injustices of this', and in which, if we but make the effort, an eternity of Progress and Endeavour awaits us. This knowledge should spur us to continual self-improvement and should enable us to accept with impatience, perhaps, but not with bitterness whatever merely transient pains and reversals we may suffer on this planet. We also have evidence that in the next world every detail of our career in this world will be open to the inspection of our fellows (should they have the poor taste to

---

[1] For Myers' views on Prayer, see *Human Personality* II, pp. 309–14, 554; and the letter quoted in James' *Varieties of Religious Experience*, London, 1925, pp. 466–7.

be curious). Just as spirits are in some way outside space, yet cognisant of different parts of it, so they may be outside time, yet able to examine different portions of it. If therefore they wish to scrutinise the past crimes of some newcomer they will be able to do so. This fact, Myers feels, will undoubtedly deter those who become aware of it from transgressing the moral law; though one wonders what sinner would be kept from crime by the prospect of having a red face in heaven.

(7) Towards Christianity Myers' feelings were mixed. On the one hand he held that the results of psychical research made the Resurrection and other miraculous events in the New Testament now seem perfectly credible; on the other hand, and by the same token, he thought that Christianity's claims to uniqueness could not possibly be upheld. *Uno itinere ad tam grande secretum non potest pervenire*. Moreover at times he felt very bitter against what he conceived to be the 'otherworldliness' of the Christian Ethic, and on one occasion he scandalised the members of the Synthetic Society by his intemperate remarks on the subject. By and large he believed Christianity to be just an adumbration of the truth, a religion useful perhaps in the nursery, but no fit home for a thinking adult. Some lines in a letter which he wrote to Lodge on 27th June 1896 put his feelings very clearly:

> Tragic and long-past circumstances connected with one now long departed enabled me with no merit of my own to see Virtue clear;—& it so happened that in that conflict and Victory Christianity in no wise came in;— . . . Christianity is a noble and beneficent incident; but how much is there in the Universe before it, after it, & beyond!

These views were not widely accepted even by Myers' colleagues. The Sidgwicks were far too cautious for such airy voyages; Podmore had become too cautious for any voyages at all; Lodge developed his own, tangential, ideas. Of Myers' immediate circle only Hodgson and William James were prepared to move with him. Hodgson did not live to express his opinions in public; but shortly after Myers' death James published his celebrated Gifford Lectures, *The Varieties of Religious Experience*. Myers' influence upon James' ideas was considerable, and is in several places explicitly acknowledged. That fact alone would give Myers' speculations some claim to be remembered; but whether they have any claim to be taken seriously I should not like to say.

XIV The Turn of the Century

WHAT IMPRESSES ONE perhaps most of all about the Sidgwick group is their sheer industry, and the scope and scale of their work. Between the S.P.R.'s foundation in 1882 and the end of the year 1900, the S.P.R. published some 11,000 pages of *Proceedings* and *Journal*, to which must in effect be added the 1,416 pages of *Phantasms of the Living* and the 1,360 pages of Myers' *Human Personality*. Of these 14,000 pages at least fifty per cent were contributed by the small group of close friends—the Sidgwicks, Hodgson, Gurney and Myers[1]—who were also the S.P.R.'s principal organisers. When one reflects that most of their papers were based upon arduous experiments or case-investigations which they had themselves conducted, and that only two of the five—Gurney and Hodgson—were in a position to give the whole, or anything like the whole, of their time and energy to the work, one's amazement passes into something like despair. How *did* they manage to do so much? It is all very well to say that they had servants and money: a good many dons today are waited upon and can lay hands on sizeable grants. Nor can one dispel one's sense of inferiority by telling oneself that their work was facile and inferior. They were able people—as able perhaps as any of their time; and their work was able—at least as able as that of the more orthodox psychologists of the day. Some might complain that their abilities could have been put to better uses; but that is another matter.

Gurney's early death had been a great blow to the hopes and

---

[1] Theodore Besterman's 'List of F. W. H. Myers's Signed Contributions to the *Proceedings* and *Journal* of the Society for Psychical Research', appended to Sir Oliver Lodge's *Conviction of Survival: Two Discourses in Memory of F. W. H. Myers*, London, 1930, mentions 87 items.

endeavours of the Sidgwick group; but they had surmounted the blow and, in 1900, with the S.P.R.'s remaining leaders active and no more than middle-aged (Myers was 57, Sidgwick 61, Hodgson 45, Mrs. Sidgwick 55, Podmore 44, and Lodge 49) it might have seemed to an optimistic outsider as if the stage was set for a decade or two of the most remarkable progress and discoveries. But by a tragic irony the band of people who had set out to penetrate death's mysteries were themselves quickly ravaged by him.

Early in May 1900 Sidgwick learned that he had an incurable cancer of the bowels. An operation for the construction of an artificial exit was urgently necessary. For about a fortnight he kept this dreadful news even from close friends, feeling that he could more easily carry on a normal life if only his wife knew of his condition. A paper (on T. H. Green) which he delivered to the Oxford Philosophical Society on 20th May, was said to have been one of his most effective ever, and in the discussion afterwards he was in excellent form. To a prominent Hegelian who suggested that the fundamental incoherence of Green's views merely indicated that the region of the ultimate difficulties of thought had been reached and that both sides of the contradiction should therefore be maintained, he replied that he had never been able to work out from the school to which he (the Hegelian) belonged how they managed to distinguish the contradictions which they took to be evidence of error from those which they regarded as intimations of higher truths.[1]

On and after 24th May he began to inform his family and closest friends. To Frederic Myers he wrote:

> I have an organic disorder which, the expert said more than a fortnight ago, must soon render an operation necessary. I am, by my Cambridge physician's advice, going to see him tomorrow. He may say 'at once.' I believe that the chances of the operation are on the whole favourable: I mean that the probabilities are that I shall not die under it: but *how long* I shall live after it is uncertain. At any rate, it will only be an invalid half-life . . .
>
> Life is very strange now: very terrible: but I try to meet it like a man, my beloved wife aiding me. I hold on—or try to

---

[1] *H.S.: A Memoir*, p. 586n.

hold on—to duty and love; and through love to touch the larger hope.

I wish now that I had told you before, as this may be farewell. Your friendship has had a great place in my life, and as I walk through the Valley of the Shadow of Death, I feel your affection. Pray for me.

This *may* be farewell, but I hope not.[1]

An operation was arranged at a London nursing home for 31st May—his sixty-second birthday. On the evening of the 30th he and his wife dined at 10 Downing Street with Arthur and Alice Balfour. Only the four of them were present. Never had Sidgwick's conversation been more brilliant.

Nothing shows more clearly the place which Sidgwick had come to hold in the affections of many different people, and the extent of his influence upon their ways of thinking and living, than the letters which he received after the news of his condition became generally known. 'My life is quite happy,' wrote Richard Hodgson, 'but I know what your presence here means for so many persons and things, and I feel how much more I owe to you in my life's way than to any other man ... even if I knew no more than that I was going into the dark, I would with absolute joy for your sake go out instead of you.'

On 25th May his sister, Mary Benson, wrote to him as follows:

Dearest Henry,

Your letter has only this moment reached me & though I feel too confused & bewildered to write yet this post must carry to you a touch of that entire utter love of my heart, which as you say, has never failed for one moment between us—I wonder whether you can ever know all you have been to me from those earliest dear years! & the love and worship in which my heart has lost itself—the strength & the stimulus & the hope with which you have filled me—

Thank God that Nora's telegram reached me an hour before your letter—her letter has not yet come. I do not quite understand but I know you will tell me all. Brother of my heart, my prayers are always yours, & now more than ever. They are winged with love, however poor a soul one is, & so they are in the Eternal Heart—your precious words touch me to the depths

---

[1] *H.S.: A Memoir*, p. 587.

—& I can only commend you with all there is of me to the Very Heart of Love—Through whatever you have to go, wherever your way lies I know that you will follow on with all the courage and the greatness & the simplicity which are your very life—and the strength of God will be yours.

Your own most loving
Minnie.[1]

At first it seemed as though the operation might have won Sidgwick an extra year or two of life in which to wind up his work. On 3rd July he was able to move to Margate, and he felt it 'something to be able to lunch, dine, and walk about among healthy human beings without a marked sense of dissimilarity'. After that he went to 10 Downing Street for a few days, and thence to Terling Place in Essex, the home of his wife's brother-in-law, Lord Rayleigh. At Terling it became apparent that the disease was still active. He grew steadily weaker, and on 13th August came a decisive change for the worse. He remained free from pain, but in great discomfort; and though he bore his sufferings with outstanding patience he longed only for the end.

On 27th August Frank Podmore, who had been of late years perhaps more a witness of and commentator upon the work of the Sidgwick group than one of that group's members, wrote to Sidgwick in these terms:

> You have counted for so much in my life: and I have valued so highly your friendship. Apart from all that you have done for our common work, I feel that I personally owe so much of my intellectual development to you: that you have helped me to see more clearly and to weigh more soberly and justly.
>
> And in other ways, that I can hardly find words for, your life and character have meant a great deal to me. I am not sure now that I very much care whether or not there is a personal, individual immortality. But I have at bottom some kind of inarticulate assurance that there is a unity and a purpose in the Cosmos: that our lives, our own conscious force, have some permanent value—and persist in some form after death. And—if you will let me say it—you and some others, just by being what you are, constantly revive and strengthen that assurance for me. I feel that there is a meaning in things.[2]

---

[1] Bodleian, Dep. Benson 3/41.   [2] Library of Trinity College, Cambridge.

It is doubtful whether Sidgwick ever saw this letter; he died the day after it was written.

Of Sidgwick's intellectual and moral qualities something has already been said, and there is little more that I can add now. He was not merely one of the ablest men of his time, but one of the most versatile. He was a Wrangler as well as a Senior Classic. He lectured at one time in both Classics and history, and his religious and theological interests led him to master Arabic and Hebrew. In later days he wrote not merely upon philosophical questions, but upon political, economic, psychological and even philological matters, whilst his literary, and particularly his poetic sympathies were wide, and the lectures on Shakespeare which he gave at Newnham were long remembered by those who heard them. He kept abreast of scientific developments, and he worked hard to promote the teaching of science in Cambridge. His interest in moral and ethical problems was not just abstract and theological; it was of a kind which impelled him again and again to public action. Thus it was in part at least from a sense of duty that he devoted time and attention to the study of politics and political economy; a sense of duty going back, no doubt, to the days when he and the other Apostles had hoped that developments in the social sciences would before long make possible an equitable and frictionless society. He served too, in one capacity or another, on many charitable and educational committees. He was a prominent advocate of women's education and university reform; and a not inconsiderable proportion of his income was given to the causes which he felt most worthy of support.

All these points, and many more, emerge from the pages of what might be called Sidgwick's 'official biography'. But I think that A. C. Benson is right in suggesting[1] that by quoting rather excessively from Sidgwick's Letters and Journal that book gives one an excessively sombre impression of his life and character. His moods of self-questioning, his doubts as to the value of his work, his recurrent sense of time frittered away, his growing pessimism about the possible solution of 'ultimate problems', are all given undue prominence. They represent, no doubt, an important side of his personality; but they do not reveal why he cast such a spell over his circle of friends. The

[1] *Op. cit.*, p. 72.

qualities which made him not merely a remarkable debater and conversationalist, but the most sympathetic and the most amusing of companions, somehow get edged out of the picture. To his friends Sidgwick was first and foremost not a dry moralist but a kindly and sociable human being. He possessed a keen 'sense of fun', and would skip with excitement whilst watching or playing in a game of croquet or tennis. His humour could be delightful and his repartee was something brilliant. Especially enjoyable is his answer to a German *savant* who complained that the English language had no equivalent to the German word *Gelehrte* (learned men). 'Oh, yes, we have,' said Sidgwick, 'we call them p-p-prigs.'[1] To someone who had remarked that a certain ecclesiastical dignitary was 'not open to the reproach of losing his temper' Sidgwick replied 'No, b-b-but he rather obviously keeps it.'[2]

Certain small eccentricities of dress and manner enhanced rather than detracted from the esteem in which Sidgwick was held. He was noted for his absent-mindedness. On one occasion when he was staying with E. W. Benson, who was then Bishop of Truro, he became absorbed in conversation after breakfast, and when the bell rang for Chapel he walked, still talking animatedly, to his seat in the stalls, only to find that he had brought his cup of tea with him.[3] He was in some ways curiously unselfconscious. He was once told by his doctor that in the interests of his health he should take up riding. Sidgwick asked if he might run instead. The doctor agreed that he could. For many years thereafter Sidgwick used regularly to run through the streets of Cambridge, sometimes even in his cap and gown. I wish someone had photographed him as he pounded along.

None the less Sidgwick was far from universally popular in Cambridge. No doubt his academic liberalism, especially as regards the admission of women to degrees, offended conservatives, whilst his widely known interest in psychical research put all kinds of orthodox noses out of joint. There were also, perhaps, some who were inclined to suspect him of being unco' guid, of splitting moral hairs unnecessarily, of being stiff

---

[1] Bertrand Russell, *Portraits from Memory*, New York, 1956, p. 62.
[2] p. 167 of Lord Rayleigh, 'Some Recollections of Henry Sidgwick', *P.S.P.R.* XLV, (1938), pp. 162–73.
[3] Benson, *op. cit.*, p. 63.

with an overbearing spiritual pride. And he did indeed occasionally show a certain prickliness and obstinacy when his position, not upon a point of theoretical ethics, but upon a question of immediate moral conduct, was challenged or invaded. One or two examples have already been given in connection with Eusapia Palladino, and a few more are to be found in Lord Rayleigh's reminiscences. Any attempt to encroach on public rights brought out this side of his character. He was once sitting in a railway carriage when two ladies got in. One said to the other in a loud aside: 'I am sure the gentleman will have too much good feeling to smoke in the presence of ladies.' 'Are you aware,' said Sidgwick, 'that this is a smoking carriage?' And, since the ladies maintained their attitude, he deliberately took out and lit a cigarette as a protest.[1]

I have not however come across anything which suggests that an accusation of spiritual pride could justly be levelled at Sidgwick. Those who knew him best would have been the last to believe it. They would, I think, have replied that since moral questions were to Sidgwick of more importance, perhaps, than any others, it is not surprising that he should sometimes have exaggerated a trivial issue, or have become involved in a slightly ludicrous *contretemps*. Had he even for a moment come to see himself as a *poseur* he would have spared no effort of self-discipline and self-examination in his endeavours to eradicate the fault.

The charge most commonly made against Sidgwick—made by his friends as well as his enemies—was simply that of ineffectiveness in both teaching and administration. And in this charge there was at least some element of truth. Sidgwick's scrupulousness and his ability to see all sides of a question prevented him from exercising a decisive influence either upon the opinions of his pupils or the outcome of committee meetings. Sir J. J. Thomson remembered that Sidgwick

> ... often took part in discussions at meetings of the Fellows when suggested changes came under consideration. His speeches were a very enjoyable intellectual treat, but they did not, I think, have much effect on the division. He was sometimes accused of sitting on the fence, but it was rather that he kept

---

[1] Rayleigh, *loc. cit.*, pp. 169–70.

vaulting over it from one side to the other, giving arguments at one time in favour of the proposal, and following them with others against. Thus whatever a man's opinion might be, he got new arguments in its favour, and voted as he had intended.[1]

Another of Sidgwick's colleagues, Alfred Marshall, the professor of political economy (who was, incidentally, said to have a croquet lawn laid out in the shape of the curve of diminishing returns), wrote to him contrasting Sidgwick's 'lecture-room, in which a handful of men are taking down what they regard as useful for examinations, with that of [T. H.] Green, in which a hundred men—half of them B.A.'s—ignoring examinations, were wont to hang on the lips of the man who was sincerely anxious to teach them the truth about the universe and human life'. Sidgwick had, as he could not but acknowledge, no truths, no answers to ultimate problems, to lay before his pupils. He used of himself Bagehot's words about Clough: 'He saw what it is considered cynical to see—the absurdities of many persons, the pomposities of many creeds, the splendid zeal with which missionaries rush on to teach what they do not know, the wonderful earnestness with which most incomplete solutions of the universe are thrust upon us as complete and satisfying.'[2] He did not even wish to be an influential teacher. To the eager questioning of young men hot for certainty he could return only the dustiest of answers.

That a man of Sidgwick's undoubted abilities and high seriousness should have devoted forty years to the problems of ethics without finding satisfactory answers; that he should almost from his infancy have sought God, yet never once have felt sure that he had found Him; that he should have taught but founded no school, have peered into the Beyond but seen nothing clearly, and should at last have died of a terrible disease leaving every major question in which he had interested himself still unsolved, and some of them apparently further from solution than before, must have seemed to many a tragic commentary upon the pretensions of both philosophy and psychical research. Yet I do not believe that in his last hours Sidgwick felt he had altogether lived in vain. He had taken a leading part in the inception and guidance of an endeavour

[1] Sir J. J. Thomson, *Recollections and Reflections*, London, 1938, pp. 294-5.
[2] *H.S.: A Memoir*, pp. 394-5.

which seemed to hold out at least a faint hope that the ancient riddles might one day be resolved; and he believed that even if the hope should in the end prove unjustified, there was at any rate no other endeavour of comparable promise to which he might have devoted his labours. And though his philosophical studies had brought him no nearer certainty, they had been fruitful in other ways. Almost his last words to Myers were these: 'As I look back on my life, I seem to see little but wasted hours. Yet I cannot be sorry that you should idealise me, if that shows that I have made my ideals in some degree felt. We must idealise, or we should cease to struggle.' What Sidgwick gave to his pupils and his friends was not a grandiose philosophy, or even a set of particular answers to particular questions, but an example; an example which few, perhaps, cared to follow, but which to those few was without parallel. It was an example not just of candour and careful judgment, and of the intellectual virtues generally, but of a constant endeavour to understand what is true and good and right, and to embody this knowledge, however painfully, into a whole way of life. Myers applied to him,[1] not inappropriately, the words in which Marcus Aurelius spoke of his tutor, the Stoic Maximus:

> From Maximus I learnt self-government, and not to be led aside by anything; and cheerfulness in all circumstances, as well, as in illness; and a just admixture in the moral character of sweetness and dignity and to do what was set before me without complaining. I observed that everybody believed that he thought as he spoke, and that in all that he did he never had any bad intention; and he never showed amazement and surprise, nor did he ever laugh to disguise his vexation, nor, on the other hand, was he ever passionate or suspicious. He was accustomed to do acts of beneficence, and was ready to forgive, and was free from all falsehood; and he presented the appearance of a man who could not be diverted from right rather than of a man who had been improved. I observed, too, that no man could ever think that he was despised by Maximus or ever venture to think himself a better man.

During the first eighteen years of the S.P.R.'s existence Sidgwick had moved from believing that there was practically no

[1] *P.S.P.R.* XV (1900), p. 452.

evidence for survival to believing that there was at least some *prima facie* evidence, though the proper interpretation of it presented almost insuperable problems. During the same period Myers moved from believing that there was *prima facie* evidence for survival to an absolutely unshakable confidence that death is not the end. However, his conviction of survival was not reached by any easy path. He had many moments of hesitation and doubt, and his doubts were of the fiercest and most despairing kind. One such mood of despair was triggered off as late as November 1887 when Sidgwick, at the extremity of one of his regular oscillations of view, declared it not improbable 'that this last effort to look beyond the grave would fail; that men would have to content themselves with an agnosticism growing yearly more hopeless,—and had best turn to daily duties and forget the blackness of the end'.[1] For a time Myers felt himself spinning on the edge of the abyss out of which he had so painfully clambered. But the mood passed. By the year 1890 the hope which he had cherished ten years before—a hope running more or less consciously in advance of his evidence—had been transformed into a certainty, and he could write to J. A. Symonds (in a letter dated 20th June): 'I do not feel the smallest doubt now that we survive death, and I am pretty confident that the whole scientific world will have accepted this before A.D. 2000.'[2] It was in part Myers' studies of phantasms of the dead that led him to conviction; but what clinched matters was a message from Edmund Gurney which he received through Mrs. Piper in 1890.[3] I have not been able to discover the precise nature of this message, which seems to have been concerned with some especially intimate matter.

Conviction of survival however was not all that Myers sought. The next world, though every whit as beautiful as Spiritualists alleged, would have been to him the emptiest of Limbos had Annie Marshall not been there to make whole his wounded heart at last. His longing for her had grown more rather than less poignant with the passage of the years. It might have been otherwise had his marriage been completely satisfactory to him; but the luckless Evie had little chance of competing with an ideal which was unattainable in

[1] *Fragments*, p. 41.   [2] Bristol University Library.
[3] *Fragments*, p. 41, and cf. above, pp. 178–9.

every sense of the word. Though Myers and his wife remained in many ways devoted to each other—towards the close Myers would write to her several times a day when they were apart, whilst Evie nursed him in his last illness with a patience that cannot have come easily to her—in other ways they were obviously drifting apart. Evie became more and more absorbed in the fashionable world of London Society—her natural habitat; and on 21st December 1900, when he was gravely ill, Myers could write to William James that he suffered 'a good deal at times with Cheyne-Stokes breathing wh. lasts through gasping nights;—but I have come rather to welcome this also, as tending to wean me from earth . . . But do not allude to all this in any letter! As my wife likes to see your letters, & I do not want to seem half-hearted in clinging to earth-life.'

It was not until 1899—twenty-three years after Annie's death—that Myers became absolutely certain that, through the mediumship of Mrs. Thompson, he had indeed made contact with her. There had however been certain previous episodes which had considerably impressed him. The most notable, perhaps, was a series of three sittings which he had in Boston with Mrs. Piper in September 1893. At the second of these sittings, on 9th September, the name 'Annie Marshall' was written over and over again, and of the third sitting, on the 10th, Myers wrote to Lodge: 'I do not say that facts *unknown* to *myself* were given:—but facts unknown to Mrs. P. were *re-combined* in a manner & with an earnestness wh. in Hodgson and myself left little doubt—no doubt—that we were in the presence of an authentic utterance from a soul beyond the tomb.' Unfortunately the record of this seance has not survived. Nor has the record of an even more intriguing seance, which Myers described to Lodge as follows, in a letter of 19th November 1894: 'I have just had a marvellous test through Arthur Labouchère (brother of Henry Labouchère, M.P!), along with Miss Wingfield. A scene—too tragic & private to tell anyone—even you—who does not already know of it—a scene wh. had been hinted at but *concealed* by the same spirit that Mrs. Piper *described, a month & time of day* given rightly. Scene is 18 years old.'

The records of Myers' own sittings with Mrs. Thompson—more than 150 between September 1898 and December 1900—

have likewise disappeared. The fullest remaining account of these sittings, and of the part played in them by a *soi-disant* Annie, is the following letter, dated 24th October 1899, from Myers to William James:

My first few sittings with Mrs. Thompson were in no way remarkable. There was little of intimacy in the communications, and Mrs. Thompson, as usual, came to herself with no recollection of the experiences of the trance state. But one day [27th April 1899] the little Nelly announced the approach of a spirit 'almost as bright as God';—brighter & higher, at any rate, than any spirit whom she had thus far seen. That spirit with great difficulty descended into possession of the sensitive's organism,—& spoke words wh. left no doubt of her identity. And when Mrs. Thompson came to herself she looked round her with an expression of startled disappointment upon a foundation of joy. 'I seem to have been taken to heaven by an angel,' she said, 'how horrid to see tables & chairs again!'

Whenever this spirit appeared the heavenly excursion was repeated. Sometimes, too, there came a tacit summons to the sensitive alone in the night. She would wake up to feel that she was *called*; look at her watch, and pass straightway into light & joy. When you get to know her she will tell you something of these 'precursory intromissions into a most holy place,' which are for her incomparably the best of all her life's experiences, & which leave her refreshed and uplifted both in body & soul. And since my presence has become associated for her with that exultation she is led by a feeling of gratitude—not to *me* but to one behind or rather above me—to offer to do all that she can in requital for this illuminating joy. When I reached you the other night, she had just been thanking me with tears in her eyes for the delight wh. my presence had—through no virtue of my own—brought to her that very afternoon.

You are the only person who have [*sic*] read my little autobiographical sketch. You know that destiny brought me into the nearness of a spirit who assuredly [?] is immeasurably far from the highest, but who, nevertheless, is as high as aught that my own limited heart & mind can grasp;—is to me indeed for all practical purposes a satisfactory object of worship, & in herself an eternal hope.

May I not feel that this adoration has received its sanction, & that I am veritably in relation with a spirit who can hear & answer my prayer?[1]

---
[1] Houghton Library, Harvard University.

Myers was the first to admit that his inability to conceive or to receive the Divine Grace except in so far as it might come to him through the mediation of Annie Marshall was a symptom of his own weakness.[1] He was also the first to admit that his creed was not perhaps an especially noble or unselfish one. But he could at any rate claim that his desire for an avenue of endless hope had led, as he wrote to Lodge on 18th December 1891, to:

> ... action when the possibility of action came;—that burning ardour, in concurrence with the conclusions wh. Sidgwick's wiser, calmer outlook on the world had led him to, has helped to initiate an experimental & positive enquiry, wh. may I hope do for other men something like what it has done for one; —transforming life from a waking nightmare into a solemn labour lit by steadfast hope.

Myers continued to have sittings with Mrs. Thompson throughout 1900, and to receive evidential messages which impressed him greatly; of the nature of the messages only a few scanty hints remain, and it is not worth pursuing them. It is likely that his wife, who seems not to have discovered until after his death the full extent to which his life had been affected by his love for Annie Marshall, destroyed all the original records. It is known that Myers had proposed to give some account of his sittings with Mrs. Thompson in his unfinished *Human Personality*; such passages as he had written were however struck out by the editors, Richard Hodgson and Alice Johnson, for reasons upon which I will not speculate.[2]

It has not infrequently been suggested that Myers was a mystic whose yearning to believe was so intense that it distorted his judgment and rendered him hopelessly credulous in his assessment of 'evidential' cases. And there is of course no doubt that in his early days he was far too optimistic. But later in life he became altogether more chastened and more cautious— see for instance his amusing paper on fraudulent physical phenomena.[3] His hopes had so often in the past proved delusory,

---

[1] Cf. *Fragments*, p. 42, and for Myers' views on prayer and mediation, above, p. 310.
[2] See *Light*, 1903, pp. 151–2 for the Thompsons' view of the matter; cf. the note by J. G. Piddington, *J.S.P.R.* XI (1903), pp. 74–6.
[3] 'On Resolute Credulity', *P.S.P.R.* XI (1895), pp. 213–43.

and his falls had been so painful, that he was now determined to test every inch of his Jacob's ladder before setting foot on it. The essential difference between Myers and a really credulous Spiritualist was that whereas the latter might respond to criticism of his views with a somewhat paranoid hostility, Myers not merely heeded such criticism but actively courted it. 'He was always ready,' said Andrew Lang, 'beyond most writers I have known, to accept criticism with candour and good humour.'[1] Nothing illustrates this point more convincingly than his reaction to Hodgson's criticisms of his records of his sittings with Mrs. Thompson, records which were undoubtedly more precious to him than any other evidence he had ever come across. On 15th November 1900 he wrote to Lodge:

> I think it [a letter of Hodgson's] is based on insufficient knowledge, & I am inclined to let all stand over until R.H. has more fully studied the evidence, & has himself had some further sittings with Mrs. T. I do not think that my records are as imperfect as he implies; nor am I conscious of any such failure of memory (by which R.H. very likely means something *more* than memory) as to vitiate my more recent work.
>
> You will understand that *if* R.H. is *right*, his plainness is the highest kindness . . . Do not let R.H.'s style set you *against* him! He writes like the friendly *surgeon*,—& with absolutely *impersonal* desire for truth. It would be a poor compliment to me if he thought that I desired *less* than absolute frankness.

That Myers believed in survival whilst Sidgwick doubted it was not to any great extent due to the former accepting phenomena which the latter dismissed as fraudulent. The evidence had reached such a state (a state in which I think it still remains) that rejecting the survivalist point of view involved about as much credulity (in the way of supposing sensitives and mediums to possess fantastic powers of telepathy and clairvoyance) as upholding it did, so that the side one took might well be decided by one's constitutional optimism or pessimism, or one's suspicions as to one's prospects in another existence. There was no doubt which way Myers would jump under these circumstances. His love of life and of experience was ineradicable. To William James he wrote on 3rd January 1894:

[1] *P.S.P.R.* XVIII (1903), p. 72.

But do not compliment me on tenacity! any more than you praise the male frog who does not release his embrace when his head is cut off. I am—as you surely know—no more than an insatiable lover of life & love, to whose earthly existence a kind of unity is given by his passionate effort to project his life & love beyond the tomb.

This is not ethical, but organic.

There was however without doubt a mystical streak in both Myers' thinking and his personality. The Platonic elements in his thought have already been touched upon; and they were no doubt partly forged out of a vein of mystical experience which he had tapped at intervals since his early youth. 'It has been my lot,' he wrote to Wilfrid Ward on 7th June 1896, '... during many years of my life, to feel in the most vivid manner almost the whole range (if I can judge from the well-known records of experience such as those of St. Augustine, St. Theresa, etc.) of spiritual conflict and ecstasy.'[1]

These experiences are not for the most part recorded in his writings, though perhaps there are occasional hints of them when he describes the effects which an especially striking scene might have upon him—as though in it and through it he could for a moment glimpse that visionary world which is at once the kernel and the archetype of our own:

> Strangely those scenes return to me, as if a part of some experience other than that of waking men. It might be a drive at dawn of day along the misty Vyrniew; the trees half seen in clinging vapour, the leaf-scented autumn chill, the sense of traversing ghostly mysteries and entering on a land unknown. Or Ludlow, clustered about the deep-cliffed river beneath a crimson sinking sun,—something of glowing and slumberous in earth and air, as if a city of the spirit-world.[2]

But however important mystical experiences may have been in determining the drift of Myers' beliefs, as an avenue to knowledge he did not trust them. He did not regard himself as being 'above the average in any real moral or spiritual merit'—rather the reverse—and he could not see why, if the experiences were what they purported to be, he should have been so

---

[1] Maisie Ward, *The Wilfrid Wards and the Transition*, London, 1934, p. 366.
[2] *Fragments*, p. 16; cf. *Fragments*, p. 42. 'Meantime the background of Eternity shows steadfast through all the pageants of the shifting world.'

singularly favoured. He was, moreover, all too keenly aware of the pathological interpretation which could be put upon them in view of his excessively emotional nature. Only through patient empirical enquiry could he reach the certainty without which he could not rest content.

And so Myers turned the ardour of soul which might have spent itself in spiritual raptures to the mundane task of organising the S.P.R. and collecting cases for its *Proceedings*. It may have been Sidgwick who for the most part laid down the straight and rigid tracks along which that Society was to move; but it was Myers who more than anyone—at least after the death of Gurney—put steam into its cylinders. He was tireless in writing and lecturing, in investigating and seeking new mediums and sensitives, in luring desirable members into the fold, in encouraging and exhorting those already recruited. William James spoke for others as well as himself when he wrote to Myers on 30th January 1891:

> Verily you are of the stuff of which world changers are made. What a despot for P.R.! I always feel guilty in your presence, and am on the whole glad that the broad blue ocean rolls between us for most days of the year, although I should be glad to have it intermit occasionally, on days when I feel particularly carefree and indifferent, when I might meet you without being bowed down with shame.[1]

If Myers was a mystic, he was at any rate a remarkably practical one. Casual acquaintances were more struck by his calmness and his everyday efficiency than by signs of any inward spiritual ecstasies. A. C. Benson, who was Leo Myers' housemaster at Eton in the late eighteen-nineties, said that there was one thing which always struck him very forcibly about Myers, and that was 'the extreme serenity and tranquillity of his face and bearing. The perfect smoothness of his brow and cheek, the absence of all lines or dints of stress or experience, his leisurely carriage, gave a feeling of self-contained prosperity and stability. It still remains to me a thing to be wondered at that so little of the eagerness or rapture of life should have been visible, and no touch of dissatisfaction or unrest.'[2]

Outward calm had not always been Myers' most marked

---

[1] Houghton Library, Harvard University.   [2] Benson, *op. cit.*, p. 180.

characteristic. That it should at the last have become so was the result not just perhaps of inward assurance, but of a sense that his destiny as participant and leader in a unique and uniquely important endeavour had already been fulfilled. 'I fear that', Myers wrote to William James on 22nd August 1899, ' . . . I illustrate what I hold to be a real danger in the future—that men will be *too happy* to work as they ought. That (other) world is too much with me; late & soon, musing & dreaming I lay waste my powers;—for that home of the soul which should act as a call & summons hangs round me rather as an entrancement, with all its brooding glory and impregnable peace.'

Myers' serenity and his undoubted social gifts did not however suffice to make him widely liked. He was indeed definitely unpopular in many quarters. Part of his unpopularity was no doubt due to the follies and excesses of his youth, and to the unfortunate business of the Camden medal; academic Cambridge was an inbred and gossip-loving community, with a long memory for the failings and transgressions of its members. And even in middle age Myers was apt to make some people feel uneasily that beneath his restrained and courteous exterior there smouldered Beltane fires which some chance gust might still whip into life. The singularity of his religious views, his transient yet unpredictable bursts of anger, the rather obviously sensual basis of his marriage,[1] were all bound to ruffle the members of the somewhat inhibited and conventional society in which he moved.

Some of those who disliked Myers seem to have done so because they found it difficult to believe that his extravagant sentiments and astonishing beliefs could be genuine; and there was unfortunately something in his manner—a hint of the theatrical, perhaps, or a rather excessive fluency—which could lend support to their suspicions. 'Frederic Myers', said Jane Harrison, discussing the founders of the S.P.R., 'rang, perhaps,

[1] Mrs. W. H. Salter, 'Impressions of some Early Workers in the S.P.R.', *J. Parapsychology* XIV (1950), pp. 23–36, comments on Myers' humour, and dramatic talents in charades, but says that he once became angry with her because she walked across the untrodden snow in his garden. I have been told by several persons who can remember Cambridge at the turn of the century that Myers' liking for the company of pretty girls caused some comment, though not exactly of a scandalous nature; he was certainly fond of Lodge's and Arthur Sidgwick's daughters. I also understand that there was an unpublished poem of J. K. Stephen's satirising Myers' tempestuous relations with his wife.

the most sonorously of all, but to me he always rang a little false.'[1] Myers was a brilliant speaker in what might be called a pulpit manner; but his rich cadences were at times too contrived even for the taste of his day. And he did not care for conventional small-talk. It was not that he never relaxed, or that he had no sense of humour; but his jokes would often have Cosmic overtones, and he tended in any case to keep them for his intimate friends. Even in his relations with his family a slightly absurd note of high seriousness would too often intrude. When Evie's first child was imminent, he started a letter: 'I begin this letter to you in this solemn season of expectation . . .' Myers' tendencies towards sonorousness and rhetoric grew upon him with advancing years and too often ruined a prose style which, at its mannered best, could be very powerful. Unfortunately the fit was most liable to seize him when he was discussing issues which he felt to be particularly important; then the measured periods would march forth with resonance and rhythm, but where they were headed, and why with such pomp, not every spectator could discern. The stiltedness perhaps arose because from childhood his highest emotions had been interwoven with his classical studies, and it had become second nature to him to express those emotions in a heavily classical vocabulary. 'I am perfectly aware of the literary defects of the style in which these chapters are written,' he said in a marginal note on the manuscript of the *Fragments*, ' . . . But I cannot feel that I am entirely candid unless I write in this emotional, over-decorated style, wh. corresponds in some subtle way to the idiosyncrasy of the soul within.' It is none the less a great pity that Myers did not make sterner efforts to curb this seeming artificiality. However flamboyant and pretentious he may have been in his youth, in later days he was passionately sincere. Yet to appreciate his sincerity, to perceive that his emotional rhetoric was no façade but a burgeoning of the man himself, one needed to know him fairly well. And it was not easy to get to know him well.

Myers was in general kindly and courteous, and he possessed great social gifts. But he was none the less extremely reserved, and he bared his inmost heart only to a small circle of close friends. They, indeed, did not despise it. Edmund Gurney said

[1] *Op. cit.*, p. 55.

of Myers to Frances Balfour: 'Only Henry and I really know what he is.' (F. Balfour to Myers, 20th July 1888.) Myers' reserve sprang no doubt chiefly from the fact that there were few who could appreciate, and still fewer who could share, the ardent hopes and the extraordinary goals which dominated his life. When he encountered someone whose aims and outlook were not unlike his own, he would cleave to him with a profound sense of comradeship in the Endless Voyage, and would give him the most unbounded sympathy and support. To Lodge he wrote, on 25th June 1900, 'It must be awfully nice to be a man like you! I don't mean you to shake me off through all eternity;—I shall stick like a leech to the highest souls I can get at.' But kindred spirits such as Lodge were rare. Adversaries were much commoner, and Myers' style of discourse was apt to turn an intellectual difference into something like personal distrust. Even his children, whom he adored, did not feel entirely at ease with him; he expected from them endeavours as earnest as his own, and preferably directed to the same exalted goals. Their mother encouraged them to take life lightly, and there was no doubt which parent was more influential. In later years Leo Myers described his father as 'Theodore [*sic*] Pontifex the Second',[1] and one cannot but sympathise with Silvia Myers' reply to a letter concerning the Spiritualist doctrine of 'guides': 'I am *extremely* sorry to hear that I have a guardian angel; I don't at all want one, and shall certainly never listen to it or follow its advice—I hope you will tell it to *shut up!* I remember that Leo's was a great bore.'

That Myers should have been somewhat unpopular is easy to understand, but it is also more than a little sad. In his later years he was a vastly improved person and, as William James remarked,[2] it was largely through his work in psychical research that the improvement had come about. He had once been every kind of a snob; he even suggested to George Eliot that she should write a novel 'in which all the people should be refined, and where the tragedy should be unmixed with vulgar elements, and depend wholly on the collision of high natures, and on such sorrows as are felt most keenly in the purest air'—

---

[1] G. H. Bantock, *L. H. Myers: A Critical Study*, London, 1956, p. 137.
[2] p. 319 of 'The Final Impressions of a Psychical Researcher' (originally written in 1909), reprinted in Murphy and Ballou, *op. cit.*, pp. 309–25.

surely the worst piece of advice she can ever have received. Now—though he still had a liking for titles and pedigrees—he would go out of his way to assist, if he could, even the humblest seeker after enlightenment, for it had often been through such people, through mediums and automatists of no outward distinction, that enlightenment had come to him. Once he had been arrogant and ambitious and selfish and proud. Now worldly fame seemed to him of no account beside the eternal advancement which awaited him, and he was keenly aware of his own shortcomings and of his unworthiness for such a splendid destiny.

Myers was at his best in the comforting of friends lately bereaved. His own absolute confidence in a future life did not betray him into assailing an uncertain mourner with tasteless expressions of certitude; rather it made his tactful indication of the various grounds for hope seem the more reassuring. His easy attitude towards the deaths or the imminent deaths of members of his own family sometimes surprised even those most intimate with him; after the death of his mother, on 6th July 1896, he wrote to Lodge: 'There is no cause for grief; but such moments make the Universe seem a solemn place.' And when his own turn came to die he faced the translation not just with serenity but with eagerness and surpassing joy.

Whether Myers' thoughts would have turned so much to the Beyond (once he was convinced of its existence) had he not come to believe that Annie Marshall was waiting for him there might be doubted; but as it was, the ties of home and family and friends were like straws beside the chains of adamant which drew him to the imagined Annie. When at last it became clear to him that death could not be long delayed, he could hardly disguise his longing to go; and one may well wonder if that longing did not, by some obscure mechanism, hasten its own fulfilment.

In March 1898 he suffered a sharp attack of influenza which passed into pneumonia; and he had another attack of influenza in February 1899. This attack left very damaging results behind it; in November Myers was found to have Bright's disease and was ordered to the Riviera for a lengthy rest. The disease led to enlargement of the heart and degeneration of the arteries. In the spring of 1900 Myers appears to have been told through Mrs. Thompson that he would waken in Annie's arms on 6th February (his birthday) 1902. He interpreted this as meaning that he would die on that day (the prophecy also seemed a sound one on medical grounds), and planned the remaining work on his *Human Personality* on that basis. However, in October 1900 Cheyne-Stokes breathing (a recurrent waxing and waning of the respiration) set in, and kept him awake through nights of misery. There followed yet another attack of influenza and, when he had sufficiently recovered, he again set out for the Riviera. In December he and his wife went to stay at Valescure with Sir Lawrence Jones, one of his colleagues on the S.P.R. Council; Miss Wingfield joined them there, and they held seances. According to Sir Lawrence Jones 'Edmund Gurney and Henry Sidgwick and others who had come through Mrs. Thompson communicated, and Myers was greatly cheered by the corroboration he received of messages already given through Mrs. Thompson.'[1]

Thence he went to Rome, which he reached on 1st January 1901. He went next day to the clinic of a certain Dr. Baldwin. Dr. Baldwin had developed a serum, concocted from the testicles and other glands of goats, injections of which were alleged to relieve atheromatous conditions of the arteries. William James was a patient at the clinic, and it was he who had induced Myers to come there, reporting that as a result of the serum his own arteries had improved, his vitality been boosted, and his skin become smoother and pinker (these effects were no doubt due to the hormones which the injections contained). Myers had agreed to place himself in Baldwin's hands, remarking in a letter to Lodge: 'possibly I shall meet my dear young female friends [Lodge's daughters] on my return as a cross between an old goat and a guardian angel'.

He received his first injection on 3rd January, and at first all seemed to go well. But on the 8th his condition deteriorated. Pneumonia set in, and the Cheyne-Stokes breathing caused him great suffering, which he endured with outstanding fortitude. On the 14th hope was abandoned. William James wrote to Mrs. Sidgwick on 20th January 1901:

His serenity, in fact his eagerness to go, and his extraordinary intellectual vitality up to the very time that the death agony

---
[1] Presidential Address to the S.P.R., *P.S.P.R.* XXXVIII (1928), p. 43.

began, and even in the midst of it, were a superb spectacle and deeply impressed the doctors as well as ourselves. It was a demonstration *ad oculos* of the practical influence of a living belief in future existence.[1]

Myers died at 9.30 p.m. on Thursday, 17th January 1901.[2] The continuation of James' letter is curious:

> From a medical point of view his case seems to have been quite anomalous. The respiratory disturbance from which he suffered agony during the past month whenever he dropped asleep, was a nervous superaddition unaccounted for by heart or arteries, and the pneumonia was equally unexplained by exposure. It began insidiously without fever or pain, and changed its seat in a way that Dr. Baldwin (from whom he got the best of care) said he had not seen in 1000 cases.

Some may think that Myers' eagerness to meet death half-way, and rather more than half-way, was the crowning symptom of a lifetime's eccentricity; others may see in it a supreme illustration of the essential spirituality of his nature. I will not venture any judgment on the question. But of Myers' last years and last hours one may confidently say at least this. He was endowed with a remarkable, indeed a dangerous, assortment of seemingly irreconcilable qualities—with an enquiring mind and a profound need for the security of a relieious belief; with the crassest sensuality and the bodiless yearnings of a mystic; with the most unruly emotions and affections, and an uncommon capacity for scrupulous self-questioning. Merely to have harnessed these divergent traits into a workable team, and to have governed them so that at the last all ran smoothly together, must have required moral and intellectual efforts of no ordinary kind.

On 20th December 1905 Richard Hodgson was seized with a heart attack whilst playing a game of hand-ball. He died almost immediately—a fitting end for a muscular Christian *manqué*.

---

[1] Houghton Library, Harvard University.

[2] The account of Myers' death-bed in Axel Munthe's *Story of San Michele* seems to be accurate in the main, though there are one or two obvious mistakes. Munthe says that Baldwin died in an asylum a few years later, but his views on professional rivals are perhaps not to be trusted.

Hodgson's undoubted talents could have brought him worldly advancement, had he striven for it. As a lawyer, defending the oppressed and attacking the oppressor, or as a doctor, exuding a contagious animal health, he would have been a great success. But he chose instead to devote his life to the unremunerative studies which he believed to be of paramount importance to the future of mankind. For that alone he would deserve respect; and there was at least one notable outcome of his devotion, namely the extensive, and for some while unique, documentation of the Piper case.

Reading about Hodgson, and reading his letters, it is sometimes hard to understand how his fellow workers found him even tolerable, let alone why they liked and admired him as much as they did. It is true of course that they would have appreciated the deep earnestness and the religious feelings which in large part inspired his interest in psychical research; but on the other hand they would hardly have cared for his loud voice, and for the inelegance of his manners, whilst his assertiveness was combined with other faults well brought out by J. G. Piddington in an unusually frank obituary notice:

> Once his mind was made up he became constitutionally unable to appreciate another point of view, and his strong convictions were accompanied by an almost righteous indignation at the perversity of the other fellow. In other words, though full of fun he was lacking in a sense of humour. He was in deadly earnest in whatever he took up. This disposition made him in his later years impatient of compromise or control. He was one of those men who, averse from and unsuited for co-operation, work best alone . . .
>
> The competitive instinct, too, was unduly developed. He hated being beaten in a game, and he would not admit defeat in an argument. And in each case I think defeat was distasteful for the same reason; namely, that at bottom he was so firmly convinced that his own side was best that when it was worsted, or in danger of being worsted, he felt a sense of injury because the righteous were not inheriting the earth. The promise of this inheritance to the meek must have been to him the hardest of Hard Sayings.
>
> Yet if he played, or wrote, or talked for victory with excessive zeal, I do not believe for one moment that egotism was the cause. *He knew* his side was in the right, and his plain duty was to

make that side prevail: a refreshing trait in these indifferent days when we lazily incline to hold that there is so much to be said for any side of a question that it matters little which gains the day.

There was something of a strain of Old Testament vindictiveness in his make-up. He must, so it seems to me, have had his moments when with the Psalmist he might have cried: 'Of thy goodness slay mine enemies: and destroy all them that vex my soul.' But, mark you, as with the Psalmist so with him, his enemies were always the Lord's enemies too: though, doubtless, he either was unconscious of the coincidence, or, if he did remark it, was not disturbed by it.[1]

Perhaps the answer is that Hodgson's colleagues simply could not fail to respect the opinions and the work of a man whose absolute sincerity, though it might support a misplaced dogmatism, was beyond doubt, and whose claims to practical expertise in all matters related to psychical research were outstanding. To William James (who had expressed an unfavourable opinion of Hodgson's philosophical work) Gurney wrote on 16th January 1887:

> His qualities are *absolutely invaluable*; & psychical research ought to insure his life for about a million pounds. His intellectual honesty is quite complete; and he combines the powers of a first-rate detective with a perfect readiness to believe in astrology. (*Don't quote this*, as it might be misunderstood. I should pity the astrologer whose horoscopes he took to tackling.)

There was, too, an altogether more human side to Hodgson's character. One source of his interest in psychical research was simply a love of puzzles, mysteries, mystifications and conjuring, in all of which he took a quite boyish delight. He had, as Piddington remarked, a great sense if not of humour, at any rate of fun. He delighted in the society of children, joining in their games, mystifying them with conjuring tricks, and giving them presents more expensive than his slender means would properly allow.

To people in need Hodgson's generosity was extreme, and to those afflicted by the loss of a loved one he gave lavishly of his time, his counsel and his sympathy. They came to meet him half-way, said Piddington,

[1] *P.S.P.R.* XIX (1907), pp. 365–6.

... but even so he won their confidence with extraordinary completeness. Many of them poured out their hearts to him without restraint; and he, though naturally a man of deep reserve where his innermost emotions were concerned, would, repaying confidence with confidence, reveal to them his own most intimate experiences and convictions, in the hope of thereby lightening the darkness or assuaging the bitterness of their despondency. And he won not only their confidence but their gratitude also, and very often their affection.[1]

His success as a comforter was heightened by his own deepening and eventually complete belief in survival. He came to accept the Imperator group completely, and to model his whole life on their teachings. He grew, so a friend said, to believe that everything in the universe, from a spot of ink to all the stars, is in and part of the infinite Goodness. In his last years he even developed automatic writing himself.[2] Through Mrs. Piper the spirits prophesied a long and healthy life for him. Soon afterwards he was dead. He had been planning a third paper on Mrs. Piper; in it he was going to expound in full the reasons for his belief that her controls were indeed the persons they claimed to be. The shorthand notes on which this paper was to have been based were indecipherable.

Of the members of what I have called the Sidgwick group Mrs. Sidgwick was now the only survivor; and as the years passed she acquired the prestige of an almost legendary figure. When she retired as Principal of Newnham in 1910 (she was then sixty-five), she became the S.P.R.'s secretary; and she retained to an advanced age her immense powers of subduing complex masses of material. The 657-page paper on Mrs. Piper which she published in 1915,[3] when she was seventy-three, is probably the most remarkable feat of this kind that she ever performed.

Many people still alive can remember the diminutive old lady, dressed in black from head to foot, with her pale, half-smiling face and thoughtful expression. She was formidable only in virtue of her seniority, and of her immense experience;

---
[1] *Loc. cit.*, p. 367.
[2] Hereward Carrington, *The Story of Psychic Science*, London, 1930, p. 66.
[3] As *P.S.P.R.* XXVIII.

an experience in whose light nothing was new or surprising, and not much was credible. In manner she remained as quiet and gentle as always. Some of the more eccentric visitors to the Society's rooms found that her calm personality had a therapeutic effect on them, and would favour her with their life histories; she was also very popular with the childish secondary personalities of various mediums. To the end of her life she retained her early habits of evangelical simplicity and austerity; even in her eighties she would not take a cab from the Society to the railway station but, whatever the weather, would set out on foot to catch a 'bus. She once said, 'mine has been a grey life'; but added, 'I think grey is a beautiful colour, and it has many colours in it.'

There is no doubt that Mrs. Sidgwick kept the S.P.R. to a high critical standard; even among her own family it was said that it was impossible to convince Aunt Nora that anything in the world had ever happened. Her immediate lieutenants in running the Society were for a long while her brother, Gerald Balfour, and J. G. Piddington. These three kept an extraordinary household at Fisher's Hill, near Woking, in which, aided by Miss Alice Johnson, they analysed an enormous quantity of communications, supposedly from their deceased colleagues, received over a period of more than thirty years through various different automatists. The psychological interest of this material is very great; but whether for the S.P.R. it was altogether good to be dominated by a group of elderly and closely linked persons whose immediate interests were in communications from their own deceased intimate friends might be doubted.

On the other hand the outstanding ability of these persons can hardly be denied, and it was perhaps no fault of theirs that psychical research did not achieve a closer *rapprochement* with orthodox psychology. In the first decade or two after 1900 such a *rapprochement*, though it did not seem imminent, did not on the other hand seem completely impossible. Three of the most distinguished English-speaking psychologists—G. F. Stout, William McDougall and William James—were members of the S.P.R.; the two last-named were Council members. On the Continent Binet, Janet, Freud, Jung, Flournoy and Bernheim all showed an interest. McDougall, James, Freud,

Jung and Flournoy contributed to the Society's *Proceedings*. Encyclopaedias and works of reference from the famous 1911 *Britannica* downwards gave psychical research on the whole a favourable treatment. The concluding volume of the popular *Harmsworth History of the World* (1909) presents the work of the S.P.R. as the culminating point in the story of Mankind. Twenty or thirty years previously psychical research had met with much derision and hostility; but now the climate of opinion seemed to be changing for the better.

Yet no *rapprochement* with orthodox psychology took place. Orthodox psychology became more experimental, more biological, more eager to be straightforwardly accepted as a science among the sciences. Its chances of being so accepted would not have been improved had it yoked itself to so eccentric a partner as psychical research; a partner who to most people spoke in the lyrical language of Myers' *Human Personality*. That language was far from typifying the tone of the S.P.R. But no book of comparable power was forthcoming to present the viewpoint of less hieratical workers. Perhaps the biggest 'if' of psychical research is, how would things have gone if Gurney had lived and had remained active until, say, 1920? Though *The Power of Sound* and *Phantasms of the Living* are little known today, I do not think that their author can be rated a less able man than the author of *Inquiries into Human Faculty* and *Natural Inheritance*; and Gurney died at an age at which Galton's outstanding works were still to come. Had Gurney lived, he rather than Myers would have written a large-scale résumé of the S.P.R.'s work, and the public image of psychical research would have been more acceptable to psychologists.

Epilogue

MOST OF THE FOUNDERS of psychical research have been in their graves for over sixty years. One might well suppose that it should by now be possible to arrive at some fairly complete and fairly unbiassed estimate of their work, to decide with reasonable certainty whether their immense efforts made a contribution of note to the sum total of things known, or whether their hopes—indeed their lives—have proved in the final reckoning altogether hollow. Had those efforts and those hopes been directed towards some branch of ordinary enquiry, such an evaluation would very likely be feasible. But their enquiries were not ordinary, and anything more than the most tentative of assessments is not feasible. For the question whether or not their work has been of lasting value is inextricably tied up with the question whether or not the strange phenomena which they believed themselves to have discovered really take place. And this is still a much disputed matter. It is hardly possible to make any firm assertions of whatever tendency to which plausible objections cannot be advanced.

To one statement however I will unhesitatingly commit myself. The endeavours of the Sidgwick group cannot against the background of their time be dismissed, as some would dismiss them, as pathetic, degrading and almost irresponsible, as the result of a hopeless or merely absurd credulity and wish to believe. The founders of psychical research were people of the highest ideals. They sought to penetrate the veil not merely, and in several cases not even principally, for their own reassurance and gratification. They hoped that their work would ultimately benefit the whole of mankind in the divers ways already touched upon. To this end they worked with great industry and perseverance, and in despite of numerous dis-

EPILOGUE

appointments and several almost crippling blows. Their sense of corporate endeavour was very strong, their indifference to personal fame most impressive. Even if their findings were illusory, their ideals unattainable, one cannot dismiss their quest as unworthy and lives devoted to it as wholly misspent. And for my part I cannot see in their work any signs of hopeless credulity, or of an overmastering will to believe. They made mistakes, it is true. They wasted time on tricksters like Mrs. Fay, they were transiently taken in by such charlatans as Mr. D. But they learned from their mistakes. They collected books on methods of deception, conducted pioneer studies in its psychology, themselves exposed impostors. And so far from being hopelessly swayed by a yearning to believe, they were all acutely aware of the pitfalls of wishful thinking and made the most strenuous efforts to avoid them. There cannot to my mind be the slightest doubt that by patient investigation and experiment, by the sifting and accumulation of first-hand testimony from responsible people, they amassed in favour of paranormal phenomena evidence which would in the case of almost any other kind of natural event have been unhesitatingly and almost universally accepted.[1]

Anyone who wants to assert that the endeavours of the Sidgwick group were entirely vain has to find some excuse for treating this evidence as a completely special case. An excuse which has been, and indeed still is, very commonly used is a principle related to or derived from Hume's famous argument against the possibility of miracles. This principle goes somewhat as follows. We have strong evidence in favour of a large number of 'Laws of Nature'—in favour, that is, of a large number of absolutely undeviating regularities in the world around us. The evidence for such laws is so overwhelming that no evidence for an occurrence contravening one of them (in other words, no evidence for a paranormal event) could conceivably outweigh it. Therefore we must always dismiss the evidence for the supposed paranormal event. Gurney devoted a considerable part of an interesting essay[2] to discussing this

---

[1] On the Canons of evidence which they applied—cf. the correspondence between Myers and Lord Acton in Appendix C below.
[2] 'The Nature of Evidence in Matters Extraordinary' in *Tertium Quid* I, pp. 227–273. First published in 1884 (see above, p. 147n).

principle as it had been deployed by W. B. Carpenter.[1] I will try to give the gist of Gurney's arguments.

Gurney admits, indeed he emphasises, that the establishment of novel and eccentric facts requires especially good evidence; but he denies that such evidence can be ruled out of court upon the principle brought forward by Carpenter. The facts adduced by psychical researchers for the most part cannot be said to conflict with established scientific laws. Scientific laws are simply statements of what happens when certain conditions obtain. Now if psychical researchers commonly alleged that under conditions already thoroughly investigated some effect other than that hitherto reported had taken place there would indeed be good grounds for dismissing their claims. But in, for instance, experiments on telepathy the conditions which obtain are for the most part quite novel—the agent concentrating on transmitting and the percipient sensitising himself to receive—and bear hardly any relation to the conditions obtaining in ordinary experiments on sensory communication. The occurrence of telepathy does not—indeed cannot—conflict with the ordinary laws of visual or auditory perception. Only if we accord negative inductions—'telepathy cannot take place because no instance of it has hitherto been reliably reported'—the status of laws would such facts as telepathy seem to conflict with scientific laws. But to dismiss the evidence for telepathy on the sole ground that it conflicted with a negative induction would be wholly inadmissible. The number of possible conditions which may obtain is infinite and we cannot claim to have exhausted them. Therefore we cannot assert positively that under no conditions can telepathy take place. Application of the sceptic's principle with the backing of a negative induction is

> ... not the vindication, by comparison, of the infinitely greater against the infinitely less amount of experience; it amounts to a positive assertion that a new fact, to which clear analogies are not forthcoming, can never be proved by testimony—what is practically nothing less than a veto on the advance of science by

---

[1] Carpenter says—*Mesmerism, Spiritualism, &c., Historically and Scientifically Considered*, London, 1877, pp. 57–8—that any evidence must be put out of court which is 'completely in opposition to the universal experience of Mankind, as embodied in those Laws of Nature which are accepted by all men of ordinary intelligence'.

EPILOGUE

a purely empirical road. The veto is pronounced, moreover—as has been well observed—in the teeth of the one induction from experience which, of all others, may be pronounced historically and scientifically valid—namely, that 'other inductions from experience, and especially negative inductions, are *not* final'.[1]

The principle is, in its customary form, so difficult to defend that the usual procedure of its upholders is to make cursory but impressive-sounding references to it, and then behind the smokescreen of pontification to apply the following covert argument to each individual case that comes to hand.

> The fact is so improbable that extremely good evidence is needed to make us believe it; and *this* evidence is not good, for how can you trust people who believe in such absurdities?[2]

The argument is never stated so baldly, but it can readily be filled out, or otherwise decorated, with some references to the psychology of dishonesty and delusion.[3] Now of course this whole procedure necessarily leads to complete deadlock, and is indeed quite absurd. Good evidence does not become bad evidence because the event involved is antecedently improbable. The antecedent improbability of an event may justifiably make us hesitate to accept even good evidence in its favour, but it cannot transform that good evidence into bad. Nor does the fact that 'good evidence' has occasionally been proved wrong show that evidence of that standard can no longer be called 'good'. Perfect evidence does not exist; the *possibilities* of conspiracy, conjuring, deceit and delusion can never be eliminated with absolute completeness. Good evidence is evidence of a standard which has in the past nearly always proved reliable. As long as evidence of that standard continues to prove highly reliable, it must be admitted to be good evidence. If one supposes that because an event is antecedently improbable any evidence for it must be bad evidence, or that because good evidence has sometimes been mistaken that sort of evidence is really not good, one makes it logically impossible for the evidence to accumulate.

---

[1] *Tertium Quid* I, p. 263.
[2] *Tertium Quid* I, p. 264.
[3] The writings of those who are addicted to this sort of argumentation can at least often be used to supply examples of the sorts of errors and illusions of memory to which they themselves commonly refer. For some examples, see Appendix B.

One slips, in fact, into paranoid reasoning, and adopts a frame of mind in which one can reconcile any turn of events whatsoever with one's preconceived beliefs. There is no doubt that the Sidgwick group forced its opponents to such extremities, and to that extent it may be said to have progressed towards its ultimate goals.

It is one thing to feel uneasy about the arguments of those who wish to dismiss out of hand all supposed evidence for paranormal phenomena. It is quite another thing to be prepared to draw from reports of such phenomena inferences relevant to issues of a moral or religious kind. There is no doubt that all the members of the Sidgwick group would have *liked* to draw such inferences, though in fact some of them were not prepared to do so. They would have liked, in particular, to assure themselves, and the world, of human survival of bodily death, with all its possibly uplifting moral and religious implications. Several would have liked to base a set of religious teachings on the information which they supposed themselves to have received from departed spirits. Whether they did indeed obtain satisfactory evidence for survival is far too difficult a question to receive even a faintly adequate discussion in the space that remains; and so, *a fortiori*, is the question of how much respect we should accord to the teachings of alleged departed spirits. I shall confine myself to a very brief examination of the evidence for survival obtained through the mediumship of Mrs. Piper.

Most people, faced with 'communicators' as realistic as some of Mrs. Piper's, would unhesitatingly assume themselves to be in contact with deceased persons. And even if they afterwards and on reflection developed doubts, they would none the less during actual sittings continue to talk to the communicators as though to the deceased persons in question. And they would do so despite occasional flaws in the personation, provided that those flaws did not become too gross.

We might look at these facts in the following way. To be a 'person', in the same sense in which, say, a decerebrate idiot, living a purely vegetative existence, is not one, is to be a centre of activities of a rather limited and very complex kind. I mean of course such activities as remembering, wishing, hoping, perceiving, fearing, knowing, believing, thinking, imagining, and the like. I shall not try to pick out a common feature which all these activities share, and in virtue of which they are to be classed together; the fact is that, for whatever reason, we *do* class them together.

These 'person-making' activities are, as no one will dispute, carried out by different people in different ways, with different relative frequencies, and with different degrees of skill. Let us call each person's particular constellation of ways of carrying out such activities his 'personality-pattern', bearing in mind that we are not using the term quite as a modern psychologist would do. On our definition a person's memory dispositions are an important differentiating feature of his personality-pattern.

Now in terms of this definition two people could obviously be said to have, or to have developed, closely similar personality-patterns; for example the man who acted as Montgomery's double during the war had not merely to look like him, but to learn to act like him and even to think like him.[1] And we could also, in fairly neutral terms, talk of the reappearance of a personality-pattern closely resembling that of a deceased person; this would not, of course, commit us to saying that the *same* person, the same centre of ongoing personal activities, was still in being, and had momentarily surfaced again.

The facts with which we began can now be expressed as follows. If, after the decease of some friend, we encounter a personality-pattern, and especially a set of memory-dispositions, closely resembling his, we almost all tend, at least in our less reflective moods, to assume that, in some obscure manner, that *person* is still with us. And here the reasoning would seem to be in some primitive way statistical. Just as it is very improbable that we shall find two people whose physical organisms are almost identical, and exceedingly improbable that we shall come across two individuals with identical fingerprints; so it is very improbable that we shall encounter two persons with closely similar personality-patterns, and exceedingly improbable that we shall encounter two persons with identical memory-dispositions. When, therefore, the personality-pattern (including the memory-dispositions) of a deceased friend reappears before us in some fullness, we are justified in supposing that that *person* is in some sense really present.

Now the line which sceptics have commonly taken against

[1] E. C. James, *I was Monty's Double*, London, 1954.

this position is somewhat as follows[1] (confining ourselves for simplicity to the case of Mrs. Piper). The personality-patterns which Mrs. Piper exhibited during her trances were decidedly like the 'secondary' personality-patterns sometimes displayed by hysterical patients. The personalities were highly suggestible, fished for information, covered up childishly when they made mistakes. The less-developed personalities could be quite absurd; in her early years Mrs. Piper had an Indian girl 'control' called 'Chlorine', and at a later seance a *soi-disant* Sir Walter Scott asserted that there are monkeys in the sun. To explain Mrs. Piper's phenomena we need to assume only three things. We must suppose firstly that she possessed remarkable powers of telepathy and probably also clairvoyance. Secondly we must suppose that when in a certain curious mental state she had a pronounced tendency to exhibit secondary personality-patterns. Thirdly we must suppose that some of these secondary personality-patterns developed into enduring entities, such as 'G.P.', whilst others remained more plastic and could take on the semblances of people with whom casual sitters wished to communicate.

Now of course there have certainly been cases of 'mediums' whose 'controls' have never given the smallest indication of being anything other than phases of the medium's personality. And one could probably arrange a continuum of cases from these, through cases in which there are occasional hints of supernormally acquired knowledge, up to cases like Mrs. Piper's, where one really is sometimes tempted to toy with the idea of possession. This fact, I think, forces one to admit that mediums are basically people who exhibit, if not exactly hysterical secondary personality-patterns, at any rate a curious proclivity for spontaneous mimicry and impersonation. Their proclivity for impersonation is played upon by many influences: their own memories of what they have heard or read; hints dropped by the sitters; information acquired telepathically or clairvoyantly; and so on. Are deceased persons ever among those influences? The practical problem round which the answer to this question revolves is whether mediums might obtain by telepathy or clairvoyance the extraordinarily detailed knowledge of the lives and personality-patterns of particular

[1] See esp. *Podmore* II, pp. 289-361.

EPILOGUE

deceased persons which they sometimes display. If they could not obtain it by telepathy, we are forced to suppose that the deceased persons may themselves be involved. Of experimental evidence for such astounding telepathic abilities there is none. In even the most impressive experiments all the percipient has been able to do is to score slightly (though consistently) above chance with a very limited range of 'target' material. Mrs. Piper, by contrast, would on a good day hardly make a mistake, even though her range of 'target' material might be enormous. So far as I know, the only data which might be held to provide evidence for the 'Super-E.S.P.' postulated by those who do not wish to accept a survivalist view of the phenomena are certain observations of performances rather resembling those of ordinary seaside and fairground fortune-tellers.[1] Not many psychical researchers would take such performances very seriously, and the evidence in most cases is certainly far from satisfactory. None the less it may be that the shortage of evidence is due to a lack of systematic enquiry; the matter is of such interest that an enquiry might be worth instituting. In the event of reliable evidence for such 'Super-E.S.P.' coming to hand, one could perhaps only establish some presumption in favour of survival by the most complex and roundabout means; by amassing, for instance, a very considerable quantity of materials validating the claims of clairvoyants and sensitives to be able to give accurate information about matters which we can verify, and then accepting their further claims to give accurate information about matters which we cannot verify—such as the aspects and occupations of the departed. I do not suppose that this could ever be done; but it has, of course, very often been suggested that the mere establishment that some people do possess powers of 'Super-E.S.P.' would itself strengthen the case for survival by showing the extent to which the activities of the mind can transcend the limitations of the brain. At the moment however we can I think only say that the evidence for 'Super-E.S.P.' is too weak to do the job required of it.

Someone who wants to persuade us to accept the 'Super-E.S.P.' theory has therefore got to find further arguments to

[1] For examples of such cases see the references to 'retrocognitive' cases, *Human Personality* II, p. 262n; and cf. E. Osty, *Supernormal Faculties in Man*, tr. S. de Brath, London, 1923.

win us to his side. The arguments employed for this purpose are, as might be expected, frequently arguments *against* a survivalist point of view rather than arguments *for* the 'Super-E.S.P.' hypothesis. I will briefly mention two.

(1) A very common argument is a neurophysiological one. It has been established that damage to parts of the brain can cause impairments in, or losses of, one's ability to carry out some or all of the kinds of activities especially characteristic of persons. That is to say, the brain damage can bring about not just simple motor paralyses and sensory deficits, but defects in such higher-order skills as thinking, perceiving, imagining, and using and understanding language. From this it is said to follow that being a 'person' (in the sense suggested above) depends upon possessing an intact brain, and that one therefore could not conceivably continue to be a person after one's brain had crumbled into dust.

However, it does not seem to me that the mere fact that damage to the brain can affect or abolish 'person-making' activities can properly be used as an excuse to set aside evidence for survival should we come upon it. The argument is based on far too crude a picture of how a person might be supposed to be related to his brain. It seems to be assumed that either a person must be related to his brain somewhat as a pianist is to a piano (you would expect the pianist to continue playing *intelligently*, even if his piano was damaged); or else there can be no person superadded to the brain; the piano must be a pianola, so to speak. But it is at least not inconceivable that a person could be related to his brain more intimately than a pianist to his piano; more intimately even than, say, a parasite to a host, or an automatic pilot to a plane. Now malfunctioning of a host may cause malfunctioning of a parasite, and vice versa; none the less malfunctioning host and malfunctioning parasite might regain their health if they were separated. Similarly, could a person disengage himself from his damaged brain, he might once more function properly, either with a new brain or else in some other environment altogether.

What most of those who believe that the known effects of brain damage rule out the possibility of survival probably have at the backs of their minds is the notion that the influence which brain injury may have upon an individual's 'person-making' activities shows that those activities are not merely *dependent* upon the intactness of his brain, but can be *fully explained* in terms of, or indeed *are*, the operations of a brain-machine. Now if such activities could indeed be thus explained, the situation would be different. I suspect that the only form of survival theory one could possibly advance under these circumstances would be to the effect that during one's life one somehow builds up an exact and gaseous copy of one's fleshy brain, a sort of ghostly surrogate brain which can in some way survive the destruction of its template, and continue the latter's functions. This would be a rather extreme hypothesis; though some Spiritualists have expressed views which approximate to it. However, it certainly seems to me altogether premature to pass from the fact that brain damage may adversely affect 'person-making' activities to a whole-hog brain-machine theory. I have suggested elsewhere that there are some difficulties of principle in the way of such a theory.[1]

(2) Another set of arguments that has of late years often been levelled against the possibility of survival is one based upon philosophical analyses of such concepts as intelligence, memory, thought, belief, imagination, perception, and so forth. It has been suggested, for instance, that whilst to remember or to perceive may not actually *be* just to behave in certain ways (as primitive behaviourists used to suggest), the concepts of thinking and of perception are so essentially interwoven with behavioural and physical concepts that it does not make sense to talk of someone's perceiving and remembering in a disembodied state. These 'personal' concepts take an essential part of their meaning from the behavioural and hence bodily ones. It may not be inconceivable that something survives the dissolution of the body; but it *is* inconceivable that that something should be a person. A bodiless entity could not properly be said to carry out the sorts of activities which would qualify it for the title of 'person'. It is just a *logical* error to ask, as Myers did:

> What, then, is to be our conception of identity prolonged beyond the tomb? In earth-life the actual body, in itself but a subordinate element in our thought of our friend, did yet by

---

[1] 'Could a Machine Perceive', *Brit. J. Phil. Soc.* 17 (1966), pp. 44-58.

EPILOGUE

its physical continuity override as a symbol of identity all lapses of memory, all changes of the character within. Yet it was memory and character,—the stored impressions upon which he reacted, and his specific mode of reaction,—which made our veritable friend. How much of memory, how much of character, must he preserve for our recognition?[1]

'Memory' and 'character' *could not* survive the dissolution of the body; for the concepts of memory and character are inextricably tied to concepts of bodily behaviour.

It might of course be pointed out in reply to these arguments that most forms of belief in survival have been in some form of *embodied* survival, to which the objections could not be applied. But for the moment I shall only suggest that it might be possible to use some of the findings of psychical research to prevent these arguments from, so to speak, getting off the ground.

Consider this passage, in which P. T. Geach tries to demonstrate that perceptual concepts are necessarily linked with physical ones:

> 'The verb "to see" has its meaning for me because I *do* see—I have that experience!' Nonsense. As well suppose that I can come to know what a minus quantity is by setting out to lose weight. What shows a man to have the concept *seeing* is not merely that he sees, but that he can take an intelligent part in our everyday use of the word 'seeing.' Our concept of sight has its life only in connection with a whole set of other concepts, some of them relating to the physical characteristics of visible objects, others relating to the behaviour of people who see things. (I express exercise of this concept in such utterances as 'I can't see, it's too far off—now it's coming into view!' 'He couldn't see me, he didn't look round,' 'I caught his eye,' etc., etc.) It would be merely silly to be frightened off admitting this by the bogey of behaviourism; you can very well admit it without also thinking that 'seeing' stands for a kind of behaviour.[2]

It seems to me that an examination of a sufficiently large number of cases of so-called 'non-optical' vision—of clairvoyance and travelling clairvoyance, exercised in normal or in trance states, or in dreams—might serve to soften up or even

---

[1] *Human Personality* II, p. 252.
[2] Peter Geach, *Mental Acts*, London, n.d., p. 112.

EPILOGUE

sever the links which the concept of 'seeing' is said to have with behavioural and other physical concepts. It might serve to soften them up in two ways. (i) Examination of a large enough quantity of well-attested cases of clairvoyance might show that even before death one may become aware of distant events and scenes in a way that is certainly difficult not to think of as perceptual, as a kind of seeing, but which seems to bear not the slightest relation to any overt bodily activity or to the laws of optics. We would seem to have here a kind of activity (whether perceptual or not) which one could carry on just as well after one's death as before it, a kind of activity which might hence provide the trans-mortem personal continuity which (according to Geach) the activity of seeing would not provide. (ii) The fact seems to be that both the people who have clairvoyant experiences and those who study such experiences almost automatically extend their concepts of vision and seeing to cover them, and indeed regard them as being a kind of vision or of seeing. Thus, reviewing such cases, Myers says: 'What we are bound to do is to generalise our conception of vision as far as possible,—no longer confining it to the definite phenomenon of retinal or optical vision,—and thus to find out by actual enquiry, what sort of messages are brought to us by each form of vision which this enlarged conception contains.'[1] Now it might be replied that extending the concept of vision in this way is illegitimate. But to say this would be very odd. For who is a philosopher to go on maintaining that the concept of 'seeing' is irrevocably linked to physical concepts in face of the fact that most people's concept of vision is quite obviously not so linked? And if the ordinary concept of vision is not so linked, it at least makes sense to talk of vision continuing after the dissolution of one's body, however hard it is to imagine such a state of affairs.

It seems to me that neither the neurological nor the logical argument against the possibility of personal survival, and hence (indirectly) in favour of a 'Super-E.S.P.' theory, is compelling. It is of course in a sense impossible to *disprove* the 'Super-E.S.P.' hypothesis. If one were to take the occurrence of the phenomena we are discussing as itself proof of 'Super-E.S.P.', one could explain away any evidence whatsoever in favour of

[1] *Human Personality* I, pp. 223-4.

survival; but the logical irrefutability of a theory is, most scientists would say, the reverse of a reason for accepting it. It is rather a reason for questioning the logic of those who propound it.

Not, of course, that one could back the survival hypothesis very strongly. The most that can be said is that if one were absolutely forced to decide (let us say in a bet with some sporting Demiurge) whether certain of the more striking of the Piper or Leonard 'communicators' were in some way manifestations or reflections of surviving deceased persons (that is, of centres of ongoing person-making activities in some sense continuous with centres previously known to us), or whether they were the results of the exercise of 'Super-E.S.P.' by the mediums—combined, of course, with a tendency towards spontaneous mimicry and impersonation—the logical thing to do would be to plump for the deceased persons.

But it is necessary to add a proviso. What Sidgwick and his friends wanted was proof of the sort of survival a man could look forward to, proof which would justify one in holding that the Universe is a friendly place. They found plenty of evidence for the survival of fragmentary and truncated persons; but of evidence for the survival of a fully developed and furthermore *developing* person they found very little. Even the G.P. personality-pattern was not complete—blundering, for example, on elementary philosophical points which the living G.P. would have comprehended readily. And most communicators fall very far short of G.P.'s level. It is of course possible to explain this fact in terms of the difficulties which a deceased person might be supposed to have in manipulating a medium's organism—difficulties, Myers suggested, perhaps similar to those which an incarnate person whose brain has been damaged may have in thinking and communicating. But there is no doubt that a good deal of the evidence can easily be reconciled with the view that not everyone survives, and that most of those who do survive, survive in some diminished manner; part-persons, blown, it may be, around the winds of the world in a state of dim and unimaginable sentience. Not a prospect to make one feel that Providence is benign.

Since it is so very difficult to come to any certain conclusions about the correct interpretation of the evidence for survival, do we have to say that the Sidgwick group totally failed to achieve its long-term aim of putting religious belief upon some kind of rational footing? Or do we at least have to suspend our judgment until firmer evidence (of which there is at present no sign) comes to hand? I think that even though Sidgwick and his friends failed to unearth clear grounds for adopting any positive set of religious beliefs, they did at least do something towards overcoming one obstacle to religious belief of any kind whatsoever, to wit the 'materialist synthesis' which had so much dominated the intellectual scene of the eighteen-seventies. They showed up what Gurney called

> ... the suicidal want of logic of the modern *cock-sure* school of Empiricists; as when an eminent comparative anatomist refuses even to take part in a trial of professed 'thought transference' on the ground that it is an impossible hypothesis, and Materialism thus lays down the law to a Universe which Empiricism humbly interrogates.[1]

Those *esprits forts* who claim that the experiences which are the basis, or rather the driving force, of religious belief—experiences which range, perhaps, from cases of spontaneous telepathy seemingly suggesting that a powerful emotion can transcend material boundaries, through cases of visions, of speaking with tongues, of automatisms of all kinds, of miraculous cures, of the sensible inflowing of Divine Grace, to moments of mystical unity with an unknown power—must each and all be mere delusions, are dogmatising in a hasty and even absurd manner. Some at least of these experiences are not always delusory, and it is far from easy to see how materialism can accommodate them. Religious belief can withstand the attacks of cock-sure materialists because the religious man's opinion that materialism cannot cope with all the data of experience is founded not on wishful thinking but on facts. William James put the point in a striking passage:

> Although ... Science taken in its essence should stand only for a method, and not for any special beliefs, yet, as habitually taken by its votaries, Science has come to be identified with a certain fixed general belief, the belief that the deeper order of Nature is mechanical exclusively, and that non-mechanical

---
[1] *Tertium Quid* I, p. 247.

categories are irrational ways of conceiving and explaining even such a thing as human life. Now this mechanical rationalism, as one may call it, makes, if it becomes one's only way of thinking, a violent breach with the ways of thinking that have, until our own time, played the greatest part in human history. Religious thinking, ethical thinking, poetical thinking, teleological, emotional, sentimental thinking, what one might call the personal view of life to distinguish it from the impersonal and mechanical view, and the romantic view of life to distinguish it from the rationalistic view, have been, and even still are, outside of well-drilled scientific circles, the dominant forms of thought. But for mechanical rationalism, personality is an insubstantial illusion; the chronic belief of mankind, that events may happen for the sake of their personal significance, is an abomination; and the notions of our grandfathers about oracles and omens, divinations and apparitions, miraculous changes of heart and wonders worked by inspired persons, answers to prayers and providential leadings, are a fabric absolutely baseless, a mass of sheer *un*truth. Now, of course, we must all admit that the excesses to which the romantic and personal view of Nature may lead, if wholly unchecked by impersonal rationalism, are direful. Central African Mumbo-Jumboism is one of unchecked romanticism's fruits. One ought accordingly to sympathize with that abhorrence of romanticism as a sufficient world-theory; one ought to understand that lively intolerance of the least grain of romanticism in the views of life of other people, which are such characteristic marks of those who follow the scientific professions to-day. Our debt to Science is literally boundless, and our gratitude for what is positive in her teachings must be correspondingly immense. But our own *Proceedings* and *Journals* have, it seems to me, conclusively proved one thing to the candid reader, and that is that the verdict of pure insanity, of gratuitous preference for error, of superstition without an excuse, which the scientists of our day are led by their intellectual training to pronounce upon the entire thought of the past, is a most shallow verdict. The personal and romantic view of life has other roots besides wanton exuberance of imagination and perversity of heart. It is perennially fed by *facts of experience*, whatever the ulterior interpretation of those facts may prove to be . . . These experiences have three characters in common: they are capricious, discontinuous, and not easily controlled; they require peculiar persons for their production; their significance seems to be wholly for personal life. Those who preferentially attend to them, and still more those who are individually subject to them, not only easily *may* find but are logically bound to find in them valid arguments for their romantic and personal conception of the world's course.[1]

The results which the Sidgwick group obtained in its twenty years of earnest labours may at any rate be used to hammer that over-zealous brand of 'mechanical rationalism' which hopes by exhibiting 'personality' as the blind output of physical forces to leave in an ordered Universe not one single Gothic protuberance on which religion can scrape a toe-hold. Against this obsessive tidy-mindedness it is possible to launch a modest arsenal of spiky facts; facts which strongly suggest that not all manifestations of personality can be understood within the accepted framework of biological science. Any rationalist who studies and thinks about these facts, dispassionately and in detail will, I should guess, find himself in deep and unsuspected waters from which no shore is clearly visible, and least of all to him.

[1] *P.S.P.R.* XII (1896), pp. 8-9.

APPENDIX A: EARLY EXPERIMENTS ON THOUGHT-TRANSFERENCE PUBLISHED BY THE S.P.R.

More extended résumés of the early experiments on thought-transference than that given below will be found in *Phantasms* I, pp. 10–85, *Human Personality* I, pp. 524–43, 598–635, and in F. Podmore's *Apparitions and Thought-transference*, London, 1894, pp. 1–142.

1. *Experiments with the Creery Family* (*P.S.P.R.* I (1882), pp. 19–30, 71–8). The first subjects with whom members of the S.P.R. conducted extended and seemingly successful experiments on thought-transference were the family of the Rev. A. M. Creery, of Buxton. The percipients were various of Mr. Creery's five daughters, acting singly. The agents generally acted in a group, and at various times included Mr. Creery himself, members of his family, Barrett, Professor Balfour Stewart (the S.P.R.'s second President), Professor Alfred Hopkinson, Gurney, Myers, and other members of the thought-transference committee. The usual procedure was as follows. The daughter who was to act as percipient would leave the room, whilst the group of agents selected a target. This would be written down rather than spoken. The girl would be called in, and the company would concentrate on the target. Targets might be a name chosen at random, an object from the house, a two-figure number, or a playing card out of a full pack.

The girls achieved some startling successes, even when members of their family were not among the agents. They succeeded not merely in their father's home (where the first experiments were carried out in 1881–2), but at Cambridge (July to August 1882) and Dublin (November 1882). For instance at Cambridge they between them guessed correctly 17 out of 216 playing cards; and at Dublin 32 out of 108.

Their ability began to wane in 1882; and in some further experiments (see *P.S.P.R.* V (1888), pp. 269–70) two of them were detected in the use of a rather weak code. Though of course it could

APPENDIX A: EARLY EXPERIMENTS

have been effective only when one of the sisters was amongst the agents.

2. *Experiments in the Transference of Pictures and Diagrams.*

(*a*) *The Smith–Blackburn Experiments (P.S.P.R.* I (1882–3), pp. 78–97, 161–7, 181–216). Three series of experiments (December 1882, January 1883, April 1883) for which Douglas Blackburn acted as agent and G. A. Smith as percipient (on Smith and Blackburn, see pp. 179–81 above). The experimenters were Myers, Gurney, and other members of the thought-transference committee. In the early experiments agent and percipient were allowed to touch each other, and in the later series they were in the same room at the time of 'transmission'. Target items included colours, names and numbers; but the successes in the reproduction of target drawings and diagrams were particularly striking.

These experiments were heavily criticised (*Proceedings* of the American S.P.R. I, p. 315) on the grounds that the results could have been obtained by the use of a code. Many years later, in 1908 and 1911, Blackburn confessed that the results *had* been obtained by a code; but Smith vigorously denied it. See T. H. Hall, *The Strange Case of Edmund Gurney*, pp. 137–49. However, neither Blackburn's confessions nor the experiments in which he participated can be readily accepted; cf. p. 180n above.

(*b*) *The Guthrie Experiments (P.S.P.R.* II (1883), pp. 24–42). The percipients were two employees of Mr. Guthrie's, Miss Relph and Miss Edwards. The agents included Mr. Guthrie and various other persons of repute from the Liverpool district; also Gurney. A drawing would be prepared in a room apart, and then brought into the room where the blindfolded percipient sat. It would then be placed on a wooden stand where the percipient could not have seen it even had she not been blindfolded. The agent, or agents, would then look at it until the percipient indicated that she was ready to try to reproduce it. A number of very striking successes were obtained. The percipients' abilities later began to wane.

(*c*) *The Lodge Experiments (P.S.P.R.* II (1884), pp. 189–200). A continuation, with positive results, of the preceding experiments. Lodge, then professor of physics at Liverpool University, simply assumed charge of the experiments for a while. He noted that very often the idea of the object depicted in the target drawing was conveyed, rather than its geometrical outline.

APPENDIX A

(*d*) *Further Experiments in the Reproduction of Drawings by Various Other Experimenters* are summarised in *Human Personality* I, pp. 614–636. See also the references p. 601n, and Podmore, *op. cit.*, pp. 38–57. I do not think that any of them could be said to be *better* than the Guthrie experiments, and there does not seem to be any point in giving details of them here.

3. *Experiments in the Telepathic Production of 'Automatic' Movements.*

(*a*) *Experiments of the Rev. P. H. Newnham* (*P.S.P.R.* III (1885), pp. 7–25). These experiments were carried out in 1871. Mr. Newnham's wife had developed the faculty of writing automatically with a 'planchette' board. Mr. Newnham would sit in the room with his wife, but in a position where she could not observe his face or notebook. He would then write down a question to be answered by the planchette board without however speaking the question aloud, or otherwise acquainting his wife with its nature. A series of 309 questions and answers (on very diverse subjects) was thus obtained. The answers were in almost all cases unmistakably appropriate to the questions. The intelligence operating the board did not claim to be separate from Mrs. Newnham; none the less answers totally unexpected by both her and her husband were on a number of occasions given; and sometimes knowledge seemingly in excess of hers was displayed.

(*b*) *Experiments of Professor Charles Richet* (*P.S.P.R.* III (1885), pp. 7–25; VIII (1892), pp. 138–48). These seem to me to be in some ways the most interesting of the early experiments. The set-up was complex. At a small table sat two persons, A and B, with the alphabet laid out in front of them. A passed a pointer continually over the alphabet. B noted down the letter over which the pointer was each time he heard a bell ring. The bell was rung automatically whenever another table in the room, at which sat three other persons, C, D and E, was tilted. C, D and E had their hands on the table in the ordinary 'table-tilting' fashion; they were so seated that they could not see the activities of A and B. A sixth person, F (usually Richet), sat apart from both groups, concentrating on a name (obtained randomly from a reference book). The letters spelled out in many cases closely followed the letters of the name on which F was concentrating. It was easy to show that the coincidences between the letters spelled out and the letters of the name greatly exceeded chance. Yet C, D and E did not know what they were spelling out, and A and B, who knew what C, D and E were spelling out, did not know the target.

APPENDIX A: EARLY EXPERIMENTS

4. *Experiments in Thought-transference under Hypnosis.*

(*a*) *Experiments in the Telepathic Anaesthetisation of a selected Finger of a Hypnotised Subject* (*P.S.P.R.* I (1883), pp. 257–60; II (1884), pp. 201–5; III (1885), pp. 457–9; V (1889), pp. 14–17; VIII (1892), pp. 577–93). The hypnotist in all these experiments was G. A. Smith. The experimenter in all except the last (conducted by Mrs. Sidgwick) was Gurney. The subject thrust his hands through a screen, and spread the fingers wide. The experimenter selected a finger, and Smith would point (or in later experiments merely look) at it. The finger would (in accordance with instructions previously given to the subject) become rigid and anaesthetic. There is at least no doubt that the anaesthesia was genuine—the fingers were subjected to severe electric shocks and to stabs.

(*b*) *Experiments in the Transference of Two-figure Numbers under Hypnosis* (*P.S.P.R.* VI (1889), pp. 128–70; VIII (1892), pp. 536–596). The principal experimenter in both these series of experiments (1889, and 1890–1) was Mrs. Sidgwick; she was assisted at various times by Miss Alice Johnson, Professor Sidgwick and Dr. A. T. Myers. The hypnotist was almost always G. A. Smith; and he also provided the subjects. Numbers were not the only targets used, but the results obtained with them were the most striking. The most successful subject was a Miss B.

In the first series of experiments 131 numbers (the numbers were drawn out of a bag) out of 664 were correctly guessed when the agent (Smith) and the percipient were in the same room. When they were in separate rooms, the number of successes dropped to 9 out of 228. In the second series striking successes were obtained when agent and percipient were not in the same room. Some of the successful trials were held at Smith's rooms; but some also in Mrs. Sidgwick's lodgings.

(*c*) *Experiments in the Telepathic Induction of Hypnosis at a Distance* (*Sommeil à Distance*). A number of experimenters reported that they had been able to induce a hypnotic trance in good hypnotic subjects known to them when the subjects concerned were in another room, or even a considerable distance away. Sometimes they had been able to influence the subject's behaviour in addition to inducing the trance. Cf. Janet's Experiments, *P.S.P.R.* IV (1886), pp. 131–7; the cases given by Gurney, *P.S.P.R.* V (1888), pp. 221–3; and the experiments of Richet, *P.S.P.R.* V (1888), pp. 32–52.

5. *Assorted Experiments on the 'Guessing' of the Suits of Playing Cards, of Two-figure Numbers, etc.* A number of persons sent in the results of

APPENDIX A

experiments of these kinds which they had carried out in response to an appeal by Gurney. Some of the results were highly significant. Cf. *Phantasms* I, pp. 33–4, and II, pp. 653–4 (where the very striking results obtained by the Misses Wingfield are recorded). In most of these cases, however, the experimenters themselves seem to have been both agents and percipients, and were no doubt in the same room during the experiments.

APPENDIX B: CRITICS OF MRS. PIPER

Writers who confine their attention to accounts of Mrs. Piper's off-days can make a black case against her. See e.g. Tuckett, *op. cit.*, pp. 321-95, and E. Clodd, *The Question: if a Man Die Shall he Live again?* London, 1917, pp. 190-214. Mrs. Piper's 'confession' has also proved popular with keen disbelievers; 'confession' was simply the heading given by a newspaper to an account of an interview with her in which she said that she herself was uncertain as to the nature of her 'controls' (see *J.S.P.R.* X (1901), pp. 192-3, 150-2). A good many of the fallacious stories about Mrs. Piper put forward by rationalist critics are strung conveniently together in C. E. M. Hansel's *E.S.P.: A Scientific Evaluation*, New York, 1966, pp. 224-7. I will quote some passages, inserting my own comments in square brackets. It is only fair to Professor Hansel to add that he has been misled by one wholly unreliable source (E. Clodd, *Rationalist P.A. Annual*, London, 1921, pp. 40-2) filtered through another wholly unreliable source (J. F. Rinn, *Searchlight on Psychical Research*, London, 1954, pp. 122-31).

After some remarks (p. 223) on 'the standard procedures of fake mediums' (all of which are inapplicable to Mrs. Piper), Professor Hansel goes on (p. 225):

'She was also able to describe the location of a tin box containing some of Pellew's private papers, which had been missing since his death. Eventually Hodgson, who up to then had been sceptical about the whole affair, was so impressed by this accumulation of evidence that he announced his conversion to spiritualism. [It was certainly not the tin box case—for which see *P.S.P.R.* XIII (1898), pp. 202-3—which particularly impressed Hodgson. His conversion to belief in paranormality of the phenomena was slow, and preceded by several years his conversion, likewise slow, to belief in the agency of departed persons.] Then, after his death in 1906 [1905], he became Mrs. Piper's control [one of them], only to be eventually ousted by the spirits of such celebrities as George Eliot and Julius Caesar [they in fact appeared almost ten years *before* Hodgson's death].

APPENDIX B

'Despite the voluminous reports and the eminence of the investigators, it is clear that the case for Mrs. Piper's extrasensory powers rests mainly on the G.P. Series.' [This, I hope, is disproved even by the tiny portions of the evidence which I have been able to quote or refer to.]

After some remarks about Phinuit's deficiencies, Hansel goes on (p. 226):

'The validity of this investigation is weakened by two points that are overlooked by writers sympathetic to the demonstration of psychic phenomena. First, it was never thought necessary to check G.P.'s statements about his earthly life. [This is nonsense. See *P.S.P.R.* XIII, pp. 295-335; it might also be pointed out that what was so convincing to many sitters was that 'G.P.' exhibited detailed knowledge of the concerns of Pellew's *friends*.] This was largely due to the tone of the reports submitted by Hodgson to the Society for Psychical Research. In them it was repeatedly implied that Pellew's parents supported the statements made by G.P. and that they were occasionally present in person at the séances. [Records of the seances which they attended are still in existence. Mrs. Pellew's answers to questions are frequently given *P.S.P.R.* XIII, pp. 295-335; but so far as I know the only expressions of opinion concerning the G.P. communicator attributed to her or her husband are those quoted from their own letters on p. 304. They are favourable.] Later, the Pellew family, which had pointedly remained aloof from the excitement and publicity about G.P., flatly denied that any material reported from Mrs. Piper's séances had any connection with George Pellew. [See the preceding comment, and also the comment on C. E. Pellew's statement below.] His mother, when refusing an invitation from Hodgson to join the American Society for Psychical Research, referred to G.P.'s communications as 'utter drivel and inanity.' [But Mrs. Pellew *did* join the S.P.R., as can be seen from its published membership lists; and she remained a member for at least ten years.]

'George's brother, C. E. Pellew, Professor of Literature [Chemistry] at Columbia ... stated that the famous tin box was in fact empty [Hodgson also states this quite clearly *P.S.P.R.* XIII, p. 303] and that the papers referred to by G.P. had been in the possession of a friend for many years. He referred scornfully to the "absolute unreliability of the believers in the Mrs. Piper cult." He wrote in a letter to a friend (Edward Clodd), "I was finally persuaded to see Mrs. Piper, and found her a bright, shrewd, ill-educated, commonplace woman who answered glibly enough questions where guessing

APPENDIX B: CRITICS OF MRS. PIPER

was easy, or where she might have obtained previous information. But whenever I asked anything that would be known only to George himself, she was either silent or entirely wrong." [This is *not* Professor Pellew's opinion of Mrs. Piper, but that of John Fiske, a noted philosopher and historian, who had had some sittings with her. Fiske is referred to in the papers on Mrs. Piper under the pseudonym of 'Marte', and his unsuccessful sittings are quoted at length in various places. I gave an excerpt from one of them above, pp. 259–60. Clodd alleges (Rinn, p. 127) that Hodgson claimed that Fiske had been completely convinced by G.P.'s answering some questions concerning his (G.P.'s) ancestors, who had been prominent in the Revolutionary wars. However, Hodgson quotes the sitting concerned in full (*P.S.P.R.* XIII, pp. 419–21); he makes Fiske's negative attitude quite plain and explicitly states (p. 422) that he does not himself regard the communications as having evidential value.]

APPENDIX C: CORRESPONDENCE BETWEEN MYERS AND LORD ACTON ON THE CANONS OF EVIDENCE TO BE APPLIED TO REPORTS OF 'MIRACULOUS' OCCURRENCES

Letter from Lord Acton to Myers, no place, no date

I have to think about certain historians and their methods; and the question arises: how do they deal with miracles when they meet them? I am thinking of Catholic writers who have no a priori difficulty about them; but who cannot help noticing that the evidence is very apt to crumble away, that the marvels increase by distance, and that Asiatic history offers some perplexing analogy.

Now the closest analogy is supplied by your system of enquiries, and I wonder whether you would tell me what light your experience tends to throw on mine. For if your scientific conclusion is that though the world is full of supernatural stories, when you examine all those of which the evidence can be really tested, so and so many break down, and a very small percentage survives, then the value of human testimony in such matters is very much impaired, and a variety of consequences ensue for the historian—the Roman Catholic historian and hagiologist—which are very obvious to anyone who has been busied in your way, and if not, not. Especially if you find that nearly all break down, and if not all, yet so many that an overwhelming presumption arises against the insoluble remainder. No-one who has not spent his life among our books has any idea of the extent to which visions, dreams, prophecies and the like, interpose in causation. And without wishing for a theory or a dogma, I want a rule for historians, who are quite ready, so far as theory goes, to accept or to reject.

From which also divers conclusions would arise touching the credibility of authorities.

Manuscript headed 'For Lord Acton: Apr 28/92', seemingly a draft of Myers' reply to the above letter[1]

The question proposed to me is virtually as follows:

[1] In the Archives of the S.P.R.

APPENDIX C: CORRESPONDENCE—MYERS AND LORD ACTON

In what way does your practical experience in sifting modern records of supernormal occurrences (let us use this *neutral* word, rather than *supernatural*,) affect your estimate of the records of similar phenomena in the Acta Sanctorum & elsewhere?

My answer sounds so like a paradox that it will need justification. It is that incidents resembling some of those in the lives of the Saints do in fact occur, but that I hold that nearly all existing accounts of such incidents are probably untrustworthy.

I. To explain this I must in the first place point out that each class of alleged supernormal phenomena must be carefully isolated, & considered on its own merits. The fact that many disparate phenomena have all been equally regarded at some time or another as supernatural, constitutes no bond between those phenomena. Their real affinities must be determined by our analysis, not by unanalytical tradition.

Alleged supernormal phenomena may be divided into four classes:—Whose respective *boundaries*, of course, will be a matter of controversy.

A. Phenomena once regarded as supernatural, or supernaturally significant, wh. cannot be proved ever to have occurred, or to have shown that significance, under proper observation.

Most of the alleged phenomena of *Magic & Witchcraft*, will come under this head. Here too we must place *augury*, & *divinatory interpretations* of common events;—et volucrum linguas, et praepetis omina pinnae.

B. Phenomena once regarded as supernatural, but now seen to fall within the operation of known physical laws, or at least to be capable of empirical reproduction.

Thus an *eclipse* falls under known laws; *stigmatization* can be empirically reproduced by hypnotic suggestion.

C. Supernormal phenomena for which there is some careful modern evidence; such as, without compelling the conviction of the world of Science, may justify the historian in refusing to reject a narrative wh. he has other grounds for believing simply because such phenomena are there alleged to have occurred. This class in my view—but many of my colleagues would shorten the list—would include many, tho' not all, forms of ecclesiastical 'miracles'. Here I should place in ascending order of evidence

1. Premonition—call it precognition & retrocognition.
2. Physical phenomena—sometimes called 'telekinetic';—as

movements of objects without contact, levitation, & *material* bilocation or unexplained transport.

3. Communications from departed souls or other unembodied intelligences.

4. Communication of a supersensory type with some unknown *region of intelligence* or World Soul—better demonstrated (as some of our group think) than communication with individual disembodied intelligences. (For this distinction see Oliver Lodge on Mrs. Piper's trances, etc., Proc. Vol VI).

5. Clairvoyance or supersensory perception of terrene scenes or objects.

D. Supernormal phenomena wh. we regard as *proved* to the candid student.

1. *Telepathy*,—or the communication of one mind with another independently of the recognized organs of sense is the main phenomenon wh. all our group wd. place in this class.

2. *Automatism*, or the action of subconscious strata of the mind may be placed here or in class B, according as it is or is not still regarded as 'supernormal. It is proved, & it is new in its present form, but it is not plainly incompatible with the materialistic hypothesis.

II. In the second place we have to consider what kind of evidence seems valid for classes C & D,—as A & B, for different reasons, may now be left out of account. Here we have simply to set forth the rules, wh. actual experience has suggested to us. On the whole, tho' with certain exceptions, we tend to reject as untrustworthy:

α. All evidence other than first-hand.

β. All evidence depending wholly on the testimony of (1) uneducated persons, (2) persons with a strong bias in favour of the supernatural, (3) Asiatics, (4) the lower races, (5) children.

γ. All evidence depending on the veracity of persons apparently hoping to receive therefrom money, fame, or reverence.

δ. All evidence not recorded on paper until ten years after the event. On this point I am myself inclined to be lenient, in dealing with good witnesses; but I think that we shall gradually draw the limit of oral tradition at 10 years, or perhaps even less. It was at first impossible to be rigid on this point.

ε. Uncorroborated evidence from informants of whom we personally know nothing. Here again the limit is hard to fix. But I calculated in 1892 that Prof. and Mrs. Sidgwick, the late Edmund Gurney, Messrs. Hodgson & Podmore & myself, had

APPENDIX C: CORRESPONDENCE—MYERS AND LORD ACTON

travelled some 20,000 miles for the sake of interviewing witnesses in India, U.S.A., Sweden, Germany, France, the United Kingdom.

The exclusion of *Asiatics*, & the addition of the expectation of *reverence* to the causes of suspicion, were forced upon us by Mr. Hodgson's exposure of Mme. Blavatsky's frauds, & of the gross credulity of some even able & educated Hindoos. Mme. Blavatsky (one may say) was within an ace of founding a world-religion, merely to amuse herself & to be admired.

We have not always been as strict as these rules imply; nor do I think that our occasional laxity has led us into serious error. But where we have admitted second hand evidence, etc., it has generally been in favour of some witness personally known to us as careful, & for some phenomenon well [illegible] in other cases [?]. We have been scrupulous about pointing out the *defects* of any evidence thus admitted. After all, we only *present* evidence to our readers; we do not claim that our judgment on it is a final one.

Broadly speaking, then, we find that,—while whole classes of phenomena are purely fictitious, & whole categories of evidence are untrustworthy,—there are left certain residual phenomena of absolutely first-rate significance. I hold that these phenomena at least break down the current materialistic synthesis—I personally believe them to indicate that each of us is a soul in a world of souls, with whom he communicates spiritually during his terrene life; & amid whom he continues to live & love after bodily death, and, I trust for ever.

F W H M

INDEX

'A.', Miss, see Wingfield, Kate
Abbott, D. P., 209n
Adams, J. Couch, 140
Adare, Viscount, 69n
Adshead, W. P., 82n, 128n
Aksakov, A., 113, 130n, 225
Albert, Prince, 67
Alexander, P. P., 69n
American Society for Psychical Research, 146, 147–8, 253, 258
Proceedings of, 173, 357
Annan, N. L., 38n
'Apostles', the, 48, 92, 317
Apparitions, F. W. H. Myers on, 288–91
    Arrival, 163, 289
    Collectively perceived, 168–71
    Crisis, 160–74; as telepathically induced hallucinations, 162–3, 289; chance coincidence explanation of, 167–9, 182–5; sources of error in testimony concerning, 164–6, 171–4; other criticisms of evidence for, 184–5
    Haunting, 170, 187–93, 196–9
    of the Dead, 186–99, 277
Armstrong, Mr., 107, 113, 127
'Arrival' cases, see Apparitions, Arrival
Ashburner, Dr. J., 70
Association of Progressive Spiritualists of Great Britain, 76
Athenaeum, The, 68
Automatic Speaking, see Mediumship, Alleged Phenomena of
Automatic Writing, see Mediumship, Alleged Phenomena of
Automatism, Motor, 288–9, 291–2; see also Mediumship, Alleged Phenomena of
Automatism, Sensory, 288–91; see also Mediumship, Alleged Phenomena of

Bagehot, W., 60n, 63, 157n, 320
Baggally, W. W., 242n, 243, 245n
Bain, A., 63
Baird, A., 202n, 253n
Baldwin, Dr., 333–4, 334n
Balfour, Alice, 315
Balfour, A. J., 64, 87, 104, 105, 110, 115, 116, 140, 141, 159, 305, 306n, 315
Balfour, Eleanor Mildred, see Sidgwick, Eleanor Mildred
Balfour, Evelyn, see Rayleigh, Lady
Balfour, Frances, 331
Balfour, Francis, 115
Balfour, G. W., 64, 115, 141, 338
Ballou, A., 15n, 20n
Ballou, R. O., 30n, 331n
Bancroft, G., 12
Banks, Mr., 129–30
Bantock, G. H., 331n
Baring, Sir T., 35
Barkas, T. P., 108, 109
    Outlines of Ten Years' Investigations into Modern Spiritualism, 107
Barnum, P. T., 11–12

INDEX

Barrett, Prof. W. F., 87, 137, 147n, 209, 211, 356
Barron, H. D., 9n
Bastian, H., 81
Bastian, H. C., 63
Bateson, W., 140
Battersea, Lady, 176, 176n, 182
Baur, F. C., 49n
Bell, C., 224n
Bell, E. M., 95n
Bell, G., 224n
Bell, J. C., 5–7
Bell, Mrs J. C., 5–6
Bell, Robert, 71
Bellier, M., 226
Benn, A. W., 62, 62n
Bennett, Sir E., 197n
Bennett, E. T., 138
Benson, A. C., 145, 145n, 317, 318n, 328, 328n
Benson, E. W., 47, 64, 116, 318
Benson, Mary (Mrs. E. W. Benson), 116, 315–16
Bernheim, H., 338
Besterman, T., 313n
Biblical Criticism, 48–53, 74
Bickersteth, E. H., 64
Bigelow, Mr., 12
Binet, A., 338
Birt, W. R., 68n
Blackburn, D., 179, 180n, 357
Blake, Mr., 113, 127
Blavatsky, Mme H. P., 203, 367
Bobbitt, M. R., 111n, 134n
Bodleian Library, 230n, 316n
Boirac, E., 241, 241n
Boldero, General, 211–13
Bourne, Canon, 290
Bradbrook, W. R., 30n
Bradley, F. H., 62
Brain, discoveries in physiology of, 58–60; effect of damage to on personality, 348–9; see also Cerebral hemispheres
'Brain-wave' explanation of telepathy, 281, 298
Breuer, J., 276
Bristol University Library, 322n

British National Association of Spiritualists, 73
British Spiritual Telegraph, 69
Brittan, S. B., 27n
Britten, E., see Hardinge-Britten, E.
Broad, Prof. C. D., 52n, 154n, 177n
Brookes-Smith, C., 106n
Brown, F. K., 35n
Brown, Robert, 221n
Browning, O., 175n
Browning, R., 71n
Bryant, W. C., 12
Bryce, J., 96, 230
Burns, J., 76
Burton, Jean, 69n, 71
Butcher, H., 64
Butler, G., 95
Butler, Josephine (Mrs. G. Butler), 95–6, 100, 106
Butler, Samuel, 36

'Cabinet', in sittings for 'materialisation', 80
Cahagnet, A., *Arcanes de la Vie Future Devoilés* (*The Celestial Telegraph*), 66
Capron, E. W., 7–10, 13
  Modern Spiritualism, 7n, 9n, 11n, 12n, 13n, 14n, 19n, 25n, 28n
Carpenter, W. B., 58n, 58–9, 87, 342, 342n
  Principles of Human Physiology, 58
  Principles of Mental Physiology, 58
Carrington, H., 71n, 209n, 223n, 238n, 242n, 243, 337n
'Carroll, Lewis', see Dodgson, C. L.
Cecil, Lady Blanche, 115
Census of Hallucinations, 174, 182–185, 196, 198
Census of Religion, 32–3
Cerebral Hemispheres, surgical separation of, 299n
Chadwick, O., 37n
Chambers, R., 45n, 68, 70
  Vestiges of Creation, 45n, 68
Chapman, J., 49, 49n
Charteris, E., 96n

Cheney, S. F., 16n
Cheney, Mrs. S. F., 16
Childs, E., 73
Cholmondeley-Pennell, H., 201n
Church Missionary Society, 35
Clairvoyance, 18, 66, 69, 70, 74, 288; see also Crystal-gazing, Retrocognition
'Travelling', 169–70, 289–90, 303
Clark, G. Kitson, 32n, 33n
Clayer, Mrs., 86
Clifford, W. K., 63, 64
Clodd, E., 361, 363
The Question: if a Man Die, Shall he Live again?, 361
Clough, A. H., 44, 320
Cobbe, Frances Power, 61–2, 64n
Cocke, J. R., 252
Coleman, B., 70, 72n
Collective Hallucinations, see Apparitions, Collectively perceived
Colley, Rev. T., 82n
Collins, B. Abdy, 197n
Colville, W. J., 75
Compton, Lord A., 64
Contemporary Review, The, 147n, 202, 202n
'Control', Spirit, see Mediumship, Alleged Phenomena of
Conway, 181
Cook, Florence, 81, 81n, 130, 224
Cook, Kate, 130
Cooper, J. Fenimore, 12
Corinthian Hall Committees, investigation of Fox sisters by, 9–10
Corner, Mrs. E. E., see Cook, Florence
Cornhill Magazine, The, 71, 157n
Coulton, G. C., 93n
Cowell, J. J., 53, 88
Cox, Serjeant E. W., 219
Creery, Rev. A. M., and family, 148 356
'Crisis' Apparitions, see Apparitions, Crisis
Crookes, W., experiments with F. Cook, 81, 81n; with D. D. Home and Mrs. Clayer, 86, 88, 89; with D. D. Home and Kate Fox, 87; and Mrs. Fay, 105, 106n; member of S.P.R. physical phenomena committee, 209; sittings with D. D. Home 213–215
Researches in the Phenomena of Spiritualism, 26n, 81n, 87, 213
Crosland, Newton, 70
Crosland, Mrs. Newton, 70
Light in the Valley, 70
Cross, J. W., 133n
'Cross-Correspondences', 274
Crowe, Mrs. C., *The Night-side of Nature*, 66
Crystal-gazing, 247–8, 269, 289
Culver, Mrs. Norman, 25

'D.', Mr., 221–2
Dakyns, H. G., 54, 88, 90n, 97n, 112
Damiani, G., 223n, 224
Darwin, C., 60–2, 108n
The Origin of Species, 50
The Descent of Man, 60–1, 61n
Darwin, F., 99n, 235
Davenport, R. B., 25n
Davey, S. J., 204–7
Davies, J. Ll., 64
Davis, A. J., 21, 24, 66
The Principles of Nature, 21, 24, 49n
The Great Harmonia, 24
De Morgan, A., 68, 74
De Morgan, Mrs. A., 70, 74
From Matter to Spirit, 70
De Musset, A., 288
De Rochas, A., 238n
Despard, Captain, 198
Despard, Rose, 197–9
Dewey, D. M., 9n, 10n, 11n
Dexter, Dr. G. T., see Edmonds, J. W.
Dialectical Society, The London, 83, 84–6
Report on Spiritualism of, 72n, 74n, 84n

INDEX

Dingwall, Dr. E. J., 69n, 79n, 81n, 104n, 209n, 223n, 224n, 238n
'Direct Voice', the, see Mediumship, Alleged Phenomena of
'Disinterested Deception', cases of, 221–2
Dodgson, C. L., 140
Doherty, Dr., 70
Donkin, Dr. C., 126
Doyle, Sir A. C., 4n, 7n, 30n
Dreams, 286–7
Duesler, W., 5
Duff, M. Grant, 197n
Dugdale, Mrs., 196n

Ecstasy, 303–4
Edmonds, Judge, J. W., 18, 29
  Spiritualism, (with Dr. G. T. Dexter), 18
Edmunds, Miss L., 258
Edwards, Miss, 357
Eglinton, W., 81, 82, 82n, 83, 200–5, 221
Eliot, George, 49, 49n, 102, 116, 175, 175n–176n, 268, 331
Elliott, C. W., 11n, 24n
Elliott-Binns, L. E., 44n, 45n
Encyclopedia Britannica, 62, 175n, 339
Essays and Reviews, 49–51
Ether, 21; see also Metetherial
Evangelicalism, characteristics of, 33–4; growth and influence of, 35; decline of, 36; influence on family life, 36–8; and early leaders of S.P.R., 115, 144–5, 338
Evans, C., 64
Evans, H. R., 209n
Evans, Marian, see Eliot, George
Everett, Mrs. Henrietta Dorothy, 250, 250n
Everitt, Mrs. Thomas, 73, 74, 200
Evidence for paranormal phenomena, sceptical arguments concerning, 341–4; quality of collected by Sidgwick group, 341; canons of, correspondence between F. W. H. Myers and Lord Acton on, 341n, 364–7; see also testimony
Ewald, H. G. A., 62

Fairlamb, Miss A., 81, 107, 108–11, 112–14, 127–8, 128n, 129
Falkner, Miss K., 194
Faraday, M.,
Farmer, J., 154
Farmer, J. S., 201n
Fay, Annie Eva, 104n, 104–6
Feilding, Hon, E., 242n, 243, 244
Ferrier, D., 59
Fish, Leah, see Fox, Leah
Fisher, H. A. L., 155n
Fisher, W., 10
Fiske, J., 363
Florentine, Abraham, case of, 79
Flournoy, Th., 241, 241n, 293, 293n, 338–9
Fodor, N., 86n, 127n
Fornell, E. W., 22n, 26n, 30n
Fortnightly Review, 59, 60n, 63, 157n, 294n
Fox, Catherine (Kate), later Mrs. H. D. Jencken, at Hydesville, N.Y., 3, 4, 5, 7; moves to Rochester, N.Y., 8; visits E. W. Capron at Auburn, N.Y., 9; influence there, 13; alcoholism of, 25; quarrels with her sister Leah, 25; present at confession of Margaretta Fox, 25; denies subscribing thereto, 26; rappings of, 26n, 72; comes to England, 72; marries H. D. Jencken, 72; object movements in presence of, 9, 72; materialisations in presence of, 9, 80; W. Crookes' sittings with, 87; investigated by S.P.R., 200n
Fox, David S., 7, 8
Fox, J. D., 3, 4, 5
Fox, Leah, later Fish, later Underhill, in Rochester, N.Y., 8; investigated by Corinthian Hall Committees, 10; at loggerheads

372

INDEX

Fox, Leah,—*continued*
with her sisters, 25; cited 4n, 11n, 13n
Fox, Margaret (Mrs. J. D. Fox), 3–5, 8
Fox, Margaretta, at Hydesville, N.Y., 3, 4, 5, 7; investigated by Corinthian Hall Committees, 10; confesses to fraud, 25; alcoholism, 25; quarrels with her sister Leah, 25; retracts confession, 26
Fox Sisters, Kate, Leah and Margaretta, W. H. Macdonald's experiences with, 10–11; visit New York under auspices of P. T. Barnum, 11–12; Mr. Ripley's account of sitting with, 12; Horace Greeley on, 13; take payment for sittings, 13; accused of fraud, 25–6; quarrels amongst, 25; rappings of, 26
Francis, Dr. J. W., 12
Free Love, supposed practice of by early American Spiritualists, 22, 22n
Freud, S., 276, 278, 278n, 295, 338
Frost, Judge, 252
Froude, Miss E. M., 121
Froude, Hurrell, 35
Furness, H. H., 208

Galton, F., 63, 339
Inquiries into Human Faculty, 339
Natural Inheritance, 339
Garrat, H. A., 128n
Garrett, Julia E., 208n, 209n
Gazzaniga, M. S., 299n
Geach, P. T., 350, 350n, 351
Genius, 288
Ghost Club, Cambridge, 67, 88
Gibbens, Mrs., 252
Gilbert, M., 81n
Gillson, Rev. E., 68, 68n
Gladstone, W. E., 140, 201
'Glove' anaesthesia, 284
God, Spirit teachings concerning, 22–3

Godfrey, N. S., 68n
Goldney, K. M., 81n, 106n
Gosse, P., 96n
'G.P.', see Pellew, George
Graham, Mr., 196
Graham, H. D. Gore, 209–10
Granville-Barker, H., 56n
Greany, Ellen M., 163–4
Greeley, Horace, 13
Green, T. H., 62, 202, 314, 320
Green, V. H. H., 35n
Gregory, W., 66
Letters on Animal Magnetism, 66
Gridley, J. A., 21, 21n, 22n
Grimbold, Alice, 251
Griswold, Dr., 12
Grosskurth, Phyllis, 90n, 95n, 102n
Grote, G., 116
Grote, Mrs. G., 116
Guidance, Spirit, 22, 310
Gull, Sir William, 121
Guppy, Mrs. Samuel, 73, 74, 80
Gurney, Rev. A., 177, 177n
Gurney, Edmund, 188, 313, 314, 356, 360, 366; as undergraduate at Trinity College, Cambridge, 64; meets W. S. Moses, 79, 104; joins F. W. H. Myers and H. Sidgwick in investigation of Spiritualism, 104; sits with Mrs. Fay, 105; sits with the Misses Wood and Fairlamb, 108–10; experiments in telepathy with W. F. Barrett and Myers, 137; and foundation of S.P.R., 138; as early member of S.P.R., 141; wealth and background, 144, 154, 156; helps to publicise S.P.R., 147n; friendship with W. James, 147–8; work on hypnosis, 153, 159n, 285, 287; secretary of S.P.R.'s Literary Committee, 154; family and upbringing, 154; as Fellow of Trinity College, Cambridge, 154–5; musical ambitions, 154–5; character and abilities, 154–6, 157, 159–60,

INDEX

Gurney, Edmund,—*continued*
174–77, 339; death of three of his sisters, 155–6; marriage, 156; studies law and medicine, 156; member of the 'Scratch Eight', 157; philosophical and religious views of, 157–9; views on vivisection, 157n–158n; becomes Hon. Sec. of S.P.R., 159; work on 'crisis' apparitions, 160–9; replies to critics, 171–4; death of, 174; as original of 'Daniel Deronda', 175n–176n; inquest on, 177–8; possibility of suicide, 178–82; supposed post-mortem communications from, 178–9, 322; and Smith-Blackburn experiments, 179–80, 357; on character of G. A. Smith, 181; views on apparitions of the dead, 193; on Myers' abilities, 276; on Myers' character, 331; on Hodgson, 336; on scepticism concerning evidence for paranormal phenomena 341–4; on 'materialist synthesis', 353; experiments on telepathy, 357, 359
Phantasms of the Living (with F. W. H. Myers and F. Podmore), 161, 162, 162n, 163n, 164, 164n, 166n, 167n, 169, 169n, 171–4, 175, 180, 185, 193, 286n, 313, 339, 356, 360
The Power of Sound, 156–7, 339
Tertium Quid, 157, 158n, 159n, 341n, 343n, 353n
Gurney, Miss Helen, 134n
Gurney, Rev. John Hampden, 154
Gurney, Kate (Mrs. Edmund Gurney), 156
Gurney, Russell, 154
Guthrie, M., 357
Gwatkin, H. M., 94n

Haddock, Dr. J., 66
Somnolism and Psycheism, 66

Haight, G. S., 175n
Halévy, E., 35, 35n
Hall, Dr., 122
Hall, Marshall, 58, 58n
Hall, T. H., 81n, 134n, 154n, 156n, 175, 177n, 179–80, 357
Hallucinations, Census of, see Census of Hallucinations
Hallucinations, Collective, see Apparitions Collectively perceived
Hammond, C., 11n, 19, 19n
Handschuschsheim ghost, 196–7
Hansel, C. E. M., 245n, 361
   E.S.P.: A Scientific Evaluation, 245n, 361–3
Hardinge (Hardinge-Britten), Emma, 27, 75, 75n, 77n
   Modern American Spiritualism, 12n, 13n, 16n, 17n, 27, 29n
Hare, A., 36
Hare, Prof. R., 16n, 20n, 21, 28n, 29, 30, 30n
Harris, T. L., 19n
Harrison, F., 50, 293, 293n, 294
Harrison, Jane, 175, 175n, 329, 330n
Harrison, W. H., 73, 80n
Hartford Times, The, 17
Hascall, Judge, A. P., 10, 11
Hatch, Cora, see Tappan, Mrs. Cora L. V.
'Haunting' ghosts, see Apparitions, Haunting
Hawks, Rev. Dr., 12
Haxby, W., 128
Hayden, W. R., 29n
Hayden, Mrs. W. R., 67–8, 69
Heitland, W., 56n
Hellis, Mr., 125–6
Henry, T. S., 128n
Herne, F., 81
Herschell, G., 204
Heslop, E., 131
Hickok, 'Wild Bill', 30
Hill, Annie Eliza, see Marshall, Annie Eliza
Hill, J. A., 276n
Hill, Rev. J. R., 116, 121

INDEX

Hitchman, Dr., 129, 129n
Hodgson, Richard, 241, 245, 311, 313, 314, 325, 362, 363, 366; as early member of S.P.R., 141; assumes management of American S.P.R., 148, 253; on death of Gurney, 178–9; early history, 202–3; character, 202, 334–7; investigates mediumship of W. Eglinton, 203–7; scepticism concerning physical phenomena, 209; views on Eusapia Palladino, 232–4, 238, 242, 293–4; detects Eusapia Palladino in fraud, 238; criticism of his 'trap' for her, 239–40; early investigations of Mrs. Piper, 253–5; views on her, 255–6, 259; in charge of her sittings, 258–61; on Mrs. Thompson, 273, 326; views on survival, 265–6, 275; last letter to H. Sidgwick, 315; death of, 334
Hodgson, Shadworth, 157
Hollond, J., 104, 104n, 113
Hollond, Mrs. J., 104, 113
Holmes, Mr. and Mrs. Nelson, 81
Holms, A. Campbell, 204n
Home, D. D., phenomena of, 15–16, 17–18, 69, 71, 86–7, 211–16; visits England in 1855, 69; works on, 69n, 71n, 216n; returns to England, 70–1; allegations of trickery by, 71, 71n; Robert Bell on, 71; as agent in the spread of Spiritualism, 71–3, 74; full-form materialisations in presence of, 80; gives evidence before Committee of London Dialectical Society, 85
Home, Mme D. D., 211
D. D. Home: His Life and Mission, 211
Hopkinson, Prof. A., 356
Hopps, Rev. J. Page, 238n
'Hornby Apparition', 185
Hort, F. J. A., 64, 64n

Houghton Library, Harvard University, 154n, 178n, 324n, 328n, 334n
Houston, Jean, 299n
Howitt, Mary (Mrs. W. Howitt), 70
Howitt, W., 29n, 70, 73, 74
Hughes, F. S., 200n
Human Nature, 76
Hume, D., 341
Husbands, J. E., 193–4
Huxley, T. H., 59, 63, 83
Hypnotism, 53, 285, 286–7, 359; telepathic induction of, 359; see also Mesmerism
Hyslop, J. H., 274n
Hysteria, 284–5

'Imperator' ('Control' of W. S. Moses and of Mrs. Piper), 78, 78n, 260–1, 267
Innes, A. T., 171–3, 180, 185
'Inspirational' speaking and writing, in early American Spiritualism, 18–19; in early British Spiritualism, 75

Jackson, H., 64
James, E. C., 345n
James, Henry, sr., 49n, 67
James, Henry, 178
James, Henry (son of William James), 202
James, William, 145, 149, 156, 166, 171, 177n, 178, 179n, 229, 251, 286, 298, 324, 326, 329, 336, 338; on contemporary attitudes to Spiritualism, 30–1; leader of American S.P.R., 147; friendship with Gurney, 147–8; on 'mental' and 'physical' phenomena, 246; sittings with Mrs. Piper, 252–3; views on Mrs. Piper, 255–6, 261; on Myers, 277, 328, 331; on unconscious mental events, 279; on stream of thought, 280; on personality, 280; on function of

INDEX

James, William,—*continued*
    consciousness, 281–2; on Myers' theory of subliminal self, 293; influence of Myers upon, 311–312; at clinic in Rome with Myers, 333; on death of Myers, 333–4; on 'mechanical rationalism', 353–5
    The Principles of Psychology, 279, 279n, 280n, 281, 282, 282n, 301
    The Varieties of Religious Experience, 310n, 311
Janet, P., 276, 285, 286, 288, 299, 338, 359
Jarman, A., 122n
Jastrow, J., 209n
Jebb, Caroline (Mrs., later Lady, R. C. Jebb), 95n, 111, 111n, 112, 134, 135
Jebb, R. C., 95, 125
Johnson, Alice, 182, 184, 209, 209n, 216n, 236–7, 239, 239n, 242, 244–5, 325, 338
Jones, Sir L. J., 247n, 333
Jowett, B., 35, 49–50
Jung, C. G., 278, 278n, 295, 338
Jung-Stilling, J. H., 23

Keble, John, 35
Kerner, J., 23
Kimball, R. B., 12
'King, John', 17, 17n, 103n, 104, 229
'King, Katie', 17n, 81
Koons, Jonathan, and family, 16–17
Kuenen, A., 62

Labouchère, A., 323
Labouchère, H., 323
Lang, A., 175, 185, 268n, 293, 293n, 294, 294n, 326
Langworthy, Dr. H. H., 10
Lankester, Prof. E. R., 126
Lape, Jane C., 6
Lawrance, W. J., 89n
Lawton, G., 22n, 29n
Leader, The, 67

Leaf, Charlotte, 108n, 154n
Leaf, W., 64, 104, 108, 141, 144, 146, 255, 275, 293, 293n, 294
Leonard, Gladys O., 247, 352
Levitation, see Mediumship, Alleged Phenomena of
Lewes, G. H., 63, 67, 116
Lewis, Angelo ('Professor Hoffman'), 209
    Modern Magic, 209
Lewis, E. E., 6
    A Report of the Mysterious Noises heard in the House of Mr. John D. Fox, 3n, 4n, 5, 5n, 7n
Light, 81n, 82n, 103n, 124n, 218n, 268, 269, 325n
Lightfoot, J. B., 64
Lincoln, Abraham, 30, 30n
Linton, C., *The Healing of the Nations*, 18
Literary Committee, see Society for Psychical Research
Livermore, C., 80
Liverpool Psychological Society, 129
Lodge, Oliver, J., 106, 142n, 162, 178, 196–7, 235, 241, 311, 313n, 314, 323, 326, 329n, 331, 332, 366; member of Council of S.P.R., 140; career and beliefs of, 142; member of S.P.R. physical phenomena committee, 209; sittings at Île Roubaud with Eusapia Palladino, 225–34; do. at Carqueiranne, 230–1; on conduct of Cambridge investigation of Eusapia Palladino, 240; Mrs. Piper stays with, 255; views on Mrs. Piper, 255–6; communications for through Mrs. Piper, 257–8; on Myers' grasp of science, 276; on Myers' theory of the subliminal self, 293, 293n; experiments in telepathy, 357
Lombroso, C., 224
Longford, E., 67n

INDEX

Losey, C. P., 5, 7
Lyman, General, 12

McCabe, J., 25n
Macalister, A., 140
Macaulay, T. B., 35, 41
McCollum, D. C., 10
MacDonald, W. H., 10–11
McDougall, W., 293, 294, 294n, 296, 338
Mackay, R. W., 49n
Mackenzie, C. F., 64
Mahan, A., 12n, 27n
Maison, M., 38n
Maitland, F. W., 64, 155, 157, 159
Mallock, W. H., 44, 63, 64, 64n, 65n, 293, 294, 294n
Manchester Guardian, 89
Manning, H. E., 35
Mansel, H. L., 54
Mapes, Prof. J. J., 29
Marcy, Dr., 29
Marshall, Alfred, 320
Marshall, Annie Eliza, Myers writes 'Account of my Friendship with Henry Sidgwick' for, 96n; and Frederic Myers, 117–24; character of, 117–18; mediumistic tendencies, 119–120; suicide of, 122–3; influence on Myers, 118–19, 309, 322, 332; supposed post-mortem communications from, 130–131, 323–5
Marshall, G. H., 121
Marshall, John (Founder of Marshalls of Leeds), 38, 116, 117
Marshall, John (Grandson of above) 116, 117
Marshall, Mrs. Mary, 71–2, 72n, 73, 74
Marshall, Susan Harriet, see Myers, Susan Harriet
Marshall, Walter J., 96n, 116–22
Marshall, William C., 145
Martin, Dr. R., 30n
Martineau, J., 49n

Maskelyne, J. N., 82n, 105n, 235, 238n
Massey, C. C., 138
Masters, R. E. L., 299n
Materialisation, see Mediumship, Alleged Phenomena of
Materialism, 142, 353–5; see also Rationalism
Mattison, H., 24n
'Maxwell Demons', 293
Maxwell, J., 238
Mayer, J. E. B., 64
Maynard, Nettie C., 30n
Medhurst, R. G., 81n, 82n, 106n, 124n
Medium and Daybreak, The, 76, 77n
Mediumship, Alleged Phenomena of:
  Automatic Speaking: in early American Spiritualism, 18; of Mrs. Piper, 252–9; of Mrs Thompson, 269–74
  Automatic Writing: in early American Spiritualism, 18–19; in early British do., 70, 74; of W. S. Moses, 78–9; of Miss Wingfield, 247; of Mrs. Piper, 252, 260–8; of Mrs. Thompson, 269–74; Myers on, 285, 291; contents of supposedly exhibiting partial independence of automatist's brain, 297–8; Newnham case, 358
  'Control' (of medium's organism supposedly by a spirit): early theory of, 18; favoured by Hodgson as explanation of Piper phenomena, 265–6; this view criticised by Mrs. Sidgwick, 267–8; Myers on, 292
  'Direct Voice', the: with Jonathan Koons and family, 16–17; with Mrs. Everitt, 73; with Mrs. Fay, 105
  Elongation: of D. D. Home, 213
  Levitation: of Mrs. S. F. Cheney, 16; of D. D. Home, 71; see also Object-movements

377

INDEX

Mediumship,—*continued*
  'Materialisation', full-form: with Home, 80; with Kate Fox, 80; in England, 80; with Florence Cook and others, 81; with F. Monck, 82-3; with the Misses Wood and Fairlamb, 107, 108-111, 112-14, 127-8; with Petty family, 108, 111-12; with Haxby, 128; with Banks, 129-130; defects in testimony concerning, 207-8; Myers on, 293
  'Materialisation', partial: with Kate Fox, 9, 16; with D. D. Home, 17-18, 69; with C. Williams, 103n; with Eusapia Palladino, 229, 236-7, 241, 242; Myers on, 293
  Musical Instruments, playing of: with Kate Fox, 9; with D. D. Home, 69, 212, 215; with Mrs. Fay, 105; with Eusapia Palladino, 231, 241, 242
  Object-movements: with Kate Fox, 8, 9, 72; with Fox sisters, 11; Podmore on, 15; with D. D. Home, 15-16, 69, 211-15; explained in terms of 'Odic' force, 27; with Mrs. Fay, 105; with Petty family, 108; with Slade, 125-7; observed by H. G. Gore Graham, 209-10; with W. S. Moses, 218-20; with Miss Wingfield and Hon. Alec Yorke, 223; with Eusapia Palladino, 224, 226-9, 231, 235, 237, 241, 242; Myers on, 292-3
  Planchette-writing: 15, 59, 250
  Possession: see 'Control', *supra*.
  Raps: with Fox sisters, 3-13, 26; with Kate Fox, 72; in early American Spiritualism, 14, 15, 27; in early British Spiritualism, 70, 73, 74; with Petty family, 108; with the Misses Wood and Fairlamb, 109; with Home, 212; with Miss Wingfield and Hon. Alec Yorke, 223; with Eusapia Palladino, 228; with Miss Wingfield, 247-50; Myers on, 292-3
  Slate-writing: with Slade, 124-6; with Eglinton, 200-7; defects in testimony concerning, 203-9
  'Spirit' photography: 80n
  Table-tipping: 15, 59, 67-9, 73, 358
  Touches: with Kate Fox, 9; with Mrs. Fay, 105; with Home, 214; with Eusapia Palladino, 227, 229, 231, 236, 241, 242
  Trance speaking and writing: see Automatic Speaking, and Automatic Writing, *supra*
  Trickery, alleged methods of: 25-7, 105n, 125, 127, 203-9, 221-2, 233, 233-4, 238
  See also: Clairvoyance, Crystal-gazing, Inspirational speaking and writing
Mediumship, Spread of in the United States, 14-15; in Great Britain, 70, 73, 81
Mellon, Mrs. J. B., see Fairlamb, Annie
Mercier, C. A., 255n
Meredith George, 96n
  Love in the Valley, 96
Mesmer, F. A., 27
Mesmerism, as precursor of Spiritualism, 13-14, 18, 23-4, 66-7
Metaphysical Society, 305
'Metetherial', the (Myers), 307-10
Methodism, 33-4, 77
Mill, J. S., 46, 48, 62
  A System of Logic, 46
Millais, J. E., 135
Miller, Betty, 71n
Mitchell, T. W., 159n
Monck, F., 81, 82n, 82-3, 130
Montebello, Duc and Duchesse de, 241
Montgomery, Field-Marshal Lord, 345
More, Hannah, 33
Morley, J., 63

INDEX

Morse, J. J., 75, 77
Morselli, E., 223n
'Morton Ghost', the, 197–9
'Morton', Miss R. C., see Despard, Rose
Moses, W. Stainton, 246, 247; forms home circle with Dr. and Mrs. Speer, 78; automatic writings of, 78; 'Controls' of, 78–9; 'evidential' cases through, 78–9; meets Myers and Gurney, 79, 104; member of Council of S.P.R., 138; physical phenomena of, 216–20; as 'communicator' through Mrs. Piper, 260–1
Psychography, 124n
Spirit Identity, 79
Spirit Teachings, 78
More Spirit Teachings, 78
Mould, Mr., 107, 127
Mount-Temple, Lady, 104
Mozart, W. A., 288
Multiple personality, see Personality, multiple
Munthe, A., 334n
Murphy, G., 30n, 331n
Myers, Dr. A. T., 38, 177, 177n, 178n, 182, 359
Myers, E. J., 38
Myers, Eveleen (Mrs. F. W. H. Myers), 101, 103n, 135–6, 146, 181, 235–7, 322–3, 333
Myers, Rev. F., 38, 43, 116
Myers, F. W. H., 153, 242, 313, 314, 355; childhood of, 38–44; meets W. S. Moses, 79, 104; career at Cheltenham College, 89; early promise as poet, 89–90; as undergraduate at Trinity College, Cambridge, 64, 89–94; character and abilities, 90, 100, 325–32; appearance, 90; as a classic, 91–4; Camden Medal affair, 92–3, 329; travels in Aegean lands, 93–4; turns to Moral Sciences, 94; wishes to read Natural Sciences, 94; elected to College Fellowship, 94; tours Canada and United States, 94; falls under the influence of Mrs. Josephine Butler, 95–6; becomes a fervent Christian, 96, 97–8; friendship with Henry Sidgwick, 96–7, 100–3; loses faith in Christianity, 99–100; work for Women's education, 100; becomes school inspector, 100; early investigations of Spiritualism with H. Sidgwick and others, 103–4; investigation of Mrs. Fay, 104–6; of the Misses Wood and Fairlamb, 107, 108–111, 112–14, 127–8; of the Petty family, 107–8, 111–12; and Annie Marshall, 116–24; sittings with H. Slade, 125–6; visits Liverpool Psychological Society, 129–30; sittings with Monck, Florence Cook, Kate Cook, 130; with Mme Rohart, 130–2; effect of Annie Marshall's death on, 122–4, 133; on pre-existence, 133, 303; belief in survival, 133n, 291–2, 322, 326; search for a wife, 134–5; marries Eveleen Tennant, 135; success of marriage, 136, 322–3, 329; experiments with Gurney and W. F. Barrett, 137; and foundation of S.P.R., 138; as organiser of S.P.R., 138, 328; his hopes for the S.P.R., 141–2, 148–9; on aims of the S.P.R., 143; wealth and background, 144; style of life, 145; subsidises S.P.R., 145–6; subsidises American S.P.R., 145–6, 258; helps to publicise work of S.P.R., 147n; secretary of Literary Committee of S.P.R., 154; writes introduction to *Phantasms*, 161; dissents from Gurney's view of collective hallucinations, 169–71;

379

INDEX

Myers, F. W. H.,—*continued*
walks with George Eliot in Fellows' garden of Trinity, 175n; on character of Gurney, 176; and Gurney's death, 177n–178n; receives alleged postmortem communications from Gurney, 178–9, 322; and Smith–Blackburn experiments, 178; on experiments at Brighton, 181; effect on of Gurney's death, 183; becomes joint Hon. Sec. of S.P.R., 182; on Mrs. Sidgwick, 186–7; views on apparitions of the dead, 193, 194–6; on ghost of Hanschuchsheim castle, 196–7; and 'Morton' ghost, 198; member of S.P.R. committee on physical phenomena, 209; collects materials on D. D. Home, 211; on physical phenomena of W. S. Moses, 216–7; and mediumship of Mr. 'D.', 221; witnesses physical phenomena in circle of his friends, 223; sittings at Île Roubaud with Eusapia Palladino, 225–34; sittings at Cambridge with Eusapia Palladino, 234–38; sittings in Paris with Eusapia Palladino, 241–2; investigates Kate Wingfield, 223, 247; and mediumship of Mrs. Everett and Mrs. Turner, 250; Mrs. Piper stays with at Cambridge, 255; views on Mrs. Piper, 251, 255–6; theory of subliminal self, 275–8, 283–99, 301–2; his knowledge of science, 276; powers of memory, 276; knowledge of psychological literature 276; prose style, 276–7, 330; on the 'unconscious', 278–9; on consciousness, 279–80; on the notion of personality, 281; on causal efficacy of consciousness, 281–3; on the soul, 300–5;
religious views, 305–12; on Henry Sidgwick, 321; receives supposed communications from Annie Marshall, 323–5; death predicted through Mrs. Thompson, 333; last illness and death, 332–4; correspondence with Lord Acton on canons of evidence, 241n, 364–7; on personal identity beyond tomb, 349–51; on supposed difficulties in communicating from beyond the grave, 292n, 352; experiments in telepathy, 357

Essays Classical, 133
Essays Modern, 133, 307n
Fragments of Inner Life, 40n, 43n, 90n, 92n, 94n, 99n, 102n, 117n, 118n, 119n, 124n, 149n, 322n, 325n, 327n
Fragments of Poetry and Prose, 99n
Human Personality and its Survival of Bodily Death, 104n, 223n, 275–8, 277n, 280n, 281, 282, 283n, 284n, 286n, 287n, 290n, 291n, 292, 292n, 293, 296, 298n, 299, 300n, 301n, 302n, 303n, 304n, 306n, 308n, 309n, 310n, 313, 333, 347n, 350n, 351, 356, 357
Phantasms of the Living (with E. Gurney and F. Podmore), see Gurney, E.
Renewal of Youth, The, 133
St. Paul, 96, 96n
Wordsworth, 133, 134n

Myers, Leo, 328, 331
Myers, Silvia, 331
Myers, Susan Harriet (Mrs. F. Myers), 38–43, 116, 121, 122, 131, 332

Nenner, Prof. and Mrs., 70
Nevill, Lady Dorothy, 197n
Newbold, Prof. W. R., 274n
Newcomb, Simon, 147
Newman, F., 35
Newman, J. H., 35

INDEX

Newnham, Rev. and Mrs. P. H., 358
Newsome, D. H., 35n, 64n
New York Excelsior, 11
New York Herald, 25
New York Tribune, 12–13
Nineteenth Century, The, 64n, 147n, 171, 202, 294n
Noel, Hon. Roden, 201
Nosworthy, E. Louisa, 130n

Object-movements, alleged paranormal, see Mediumship, Alleged Phenomena of
Ochorowicz, J., 226, 228–9, 230–1, 234, 240
O'Connor, R., 30n
Odic force, as explanation of Spiritualistic phenomena, 27–8, 68, 68n
Odyle, see Odic force
Olive Branch, The, 14
Osty, E., 347n
Owen, Sir Richard, 45
Owen, Robert, 68
Owen, R., Dale, *The Debateable Land*, 26n, 78, 80n
Oxford Movement, 36, 46
Oxley, W., 82

Page, C. G., 24n
Palladino, Eusapia, works on, 223n; early history and character, 223–4; Lombroso's sittings with, 224; sittings at Milan, 224–5; sittings at the Île Roubaud, 225–34; sittings at Carqueiranne, 230–1; sittings at Cambridge, 234–40; sittings at Paris, 241–2; sittings at Naples, 242–3; Sidgwick's attitude to, 230, 241–1, 319; Miss A. Johnson on phenomena of, 245
Parish, E., 184, 184n, 185
Pattison, M., 35, 36
Peirce, C. S., 173–4, 180
Pellew, C. E., 362–3

Pellew, George ('G.P.'), 259–60, 265, 266–8, 346, 352, 362–3
Pellew, Mrs. H. E. (step-mother and aunt of George Pellew), 362
Perception, concept of, 349–51
Perovsky-Petrovo-Solovovo, M., 26n, 71n, 216n
Personal identity and survival, 349–51
Personality, 280–1, 285, 289–90, 344–6; see also Survival, question of
Multiple, 285–6, 294–5, 297
Petty family, 107–8, 111–12
Phantasms of the Dead, see Apparitions of the Dead
Phantasms of the Living, see Apparitions, Crisis
'Phinuit', Dr., 252, 256, 257, 258, 260, 262–4, 267
Photography, 'spirit', 80n
Physical phenomena of mediumship, see Mediumship, Alleged Phenomena of
Piddington, J. G., 242, 273–4, 325n, 335–6, 338
Piper, Alta, L., 251n
Piper, Mrs. L. E., 199, 247, 335, 337, 352, 366; supposed post-mortem communications from Gurney through, 178–9, 322; mediumship of, 251–68, 344–6; character and intellect, 251; investigated by W. James, 252–3; early investigations of by R. Hodgson, 253–5; shadowed by detectives, 255; visits England, 255–8; early views on of Lodge, Myers, Leaf, Hodgson, James and the Sidgwicks, 255–6; Hodgson assumes charge of sittings with, 258; emergence of 'G.P.' communicator, 259; development of automatic writing, 260; F. Podmore on, 261–2; alleged communications from Katherine Sutton through, 262–4;

381

INDEX

Piper, Mrs. L. E.,—*continued*
and cross-correspondences, 274; Myers on, 277; and phenomenon of 'ecstasy', 304; supposed communications from Annie Marshall through, 323; status of 'communicators', 264–266, 344–52; critics of, 361–3; 'confession' of, 361
Planchette-writing, see Mediumship, Alleged Phenomena of
Plato, 276
Phaedo, 94, 119
Podmore, F., 224n, 246n, 311, 313, 366; on spread of Spiritualism in United States, 13–14; on physical phenomena of Spiritualism, 15; on theology in spirit communications, 22; on Robert Owen and Spiritualism, 68n; on W. S. Moses' *Spirit Teachings*, 78; career, 142–3; aims, 143; role in preparation of *Phantasms*, 161; becomes joint Hon. Sec. of S.P.R., 182; attacks Myers' views on apparitions of the dead, 195–6; scepticism concerning physical phenomena, 209; on physical phenomena of W. S. Moses, 217–18; on cases of 'disinterested deception', 222; on Eusapia Palladino, 245n; on mediumship of Mrs. Piper, 261–2, 346; on Mrs. Thompson, 273, 273n; last letter to Henry Sidgwick, 316
Apparitions and Thought-Transference, 356, 358
Modern Spiritualism, 13n, 15n, 16n, 22n, 27n, 67n, 68n, 69n, 73n, 80n, 85n, 126n, 128n, 143, 216n, 217, 217n, 218n, 222n, 346n
Phantasms of the Living (with E. Gurney and F. W. H. Myers), see E. Gurney
Pollock, F., 157

Pond, Mariam B., 7n
Post, Isaac, 8, 9, 20, 20n, 22, 23n, 30
Pre-existence, Myers on, 133, 303
Prevorst, Seeress of, 23
Price, Harry, 209n
Prince, W. F., 30n
Progress, as keynote of Spiritualism, 22, 74
Prosser, J., 28
Prothero, G., 64
Pulver, Mrs. Anna, 6
Pulver, Lucretia, 5–6
Pusey, E. B., 35

Quarterly Journal of Science, 86, 87, 213

Raps, alleged paranormal, see Mediumship, Alleged Phenomena of
Rationalism, growth of in England, 44–65; 'mechanical', W. James on, 353–5
Raverat, Gwen, 99n
Rawcliffe, D. H., 245n
Rayleigh, Lord (third Baron Rayleigh), 72n, 87, 104, 106, 115, 138, 140, 235, 237, 316, 318n, 319
Rayleigh, Lady, 104
Rayleigh, Lord (fourth Baron Rayleigh), 240n
Read, Carveth, 157
Reade, Winwood, 62–3
The Martyrdom of Man, 63
Redfield, W., 5
Redière, Mme, 132
Religion, and Science in Victorian England, 44–7
Religious revival in England, 32–3
Relph, Miss, 357
Renan, J. E., 51
'Retrocognition', 248–9, 347, 347n
Richet, C., 223, 223n, 224n, 224–230, 233–4, 235, 238n, 240n, 241, 358, 359
Richet, Mme C., 241, 241n, 242

INDEX

Richmond, B. W., 27n
Rimmer, W. G., 116n
Rinn, J. F., *Searchlight on Psychical Research*, 361, 363
Ripley, Mr., 12
Rita, A., 81
Robertson, G. C., 154n, 157
Rogers, E. C., 27n
Rogers, E. D., 137n, 200n
Rohart, Mme, 130-2
Roubaud, F., 68n
Ruskin, J., 36, 45, 140, 140n
Russell, Bertrand, 84n, 318n
Russell, C., 38
Russell, G. W. E., 38n
Russell, Patricia, 84n
Rymer, T., 69

'S.', Mr., 206-7
Sage, M., 251n
Salter, Helen (Mrs. W. H. Salter), 329n
Salter, W. H., 67n, 84n, 137n
Sangster, P. E., 36n
Sargent, E., 80n
    Planchette: the Despair of Science, 30
Schiaparelli, G. V., 224
Schiller, F. C. S., 293, 294n
Science and Religion in Victorian England, 44-7
Scott, C. B., 64
Seeley, J., *Ecce Homo*, 52, 54
Ségard, Dr., 230
Sexton, G., 82n
Sherwood, Mrs. Mary Martha, *The Fairchild Family*, 37
Shorter, T., 73
Showers, Mary, 81, 81n
Sibley, Kate, see Gurney, Kate
Sidgwick, A., 90, 90n, 92, 95, 96, 97, 329n, 366
    H.S.: A Memoir (with E. M. Sidgwick), 47n, 48n, 51n, 52n, 53n, 54n, 55n, 56n, 57n, 88n, 100n, 104n, 112n, 120n, 314n, 315n, 317, 320n
Sidgwick, Eleanor Mildred (Mrs. Henry Sidgwick), 311, 313, 314, 333; early investigations of Spiritualism with H. Sidgwick, Myers and others, 104; investigation of Mrs. Fay, 105, 105n; sittings with the Misses Wood and Fairlamb, 110-11, 112-14, 127-8; upbringing, 115; character and abilities, 115-116, 186-7, 230, 337-8; engagement and marriage to Henry Sidgwick, 115-16; appearance, 115, 337; sittings with H. Slade, 124-5; views on W. Eglinton, 138, 202, 203-4; Principal of Newnham, 139, 337; early member of S.P.R., 141; wealth and background, 144; austerity and absence of display, 116, 145; on Hodgson's views concerning Gurney's death, 178, 178n; member of committee on census of hallucinations, 182; on apparitions of the dead, 186-93; and alleged mediumship of 'Mr. D.', 221-2; sittings with Eusapia Palladino at Carqueiranne, 230-1, 232; sittings with Eusapia Palladino at Cambridge, 236; defends conduct of Cambridge sittings, 239, 239n; views on Mrs. Piper, 255-6, 267-8; views on survival, 275; as Hon. Sec. of S.P.R., 337-8; experiments in telepathy, 359
H.S.: A Memoir (with A. Sidgwick), see Sidgwick, A.
Sidgwick, Ethel, M., 115n
Sidgwick, Henry, 120, 121, 143, 241, 311, 313, 314, 352, 359, 366; on influence of J. S. Mill at Cambridge, 46-7; at Rugby School, 47; as undergraduate at Trinity College, Cambridge, 47; elected College Fellow, 47; religious doubts, 48-57; membership of the 'Apostles', 48; letter to *Times* on *Essays and*

Sidgwick, Henry,—*continued*
Reviews, 50–1; views on miracles, 51–3; studies Arabic and Hebrew, 51; appointed College Lecturer in Moral Science, 53; philosophical studies, 53–4; leans towards Theism, 55; influence at Cambridge, 55–6, 57, 64; character and appearance, 56–7, 100, 138–40, 317–321; and contemporary science, 64, 64n; early interest in Spiritualism, 87, 88–9; friendship with F. W. H. Myers, 96–97, 99–103; on Myers' *St. Paul*, 96, 96n; work for women's education, 100, 317; early investigations of Spiritualism with F. Myers and others, 103–4; investigations of Mrs. Fay, 104–6; of the Misses Wood and Fairlamb, 107, 108, 111, 112–114, 127–8; of the Petty family, 108, 111–12; engagement and marriage to Eleanor Balfour, 115–16; sittings with Slade, 124–5; gives Myers test questions for Mme Rohart, 132; becomes President of S.P.R., 138; as President of S.P.R., 138–40; becomes Professor of Moral Philosophy at Cambridge, 139; his hopes for S.P.R., 141, 142, 148–9; wealth and background, 144; economy with money, 145; on plan of *Phantasms*, 161; on death of Gurney, 178; member of committee on census of hallucinations, 182; member of S.P.R. physical phenomena committee 209; and mediumship of 'Mr. D.', 221–2; sittings with Eusapia Palladino at Carqueiranne, 230–1, 232; sittings with her at Cambridge, 236; defends conduct of Cambridge sittings, 239n, 239–40; views on Mrs. Piper, 255–6, 266–7; views on survival, 275, 321–2, 326; last illness and death 314–17; and University reform, 317

The Methods of Ethics, 53n, 54, 55, 88

Slade, H., 124–7
Smith, G. A., 179–81, 196, 258, 357, 359
Smith, Rev. J., 70
Smith, J. G., see Piddington, J. G.
Smith, R. Pearsall, 253
Smith, W. Robertson, 62
Snow, Rev. H., 16n, 18, 18n
Socialism, linked with Spiritualism, 22, 75
Society for Psychical Research, foundation of, 137–8, 153; official aims and objects of, 137–8; resignation of Spiritualists from, 138; membership of, 140; background of its early leaders, 141, 144; hopes of its early leaders, 140–3, 148–9; Myers on its aims, 143; wealth of its early leaders, 144–5; subsidised by them, 145–6; committees set up at foundation of, 146–7; work of, 153 and *passim*; in early decades of twentieth century, 338–9

Journal of, 138, 139, 313, *passim*
Literary Committee of, 147, 153–154, 161, 167
Physical Phenomena committee of, 200, 209, 211, 213
Proceedings of, 138, 139, 313, *passim*

Soul, nature of in Spiritualist doctrine, 20–1; Myers on, 290, 300–5
Speer, Dr. and Mrs. Stanhope, 78, 216–17, 218–19
Spencer, Herbert, 60, 120–1, 202
Spheres, spirit, 21
Spicer, H., 15, 15n, 19n, 25n
Spirit, nature of in Spiritualist doctrine, 20–1; see also Soul

INDEX

Spirits, departed, supposed teachings of in early American Spiritualism, 19–23; alleged occupations of, 22; relations between sexes amongst, 22; moral and political ideas of, 22; 'control' by favoured by Hodgson as explanation of Piper communications, 265–266; Mrs. Sidgwick's arguments against this view, 267–8; Myers on possible 'control' by, 291–2; Myers on state of, 308–10; Myers on relations of with the living, 310

Spiritual Herald, 69

Spiritualism, Modern, its rise in the United States, 1–31; its rapid spread there, 13–15; modes of alleged communication with the departed, 18–19; doctrines of, 19–24; rival explanations of its characteristic phenomena, 24–9; number of adherents in United States, 29; prominent adherents there, 29–30; in England, 66–87; table-tipping epidemic, 67–8; developments 1855–9, 69–70; spread of after 1859, 70–77; among working men, 74–7; draws converts from nonconformists and in industrial regions, 77; number of adherents, 77; W. S. Moses and, 78–9; materialisation phenomena, 79–83; phenomena of neglected by scientists, 83–4

Phenomena of, see Mediumship, Alleged Phenomena of

Spiritualist, The, 72n, 73, 78, 80n, 83n, 86n, 107n, 223n, 224, 224n

Spiritual Magazine, The, 72–3, 74, 77n, 82n

Stanley, Dorothy (Mrs. H. M. Stanley), 236–7

Stephen, James, 38

Stephen, J. K., 329n

Lapsus Calami, 96

Stephen, Leslie, 47n, 63, 157
Stephenson, C. J., 106n
Stevenson, R. L., 288
Stewart, Balfour, 21n, 137n, 140, 356
Storer, W. D., 7
Stout, G. F., 293–6, 294n, 338
Stowe, Harriet Beecher, 29
Strutt, Admiral Hon, A. C., 56n
Subliminal Self, Myers' theory of, 275–78, 283–99, 301–2
Sully, James, 157
Summerfield, Mr., 11
Survival, question of, 265–7, 275, 278, 292, 344–52
Sutton, Katherine, 262–4
Sutton, Rev. and Mrs. S. W., 262–4
Swedenborgianism, as precursor of Spiritualism, 14
Swedenborg Society, 49n, 67n
Swinburne, A. C., 108
Swinhoe, Imogen, 197
Symonds, J. A., 44, 90n, 95n, 102n, 140, 142, 322
Synthetic Society, 305–6, 311

Table-tipping, see Mediumship, Alleged Phenomena of
Tait, A. C., 38
Tait, Catharine (Mrs. A. C. Tait), 38n
Tait, P. C., 21n
Talmadge, N., 29
Tappan, Mrs. Cora L. V., 75
Taylor, Mr., 81
Taylor, Una, 100n
Telekinesis, see Object-movements, under Mediumship, Alleged Phenomena of
Telepathy, 132, 137, 138, 148; as explanation of crisis apparitions, 162–3, 177; as explanation of 'haunting' ghosts, 195–6; as explanation of veridical 'communications', 257–8, 259, 264–265, 347–52; as function of subliminal self, 288; as independent of brain, 298; and 'metetherial',

INDEX

Telepathy,—*continued*
  307–8; supposed conflict with ordinary scientific laws, 342; experiments on, 356–60
'Telepathy', term coined by Myers, 137n
Tennant, Dorothy, see Stanley, Dorothy
Tennant, Eveleen, see Myers, Eveleen
Tennyson, Alfred Lord, 45, 140
  In Memoriam, 45
  The Voyage, 55
Testimony, sources of error in, 164–166, 171–4, 203–9, 244; see also evidence
Theological Review, 61
Thompson, J., *History of Leicester*, 251
Thompson, Rosina (Mrs. Edmond Thompson), physical phenomena of, 247, 268–9; development of mediumship, 268–9; investigated by Myers, 269; sits for F. van Eeden, 269–72; for Mrs. A. W. Verrall, 272; for R. Hodgson, 273; defended against Hodgson by Podmore, 273–4; alleged communications from Annie Marshall, through, 269, 323–5; and cross-correspondences, 274; and phenomenon of 'ecstasy', 304; prediction of Myers' death through, 333
Thompson, W. H., 155
Thomson, J. J., 140, 235, 237, 319, 319n
Thought-transference, see Telepathy
Times, The, 50, 68, 84, 147, 153, 156n, 171
Toplady, A., 33n
Trance, mediumistic and mesmeric, 18; see also Mediumship, Alleged Phenomena of
Trethewy, A. W., 78n
Treves, Sir F., 156n
Trickery, methods of, see Mediumship Alleged Phenomena of

Trinity College, Cambridge, 47, 54–5, 56, 64, 110n, 140, 154, 155, 175n, 316
Truesdell, J. W., 105n, 126n, 209n
Tuckerman, H. T., 12
Tuckett, I. Ll., 185, 361
Turner, Mrs. C., 250
Twining, Elizabeth, 22
Tylor, E. B., 62, 63
  Primitive Culture, 62
Tyndall, J., 63

Unconscious, the, Myers on, 278–9; James on, 279
Underhill, Leah, see Fox, Leah
Universalism, as precursor or Spiritualism, 14

Van Eeden, F., 269–72
Varley, C., 26n, 84
Vaschide, N., 185
Venn, J., 140
Verrall, A. W., 64
Verrall, Mrs. A. W., 272
Victoria, Queen, 67
Von Reichenbach, K., 27, 27n

'W.', Mrs. 189–90
'W.', Miss, 190–1
Wallace, A. Russel, 73, 82n, 83, 84, 126, 137, 140, 215
Ward, Maisie, 327n
Ward, Wilfrid, 305, 327
Waters, E., 28
Watts, A., 70
Watts, Anna Mary Howitt, *Pioneers of the Spiritual Reformation*, 70
Wedgwood, Hensleigh, 108, 108n, 201, 204, 250
Weekman, Mr. and Mrs. M., 6
Wellhausen, J., 62
Werner, H., 23, 23n
Westcott, B. F., 64
Whewell, W., 41, 41n
White, A. D., 45n
Whittlesey, Hon. F., 10
Wilberforce, R. I., 35
Wilkinson, J. J. G., 49n, 67, 70

Wilkinson, W., 70–3
  Spirit Drawings, 70
Willets, G., 9
Williams, C., 81, 103n, 104
Willis, N. P., 12
Willmore, Mr., 72n
Wingfield, Kate, 223, 247–50, 269, 293, 333, 360
Wood, Miss C. E., 81, 107–8, 111, 112–14, 127–8, 128n, 129
Wordsworth, W., 40, 133, 276
Wright, Chauncey, 259

Wyld, G., 137n
Wyndham, H., 69n
Wyndham, P., 201

Yorke, Hon. A., 223
Yorkshire Spiritual Telegraph, 69
Young, E. M., 53
Young, G. M., 35, 35n
Young, K., 116n

Zoist, The, 66
Zöllner, J. C. F., 124n